SHIPS AND SHIPWRECKS
OF THE AMERICAS

SHIPS AND SHIPWRECKS OF THE AMERICAS

A History Based on Underwater Archaeology

Edited by GEORGE F. BASS

With 376 illustrations, 80 in color

Thames and Hudson

To John H. Baird,
*pioneer patron of nautical archaeology,
and friend*

Editor's Note

We have tried to be consistent in the spelling of placenames, using those which appear most frequently in English, or those used by accepted authorities, although these may not have been the first choices of individual authors in this book. Both English and metric measurements are given, which has led to minor problems. Archaeologists normally use the metric system in recording their sites, whether watercraft or not, but many of these watercraft were built to the English standard. We have, therefore, for instance, given the metric measurements first in Chapter One, which concerns pre-Columbian watercraft not built by people using feet and inches, whereas in Chapter Ten, discussing nineteenth-century steamboats, English measurements are listed first. Approximate figures present a problem: a vessel 'around 45 ft long' becomes an overly precise 'around 13.7 m' long when converted literally, and the measurement cited first should be taken to be the more correct one.

Title page A diver dismantles a floor timber from a sixteenth-century Basque galleon found in Red Bay, Labrador. See Chapter Four.

© 1988 Thames and Hudson Ltd, London

First published in the USA in 1988 by
Thames and Hudson Inc.,
500 Fifth Avenue, New York, New York 10110

Library of Congress Catalog Card Number 88-50246

Printed and bound in Spain by
Artes Graficas Toledo S.A.
D.L.: TO-1187-1988

Contents

Introduction

George F. Bass

INSTITUTE OF NAUTICAL ARCHAEOLOGY
TEXAS A&M UNIVERSITY

pages 9–12

CHAPTER ONE

The Earliest Watercraft: From Rafts to Viking Ships

Margaret E. Leshikar

INSTITUTE OF NAUTICAL ARCHAEOLOGY
TEXAS A&M UNIVERSITY

pages 13–32

SIBERIA

ARCTIC OCEAN

GREENLAND

ICELAND

Bering Strait
Point Barrow

ALASKA

CORNWALLIS I.
× BREADALBANE
(1853)

BAFFIN I.

KING WILLIAM I.

N
O
R
T
H

C
A
N
A
D
A

LABRADOR

Yukon R.

PACIFIC

RED BAY WRECKS (c.1565)
× L'ANSE AUX MEADOWS (c.1000)
NEWFOUNDLAND

NOVA SCOTIA

Fort Benton
Missouri R.

The Great
Lakes

A
M
E
R
I
C
A

Appalachian Mountains

× TITANIC (1912)

Coloma

U   N   I   T   E   D

CAPE COD
× ANDREA DORIA (1956)

San Francisco
× NIANTIC
(1851)

CALIFORNIA

S   T   A   T   E   S

× BERTRAND
(1865)
Omaha
Mississippi R.

CAPE
HATTERAS

BERMUDA

Colorado R.

Rio Grande

Spiro

CHANNEL IS.

O
C
E
A
N

GULF
OF MEXICO

M   E   X   I   C   O

CARIBBEAN SEA

CENTRAL AMERICA

VENEZUELA

Orinoco R.

COLOMBIA

S
O
U
T
H

CABO DE
SÃO ROQUE

Rio Esmeraldas

Amazon R.

MANABI
PROVINCE

ECUA-
DOR

B   R   A   Z   I   L

Salvador
(Bahia)
× SACRAMENTO
(1668)

Paita

P
E
R
U

A
M
E
R
I
C
A

SECHURA
DESERT

Andes Mountains

Lake
Titicaca

Rio de Janeiro

BOLIVIA

C
H
I
L
E

Rio de la Plata

FALKLAND IS.
Port Stanley
SNOW SQUALL (1864)

Straits of le Maire
CAPE HORN   TIERRA DEL FUEGO

A
T
L
A
N
T
I
C

O
C
E
A
N

0   1400 MIs
0   2000 Km

HAWAII

Pearl Harbor ×
USS ARIZONA
(1941)

0   150 MIs
0   250 Km

YUKON   N.W. TERRITORIES

NEWFOUNDLAND

BRIT.
COL.

ALB.   SASK.   MAN.

ONTARIO   QUEBEC

N.B.
WASH.   ME.   NOVA
MONTANA   N.DAK.   MINN.   MICH.   N.Y. N.H. SCOTIA
OREGON   WIS.   MASS.
IDAHO   WYO.   S.DAK.   PA.   R.I.
NEBR.   IOWA   ILL. IND. OHIO   N.J. CONN.
CALIFORNIA NEV. UTAH COLO. KANSAS MO. KY. WVA. VA. DEL.
ARIZ.   N.MEX.   OKLA. ARK. TENN. N.C. MD.
MISS. ALA. GA. S.C.
TEXAS   LA.
FLA.

PROVINCES
AND STATES
OF CANADA
AND USA

0   800 MIs
0   1200 Km

Introduction

George F. Bass

It is impossible to imagine a history of the Americas without ships and boats.

The European discovery, exploration, colonization, commercial development and defense of this New World have all depended on ships.

But European explorers, even as early as Leif Eiriksson, were not the first to use water transport in the Americas. Columbus' ships were met by Caribbean watercraft, and Europeans who followed the great admiral encountered specialized local craft – birchbark canoes, log dugouts, skin-covered kayaks and reed *balsas* – as they pushed overland from the Atlantic to the Pacific.

The soldiers, priests, merchants and adventurers who both westernized and plundered much of South and Middle America arrived by sea. Columbus himself founded the first Christian town in the Americas, La Isabela in the Dominican Republic, in 1494. Cortés, Cabral, Balboa and Pizarro were among those who followed in his wake.

Farther north, discoveries by other intrepid mariners led to the colonization of what today are the United States and Canada. Ponce de León discovered Florida in 1513 by sea, and eleven years later Verrazzano made landfall in present-day North Carolina before sailing all the way up the coast to Maine. Basque seafarers entered still more northerly waters, not for what the land could yield, but for whales.

The first permanent European settlers in North America reached Jamestown in the *Susan Constant*, *Godspeed* and *Discovery*. A replica of the *Mayflower*, which not long ago duplicated the Pilgrims' transatlantic crossing, represents the interest we still have in the vessels that populated our early colonies. The replica of a Manila galleon, recently built in Mexico, demonstrates an equal interest in the ships that once brought goods from across the Pacific, goods that were transshipped overland to cargo holds waiting to ferry them on to Europe.

Throughout the Americas, ships made possible the wretched trade in African slaves.

When some of the North American colonies opted for independence from the Old World, a naval blockade of the York River was decisive to the outcome of the battle of Yorktown, which led to Cornwallis' final surrender of British forces.

Much later, when these colonies had become united states on the verge of becoming disunited, naval forces again played a crucial role in the outcome. In his book, *The Civil War* (1971), the eminent historian Bruce Catton writes:

> While the rival armies swayed back and forth over the landscape . . . a profound intangible was slowly beginning to tilt the balance against the Confederacy. On the ocean, in the coastal sounds, and up and down the inland rivers the great force of sea power was making itself felt. By itself it could never decide the issue of the war; taken in conjunction with the work of the Federal armies, it would ultimately be decisive. In no single area of the war was the overwhelming advantage possessed by the Federal government so ruinous to Southern hopes.

Even today, the most powerful military deterrent in the Americas probably lies in the fleet of Trident submarines gliding silently beneath the waves. Even today, immigrants disembark onto American shores from ships and boats. Even today, bulk cargoes, from oil to the automobiles that devour it, reach our coasts by sea.

More than a dozen years ago, I edited *A History of Seafaring Based on Underwater Archaeology*, a book intended to combine and supplement existing information with the latest results of the new field of nautical archaeology. I had not anticipated the public interest that led, eventually, to the book's publication in six languages.

That original volume emphasized mostly earlier ships and boats, watercraft about which we would have had few details without archaeology. Only the last two of twelve chapters dealt with watercraft in the Americas. There were two reasons for this. The first was that nautical archaeology was pioneered in and matured in the Mediterranean and in Northern Europe. The second was that I believed archaeology had far more to offer to, say, the study of classical or Viking ships than to the study of ships of the modern era. What new information could shipwreck archaeology offer us about much more recent vessels?

The answer came to me several years ago when I was asked to give a paper on 'Shipwreck Archaeology in the Eastern United States' at a published symposium organized by Louisiana State University. My own experience as an underwater archaeologist had been mostly with ancient Mediterranean shipwrecks. Thus, I was surprised to learn that we know more about the construction of Greek and Roman ships than we do of relatively modern Spanish and Portuguese ships of exploration. I found how vividly careful excavation can bring to life the crews and passengers of even more recent vessels. I was heartened to learn that a small but growing number of nautical archaeologists are conducting excavations in the New World to the same exacting standards as those established earlier in Europe.

Why nautical archaeology in the Americas has lagged behind that in Europe is not easily explained. Perhaps it is because New World archaeologists traditionally have been most interested in pre-Columbian sites and cultures. Thus, it went almost unnoticed by many of them that historic shipwrecks were being looted by treasure-hunters who would have been prohibited by law from bulldozing Indian mounds for pottery or dismantling historic dwellings for souvenirs they might sell for personal gain. At last, largely through the work of the authors of this book, nautical archaeology in the Americas has a bright future, a future to benefit historians, other archaeologists and, most importantly, the general public.

Archaeologists trained on Mediterranean shipwrecks, in fact, are playing a major role in starting scholarly underwater archaeology in the New World. I had a modest part in beginning the first scientific excavations of both American and British shipwrecks from our War of Independence. David Switzer, director of the *Defence* excavation in Maine, was trained on a Late Roman wreck in Turkey. John Broadwater, now excavating one of Cornwallis' ships in the York River, Virginia, earlier dived on wrecks in Turkey, as well as in North Carolina and Truk. The first hull Richard Steffy ever restored was that of a classical Greek ship in Cyprus. Donald Keith had excavated wrecks in the Mediterranean before beginning the first full-scale, thorough excavation ever conducted of a ship of the exploration period in the Caribbean. Their work is described in the following pages.

The chapters here, as in the original *History of Seafaring*, are all written by scholars who have studied firsthand ships and shipwrecks of the periods they cover. By good fortune, all are friends. I have personally explored with them some of the sites they describe, and in other cases they have worked on my underwater projects.

Margaret Leshikar describes indigenous watercraft from Peru to the northwest of North America, illustrated by evidence ranging from Maya reliefs to descriptions and drawings of early explorers in the New World; she has studied surviving Aztec dugouts, and has recorded in detail present methods of building dugouts in the Caribbean. **Roger Smith**, who is conducting a search for two of Columbus' ships abandoned off the north coast of Jamaica, presents evidence for locations of other Columbus shipwrecks, and what might be learned from them to supplement existing information from contemporaneous models and paintings.

Donald Keith moves the story forward by writing on the ships of exploration that followed immediately after Columbus, and the knowledge gleaned from the wrecks of such ships he has examined off the Bahamas, the Turks and Caicos Islands, and Mexico. Hulls of Iberian ships locked in the frozen north are better preserved than those of ships sunk in the shipworm-infested Caribbean, and these are described by **Robert Grenier**, director of the excavation of a remarkable Basque whaler in Labrador. **Roger Smith** then combines both field and archival research to present a vivid picture of the treasure-laden Spanish galleons that carried the riches of the Americas back to Europe.

Shipping in the English colonies was involved with the transport of more mundane goods – and with people. **J. Richard Steffy** describes modern replicas of the famed *Mayflower*, *Susan Constant*, *Godspeed* and *Discovery* mentioned above, and provides construction details from shipwrecks of both coastal and transoceanic vessels of the period. **Kevin Crisman**, who pioneered the excavation and study of wrecks in the lakes of the northern United States, draws on an abundance of well-preserved ships to describe the role of watercraft in the westward movement of Europeans during the French and Indian War. **John Sands**, who is engaged in current excavations of British ships lost by General Cornwallis in the York River, Virginia, describes these ships in their historical context, and illustrates other ships from the War of Independence, including the American brig *Defence*, recently excavated in Maine, and the famous *Philadelphia*, raised from Lake Champlain.

Perhaps the most perfectly preserved early ships ever found in the Americas are those of the *Hamilton* and *Scourge*, sitting upright at a depth of 300 ft (90 m) on the bed of Lake Ontario in Canadian waters. Even their painted figureheads have survived in excellent condition since the War of 1812, as **Kenneth Cassavoy** and **Kevin Crisman** show.

Joe Simmons, in writing on the steamboats that carried bulk cargoes and passengers throughout North America, concentrates on the wreck of the *Bertrand*, a stern-wheeler sunk in the Missouri River in 1865; its excavation yielded 140 tons of mid-nineteenth century artifacts, more than a million items! **Gordon Watts** combines space-age technology and Civil War history in discussing his dives from a special submarine on the famed ironclad *Monitor*, 200 ft (60 m) below the stormy waters off Cape Hatteras. He relates his own experiences on blockade runners sunk off the same North Carolina

coast, but ranges from Texas to Mississippi in describing other wrecks from the war between the states.

Paul Johnston describes the great sailing vessels that made America a commercial power in the nineteenth century, from eastern whalers and Clipper ships to the wrecks of Gold Rush ships in California. Finally, I found myself so dependent on the vast knowledge of marine salvage stored by **Captain W. F. Searle**, USN (ret), who was Director of Ocean Engineering, Supervisor of Salvage, and Supervisor of Diving for the United States Navy between 1964 and 1969, that I prevailed upon him to write with me a chapter about the future of underwater archaeology in the Americas.

Many of the authors share a common training. Smith, Crisman, Cassavoy and Simmons received their MA degrees in nautical archaeology at Texas A&M University, where Steffy and I were among their professors, and where Smith and Keith are now completing doctorates. Leshikar, Sands, Watts and Johnston have assisted field projects of the Institute of Nautical Archaeology, now based at Texas A&M, where Grenier visits for consultations with Steffy. Searle, who had lent Navy support to some of my own early efforts in underwater technology, was a founding director of the Institute, and the driving force behind the Institute's first New World project – the excavation of the *Defence*. The family of nautical archaeologists remains small.

Nautical history, however, is not simply for scholars. We cannot and should not deny the simple romantic appeal of experiencing the past. As I wrote some of this introduction I was sailing through the Virgin Islands, struck by the awesome isolation of the landfalls that Columbus saw on his second voyage. One night there was a rough crossing. Most of us did not sleep. A few were seasick. Yet we were stabilized and air-conditioned, guests on the 170-ft motor yacht *Michaela Rose*. I wondered idly what it was like for the crews of early caravels and *naos* in these Caribbean waters. Later, from my porthole, I could see a future archaeological site – the rusting hulk of *Sarah*, on her side, half above and half

below the surface of the harbor of Aquilla in the British West Indies. Civilization now is near at hand. But what was it like to be wrecked centuries ago? Within sight of *Sarah* is a desert island – a few palm trees in the midst of white sand – a cartoon island out of the pages of *New Yorker* or *Punch*. One morning, sitting on the sand while my companions swam and dived, I tried to imagine the loneliness of being marooned. Even there my imagination was not vivid enough.

It was not until I had edited almost the entire manuscript and written the above words that, at last, the significance of seafaring to almost all Americans of European, African or Asian descent really struck home. Going through old family papers for the first time, I discovered that my great-great-grandfather, the Reverend William Jessup Armstrong, drowned in November 1846 when the side-wheel steamer *Atlantic* was wrecked in Long Island Sound with the loss of forty-two souls. And that my great-great-great-great-grandmother, Nancy Alexander Wauchope, gave birth to a son on 15 December 1727 during a three-month crossing from Ireland to Pennsylvania. Having made a December crossing of the North Atlantic on the *Queen Mary*, I shudder to imagine *that* experience! That ships of almost every century covered in this book affected my forebears later came to light when I found that the first European in my family to reach the New World, Captain Nathaniel Basse, arrived by ship at Jamestown on 27 April 1619. And when I learned that some of my ancestors on that paternal side were Algonkian-speaking Indians, I realized that even native American canoes and dugouts must have played a role in my distant past. I had been a nautical archaeologist for more than a quarter of a century, but it was through these dry-land discoveries that the importance of watercraft to my life, and to the lives of virtually all Americans, finally made an emotional impact. Those who want to understand the Americas and Americans cannot distance themselves from the ships and boats described in the following pages. They have touched us all.

George F. Bass

CHAPTER ONE

The Earliest Watercraft: From Rafts to Viking Ships

Margaret E. Leshikar

Human beings have lived on the American continents for at least 12,000 years. They traveled from East Asia by land and, perhaps, at times by sea in more than a single migration. They came via the Bering Strait, today a 53-mile-wide passage of water that separates Alaska and Siberia, but twice in the past 38,000 years the site of a 'land bridge' connecting the continents when sea levels were lower. Exhibiting flexibility and ingenuity, they adapted to varied natural environments and their populations diversified culturally as they spread across the landscape.

In the thousands of years before Columbus reached America, its inhabitants had not developed use of the wheel for transportation, and beasts of burden, such as dogs and llamas, were used only on a limited basis. Yet there was scarcely a populated place where land met river, lake or sea – from the North American Arctic to Tierra del Fuego – that some form of watercraft was not used by pre-Columbian residents. Today we have a wealth of information about these indigenous vessels of the Period of Contact, from letters, books, journals, sketches and paintings of early European explorers. Modern ethnographic data, used with caution, provide additional insight into some pre-Columbian traditions that survived contact. We must depend on archaeology, however, for more concrete knowledge about the very earliest American watercraft. In some areas their use can be inferred simply because islands were settled. In others, representations of vessels have been discovered in the form of pictographs, petroglyphs, engravings, murals and models. We even have surviving aboriginal boats.

In the Americas there is evidence for pre-Columbian use of floats, rafts, dugout canoes, bark canoes, plank canoes, reed boats and skin boats. Environment dictated need and provided natural resources for tools and building materials. It played a major role in the development of specialized local watercraft in diverse regions of the Western Hemisphere.

North America: Skin Boats and Canoes

Skin boats. Eskimos occupied the demanding North American Arctic from the Bering Strait to Greenland prior to European arrival. Their maritime culture has roots in Alaska, where archaeological evidence of whale hunting from around 2000 BC has been found. Exploitation of the sea implies the use of watercraft, and as the Eskimos spread from Alaska to Greenland they took with them a tradition of building skin boats. Though regional styles evolved over time and distance, two distinct types of boats, the kayak and the umiak, were built from coast to coast. We do not know when Eskimo skin boats first evolved into kayaks and umiaks, but we do have evidence that 1,500 years ago they had developed into forms similar to their more modern counterparts. Toy or model kayaks and umiaks, dated to about AD 500, have been discovered in excavations near Point Barrow in northern Alaska.

The earliest historical mention of Eskimo skin boats comes from the medieval Icelandic sagas, but the voyages of English navigator Martin Frobisher between 1576 and 1578, in his search for the Northwest Passage to India, provide greater detail. A watercolor attributed to John White, of Frobisher's battle with Eskimos, depicts an actual sixteenth-century kayak.

Though regional styles differ, and many varieties have gone out of use, original Eskimo kayaks and umiaks are still in existence. Historian and naval architect Howard I. Chapelle recorded detailed information about a wide range of skin boats, and states that, in skilled hands, they are perhaps the most seaworthy of all primitive small craft. Since the kayak and umiak are very different from European watercraft, there is little chance that European ships influenced their basic construction. Both are built with a lashed framing system, usually of driftwood, that is first erected and then fitted with a skin cover oiled with animal fat. The seams also are treated with blubber or animal fat.

The kayak, a small decked canoe, was used primarily by men for hunting and fishing. The gunwale gives the vessel its strength, while light longitudinal battens and light frames support the skin cover. The unique vessel is made watertight when the occupant laces his skin clothing over the rim of a 'manhole' through which he sits. If the kayak capsizes, the Eskimo can right himself and the kayak with a stroke of his paddle. The craft combines great strength, lightness and seaworthiness, and is ideal for hunting, fishing and portaging. It is maneuvered with paddles.

In contrast, the umiak – larger than the kayak – has a strong keelson, strong longitudinal chine timbers, and transverse frames in three sections (two on the sides and one on the bottom). The umiak has great elasticity in that its seal- or walrus-skin cover is completed as a unit and then secured only to the gunwales, the stem and the stern, and not rigidly attached to the frame. Such construction makes the umiak especially seaworthy in a sea of floating ice. The umiak was made for carrying cargo and passengers long distances, qualities suited to family migration by sea. In some areas, streamlined versions of umiaks were also used for whaling and hunting walrus. Primarily propelled by paddles, umiaks with sails of animal skins or bladders were reported by participants in the sixteenth-century voyages of Frobisher. Whether knowledge of sail spread to the eastern coast from Alaska, where grass-mat sails may have been used, or whether east-coast Eskimos adopted the technology of sail from early sixteenth-century European ships, or even earlier Viking vessels, is not known.

Skin boats were also built by North American Indians in regions where bark canoes were more common, but these usually were temporary craft made when bark was not readily available. Rather than following the Eskimo technique of fitting a skin cover over a framework already lashed together, the Indians made a skin boat with the same methods as for bark canoes, so that the skin cover held the framework together.

The simplest skin boat used in North America was actually a coracle called a 'bull-boat'. Generally made from one or two buffalo hides stretched over a basket-like framework of willow or other boughs, it was widely used for crossing rivers and streams by the Plains Indians, including the Mandan, Cherokee, Omaha, Kansas, Hidatsa and Assiniboin. It was either towed by a swimmer or propelled with short-handled paddles or with poles.

Bark canoes. One of the most romanticized creations of North American Indian culture is the birchbark canoe, the primitive watercraft which later captured the imagination of artists, poets and novelists. Although information from the Contact Period on the Indian bark canoe is limited, it may be assumed that the highly evolved canoe in use at that time had a very long history of development. The French explorer Jacques Cartier reported seeing bark canoes as early as 1534, and in 1603 Samuel de Champlain measured an Algonkin vessel near Quebec that was about 20 ft (6 m) long and 3 ft (1 m) wide. He was impressed by the great speed of the canoes, as was Captain George Weymouth in 1603 off the coast of Maine. Weymouth reported that Indian bark canoes propelled by only three or four paddlers could overtake the English ship's boat with its four oarsmen.

From the earliest accounts we learn that Europeans were impressed not only with the speed of Indian bark canoes, but by their usefulness in river rapids, in shallow water and even at sea. Being very lightweight, they could be portaged easily around waterfalls and dangerous rapids. They were strong and stable and even when loaded were not easily capsized. Though bark was somewhat fragile, it was plentiful, so repairs were not difficult. Such characteristics made the Indian bark canoe well suited to wilderness travel, and it was adopted quickly by Europeans for that purpose because it was superior to their wooden boats; they used the bark canoe for exploration and later for the fur trade, and though sometimes they made larger vessels, the basic Indian design remained unchanged.

The range of the bark canoe was as wide as that of the paper birch trees from which the bark was taken. The area includes, coast to coast, most of Canada and Alaska north to the Arctic environment, and extends south through the northern states of the United States. Bark canoes were made by the Micmac, Malecite, St Francis-Abnaki, Beothuk, Eastern and Western Cree, Algonkins, Ojibway, Chipewyan, Beaver, Têtes de Boule, Nahane, Sekani, Kutenai, Salish and other Indian tribes.

The Indian tradition of building bark canoes, still practiced in the nineteenth century, was carefully recorded by Edwin Tappan Adney, who was born in 1868. Howard Chapelle organized Adney's notes and drawings in order to provide great detail about such construction. Though bark canoe styles varied from tribe to tribe, the data we have suggest that those forms changed very little over time, and the basic building methods for such vessels are probably pre-Columbian.

The distinctive characteristic of bark canoes is that they were built by forcing a framing system into a previously assembled tree-bark cover. First the gunwales and thwarts were built and laid on the wet bark, holding it fast as the outer edges of the bark were bent up into the rough shape of the canoe and held in place by vertical stakes. The gunwale was then lifted and sewn to the bark, and finally the ribs were inserted.

Though paper birch provided the superior and preferred bark for canoes, the bark of elm, hickory, chestnut, cottonwood, spruce and other types of birch was sometimes used. The bark was peeled from the trees and was usually sewn together with roots of the black spruce. The seams were made watertight with gum from the black or white spruce, the sealant being tempered with a little animal fat and powdered charcoal. Wood from other local trees was used for ribs, thwarts, gunwales, end pieces and interior sheathing. Among the pre-Columbian tools used for building bark canoes were axes, wedges, hammers, knives and scrapers of stone, bone awls and wooden mauls.

Dugout canoes. Dugout canoes were used extensively in two major areas of America north of Mexico. The

Skin Boats and Bark Canoes

Watercraft made from skins or bark were widespread in pre-Columbian North America, from Eskimo kayaks and umiaks in Arctic regions, bull-boats among the Plains Indians, to the famous birchbark canoes of Canada and the northern United States.

1 (*above right*) The Swiss artist Karl Bodmer drew this scene in the 1830s of two Mandan Indians with their bull-boats on the Missouri River in North Dakota. Such vessels were created out of buffalo hides stretched over a basket-like framework.

2 (*center right*) A group of Hudson Bay Indians beside their tepee and birchbark canoe in 1888. So impressed were Europeans by the strength and lightness of this type of canoe that they adopted it for their own use in exploration and the fur trade.

3 (*below*) Greenland Eskimos of 1905 display their kayaks (foreground) and an umiak. The agile kayak was the supreme craft for hunting and fishing in Arctic waters; the umiak transported cargo and passengers long distances.

southeastern region extends roughly from the Great Lakes southward to the Gulf of Mexico, east to the Atlantic Ocean, and west to encompass the major river systems which discharge into the Gulf of Mexico. The northwestern region is a rich coastal strip that borders the Pacific Ocean, is cut off on the east side by extensive mountain ranges, and stretches from Alaska through northern California.

In the southeast there is archaeological evidence of the early use of dugout canoes. On the wall of a rock shelter near the Rio Grande in Texas is a pictograph, attributed to the Pecos Style of several thousand years BC, thought to represent such a canoe. Actual aboriginal dugouts, primarily of cypress or pine, have been discovered in southern Ontario, Michigan, Ohio, Vermont, North Carolina, South Carolina, Florida, Georgia, Kentucky, Mississippi, Alabama, Louisiana and possibly Texas. The

oldest known, from Florida, has been dated by radiocarbon to around 3000 BC. A vessel of white oak known as the Ringler Archaic dugout, from Savannah Lake in Ohio, has been dated by radiocarbon to around 1500 BC, and a dugout from near Lakeland, Florida, has been dated to around 1100 BC. These attest to the widespread use of such canoes in North America before the first millennium BC.

Archaeologist David Brose points out that the Ringler dugout exhibits construction techniques that involve the use of fire and stone axes. This is similar to a method used by Indians in Virginia to build a dugout canoe 3,000 years later. In the late 1500s Thomas Harriot described how the Indians first selected a tree and made a controlled fire on the ground around its roots. When the tree eventually fell, they burned off the top and branches. Then they laid it upon horizontal poles held up by forked posts and

Discovering Dugouts

New finds over the last two decades have brought to light evidence for North American dugouts several thousand years old.

4 (*left*) A diver lifts part of the 5,000-year-old dugout found at De Leon Springs, Florida.

5 (*below left*) A 3,500-year-old dugout was accidentally discovered in 1976 on the Ringler property at Savannah Lake, Ohio, a peat-filled bog that earlier had yielded two similar canoes. This example had been made by charring and scraping the wood.

6 (*below*) This copy of a rock-shelter sketch in Val Verde County, Texas, may show an early dugout. Painted in the so-called Pecos Style, the sketch is probably 3,000–6,000 years old.

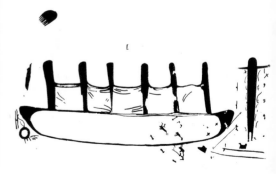

The manner of their fishing

A Vanishing Tradition

Nearly two centuries apart, the artists John White and Paul Kane recorded the native boatbuilding tradition.

7 (*above*) White's watercolor of the English explorer Frobisher's fight with Eskimos in 1577 shows a kayak.

8 (*right*) Eight years later, in 1585, White painted this scene of Indians fishing from a dugout off the North Carolina coast.

9 (*below*) The Canadian artist Paul Kane traveled overland in the mid-nineteenth century to document the Indians of the Pacific Northwest, who relied on fishing for their livelihood using canoes such as these.

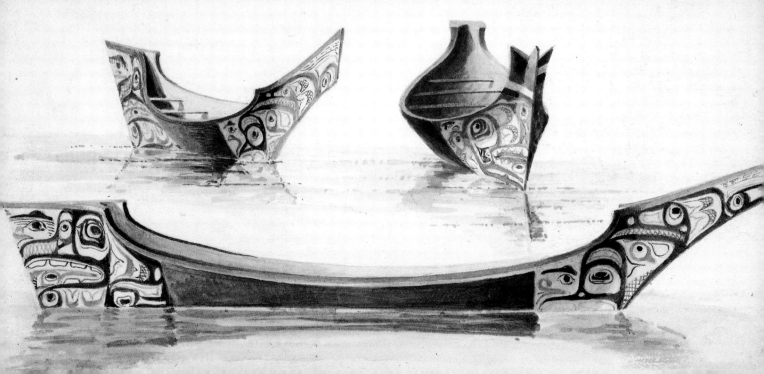

10 (*left*) A sixteenth-century engraving of native Americans building a dugout canoe by means of fire.

11 (*right*) This pre-Columbian paddler appears on a conch-shell fragment from the site of Spiro, Oklahoma, a major North American ceremonial center some 600 years ago.

removed the bark with shells. Finally, the canoe was shaped by repetitive burning and scraping out of the resulting coals with shells.

Archaeological evidence of dugouts has been found also in the form of engravings on conch shells from the Late Prehistoric Period at Spiro, Oklahoma. These illustrations reveal that some canoes were decorated and carried standards, and that one method of propulsion was by short-handled paddles.

One of the most colorful descriptions we have of sixteenth-century dugout canoes comes from Garcilaso de la Vega, who recorded the information from a member of Hernando de Soto's 1539–43 expedition to what is now the southeastern United States. De la Vega wrote that the Indian canoes which pursued the Spaniards down the Mississippi River were unusually large, the smallest having 14 paddlers on each side, the largest having 25 paddlers on each side and 25 to 30 warriors in between. He said that the canoes were made from single pieces of wood and that they were so swift that a horse running at full speed would hardly have advantage over them. The Indians sang many songs in rhythm so that they could paddle in unison, and their decorated canoes, he emphasized, were each tinted a single color, even down to the occupants and paddles.

Other early illustrations and accounts reveal that dugout canoes were used in the southeast for hunting, fishing, commerce, warfare and as basic transportation. John White's 1585 watercolor shows Indians fishing off the North Carolina coast. We also see the style of dugouts in use there, and the long-handled paddles that were used for propulsion. Two Indians are shown building a small fire, probably on a base of clay in the center of the canoe.

In contrast to other advanced cultures in the New World, many Indian tribes on the Northwest Coast of North America, including the Nootka, Makah, Wishram, Kwakiutl, Quinault and Haida, developed a very advanced culture that was not based on agriculture. In a damp and relatively mild environment of dense forests,

rivers and innumerable inlets filled with islands, they fished for salmon, halibut, cod, herring and shellfish. Several tribes even became efficient in capturing whales, seals and sea lions. In short, the Northwest Coast people were principally fishermen, their other methods of food gathering being secondary. In perhaps no other area of North America was the canoe so essential to Indian lifeways.

Archaeology suggests that these coastal fishermen were related to the early Eskimos, but that by 1000 BC they had developed a separate and distinct culture on the Northwest Coast. In an environment that made water transportation easier and more efficient than that on land, they became expert in the building of dugout canoes. Their vessels, generally made of red cedar, ranged from canoes built for one person to great seagoing war, ritual and trade canoes usually about 39 ft (12 m), but also up to 59 ft (18 m), in length. Lewis and Clark noted in 1806 that the Northwest Coast Indians had a number of different types of dugout canoes. Modern scholars, attempting to determine the pre-European canoe types, have proposed as few as two ('ocean canoes' and 'river canoes') to as many as five or six distinct types, suggesting that Northwest Coast canoes evolved into specialized forms. It is noteworthy that Lewis and Clark remarked that the oceangoing canoes rode better at sea than did the white man's boats.

Construction of Northwest Coast canoes involved a stone tool assemblage. The basic vessel was carved from a single tree, but bow and stern pieces designed to throw aside the seas were pegged and lashed to the hulls of some of the large canoes. The advanced development and large size of these canoes was in part made possible by the abundance of trees of vast size in the coastal forests.

Northwest Coast Indian culture survived until the first part of the twentieth century. Because of this we have been left with both ethnographic examples and photographs of their vessels, which probably exhibit little European influence.

Sewn-plank canoes. In the early twentieth century John P. Harrington documented sewn-plank canoes made by the Chumash and Gabrielino Indians of southern California. Built outside the redwood belt, where trees large enough to make dugouts are found, they were constructed of redwood driftwood from the north and from a poor variety of local pine. The larger and more stable vessels seen by Europeans at first contact probably evolved from small dugouts to which boards of driftwood were added. Eventually, the dugout portion was reduced to a single thick plank with prow and sternpost continuing its line; small planks were then lashed together with red milkweed string or deer sinew and asphalted in place to form a hull. The sewn-plank canoe was propelled by double-bladed paddles. Although generally used for coastal travel, it was used in fair weather for open-sea crossings to the Channel Islands, the nearest lying 25 miles off the southern California coast. Archaeological finds suggest that such vessels may have been in use by AD 500. There are no known drawings or surviving specimens of the early planked canoes, but a few perforated canoe planks and possible models have been found.

Reed boats. Boats of tule, a local bulrush, were used in bays and off the coast of California for fishing and hunting. The simplest style was made of three bundles of tule bound together, but larger craft were also constructed. These reed boats were propelled by double-bladed paddles.

Rafts. Rafts were also used in North America. Having a distribution that is almost universal, these craft, constructed from available regional resources such as reeds, logs or other materials, were usually improvised for fishing or for crossing streams.

The Caribbean Islands

Dugout canoes. Some of the earliest archaeological evidence for settlement of the Caribbean Islands occurs in the form of pre-pottery sites, dated as early as 2700 BC, on Hispaniola. Though the first prehistoric settlers obviously traveled by sea, nothing is known about the watercraft they used to reach their destinations. By the time the Spaniards arrived in 1492, however, dugout canoes were used widely by the two most prominent linguistic-cultural groups in the West Indies: the Arawak who populated the Bahamas and the Greater Antilles, and the Carib who lived in the Lesser Antilles. The Arawak entered the West Indies from South America shortly before the time of Christ and had spread from the Lesser Antilles as far as the Bahamas by about AD 1000. They were eventually displaced from the Lesser Antilles by the Carib who, according to their own tradition, came to the West Indies about a century before the arrival of Columbus.

Numerous interpretations of Arawak and Carib canoes have been attempted by modern scholars. Substantive archaeological material for direct evidence is lacking, but a few clues about the vessels are available in the earliest first-hand accounts. In the journal of Columbus for 13 October 1492, there is a description of Arawak canoes recorded during the first European encounter with people of the Caribbean:

> They came to the ship in boats, which are made of a tree-trunk like a long boat and all of one piece. They are very wonderfully carved, considering the country, and large, so that in some forty or forty-five men came. Others are smaller, so that in some only a solitary man came. They row them with a paddle, like a baker's peel, and they travel wonderfully fast. If one capsizes, all at once begin to swim to right it, bailing it out with gourds which they carry with them.

One of the few archaeological recoveries associated with canoes in the Caribbean is an Arawak paddle, carved from a single piece of cedar and found in a cave on Mores Island on the Little Bahama Bank. Another paddle has been found in Cuba, and a petroglyph depicting a paddle has been found in a cave on Rum Cay in the Bahamas.

Dugout canoe design and use in trade are revealed in a Columbus letter of 1493:

> They have in all the islands very many canoes, like rowing *fustas* [small European vessels], some of them larger, some of them smaller, and some larger than a *fusta* of eighteen benches. They are not as broad because they are of only one piece of wood. Moreover, a *fusta* does not catch them because their speed is something unbelievable. And with them they navigate all the innumerable islands, and trade their merchandise. I have seen one of these canoes with seventy and eighty men in her, each one with his paddle.

The canoes were probably double-ended vessels with tapered bows and sterns. It is of great interest that Columbus, the experienced mariner, judged the Indian vessels to be swifter than the small Spanish boats. The Arawak were experienced seafarers and navigated frequently by canoe between the islands of the Greater

Antilles even though, according to Columbus, their canoes had no sails. Perhaps the largest canoe described by Columbus during his voyages was encountered among the Arawak in 1492. It was described as 63 ft long (*c.* 19 m), carved from the bole of a single tree, and capable of holding 150 people. Unfortunately, the island Arawak populations and their seafaring heritage died out within several decades of the arrival of the Spanish.

When Columbus traveled into the Lesser Antilles, he encountered the other dominant Caribbean Indians, the Carib. Of them Dr Diego Alvarez Chanca, physician on Columbus' second voyage, wrote:

> One and all make war against all the neighboring islands, traveling by sea a hundred and fifty leagues to attack with their many canoes, which are small *fustas* of a single piece of wood.

There is no mention of sails used on Indian watercraft encountered by Columbus (the 'mast' mentioned in a nineteenth-century English version of this passage is a mistranslation), but later Contact Period accounts suggest to modern scholars that the Carib did have sails. The statement that the Carib could make voyages of 150 leagues implies that they could navigate about 600 miles from home in their canoes, for Columbus mentions that

the system used at sea was 4 miles to the league. If the Carib did not use sails, they traveled prodigious distances among the islands by only paddle propulsion.

Early accounts also give us information about dugout canoe construction in the West Indies. Dr Chanca recorded data about tools available for such work:

> None of the people of these islands, as far as we have yet seen, possess any iron; they have many tools, such as axes and adzes, made of stone, so excellent and so well finished it is a marvel that they can be made without iron.

Sixteenth-century Spanish historian Gonzalo Fernández de Oviedo y Valdés wrote that Arawak dugout canoes were made from logs repeatedly burned out in their interiors, the charred areas being removed with stone axes. Another Spaniard of this period, Bartolomé de Las Casas, wrote that in Cuba and Hispaniola canoes were made from cedar and ceiba. Though present-day canoes cannot provide direct evidence of ancient construction methods or design, it is of interest that Jamaican canoes are still often carved from cedar and ceiba. My documentation of the construction of one such vessel made it evident to me that the wood of the ceiba, locally known as 'silk cotton', is very light textured and that even stone tools would be quite efficient in working it.

12   Caribbean canoe construction: modern boatbuilding methods help shed light on earlier practice. Here a ceiba tree trunk is being hollowed out by Jamaicans using metal axes. The wood is soft enough even for stone axes to be quite effective, without resorting to fire. Sixteenth-century Spanish historians mention the use of this same tree by the indigenous Arawak to make their dugouts.

Maya Navigation

The creators of pre-Columbian America's greatest civilization, the Maya transported many of their goods by canoe along coasts and rivers.

13 (*right*) Tulum's El Castillo, with its illuminated windows, can guide vessels through a narrow opening in the coral reef opposite, and perhaps served as a pre-Columbian lighthouse.

14 (*below*) A coastal scene depicted on a fresco of about AD 1000 in the Temple of the Warriors, Chichén Itzá. Three canoes with high bows and sterns – reminiscent of those shown on Maya bone engravings (ills.15–17) – carry warriors past a village.

Rafts. Rafts were not commonly used in the West Indies. Las Casas, however, mentions that on one occasion, when Spaniards deprived the Arawak of their canoes, the Indians fashioned a raft by binding hollow stakes together. Though the raft was probably used for limited purposes, Indians of the Caribbean Islands were familiar with the methods employed in its construction.

Middle America: Vessels of the Maya and Aztec

Dugout canoes. Maya civilization flourished from the Yucatan Peninsula south to the Guatemala highlands in the first thousand years AD. Although its great cities – Tikal, Copan, Palenque – subsequently collapsed, Maya culture was still in existence when the Spaniards arrived at the beginning of the sixteenth century. The region was well suited to water transport. Dense forests discouraged land routes while favoring coastal and riverine traffic, and there were numerous large rivers in its central part. Archaeologist Norman Hammond concludes that the Caribbean coastal route ultimately reached from north of Mexico City along the entire length of Mexico and Central America to the present-day Panama Canal, linking all areas in commercial contact. He hypothesizes that large, seagoing canoes stopped at offshore facilities such as the islands of Cozumel, Wild Cane Cay and Moho Cay, where evidence of exotic trade goods (obsidian, metalwork and pottery) has been found, some dating as early as AD 250–900, and that transshipment of goods to smaller river and shore-going canoes occurred.

A scatter of stone axes that may represent the cargo of a wrecked canoe has been reported on the sea bed off the east coast of Cozumel, and archaeologists have tried to locate canoes by remote-sensing techniques in the Maya area. At present, however, our sources of information on Maya canoes are limited to engravings on bone and stone, bone models, metal reliefs, painted murals, Maya codices and ethnohistoric accounts.

Depictions of canoes occur in seven scenes engraved on bones recovered from the grave of Ruler A at Tikal, Guatemala, a site located near a river but some 90 miles from the coast. Dated to AD 700, the seven scenes show two or three different styles of canoe. Two scenes show Maya deities fishing from canoes that have flat and extended bows and sterns. One god gathers fish while the other uses a paddle that has a blade widened on only one side of the shaft. Above the canoe is a series of glyphs; the first is a 'canoe glyph' that probably represents a journey by canoe, the second identifies the god in the canoe, and the third is the place glyph for Tikal. Another engraving from Tikal shows a canoe with a very high stern. The vessel dives below the surface of the water. In it, Ruler A is propelled by animal- and human-headed deities, possibly to the underworld. In the last example from Tikal, the canoe has a very high bow and stern, the bow ornately decorated and carved in the form of a Maya god.

At least two manatee-bone canoe models, interpreted as children's toys, have been found near the coast in Maya territory. The first, dated to AD 650–750, was found at Altun Ha, Belize, and the other, from an undated context, was found at Moho Cay, Belize. The models are similar in appearance. Both vessels show platform-ended canoes that are somewhat flat bottomed although rounded at the bilges. They are similar in profile to one of the Tikal styles engraved on bone.

A wall mural of *c.* AD 1000 from the Temple of the Warriors at Chichén Itzá, a site with central Mexico Toltec influence, depicts three canoes with high and slightly projecting bows and sterns. The canoes are reminiscent of the canoes with high bows and sterns represented in the Tikal bone engravings. In each are two warriors and a person engaged in propelling the vessel with a long-handled paddle, used somewhat like a punting pole. That the scene depicts coastal activity is shown by the presence of marine creatures such as crabs and stingrays. Another mural in the temple shows the bow of a canoe carved in the shape of an animal head.

At the time of the fourth voyage of Columbus, east of the Yucatan Peninsula and near the Bay Islands of Honduras, it was apparent that people of advanced cultures were engaged in extensive coastal waterborne trade in the New World. Ferdinand Columbus, Christopher's son, wrote:

> The Adelantado [Christopher Columbus] being eager to learn the secrets of that island, by good fortune there arrived at that time a canoe long as a galley and eight feet [2.5 m] wide, made of a single tree trunk like the other Indian canoes; it was freighted with merchandise from the western regions around New Spain. Amidships it had a palm-leaf awning like that which the Venetian gondolas carry; this gave complete protection against the rain and waves. Under this awning were the children and women and all the baggage and merchandise. There were twenty-five paddlers aboard.

Ferdinand Columbus continued with a description of the contents of the canoe: cotton mantles, embroidered shirts, copper axes, hawks' bells, wooden swords with flint knives embedded in their edges, roots, grain, wine made from maize and cacao. The origins of the goods range from central Mexico and the Yucatan Peninsula to the nearby coast of Honduras.

It is possible that coasting vessels were navigated in part by signals from shore. An archaeological investigation of this possibility has been initiated by Pilar Luna of Mexico's Departamento de Arqueología Subacuática del Instituto Nacional de Antropología e Historia, working with Michael Creamer. This study of small buildings along the coast of the Yucatan Peninsula, interpreted variously as religious shrines and defensive watchtowers, may reveal that the structures served also as lighthouses and other types of navigational signal beacons. It is known that bonfires were lit at some of these structures during the period of Spanish contact. That the Maya did use navigational aids is evident in Diego de Landa's comment that 'the Indians put signs on the trees to mark the way going or coming by boat from Tabasco to Yucatan'.

Reported archaeological evidence of the use of watercraft on the Pacific Coast of Middle America is limited, although sixteenth-century sources such as Nuñez de Balboa and Oviedo y Valdés mentioned Indian canoes there.

In addition to dugout canoes on the rivers and coasts of Middle America, variations of such vessels plied some of the inland lake systems. One such lake system saw the development and, ultimately, the intensive use of such watercraft by the most powerful pre-Columbian civilization of late Mesoamerica, the Mexica-Aztec, whose capital was Tenochtitlan, in the Basin of Mexico. (The Aztecs knew themselves as the Mexica but will, for convenience, be referred to here by their more widely known name, the Aztecs.) Use of the canoe in this area deserves special attention because evidence for its method of construction is supported by one of the few archaeologically recovered examples of Middle American

watercraft, and because descriptions of Aztec canoes and their use are abundant in ethnohistorical sources.

The natural environment of the Basin of Mexico was conducive to the development and support of populations who used watercraft. A volcanic basin of interior drainage, its lake system of both fresh and salt water contained many edible plants and attracted animal resources. It was also surrounded by abundant timber suitable for vessel construction. Thus, it is not surprising that use of canoes developed quite early. Studies of settlement patterns have shown that the basin supported human populations from at least as early as 1700 BC. Settlements are known to have existed on Tlapacoya Island between 1500 and 1150 BC. Since there is no evidence of watercraft other than canoes and rafts in the pre-Columbian Basin of Mexico, it is probable that canoes

Canoes in Miniature

15–17 (*above* and *left*) Three scenes engraved on bone objects from the burial of Maya Ruler A at Tikal, Guatemala, AD 732. In the first (top) two gods gather fish while another paddles the canoe. The second engraving shows Ruler A in a high-sterned canoe, apparently being propelled down into the underworld by animal and human-headed deities. The third canoe has a high bow and stern, the bow decorated in the form of a Maya god.

18 (*center left*) Possibly a child's toy, this manatee-bone canoe model was found in Maya territory on Moho Cay, an island off the coast of Belize. It resembles the platform-ended canoe in one of the Tikal engravings (ill. 15).

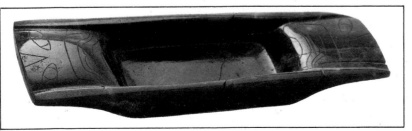

19 (*below left*) The Olmecs, who flourished along the Gulf Coast over 2,000 years ago, also used dugouts, as this jade carving shows.

Wooden Dugout, Golden Raft

20 (*left*) Part of a full-size canoe was excavated in 1959 from beneath modern Mexico City and recent work has emphasized its importance as an authentic Aztec vessel. Hewn from a single *ahuehuete* tree, it would have been capable of carrying up to five people.

21 (*below*) El Dorado, 'the gilded man', sits enthroned on a raft surrounded by attendants. This magnificent gold model from Colombia, 19 cm (7½ in) long, recalls the legend of the Muisca Indian accession ceremony on Lake Guatavita, where a reed raft was set afloat bearing the new ruler, who was bedaubed with clay and gold dust.

were already in use at that early date. There is support for this assumption in that Tlapacoya Island had affinities with the Olmec culture which dates from about 1500 to 300 BC, and a jade carving of a canoe in Olmec style was recovered during archaeological investigations at Cerro de las Mesas in Veracruz. The basic flat-bottomed, square-ended style of the Olmec canoe carving is very similar to that of later canoes in the Basin of Mexico.

Aztec mythology suggests that the tribe left Aztlan, their paradisiacal island homeland in a lake, via canoes to fulfill the destiny revealed by their patron god, Huitzilopochtli. After much wandering the god led them to the vicinity of the Basin of Mexico which, unsurprisingly, was much like Aztlan. Here they were to become legitimate heirs to power in the basin.

In actuality, the Aztecs arrived in the basin in approximately AD 1100 and, after living among the prior residents of the area for 200 years, retreated to a small island in Lake Texcoco. Making themselves useful to more powerful towns, and existing on the borders of three major centers in a somewhat neutral zone, they were able to develop their city of Tenochtitlan. They had an uncanny ability to incorporate and improve upon existing knowledge of the lake area that they had gained from the people who had long lived there. In the early days of settlement on the island, the Aztecs obtained natural resources from the lakes in canoes and transported them to the three major centers on the lakeshore, where they traded them in the market places. Payment was often in items of construction on materials for development of the island city, Tenochtitlan, because Aztec society was centrally organized and promoted the building of great public works. Canoes were essential both to transporting materials for building monumental structures and to major hydraulic engineering modifications such as the extension of land by drainage, construction of *chinampas* (floating gardens), digging of ditches and canals, and building of bridges, causeways, dikes and dams.

The city of Tenochtitlan, constructed in the midst of the lake, thus evolved in an environment which demanded that many activities be conducted via water transport. Canoes, therefore, were integrated closely into the lives of the Aztec population. The *Codex Mendoza*, an Aztec manuscript prepared by an Indian artist for the Spanish conquerors, suggests that Aztec boys were expected, by their early teens, to be able to travel alone in canoes to accomplish certain tasks. Examples of daily activities for which canoes were necessary include the transport of building materials, household materials and water; gathering fish and other aquatic plant and animal resources; transporting goods to and from the market places; and transporting goods on local and coastal trading expeditions. Canoes were also decorated and used during ritual activities, particularly in ceremonies devoted to Tlaloc, the major god associated with water, and to other water-related deities. One of the prime functions of the Aztec canoe, however, was its use in warfare. The

Aztecs consciously built up their fleets of war canoes and practiced military maneuvers. With canoes, the Aztecs were able to launch offensive conquest without fear of being attacked in their well-guarded city, which was approachable (when the bridges linking the main causeways to the island were removed) only by boat. As other Indians in the basin were not as aquatically oriented in warfare as the Aztecs, Tenochtitlan became mistress of Lake Texcoco. Control of the lake system made Tenochtitlan indomitable in the eyes of contemporary Indian societies.

Sixteenth-century sources reveal much about the design of Aztec canoes. Like the canoes previously seen by Europeans in the New World, Aztec canoes and *piraguas* (large canoes) were dugouts carved from single logs by the use of only stone or copper tools. Timber for their construction was available in the form of wood from the *ahuehuete*, American cypress and pine. In addition to vessels which may have been shaped like those used by the Maya and Caribbean peoples, the Aztecs used flat-bottomed canoes with hard-chined bows and sterns which were squared off in punt-like fashion. Records indicate that Aztec canoes did not reach the extensive proportions of the canoes reported by Columbus. The Aztec vessels are typically described as capable of carrying from one to ten people, and may have carried twenty or more. Some Aztec canoes had shelters or awnings, and the vessels were propelled by several types of devices. In addition to paddles with standard-length shafts and rounded blades, the Aztecs used long-handled, flat-bladed paddles as well as poles in their shallow-water lakes. Some Aztec vessels were decorated for warfare and ritual, and occasionally seats were used, although we cannot be certain whether these seats were part of the canoe's structure or were added, litter-like features. There is no evidence that sails were ever used on canoes in the pre-Columbian Basin of Mexico.

Archaeological data further support the ethnohistorical record concerning the features of some Aztec canoes. Two clearly pre-Columbian stone carvings in the shape of canoes were found among a cache offering to Tlaloc in a box buried in the Great Temple (Templo Mayor) of Tenochtitlan, the major Aztec ceremonial center recently excavated in the middle of Mexico City. They confirm the ethnohistorical record that some canoes correspond to the flat-bottomed punt-like shape described above for some Aztec vessels. The canoe carvings further support the thesis that such boats were used for procuring aquatic resources, as there are small carvings of a three-pronged harpoon and an atlatl (spear-thrower) in each vessel, with small fish in one. Each canoe carving also contains a paddle.

Of primary importance, the features of an archaeologically recovered dugout canoe are also compatible with the ethnohistorical data. This canoe, excavated in 1959 from a site several meters below present-day Mexico City, is carved from a single ahuehuete log. It is shaped much like

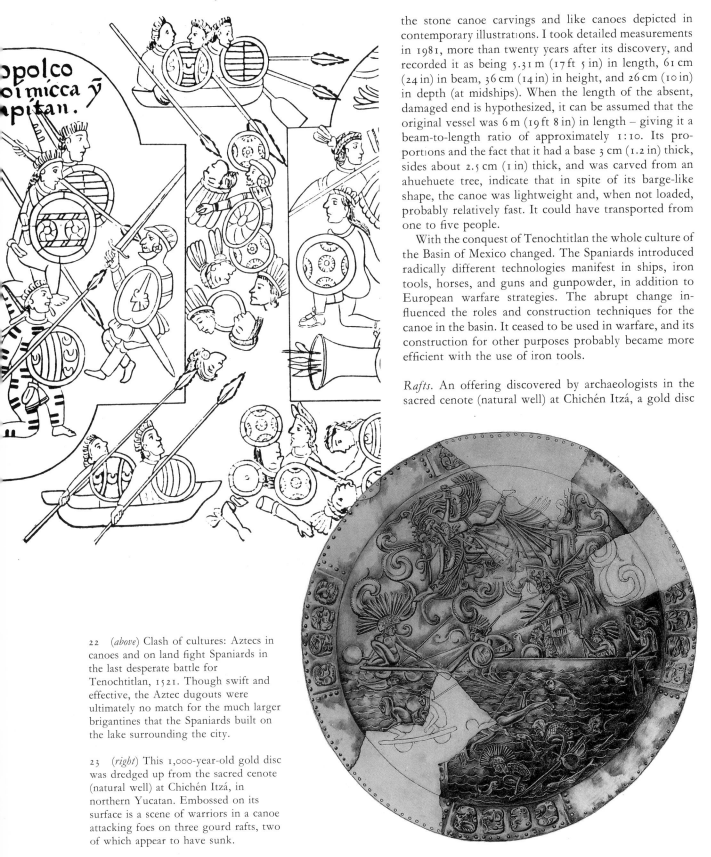

the stone canoe carvings and like canoes depicted in contemporary illustrations. I took detailed measurements in 1981, more than twenty years after its discovery, and recorded it as being 5.31 m (17 ft 5 in) in length, 61 cm (24 in) in beam, 36 cm (14 in) in height, and 26 cm (10 in) in depth (at midships). When the length of the absent, damaged end is hypothesized, it can be assumed that the original vessel was 6 m (19 ft 8 in) in length – giving it a beam-to-length ratio of approximately 1:10. Its proportions and the fact that it had a base 3 cm (1.2 in) thick, sides about 2.5 cm (1 in) thick, and was carved from an ahuehuete tree, indicate that in spite of its barge-like shape, the canoe was lightweight and, when not loaded, probably relatively fast. It could have transported from one to five people.

With the conquest of Tenochtitlan the whole culture of the Basin of Mexico changed. The Spaniards introduced radically different technologies manifest in ships, iron tools, horses, and guns and gunpowder, in addition to European warfare strategies. The abrupt change influenced the roles and construction techniques for the canoe in the basin. It ceased to be used in warfare, and its construction for other purposes probably became more efficient with the use of iron tools.

Rafts. An offering discovered by archaeologists in the sacred cenote (natural well) at Chichén Itzá, a gold disc

22 (*above*) Clash of cultures: Aztecs in canoes and on land fight Spaniards in the last desperate battle for Tenochtitlan, 1521. Though swift and effective, the Aztec dugouts were ultimately no match for the much larger brigantines that the Spaniards built on the lake surrounding the city.

23 (*right*) This 1,000-year-old gold disc was dredged up from the sacred cenote (natural well) at Chichén Itzá, in northern Yucatan. Embossed on its surface is a scene of warriors in a canoe attacking foes on three gourd rafts, two of which appear to have sunk.

embossed with the form of a canoe and what appear to be three gourd rafts, tells us that at least two kinds of watercraft were used by residents of the Yucatan Peninsula. J. Eric S. Thompson reported rafts made in modern times with a square frame of bamboo on top of which stalks were laid together to form a platform; these rafts were supported by gourds enclosed in net bags. Thompson states that such rafts, used widely throughout Mexico for fishing and for crossing streams, probably have a long history. He also suggests that rafts made from reeds, wood and other materials in modern times were known and used in Middle America in much earlier times.

South America: From Rafts to Dugouts and Reed Boats

Dugout canoes. It has been shown that dugout canoes were the primary form of pre-Columbian water transport used in the Caribbean Islands and Middle America. Their use extended even farther south to the north and east coasts of South America and to her major river systems, including the Orinoco, the Amazon and the Rio de la Plata. The first recorded sighting of dugout canoes near the mainland of South America was made during the third voyage of Columbus, in 1498, off the north coast of Venezuela. In addition, the Carib who occupied the Lesser Antilles at the time of Spanish contact continued to make visits via dugout canoes to the coast of South America, from which they had emigrated.

Dugouts are documented also on the Pacific Coast of South America, with continuous distribution from Colombia through northern Ecuador. According to Oviedo y Valdés, Indians near the Rio Esmeraldas in northern Ecuador had large canoes with structures the height of a man on their bows and sterns. Propulsion was by means of paddles and sails. Though this Indian use of the sail was observed more than twenty years after the first Spaniard arrived in the New World, many scholars believe that Oviedo's statement supports the theory that the sail was known to pre-Columbian people on the Pacific Coast of South America.

Two pre-Columbian pottery seals or stamps from Manabi Province, Ecuador, have been attributed to the Manteño culture and are thought to represent dugouts. Geographer Robert C. West suggests that the Manteño may have launched seagoing trading ventures by dugout canoe as far as the Zacatula coast of central Mexico, roughly 2,000 miles away, if a 1525 letter by Rodrigo de Albornoz does indeed refer to the Manteño.

Log rafts. Simple log rafts, similar to a model dating from approximately AD 1200 from northern Chile, were probably known from very ancient times in western South America. Sixteenth-century accounts describe these rafts

24 (*above*) Do these two vivid figures from an Ecuadorian pottery seal or stamp hold paddles in their hands and stand beside a dugout? If so, they add to the strong evidence for pre-Columbian canoes in South America.

25 (*right*) A model dating to about AD 1200 of a log raft with double-ended paddle, now in the Arica Museum, Chile. Simple rafts like this must have been used from earliest times in western South America.

as composed of an uneven number of logs, the center one, acting as a bow, being longer than the others. Such rafts were used on rivers and along the coast.

Balsa-log sailing rafts are known from early Contact Period sources, including the widely quoted accounts of Francisco de Xeréz and Miguel de Estete, who accompanied Francisco Pizarro on his second voyage towards Peru. These great trading rafts, in use when Pizarro arrived in South America, were probably adapted from pre-existing simple log rafts. Girolamo Benzoni, who traveled in the New World between 1541 and 1556, illustrated and described the rafts:

> All along this coast the Indians are great fishermen. The boats they use are a kind of raft, both for fishing or navigating, consisting of three, five, seven, nine, or eleven very slender timbers, forming a sort of hand, with the longest in the middle. They are made of various lengths, and thus carry sails according to their size; and a proportionate number of rowers. When they are becalmed at sea, they throw bread, fruit and other things over board as a sacrifice, praying for fair wind, they being too tired to row any more.

In his illustration two simple log rafts appear in the background while a balsa-log raft under sail and paddle appears in the foreground. While most scholars agree that the sail was probably known on the Pacific Coast of South America from the Manabi Province of Ecuador to the Sechura coast of Peru in pre-Columbian times, they still disagree on the shape of the Contact Period sail. Basing his opinions on extensive scholarly research and on first-hand accounts, cultural geographer Clinton R. Edwards maintains that log rafts with triangular, fore-and-aft rigged sails, and a system of centerboard navigation, were known.

Other rafts. Though distribution may have been wider, early chronicles mention the use of gourd rafts only in northern Peru. The descriptions of these rafts suggest that they were made simply by fitting large gourds tightly into net bags. These gourd rafts loaded with passengers or cargo were guided across rivers by swimmers.

Evidence for the use of an elaborately constructed and ornamented raft made of rushes exists in the form of a gold model. Actual use of the raft is known through myths and legends surrounding the accession ceremony of chieftains that took place on Lake Guatavita in Colombia and gave rise to the legend of El Dorado (which means 'the gilded man').

Reed boats. Reed boats or 'balsas' were used in pre-Columbian times along the coasts of Peru and northern Chile, and on some of the large inland lakes in the highlands, such as Lake Titicaca in the Andes on the border between Peru and Bolivia. In its simplest form, two tightly bound bundles of *totora* reeds were lashed together to make a reed float with upturned bow and truncated stern. A 2,000-year-old model of such a vessel has been excavated from a burial site in Chile. Fishermen rode astride these craft while paddling them. Simple reed floats were the most common type of reed boat used in coastal areas, though ceramic models from the Moche (AD 800–1000) and Chimú (AD 1000–1450) cultures depict a slightly larger craft, perhaps the precursor of Lake Titicaca craft upon which fishermen could sit.

The reed boats of Lake Titicaca, much larger than the coastal reed floats, have been used by Uros and Aymara Indians for fishing and transport from pre-Columbian times up to the present. Variations on the vessel occur, but most are double-ended with pointed, upturned bows and sterns.

26 (*far left*) Early chronicles describing South American life suggest that gourd rafts – similar to the ceramic model shown here – were used in northern Peru.

27 (*left*) A woodcut of 1565 depicts a Peruvian lake scene with a large balsa raft in the foreground and, in the distance, men astride three-bundle balsas towing a fishing net.

28 (*right*) A photograph taken in 1897 provides an invaluable record of the kind of reed boats used by the highland peoples of Peru since pre-Columbian times. Each boat consisted of two tightly bound bundles lashed together.

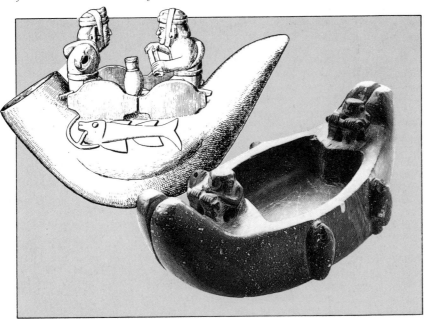

29 (*far left*) Some of the finest and most famous pre-Columbian ceramics were produced by the Moche culture 1,000 years ago in northern Peru. This pottery model shows two men fishing from the kind of reed boat used in coastal waters.

30 (*left*) Another Peruvian model, this time in stone and about 500–700 years old, represents a different type of vessel: a float made from marine mammal hides.

Skin floats. In arid and treeless coastal Peru and northern Chile, double-pontoon floats made from marine mammal hides were used in pre-Columbian times. Sixteenth-century sources suggest that the sealskin vessels were used for fishing, and later observers described how well adapted the vessels were for use in the surf zone and along rocky shores.

Sewn-bark canoes and sewn-plank canoes. According to cultural geographer Clinton R. Edwards, double-ended canoes made of bark slabs sewn together, and *dalcas* made similarly but of wooden planks sewn together, were used in southern Chile at the period of European contact. Mid-sixteenth-century witnesses refer to such vessels and relate that the bark canoes and dalcas were sewn with strips of baleen.

Pre-Columbian Visitors to the New World

Ships were central to discoveries of the Americas. Because of the impact it had on world history, the fifteenth-century discovery by Columbus deserves its pre-eminence. There is evidence, however, that other Old World seafarers encountered the vast New World still earlier. Greenland was explored and settled by Vikings from the tenth until the fifteenth century, when their colonies were abandoned, and a Norse site from about AD 1000 has been discovered and excavated at L'Anse aux Meadows on the northern tip of the Great Northern Peninsula of Newfoundland.

The settlement at L'Anse aux Meadows consisted of eight houses (one a smithy), a kiln, several large cooking pits and a boat shed. Archaeological evidence is supported by two Icelandic sagas. *The Greenlanders' Saga* and *Eirik the Red's Saga* describe early eleventh-century voyages to Helluland, Markland and Vinland, regions generally ac-

cepted today as Baffin Island, Labrador and Newfoundland. Later historical accounts, accurate geographical descriptions and modern archaeology have convinced scholars that the sagas' accounts of Leif Eiriksson's voyages to North America around AD 1000 are generally accurate. The sagas tell what appear to be two versions of the same story, but both indicate that eleventh-century Vikings crossed the sea in their ships.

The local inhabitants, whom the Norse called 'Skraelings', used skin boats. They were probably Eskimos with kayaks or umiaks, but Indians with bark canoes may also have been met. The accounts suggest that the Vikings engaged in some trading, but that most encounters with the locals ended in skirmishes. From the sagas, and from the very scarce archaeological material available, it can be assumed that exchanges of cultural and technological ideas between the two groups were limited. Following aborted efforts at colonization, the Norse attempted no other permanent settlements, although periodic trips were probably made to the great forests of Labrador from Greenland because wood was so scarce in Greenland. This is a reasonable hypothesis – Labrador was only a short distance away, and isolated Norse artifacts have been encountered in indigenous sites in probable areas of Viking exploration in North America. Also, a small chert point in the style consistent with points made by Indians in southern Labrador and Newfoundland between AD 1000 and 1500 was found in a Norse graveyard in Greenland. Vikings may, therefore, have visited North America over a period of several centuries.

Viking ships had little influence on a native population which already had watercraft that served its needs. Even the smaller wooden boats which the Norsemen must have used in coastal exploration were probably no better suited to the Arctic environment than were Eskimo skin boats.

The Vikings and America

Some 500 years before Columbus the Vikings explored the Atlantic shores of North America and established at least one settlement there.

31 (*right*) On the northern tip of Newfoundland, at a site known as L'Anse aux Meadows, archaeologists have discovered and excavated the only known Viking settlement in North America. This model reconstructs what part of the site might have looked like, with turf-roofed houses and ships drawn up away from the exposed shore, in accordance with West Norse custom.

32 (*center right*) A modern replica of the Viking *knarr* excavated at Roskilde Fjord, Denmark, provides a vivid picture of the type of vessel that carried Viking sailors to the New World. Here, in June 1986, *Saga Siglar* approaches Roskilde after a round-the-world passage that had begun in 1984.

33 (*below*) The *knarr*, a cargo ship, was strongly built to withstand the heavy seas of the North Atlantic – although, as this cross-section of the Skuldelev vessel shows, no shelter from the elements was provided for either cargo or passengers.

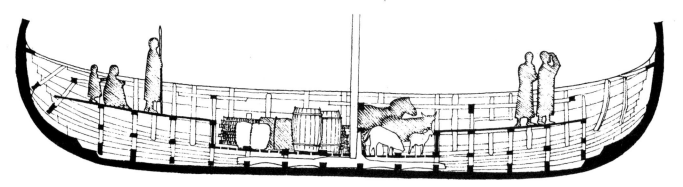

In addition, if we trust the sagas, the Vikings showed little interest in sharing their technology. Nevertheless, the vessels that carried the first known Europeans to America's shores are part of the history of watercraft in the New World.

Thousands of miles from L'Anse aux Meadows, archaeological excavation has revealed details of the kind of vessel probably used by the Norse settlers in Newfoundland. Divers discovered in Roskilde Fjord near Skuldelev, Denmark, the wrecks of five Viking ships of around AD 1000, the time of the settlement. One wreck was of a *knarr*, a heavy, seagoing cargo ship often mentioned in Icelandic sagas. Unlike many other Viking ships, which were made very light for ease in pulling ashore, the knarr was more stoutly constructed, made to withstand the beating seas of the North Atlantic.

The solidly built Skuldelev knarr, excavated between 1957 and 1962 by the Danish National Museum, is about 16.5 m (54 ft) long and 4.5 m (14 ft 10 in) wide, with a full rounded stem and stern. It is built of large planks of pine, pointing to southern Norway where such timber was plentiful. The keel and lower frames (ribs) are of oak, and the remaining parts of lime wood. The overlapping strakes, or side planks, are fastened in the clinker fashion with round iron rivets and attached to the frames with treenails. Although this knarr has several oar-holes fore and aft, it was primarily a sailing vessel, with a spar which made it possible to set the single square sail in three different positions. The midship cargo hold is open, and although there was deck space fore and aft for passengers, there were no shelters to protect either cargo or passengers from the elements of the North Atlantic.

There are other claims of pre-Columbian visitors to the Americas. Among candidates for Atlantic crossings are the Irish, British, Italians, Portuguese and, much earlier, the Phoenicians, Carthaginians, Greeks and Romans. To date, there is no conclusive evidence that such crossings were ever made. On the western side of the continents, however, archaeological evidence may link the Pacific coasts of America with Japan. Pottery of the Valdivia phase used around 3000 BC in coastal Ecuador occurs in developed form with no antecedents in a style comparable to the contemporaneous Middle Jomon phase pottery of Japan. Perhaps future archaeological research will reveal if styles of pottery – and perhaps even particular types of watercraft – were brought to the Western Hemisphere by early trans-Pacific voyagers.

Conclusion

When Europeans first explored the New World, they encountered local peoples who used watercraft. Throughout the Western Hemisphere, in both coastal and riverine environments, vessels were made from locally available materials and ranged from those intended for merely keeping something afloat for short periods to those capable of making extended sea voyages.

There are already many kinds of evidence for pre-Columbian watercraft in the archaeological record of the New World – from models or toys to actual recovered craft – and this evidence is greatly enhanced by ethnohistorical and ethnographical data. Much of the hope for future study of pre-Columbian craft lies in the emerging field of underwater archaeology, although there are problems in the search for such vessels: most are relatively small when compared with other shipwrecks, and they have no metal parts for detection by magnetometry. When sunken craft are located, however, there is great potential for their excellent preservation in the underwater environment. Ultimately, study of actual vessels and how they developed and were used under local conditions will provide insights into man's adaptation and remarkable technological advances through the ages.

CHAPTER TWO

The Voyages of Columbus: The Search for His Ships

Roger C. Smith

Before 1492, Spain's only possessions outside Europe were the Canary Islands; within a half-century, she controlled most of the West Indies, a large portion of the American continent, and outposts in Africa. During that time her mariners had sailed from the New World to the Far East. The voyages of Columbus were not isolated events in their time, but rather part of a continuous process of exploration. They stand out today because they paved the route for Spanish exploitation and empire in the Western Hemisphere.

A man of humble Genoese origins, Columbus had traveled to the eastern Mediterranean, northwestern Europe, the Guinea coast, and had lived on Madeira and in Lisbon. He was a navigator, chartmaker and self-made cosmographer. Above all, he offered Europe a theory and a vision: '... I should not go by land, which is the usual way, to the Orient but by the route of the Occident, by which no one to this day knows for sure that anyone has gone.'

The Enterprise of the Indies consisted of four voyages 'to discover and acquire certain islands and mainlands in the Ocean Sea'. The first was a deep-water passage of distance and duration unequaled since the Norse explorations. On 12 October 1492, Columbus found himself in the Bahamas, among naked and primitive peoples instead of the civilizations of Marco Polo's Asia. In search of China, his fleet found Cuba and Hispaniola, where he established the first European outpost in the New World since the Vikings. Returning with reports of his achievements, tales of gold and potential slaves, Columbus became Admiral of the Ocean Sea and Viceroy of the Indies, commissioned to command a second voyage to settle a trading post and convert the 'Indians'.

A colonizing force of seventeen ships and 1,500 men arrived at Hispaniola in November 1493, hastily founded a new colony, then proceeded to exploit the natives. Convinced that Cuba was Japan, Columbus continued his maritime quest of the Antilles, discovering Jamaica in 1494. But reports of widespread discontent among the gentlemen colonists of Hispaniola and increasing Indian resistance had already begun to raise doubts about

Columbus' enterprise in the minds of King Ferdinand and Queen Isabella back in Spain. The Admiral thus found it more difficult to organize a third expedition, which put to sea in May 1498 aboard six ships. Three of the vessels were dispatched to Hispaniola, while the remainder headed southwest, where Columbus believed there to be a landmass counterbalancing that of Africa. Off the coast of South America, he found the island he named Trinidad, and venturing farther his ships sailed into the massive outflow of the Orinoco River. The Admiral believed he had discovered the mythical Terrestrial Paradise, but he was not so fortunate. Open rebellion had erupted on Hispaniola. The monarchs sent an official to investigate the situation, and Columbus with his brother and son were returned to Spain in chains. Already the Crown had revoked the Discoverer's monopoly and had begun to issue licenses for other exploratory expeditions.

Despite these setbacks, there would be one last chance to find a sea route to China. But the fourth voyage, rather than reaching the elusive strait and opening the way to Jerusalem, was to end in illness and despair.

The nautical legacy of Columbus is perhaps best expressed by a prophecy in Seneca's *Medea*: 'An age will come after many years when the Ocean will loose the chains of things, and a huge land lie revealed; when Tethys will disclose new worlds and Thule no more be the ultimate.' Next to that passage, in the Admiral's own copy of Seneca, his son Ferdinand later wrote: 'This prophecy was fulfilled by my father the Admiral in the year 1492.' Today the tangible remains of that fulfilled prophecy lie in the timbers of ships left behind by the Discoverer on three of his four voyages.

Ships of Discovery

Identification of shipwrecks belonging to Christopher Columbus in itself would be a landmark of discovery. Surviving relics associated with the most famous explorer today consist only of books and bones. Archaeological finds from his voyages would add much to the 1992 Quincentennial observances, but discovery of the ships themselves would present the greatest gift to history,

since their remains might help to explain the methods by which ships of exploration were built. Because they have been excavated archaeologically, we know more about Greek and Roman ships than we do about the vessels that propelled men from the Middle Ages into a nautical Renaissance.

Preferred by almost all Iberian maritime explorers were *caravels* and *naos*. Columbus used them exclusively in his voyages to the New World, constantly making refinements and improvements in their design. However, while we can glean general features of these famous craft from crude depictions and vague documents, detailed knowledge about their construction is nonexistent, since formal plans of ships had not yet been developed.

We know that coastal fishing *barchas* and *barineles*, heavily planked against the swells of the western ocean, propelled Portuguese mariners down African shores in the early fifteenth century until headwinds and currents from the Gulf of Guinea slowed the progress of exploration under square sail and oar. A slightly longer, larger and lighter vessel, with finer lines and partial decking, then emerged to ride over heavy seas and to venture up equatorial river mouths. Greater sailing distances prompted a need for increased crews, provisions and trade goods, and also swifter and more maneuverable craft in which to return home.

The most important improvement in ship design, however, was a change from single-masted square-rigging to multiple lateen sails. The fore-and-aft triangular sail, employed on small Mediterranean craft from the seventh century, most likely was brought from the Indian Ocean by Arab conquests in Egypt. The segmented spread of triangular canvas distributed over a longer hull allowed a craft to point, pivot, tack and run as wind directions necessitated. Preconstructed framing, upon which flush 'carvel' planking was nailed, provided support for the multiple rig and created a stronger, larger southern European hull tradition. An axial stern rudder, like that used to keep the flat bottoms of northern lapstrake ('clinker') vessels on course, was added for maneuverability in the open ocean.

It was this combination of rig, hull and rudder, adapted from different regions by Portuguese mariners through seagoing trial and error, which comprised the characteristics of the distinctive craft, the *caravela*, built for seaworthiness rather than cargo capacity. Expeditionary voyages launched the use of three lateen yards set on raked masts for clawing to windward and making rapid steering maneuvers. Aerodynamically, this grouping of triangular sails increased a *caravela latina*'s speed, especially if the mizzen sail was trimmed to spill wind into the mainsail.

The shallow draft of early caravels proved useful for coastal and riverine exploration. Traditional oars of shorter-ranging craft were retained in the form of light sweeps to row in shallow estuaries and in becalmed conditions. However, with the addition of deck-mounted naval artillery to carry out conquest in the Indian Ocean, a

caravela de armada encountered problems of stability. A squared and beamier sterncastle with slight tumblehome (progressive narrowing of the ship above the waterline) was evidently adopted to provide a sturdy platform for conning and defending the vessel. Heavy artillery and ground tackle were stowed below at sea, but readied on decks as land was approached.

Caravels had proven themselves off Africa and across the Indian Ocean, but soon they faced a broader challenge – the Atlantic. During Columbus' first voyage, square sails were added to the caravel, changing the *caravela latina* to a *caravela redonda* to take advantage of following trade winds. Columbus altered his caravel named *Niña* in this way as soon as he reached the Canary Islands. Contemporary depictions of the first Spanish ships in the New World, such as those on the Juan de la Cosa map of 1500, show caravels with square-rigged fore and main masts and a lateen mizzen. Thus began a combination of canvas and spars which represents the ancestor of the traditional 'ship rig' that climaxed with the clipper.

The secret of the caravel's successful role in seafaring history, however, was its hull design and construction. Proportions of caravels recorded in the sixteenth-century

Ships of Discovery

Paramount among Iberian vessels of exploration were sleek caravels and sturdy *naos*.

1 (*left*) Typical sixteenth-century vessels are shown in this woodcut from a Venetian book on navigation of 1555. Clockwise from top left: a carrack, lateen-rigged caravel, square-rigged caravel, *nao*, lateen-rigged caravel and galley.

2 (*right*) The Mataró votive model, thought to date from the mid-fifteenth century. The model, now in Rotterdam, represents a Catalonian *nao* of southern Spain and provides the basis for what little we know about ship design of the period.

3, 4 (*below right*) Sixteenth-century illustrations depict a *caravela latina* (with a lateen rig) and beneath it a *caravela redonda* (with a square rig). During his first voyage, Columbus altered one of his caravels from the lateen to the square rig to take advantage of Atlantic trade winds. This combination of square-rigged fore and main masts and a lateen mizzen gave rise to the traditional 'ship rig' that has lasted into modern times.

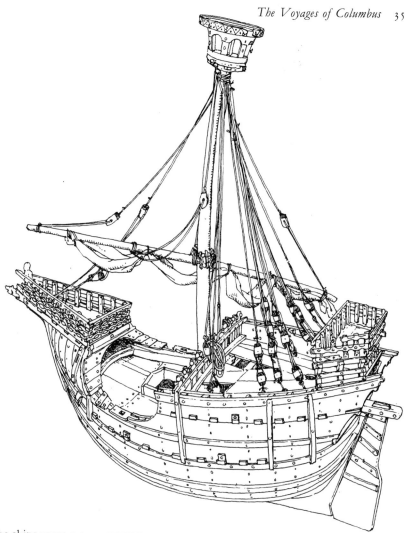

Portuguese *Livro Nautico* indicate that the ships were 2.3 times as deep as they were wide, their keels 2.4 times as long as their beams, and their decks 3.3 times as long as their beams. A Renaissance expression of nautical design, this sleek hull shape allowed transoceanic voyages to become routine, and the globe to be circumnavigated for the first time. Slightly more beamy but rigged similarly, the larger workhorse *naos* carried colonists, arms, tools and provisions, and paved the way for commercial maritime empires in the East and West Indies.

Nautical technology. What little we know about fifteenth-century hulls and the way in which they were formed and fastened comes from a votive model found in a church in the small Catalonian town of Mataró. The model builder employed construction techniques of his day, but with scaled-down timbers, frames and planking put together with tiny iron and wooden fasteners. Hull features such as bilge stringers, dead wood, knees, internal stanchions and external fender wales were carved and fixed in place to reproduce in miniature an actual ship of the period.

The Mataró model demonstrates how the backbone of an Iberian ship may have been notched to accept key

framing ribs sandwiched between keel and keelson, and fastened with forelock bolts secured by wedges and washers. It tells us how the masts were stepped in the hull and stayed to the topsides. The internal details of forecastle and sterncastle not depicted in illustrations are revealed for the first time. But the model, like an ancient shipwreck, has suffered over time; pieces are missing, and questions not answered by a church effigy await further evidence.

Reconstructions. Larger than her caravel consorts *Pinta* and *Niña*, Columbus' flagship, *Santa María*, was most likely either a *nao* or a light carrack. Although we have no records of her tonnage or dimensions, she must have been slightly less than 100 tons in cubic capacity, as measured in the number of *tuns*, or wine barrels, that could be carried in the hold. From graphic sources such as contemporary paintings, engravings, maps and models, scholars have long attempted to reconstruct the appearance of *Santa María* and her consorts. Models displayed in Genoa were made from hypothetical plans published by Enrico d'Albertis for the Italian Columbus Commission of 1892.

Concurrently, the Spanish Commission, under Cesáreo Fernández Duro, drew up plans for reconstructed 'replicas' of the *Santa María*, *Pinta* and *Niña*. Launched in 1892, the flagship was sailed across the Atlantic in 1893 for display at the World Columbian Exposition in Chicago. It was joined by replicas of the two caravels, which were towed across the ocean under command of the U.S. Navy.

For the 1929 Ibero-American Fair of Seville, features of *Santa María* were re-evaluated by Julio Guillén Tato, who considered her to be a large caravel. Published in 1927, Guillén's research prompted the building of another 'replica', which was exhibited for many years until it sank in 1945 while en route to be repaired. A copy of this ship was built in 1951 for a Columbus film and afterwards was moored at the Museo Marítimo in Barcelona, where it can still be seen. Another experimental replica, this one of the caravel *Niña*, was constructed in Spain under the direction of Carlos Etayo Elizondo. The vessel set sail from Palos in 1962 and reached San Salvador in 97 days – much longer than the 36 days it took Columbus.

These hypothetical plans of Columbus' ships differ primarily in the overall size of the vessels and details of

superstructure and rigging, since most are based on pictorial evidence and fragmented references in narratives. Ocean sailing of the replicas proved how little is known about properties of the hull below the waterline, its construction and ballasting, and its center of gravity in relation to spars and sails. The 1892 replica of *Santa María* yawed heavily and had a tendency to run almost 90 degrees off course; replicas of *Pinta* and *Niña* were built from the used hulks of modern boats and had to be towed across the ocean. During sea trials, Guillén's *Santa María* pitched and rolled excessively, probably due to the shortness of her keel and rounded bilges. Etayo's *Niña* gave her modern crew constant problems; aside from being top heavy and much too small, the replica sailed poorly despite alternate use of both lateen and square rigs.

With new replicas of Columbus' ships planned for 1992, examination of the remains of ships associated with the Admiral's voyages could show archaeologists how the hulls were built. True reconstructions must be based on authentic fragments of the 'Mercury space capsules' of transoceanic history. And such fragments today lie off Haiti, the Dominican Republic, Panama and Jamaica.

Columbian Voyages

5 (*facing page*) A 'replica' of *Santa María*, Columbus' flagship on his first voyage, was built in 1892 under the direction of naval architect Cesáreo Fernández Duro and sailed by the Spanish navy across the Atlantic to take part in the World Columbian Exposition in Chicago.

6 (*below*) Map showing the voyages of Columbus (with two Spanish *naos* inset, from the first chart of the New World published in 1500). No vessels were lost on the third voyage; nautical archaeologists have therefore concentrated their efforts on the other voyages. The precise routes of the voyages are the subject of much scholarly debate.

The First Voyage

Santa María and her two consorts reached the Bahama Islands in October 1492; cruised the north coast of Cuba in November; and reached the shores of another island, 'Bohio', in December. Finding the land as beautiful as Spain, the Admiral named it La Isla Española (Hispaniola). Naked Taino Indians wore ornaments of gold and were friendlier than neighboring Cuban natives. The Spaniards' arrival made such an impression that Guacanagari, chief of northwestern Hispaniola, invited them to his village in Cibao. This was what Columbus had been waiting for, since Guacanagari's region sounded like Cipango, the name Marco Polo had given to Japan, where palaces were roofed with gold.

The ships made for Cibao, eastward along the coast. In the middle of a calm night, on Christmas Eve, with all asleep aboard the *Santa María* except a boy at the helm, the flagship passed inside the reefs of Cap-Haïtien and gently grounded on a shoal. She could not be pulled off, and Columbus was forced to empty her of stores and hardware. A fortified outpost was constructed from her timbers ashore near Guacanagari's village and named La Navidad in honor of the day of the disaster. Thirty-nine men were chosen to occupy the fort, while Columbus and the remainder returned to Spain. The lower hull and ballast stones comprising the grave of the *Santa María* remained on an unmarked reef a league and a half from shore, the first recorded European shipwreck in the New World.

The search for the 'Santa María'. The first evidence of the *Santa María* was found by the eighteenth-century French historian, Moreau de St-Méry, who recorded the discovery of one of *Santa María*'s anchors in the muddy bottom of Grande Rivière a mile from its mouth and 2 miles from the present-day fishing village of Limonade Bord-de-Mer, Haiti. St-Méry conjectured that the anchor, now on display at the National Museum in Port-au-Prince, was the one reported by Dr Chanca, physician of Columbus' second voyage, near the burned ruins of Navidad, '... an anchor belonging to the ship which the Admiral had lost here on the previous voyage'. Over the centuries, the mouth of the river apparently had gradually accreted out into the sea.

Some 150 years later, in 1939, American historian Samuel Eliot Morison, following in the wake of Columbus, carefully studied the contour of the Haitian coastline to retrace the final course of the *Santa María*. Concluding that Guacanagari's village was situated near Limonade Bord-de-Mer, he hypothesized that the flagship had wrecked on one of three small shoals between the shore and the barrier reef. Unfortunately, the archaeological means by which to test his theory had yet to evolve.

A decade after Morison's visit, pilot Don Lungwitz glimpsed from the air a dark oval blur inside the barrier reef that shelters the wide harbor of Cap-Haïtien. Unlike coral mounds scattered throughout the reefline, the blur lay at a right angle to the surf zone and was oval-shaped, like a ship.

In 1955, underwater explorers Edwin and Marion Link visited Cap-Haïtien to search for the *Santa María*. Diving far to the west of Morison's hypothesized location, they recovered an early anchor from a reef in the harbor entrance. Although the ring, part of the shank, and the palms were missing, the Link anchor generally resembled the anchor found by St-Méry. It was covered with an encrustation of sand, suggesting that it once had been lying on a sandy bottom rather than on the reef where it was found. Examined by Mendel Peterson of the Smithsonian Institution, both the St-Méry and the Link anchors were conjectured to have come from the same ship, possibly the *Santa María*. Metal samples tested at the U.S. Bureau of Standards indicated that both anchors had been fashioned from iron of the same type and period.

But what of the mysterious ship-shaped mound spotted by Don Lungwitz in 1949? Fred Dickson, another explorer in quest of history, came to the north coast of Haiti in 1967. Knowledgeable about the Morison and Link expeditions, Dickson also met Lungwitz, and exploratory excavations of his mound began within the year. Under 12 ft (3.7 m) of coral and ballast rock, divers recovered wood, copper and iron fastenings, lead sheathing and ceramics.

It was not until 1970 that a magnetometer was employed on the coral mound, revealing to Dickson a major anomaly some 82 ft (25 m) to the northwest. Test excavations produced more wood, ballast, fasteners and ceramics, but also glass fragments, grapeshot and two large, square iron bars of a type carried as ballast on warships. Archaeologist Carl Clausen concluded that the artifacts were consistent with an eighteenth- or nineteenth-century shipwreck. The following year additional excavation produced similar shipwreck materials, but radiocarbon dating of surrounding sediments indicated the earliest to be only 320 years old. Persisting in his search for the *Santa María* in 1972, Dickson tragically died following a diving accident.

Discovery of the precise location of the fortified outpost, La Navidad, now being sought by archaeologists from the Florida State Museum, by narrowing the search area would be of the greatest benefit to those who continue the quest.

The Second Voyage

Columbus' second expedition mustered a fleet of seventeen ships which he loaded with settlers, soldiers, livestock, seeds and tools to establish a trading colony on the north shore of Hispaniola, whence the interior gold-bearing region of the island could be mined. The small fortress of La Navidad, built the previous year from timbers of the shipwrecked *Santa María*, was found in ruins, her thirty-nine men dead or missing. The Admiral pushed on, but after a month of tacking against the wind,

A Land as Beautiful as Spain

7 (*right*) On this promontory in Hispaniola (in the present-day Dominican Republic) was built the first Christian town in the New World – Isabela. Several fifteenth-century vessels associated with Columbus are recorded as having been lost in Isabela Bay during a hurricane shortly after the Admiral established the settlement on his second voyage in 1494. Brief surveys in 1980 and 1983 determined that the sediments of the harbor bottom contain the potential to preserve organic remains of sunken ships.

8 (*below right*) Isabela is clearly depicted on this 1534 map of Hispaniola from Benedetto Bordoni's *Isolario*.

his ships had traveled less than 40 miles along the coast. With crews exhausted, livestock dying and would-be colonists falling ill, the fleet anchored in an open bay behind a small wooded peninsula that gave some protection from the wind. A slightly raised promontory overlooking a shallow harbor and a fresh-water river seemed suitable for America's first townsite, which Columbus named La Isabela after his queen.

Not wanting to keep the ships' crews on the royal payroll longer than necessary, the Admiral sent all but five of the vessels home to Spain after disembarking colonists and cargo. To minimize Crown expenses, he had purchased a share in the flagship, *Mariagalante*, and had bought outright the ship *Gallega*, the veteran *Niña*, and two smaller caravels, *San Juan* and *Cardera*. Columbus hastily established a council to govern Isabela, then outfitted the three caravels in the spring of 1494 to resume exploration. Sailing toward Cuba, he left the two larger,

armed ships at anchor to protect the new settlement.

The Admiral returned in five months to find the colony rife with discontent and local Indians cruelly mistreated. Many of the settlers elected to return to Spain aboard the first available ships, which sailed in February 1495 with over 500 captive natives to be sold into slavery. In June, a hurricane struck the struggling colony, adding to its misery. Three anchored ships, *San Juan, Cardera* and probably *Gallega* were swept to destruction, but the sturdy *Niña* rode out the storm. Historical accounts differ concerning the ship losses at Isabela, with some including *Mariagalante*, and others reporting as many as seven ships lost in two different hurricanes in 1494 and 1495. From the timbers of the wrecked vessels was built a small caravel, *Santa Clara*, nicknamed *La India* since she was the first ship constructed in the Indies. Together with *Niña*, she sailed under the Admiral's command back to Spain to complete his second voyage.

La Isabela. The larger vessels in Columbus' fleet could not anchor closer than a half-mile from shore in the shallow waters of the bay at Isabela. I found this to be true in 1980, when, aboard the research vessel *Morning Watch*, captained by former U.S. Ambassador Sumner Gerard, we anchored at Isabela to conduct a preliminary reconnaissance of the townsite and harbor. The first European town in the Americas looked barren. Once we were on the promontory, however, historical data, including a survey report and plan produced in 1891 by U.S. naval officers shortly before Isabela's 400th anniversary, helped us to trace many of the townsite's original stone foundations. Brick and ceramic fragments eroded from the ruins lay in the surf below us.

Our goal was to learn the potential of the harbor to preserve wreckage associated with Columbus. Mapping harbor depths and sampling sediments, we found the sea bed covered with soft organic mud and silt. Soundings indicated extensive layering of alluvial and marine deposits, with the exception of a small reef at the seaward edge of the harbor.

In 1983, *Morning Watch* returned to Isabela to conduct more extensive explorations under the direction of Donald H. Keith. Several magnetometer and sub-bottom sonar targets, some of which appeared characteristic of shipwrecks, were located in the bay. One contained a modern anchor. Test excavation of another, dug to a depth of 11 ft 6 in (3.5 m) through silt, sand and clay, contained no cultural material. Cores were taken to determine the nature of the sediments and ecology of the harbor.

Although reconnaissance at Isabela has yet to produce remains of wrecked vessels, it has demonstrated the bay's potential to preserve them.

The Fourth and Final Voyage

Sailing from Spain in 1502 with four caravels, the Admiral hoped to find a strait to the Orient beyond the islands discovered during his three previous voyages. For nearly a year the expedition cruised the coast of Central America, suffering storms and Indian hostilities. He attempted to establish a small fortified garrison in Panama, named Santa María de Belén, but was forced to abandon the caravel *Gallega* inside the mouth of the Belén River when the tiny beachhead was overrun by natives who killed several of his crewmen, including the ships' caulkers. (A combined aerial and land reconnaissance of the river mouth in 1987, by Mark Myers and Bruce Thompson of the Institute of Nautical Archaeology, suggests that the area in which *Gallega*'s remains must lie is relatively small.)

Shortly thereafter, shipworms took their toll on the vessels' planking: *Viscaína*, leaking badly, was stripped and left behind near modern Portobelo. The two remaining caravels, *La Capitana* and *Santiago de Palos*, continued along the South American coast, seeking enough windward room to turn northeast in order to reach the safety of Hispaniola.

But prevailing Caribbean winds and currents carried the tired explorers too far west. By the time they reached the south coast of Cuba, the ships were so rotten that, as one crew member recalled, '. . . all the people with pumps, kettles, and other vessels were insufficient to bail out the water that entered by the worm-holes'. The explorers suffered further misfortune when, after losing all but one anchor, their two ships smashed together while riding out a storm on a single mooring.

The leaking caravels limped eastward on a port tack to avoid bucking headwinds on the way to Hispaniola, but water rose so quickly in *Santiago* that both ships turned downwind in a desperate run toward Jamaica. Columbus remembered a sheltered bay discovered and named Puerto Santa Gloria on his second voyage; the caravels headed for its entrance under a land breeze, and, as the Admiral's son Ferdinand later recalled:

> Having got in, and no longer able to keep the ships afloat, we ran them ashore as far as we could, grounding them close together board on board, and shoring them up on both sides so they could not budge; and in this position the tide rose almost to the decks. Upon these and the fore and stern castles, cabins were built where the people might lodge, intending to make them strong so that the Indians might do no damage; because at that time the island was not yet inhabited or subdued by Christians.

Columbus and 115 men and boys remained on the north coast of Jamaica for a year. Depleted of provisions, they bartered from Taino Indian villages, and sent two Europeans eastward in local canoes jury-rigged with washboards and sails to attempt a crossing to Hispaniola, where a rescue vessel might be obtained. Meanwhile, despair and discontent erupted into mutiny, and more than half of the castaways left the caravel camp to venture on a fruitless escape voyage.

The Admiral, now ailing, remained in his cabin awaiting word from Hispaniola while the natives increasingly refused to feed the foreigners. Consulting his German almanac, he noted that a lunar eclipse was due to occur on the night of 29 February 1504. He summoned local chiefs to the grounded *Capitana*, telling them through an interpreter that his Christian God would send a token from Heaven to demonstrate His disapproval of their behavior. The natives scoffed at the old man, but as the rising moon began to disappear, they assembled in panic around the caravels and begged Columbus to intercede on their behalf. From that night the Spaniards continued to receive provisions from the Amerindians.

Meanwhile, having failed in their attempted canoe escape from Jamaica, the mutineers returned to Santa Gloria with the intention of seizing the caravel post; instead they were defeated in a pitched battle with the loyalists. Finally, in June 1504, a rescue ship from

Hispaniola ended the long ordeal. Leaving his last two exploratory vessels in the soft mud of the bay, Columbus returned to Spain to find his royal patronage evaporated with the death of Queen Isabella. His own death followed shortly thereafter.

The location of the first European outpost in Jamaica was not immediately forgotten. Four years later, Diego Columbus caused the settlement of Sevilla la Nueva to be established at Santa Gloria, near the place where his father had been marooned. But the town was inhabited for a mere quarter-century before being abandoned for more favorable ground on the south coast, and eventually the site was consumed by tropical flora. Centuries afterwards, in 1932, the overseer of the English plantation named Seville at St Ann's Bay on the north coast of the island was riding through canefields aligning the shore when his horse stumbled on the masonry lip of a buried storage cistern. Exploratory excavations at the site by amateur archaeologist C. S. Cotter confirmed buried stone and masonry foundations as the remains of Sevilla la Nueva, and St Ann's Bay as Columbus' Santa Gloria.

St Ann's Bay. In 1935 amateur archaeologist William Goodwin initiated a search for Columbus' caravels in Don Christopher's Cove adjacent to St Ann's Bay, but abandoned it three years and 150 test holes later. Samuel Eliot Morison was at the same time preparing his Harvard University expedition to retrace the four voyages of discovery. When Morison sailed into St Ann's Bay in 1940, he set out to reconstruct the surroundings of

Surveying St Ann's Bay

9 (*right*) Archaeologists run a proton magnetometer into St Ann's Bay, Jamaica, in order to detect iron remains beneath the harbor bottom. Project director Roger Smith is seen in the foreground at left.

10 (*below*) An archaeologist surveys the ruins of the sixteenth-century Spanish townsite of Sevilla la Nueva on the north coast of Jamaica. Foundations of what is thought to be the governor's fortified residence were discovered in 1932, when the plantation overseer's horse stumbled into this brick-lined Spanish cistern.

On the Track of Columbus

To date no certain remains of Columbus' vessels have been found – but the search continues.

11, 12 (*right*) St Ann's Bay, Jamaica, site of Columbus' enforced exile of 1503–4, and later the first Spanish townsite on the island, Sevilla la Nueva. Somewhere beneath the sediments of this enclosed lagoon may lie the remains of *Capitana* and *Santiago de Palos*, the last two ships commanded by the great Admiral (inset, Columbus in his later years, a 1525 portrait considered to be the closest existing likeness).

13 (*below*) Archaeologists lay out a 30-sq.m survey grid along the shoreline at St Ann's Bay, in order to employ electronic sensing instruments in the search for Columbus' caravels. Ruins of an eighteenth-century English plantation wharf and warehouse in the background show the extent of sediment accretion since that time.

14 (*right*) Columbus abandoned the caravel *La Gallega* in Panama's Belén River during his fourth and final voyage. The remains of the hull probably lie here in the mouth of the river, just before it flows out into the Atlantic Ocean.

Columbus' unintentional exile. Both he and Cotter rejected Goodwin's choice of Don Christopher's Cove as a possible location for the beached ships because of the inlet's narrow shape and shallow water. They determined that the name had been derived not from the famous Admiral, but from Don Cristóbal Yssasi, the last Spanish governor of Jamaica, who used the cove as a hide-out and smuggling rendezvous when pursued by Cromwellian troops in the seventeenth century. Morison and Cotter concurred that Columbus' ships probably lay in the western section of St Ann's Bay, where deep and tranquil water came close to shore near an old stone wharf close to the ruins of Sevilla la Nueva.

Twenty-six years later, while conducting excavations at the sunken city of Port Royal on the south coast of Jamaica, Robert Marx visited St Ann's Bay. Probing the mud with a metal rod in Morison's proposed area, Marx recovered fragments of wood, stones, ceramics and obsidian. Two years later, Marx returned with Dr Harold Edgerton, who produced sonar images of several targets in the bay. Core samples of a target in the area Marx had probed yielded the same materials as before, as well as glass, charcoal, flint, an iron tack and a black bean. When examined by different laboratories, the samples were judged to be of varying dates and ambiguous origins, but that did not preclude the possibility of their having come from one of Columbus' caravels. The existence of an adjacent and similar sonar target raised hopes and led to public reports that both vessels had been found.

At Marx's urging, the Jamaican government sought international support to begin test excavations of the caravels. During several days of dredging at the site in 1969, veteran French diver Frederic Dumas mapped ballast stones, artifacts and glass fragments in a gradual curve on the sloping mudbank near the old wharf. Because of the number of different rock and artifact types, and because an old chart showed two anchors at the location he had tested, Dumas concluded the site was an anchorage midden associated with the wharf. Recovery of eighteenth-century wine bottle bases and clay pipe fragments reinforced this hypothesis, and the government was told that Columbus' ships were probably buried elsewhere.

Armed with historical documentation, a chronology of charts and aerial photographs of the bay, geologist John Gifford and I took up the search in 1981 by trying to determine the changes that had taken place since the time of Columbus in the shoreline of St Ann's Bay. Mangroves disguised the former beach, and Spanish and English ruins had been overgrown. Initial coring along the coast indicated that some stretches of the shoreline had variously eroded or accreted in time, due to marine and alluvial action. The possibility thus existed that the remains of Columbus' ships could be buried under the present-day beach.

On and off shore, a systematic magnetometry survey combined with a survey employing sub-bottom penetrating sonar detected buried targets. Several were found to be natural features, but others, when probed and cored, produced artifacts. A cluster of five subterranean sonar images was charted offshore of the old wharf where Marx and Dumas had worked. Test excavations confirmed the site as an anchorage midden with two discrete layers of cultural debris deposited during periods of intense plantation activity in the eighteenth century.

Elsewhere, under almost 6 ft 6 in (2 m) of mud and silt, we discovered a well-preserved English trading vessel from the mid-eighteenth century. Near the ruins of an old fort farther along the shore, coring and test excavation of a magnetic anomaly, which appeared to be the correct size and configuration for two buried ships when plotted on three-dimensional computerized maps, revealed upon excavation only modern trash, ballast, bricks and metallic debris. Additional research indicated that the area had served as an anchorage early in this century for small lighters employed in lading ships anchored in the bay.

In addition to magnetometry and sonar, infrared photography and ground-penetrating radar were employed along the shore and in the vicinity of the ruins of Sevilla la Nueva. An experimental computer-enhanced, color-coded sonar device was used in 1984 to resurvey several offshore areas. Additional shipwrecks were discovered, but each was dated later than the sixteenth century, and none was Spanish in origin.

The area of the eighteenth-century English stone wharf had witnessed intense maritime activity. We hypothesized that the wharf had possibly been built on top of an earlier pier, belonging to Sevilla la Nueva, that had been made from the combined ballast piles of two abandoned caravels lying side by side on the shore.

Unwilling to disturb the historic ruins by undermining the old wharf, and unable to penetrate rock-strewn sediments in the vicinity with our coring device, we tested this theory by tunnelling downward inside aluminum culverts 4 ft (1.2 m) in diameter, which we placed upright on the bay bed. As the contents of these miniature caissons were removed, the tubes sank deeper into the water-saturated soil.

In this manner, more than a ton of river and ballast rock intermixed with hundreds of artifacts was extracted by hand during two summers of diving in tight quarters with no visibility. Digging deeper, we encountered debris from generations of trade goods that had passed across the plantation wharf. As each 5-ft (1.5-m) section of aluminum culvert sank to its limit, another was bolted atop and the process continued downward. Fragments of fine porcelain and glassware intended for the Seville Plantation; rough earthenware pottery and locally made bricks; pieces of wooden barrels containing muscovado sugar boiled from the canefields; Pacific cowry shells traded in West Africa for slaves brought to Jamaica – all interspersed among countless broken rum bottles and clay pipes – testified to the once-prosperous commerce of St Ann's Bay.

We had not intended to pursue colonial English archaeology, and thus excavated deeper with a 3-ft (0.9-m) diameter tube placed inside the larger culverts. Preservation of organic materials was astonishing: wooden buttons, wisps of fabric, shoe leather, twists of rope, shredded coconut husks and countless seeds were cataloged. However, as artifacts from the mid-seventeenth century began to emerge we noticed the layers were no longer discrete. Still deeper, the soil became sterile. Even a core driven to a total depth of 33 ft (10 m), starting inside the caisson, encountered no sixteenth-century materials. Our hypothesis about a Spanish wharf in that location had been disproven.

Although the latest data from St Ann's Bay have yet to be analyzed, we cannot at the time of writing report that Columbus' lost caravels have been discovered. My colleagues and I continue to pursue the ships associated with the Admiral's voyages, however, in hopes of unearthing remains of the fifteenth-century vehicles that made possible the discovery and colonization of the New World. We are also studying known sixteenth-century shipwreck sites, some of which are the earliest yet found in the Americas, so as better to understand the maritime legacy Columbus brought across the Atlantic.

CHAPTER THREE

Shipwrecks of the Explorers

Donald H. Keith

It did not take long for the New World discovered by Columbus to beckon other explorers. After Columbus' third voyage, in 1498, the Spanish Crown began to license voyages by others, many of them men who had sailed with the Admiral and seen the wonders of the New World at first hand. Most of these voyages were not authorized by Columbus, despite the fact that the Crown had granted him the titles of Viceroy and Governor of the territory he had discovered. In the 1494 Treaty of Tordesillas – which established a line running from pole to pole 370 leagues west of the Cape Verde Islands, with Portugal having rights east of the line and Spain rights to the west – the Spanish recognized that the New World was too vast to be monopolized by a single nation. Now, in 1499, the Crown demonstrated its conviction that lands on the Spanish side of the Line of Demarcation were too vast to be monopolized by a single man: it authorized four voyages by explorers other than Columbus. The story of what happened can be gleaned from the earliest maps attributed to the explorers, and from surviving letters, legal documents, tax records and accounts.

Early Maps of the New World

The earliest known maps of the New World present difficulties to historical geographers who attempt to retrace early voyages of exploration. Few explorers produced or otherwise authorized maps representing their discoveries. Navigation still lacked precision. And literary descriptions of discoveries attributed to the explorers themselves survive today only in second- or third-hand versions. Cartographers coped as best they could with the information provided them, but the maps they produced contained many ambiguities, the landforms they traced sometimes difficult to match with geographic reality. The maps that have come down to us were almost certainly never intended to be used at sea, but were rather to impress potential backers, politicians and perhaps even geographers. What sort of schematic diagrams were used by exploration pilots and navigators themselves when they were actually trying to steer a course is anyone's guess.

The most famous early map is the earliest known – the Juan de la Cosa map of about 1500. On it the New World is shown as two obscure masses separated by the Caribbean Sea, while the Greater Antilles, Bahamas and other well-known islands are represented in the same fashion as familiar Old World lands. The cartographer masked his uncertainty as to whether the northern and southern continents were contiguous by placing a representation of St Christopher between them over the western end of the Caribbean Sea.

Paradoxically, some early maps seem to show coastal profiles of New World lands that, according to conventional history, had not yet been visited by Europeans. For example, the Cantino map of *c.* 1502 shows Cuba correctly represented as an island, even though it was not circumnavigated until 1509. Still more perplexing is a peninsular landform northwest of Cuba. Could it be Florida? Perhaps. But as far as history is concerned Florida was not charted until the 1513 voyage of Ponce de León. Could it be the Yucatan? There is no reference to Yucatan until the 1517 voyage of Hernandez de Cordobá.

The Contarini Map of 1506 shows the Greater Antilles, the north coast of South America, and a land mass to the north that grades into the east coast of Asia. A globe and a set of maps produced in 1507 by the cartographers of St Dié show a more accurate perception of the New World. On the main map and the globe the northern and southern continents are separated by an ocean strait, but an inset of the Western Hemisphere shows that the continents are connected. Cuba is called 'Isabella', and its shape is recognizable. A peninsula extending from the mainland to the northwest could be Florida or the Yucatan. On the globe the southern continent is labeled 'America', in honor of the discoveries made by the Italian merchant and adventurer Amerigo Vespucci.

The suggestion has been made that early cartographers had access to information supplied by unknown or now lost explorers. The probability of 'extra-legal', clandestine voyages is supported by circumstantial evidence and the certainty that human nature was the same 500 years ago as

A New World in Maps

The voyages of the early explorers brought about a cartographic revolution.

1 (*right*) A detail from Juan de la Cosa's New World map of 1500, the earliest known, indicates the restricted understanding of Caribbean islands at that time.

2 (*below*) The magnificent Miller Portuguese Atlas of 1519 reveals how quickly knowledge of New World geography had improved – even if North America itself was still largely a blank, taken up by an imaginary scene of animals in a kind of paradise. Out in the Atlantic we see numerous Spanish and Portuguese vessels under sail.

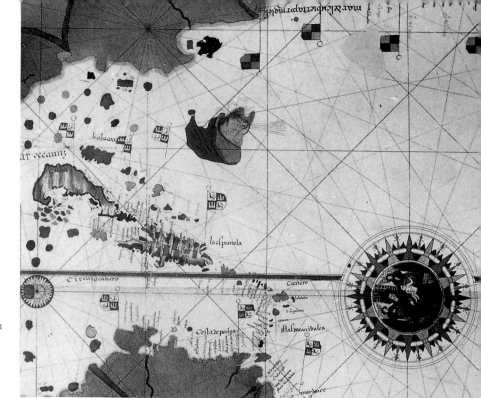

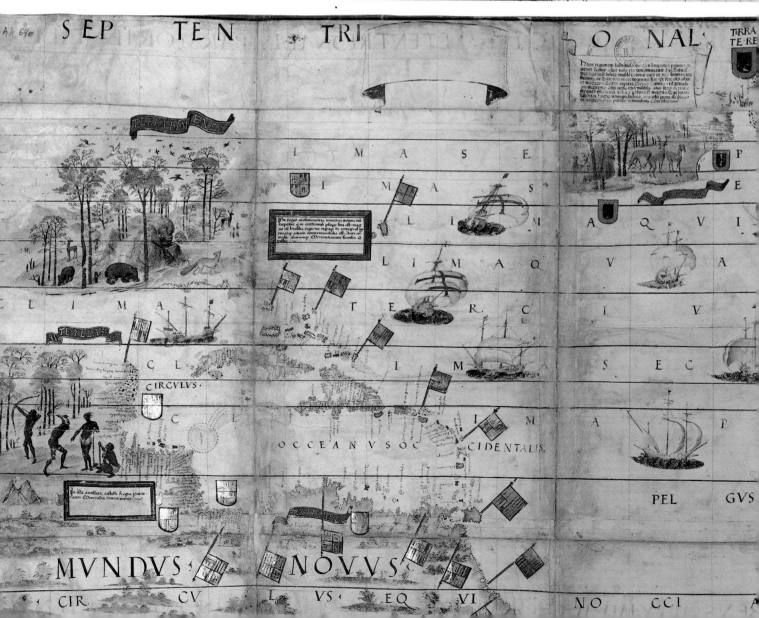

it is today. Historians have argued that, given the expense of preparing transatlantic voyages, it would have been difficult, it not impossible, for clandestine, unrecorded voyages to have taken place. However, it is known that at least some resourceful explorers hijacked, built or otherwise acquired ships *en route*. During the course of his perfectly legitimate voyage of 1499, for example, Alonso de Hojeda began by hijacking a ship in Puerto de Santa María, Spain, where his voyage began, picked up another 60 miles up the coast in Huelva, stripped equipment from vessels he encountered in European waters and pillaged additional stores on the island of Lanzarote in the Canaries. Once in the New World he built a *bergantín* somewhere on the Pearl Coast of South America. Examples such as this contradict the theory that exploratory voyages had to be carefully staged and that only officially sponsored – and therefore well-recorded – expeditions were possible. More likely, the records pertaining to some discovery voyages have fallen through the cracks of history and become lost to us.

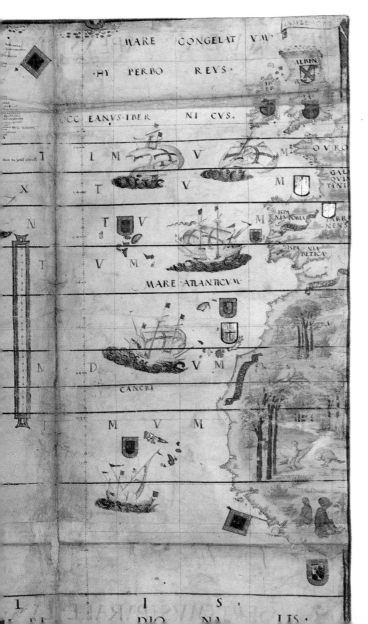

English and Portuguese Seafarers

Spain held no monopoly on seafaring adventure. European codfishermen probably touched on the northeastern shores of the North American continent before Columbus' first voyage. Sailing from Bristol in a single ship in 1497, John Cabot – like Columbus a transplanted Genoese – landed somewhere on the coast of New England and claimed possession for England. His disappearance during a subsequent voyage in 1498 dampened English enthusiasm for exploration and colonization of the new lands he discovered.

The fertile fishing banks off Newfoundland were also known to Breton, Biscayan and Portuguese fishermen. They did not perceive that they were exploring, had no reason to establish permanent colonies on the mainland, and left no official record of their discoveries. Three voyages to the northern coast of North America were undertaken between 1500 and 1502 by the Portuguese brothers Gaspar and Miguel Corte Real, who may have reached Greenland, Newfoundland and Nova Scotia. Like Cabot, the Corte Reals disappeared without a trace. Thereafter, Portuguese efforts focused on the southern route around Africa to the Indies, and on the New World land of Brazil, accidentally discovered in 1500 by Pedro Álvares Cabral attempting to follow this route.

At virtually the same time, in 1501 and 1502, at least two voyages to the north coast of Newfoundland were undertaken by Bristol-based explorers, three of whom were Azorian Portuguese. Historical geographer Carl Sauer noted that the nickname of one of the Portuguese explorers, João Fernandes, was 'El Lavrador' (the 'farmer' or 'herdsman'), and that although he took part in the first of these voyages, he is not mentioned after 1501. Sauer speculates that Fernandes died on the voyage and that his fellow explorers named the new land for him. John Cabot's son, Sebastian, claimed to have explored the coast of Canada in 1508 or 1509, but some authorities doubt the report as it is not supported by primary documentation.

Spanish Exploration of the New World

Between 1499 and 1505 at least eleven 'Minor Voyages' of discovery to the New World were made from Spain. All originated in Andalusian ports, and each consisted of fleets of from one to five ships; the number of vessels involved may have been greater, as only the principal ships in a fleet are mentioned in historical records.

At first the 'companions of Columbus' followed almost directly in the Admiral's footsteps, seeking to exploit the lands he had discovered. Whether by intent or accident, however, they later ventured further into true *terrae incognitae*. Searching for a western passage to the Indies, Columbus had by 1498 discovered the Greater Antilles, the southern Bahamas, the Leeward Islands and the northwestern tip of South America. But it was almost twenty years before the coasts bordering the Caribbean

Sea and the Gulf of Mexico had been run out, proving that no such passage existed.

The first of the 'Minor Voyages' was that undertaken by Alonso de Hojeda, Juan de la Cosa and Amerigo Vespucci, who sailed from Spain on 18 May 1499 with a fleet of five ships. Reaching the coast of South America at a latitude of about 5 or 6 degrees N, the explorers split up. Hojeda and la Cosa turned north and coasted as far west as Cabo de la Vela, at the tip of the Peninsula de Guajira, while Vespucci sailed south beyond the mouth of the Amazon before doubling back and rejoining the others. Apparently, Hojeda, la Cosa and Vespucci did not sight the single ship of Peralonso Niño and Cristobal Guerra which had departed Spain only two weeks later and was at the same time harvesting pearls off the island of Margarita.

A third exploratory fleet, comprising four caravels, left Spain in December of the same year under the command of Vicente Yañez Pinzón. The fleet first touched land in the vicinity of Cabo de São Roque in northeastern Brazil, then coasted northwest past the mouth of the Amazon to Paria where Pinzón left South America and picked his way through the Windward Islands, eventually reaching Hispaniola. On the return trip to Spain, Pinzón lost two caravels somewhere in the Bahama Islands. The fourth voyage of 1499 followed Pinzón by about two weeks. Diego de Lepe, commanding two ships, seems to have covered about the same ground as had Pinzón, except that he sailed a little farther south along the coast of Brazil, rounding Cape Santo Agostino.

The next year Alonso Vélez de Mendoza and Luis Guerra (Cristobal's brother) took two caravels past Cape Santo Agostino, possibly reaching latitude 39 degrees S. They were unaware that Cabral had touched the coast of Brazil in April, before they left Spain, and had claimed it for Portugal. Sailing for Portugal a year later, in 1501, Gonçalo Coelho and Vespucci explored the South American coast to a point 25 or 30 degrees south of the equator. About the same time Rodrigo de Bastidas and Juan de la Cosa followed the northern coast of South America to the Isthmus of Panama, extending Hojeda's 1499 explorations. All four of their ships were wrecked and abandoned on the south coast of Hispaniola, but the survivors managed to make their way overland to the Spanish New World capital of Santo Domingo. They arrived in May 1502, just in time to obtain passage in a fleet returning to Spain. But their adventures were not yet over. Two days east of Santo Domingo the fleet was caught in a hurricane that destroyed more than nineteen ships. Incredibly, theirs alone made it safely to Spain.

During his fourth voyage, in 1502–3, Columbus explored the Caribbean coast of Central America from the Gulf of Urabá to the Gulf of Honduras. This was his last voyage, but it was the proving ground for a man who became perhaps the finest pilot in the Caribbean and to whom may be attributed credit for the successes of numerous exploratory voyages to Florida, Yucatan and Mexico. Antón de Alaminos, who may have first come to the New World with Columbus' second voyage, piloted one of Columbus' ships during the fourth voyage, and guided Ponce de León through the treacherous Bahamas to Florida in 1513. Undoubtedly he noted the circulation patterns of wind and sea, because later he pioneered the use of the Gulf Stream to make swift passage out of the Gulf, through the Straits of Florida and on to Spain. He piloted the voyages of Cordobá in 1517 and Grijalva in 1518, and guided Cortés to Villa Rica de Veracruz in 1519. Utilizing the Gulf Stream to by-pass Cuba, Alaminos piloted the vessel carrying Cortés' first shipment of Aztec treasures back to Spain.

By 1508 the growing Spanish population and dwindling native labor force on Hispaniola caused Governor Nicolás de Ovando to consider expanding into other islands, notably Cuba and Puerto Rico. The depredations of the hurricanes of 1508 and 1509 on shipping in the harbor of Santo Domingo may also have had some bearing on this new interest in the other islands of the Greater Antilles. Cuba was officially circumnavigated in 1508–9 by the independent explorations of Pinzón and Juan Díaz de Solis and Sebastian de Ocampo, which proved that it was not connected to a larger mainland in the north and that a vast sea lay to the north and west. Diego Columbus, who replaced Ovando in 1509, appointed Diego Velázquez de Cuellar to lead the conquest of Cuba. Juan Ponce de León was already establishing a colony on Puerto Rico.

In 1512 King Ferdinand ordered his subjects in the Spanish New World to search for a westward passage to the Orient. Perhaps this led to the 'discovery' of Florida by Ponce de León, although cartographic and other evidence suggests that the presence of a large land mass to the north of the Greater Antilles was long suspected. Departing Puerto Rico in 1513, Ponce de León sailed up the Bahama chain, crossed the Gulf Stream and coasted up the east coast of Florida to the latitude of St Augustine. He then turned south, hugging the coast to the western terminus of the Florida Keys, and continued up the western side of the peninsula to about Bay San Carlos before returning to San Juan.

Ponce de León's voyage failed to find a passage to the west, but when word of Vasco Núñez de Balboa's discovery of the Pacific Ocean reached King Ferdinand in 1513, he authorized an exploratory voyage to round South America and report to the governor of Panama from the south (Pacific) side of the Isthmus. Provisioned for two-and-a-half years, the three ships in this fleet under the command of Solis pushed farther south along the coast of South America than anyone had gone before. But the expedition ended in failure in 1516 after reaching the mouth of the Río de la Plata when Solis was killed and one of the three ships was lost; ten years later, subsequent explorers were still picking up the marooned survivors.

The conquest of Cuba provided a new base for Spanish slave-raiding expeditions to Central America and the

3 (*right*) 'Replicas' of Columbus' vessels for his first voyage, *Santa Maria*, *Pinta* and *Niña*, built in Spain for the 1892 Columbian Exposition. *Santa Maria* was sailed successfully across the Atlantic, although she did not respond well to the helm. The other two vessels had to be towed.

4 (*below*) This sheer plan of a late sixteenth-century Spanish vessel is one of the earliest published plans dealing with ship construction.

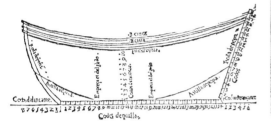

Bahamas. But what lay beyond Cuba to the west? In 1517 two caravels and a *bergantín* under the command of Francisco Hernández de Cordobá sailed westward from Santiago de Cuba and discovered the northern coast of the Yucatan peninsula. The natives of this new land were both hostile and formidable: the Spaniards left fifty-seven dead soldiers behind and many more were wounded. Valázquez de Cuellar, Governor of Cuba, immediately launched a second expedition to the west under the command of his nephew, Juan de Grijalva. The four caravels that made up the expedition sailed from Santiago in January 1518, and proceeded to run out the coast of Mexico from Tulum to Cabo Rojo. Eight months later no word had been received from Grijalva. Velázquez hastily organized a rescue expedition under the leadership of Hernán Cortés. It was too late to call off the new expedition, which amounted to eleven ships carrying about 600 Spaniards, when Grijalva arrived in Santiago before Cortés departed. The monumental consequences of Cortés' 1519 expedition to Mexico signaled the beginning of the Spanish conquest of the mainland and provides a convenient cut-off date for the period of maritime exploration and discovery in the Caribbean.

Little is known of the 1519 voyage of Alonso Alvarez de Pineda, except that he explored more of the Gulf of Mexico than any other navigator. Under the authority of Francisco de Garay, newly appointed Governor of Jamaica, Pineda set sail from Sevilla la Nueva, Jamaica, with a fleet of four vessels a few weeks after Cortés left Cuba. Pineda's explorations began on the west coast of Florida, and proved that it was not an island but a peninsula attached in the north to a vast mainland. The fleet coasted the Gulf Coast of North America, passing the mouth of the Mississippi River and continuing along the coast of Texas to link up with Cortés' outpost at Villa Rica de Veracruz. A landmark sketch map produced by the voyage, faithfully portraying the shape of the Gulf of Mexico, demonstrated that the coastline was unbroken.

The same year that Pineda proved the Gulf of Mexico had no outlet to the west, Magellan's fleet departed Spain on the voyage that would discover the only practical western route to the Indies. But it would be three years before the survivors of this, perhaps the greatest exploratory voyage of all time, returned to tell their tale.

Evidence from Shipwrecks

Given the immeasurable impact these explorers and conquerors had on world history and geography, it is singularly remarkable that we know so little about the ships which made their voyages possible, and which transmitted important characteristics to the oceangoing ships that followed. But the types of ships first capable of making reliable, round-trip, oceanic voyages, designed by Iberian mariners in the fifteenth century, lasted only a few decades. As the impetus for exploration gave way to the necessity of supplying the colonies founded in the explorers' wakes, these ship types disappeared completely. And no one had thought to make a good record of what they looked like, how they were constructed and sailed, or how they evolved through time.

When all the evidence from archival references, depictions and models is compiled, interpreted, re-compiled and re-interpreted, it remains clear that questions about the appearance, construction and performance of ships of exploration can be argued endlessly. Attempts by historians, naval architects and

5 (*left*) The astrolabe, an ancestor of the sextant, was used for determining latitude by measuring the altitude of heavenly bodies. A centrally mounted sighting device was moved around a series of graduations on the outer disc to take the measurement. Developed on land by Arabs, the device was modified by Portuguese mariners for use at sea during fifteenth-century explorations down the west coast of Africa. This astrolabe, recovered from the 1554 fleet off Padre Island, Texas, may be Portuguese and is among the oldest such devices found in the New World.

shipwrights to reconstruct and replicate the vessels used by Columbus in his first voyage across the Atlantic, to celebrate its 400th anniversary, demonstrated how even a century ago research on the ships of exploration was reaching a point of diminishing returns. All available evidence was synthesized and the ships were built as authentically as possible, but the effort was akin to paleontologists trying to recreate the appearance of a species of dinosaur from the evidence of its fossilized footprints and a cluster of gizzard stones. The sailing performances of these and subsequent 'replicas' left little question that something in their design and rig was dreadfully amiss.

Beginning in the 1950s, pioneers like Edwin Link, Pablo Bush Romero, Teddy Tucker and Mendel Peterson began to look to underwater archaeology as a new source of evidence which could supplement artistic depictions, votive models and written descriptions. If wrecks of documented exploratory vessels could be excavated and analyzed, they could supply incontrovertible evidence of how these ships were built, what they carried and how they carried it.

Starting with the first fleet to reach the New World, in 1492, many ships of exploration and their crews were lost. In addition to the hazards of threading the islands and reefs guarding the entrances to the Caribbean Sea and the Gulf of Mexico, there were powerful and unfamiliar currents, incredibly violent hurricanes, and tropical waters infested with voracious boring molluscs that could riddle an unprotected ship's bottom in a matter of weeks.

Contemporary histories mention more than fifty exploratory vessels lost to these and other causes between 1492 and 1520. Some of them, such as Columbus' *Santa María*, ran aground and were subsequently stripped and abandoned. Others, such as Alonso de Hojeda's caravel *Magdalena*, simply disappeared at sea. Still others, such as the four caravels of Juan de Aguado, sank in protected anchorages and were swallowed up by soft bottom sediments.

The ideal wreck would be of a fully equipped vessel sunk in a protected harbor and never salvaged, but efforts to find the remains of Columbus' caravels in St Ann's Bay, Jamaica, have been unsuccessful (Chapter Two) and few other known wrecksites fit that description. At the same time, fortuitous discoveries of very early but unidentified shipwrecks have begun to compete for attention.

Not one of the historically recorded vessels lost in the New World between 1492 and 1520 has been positively identified. Very few early shipwreck sites have even been reported. But how would we recognize the wreck of an exploratory vessel if we stumbled across it? What are the diagnostic artifacts that can key us in to the right sites? The touchstone used to assay the antiquity of shipwreck sites is the collection of artifacts from two ships of the New Spain fleet wrecked on Padre Island, Texas, in 1554. Although not ships of exploration, these are the earliest wrecks of certain date so far explored in the New World.

An Archaeological Benchmark: The Padre Island Wrecks

The artifact assemblage from two wrecks of the 1554 fleet was painstakingly conserved, analyzed and thoroughly published by the Texas Archaeological Research Laboratory (TARL) in the 1970s, greatly enhancing the world's knowledge of mid-sixteenth-century Spanish colonial seafaring (see also Chapter Five).

The wrecks are the physical remains of the kind of tragedy that was the common lot of sixteenth-century seamen and settlers, even those joyfully returning to Europe with riches from the Americas. Four ships sailed for Spain from Veracruz in 1554 carrying 2 million pesos. Struck by a violent April storm, three of the ships were driven aground just off Texas' great barrier bank, Padre

Treasures of the 'San Estebán'

A violent storm in 1554 drove *San Estebán* aground off Padre Island, Texas, with two other Spanish vessels. The earliest historically attested shipwreck of certain date to have been explored in the New World, her salvaged artifacts provide a benchmark against which other archaeological discoveries can be judged.

6 (*above*) A gold crucifix discovered on the wreck.

7 (*above right*) Other finds from the ship included silver bullion, silver coins and a gold bar.

8 (*right*) A museum display on the *San Estebán* shows the remains of her keel (at left), anchor and a type of breech-loading cannon known as a *bombardeta*. The 'spindliness' of the anchor shank is one of several features diagnostic of Spanish anchors used in the New World during the first half of the sixteenth century.

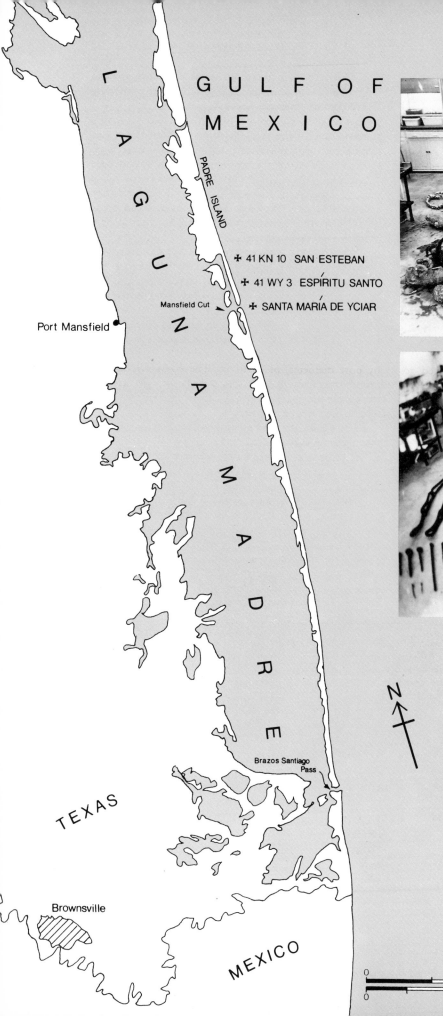

GULF OF
MEXICO

L A G U N A   M A D R E

PADRE ISLAND

✝ 41 KN 10   SAN ESTEBAN

✝ 41 WY 3   ESPÍRITU SANTO

✝ SANTA MARÍA DE YCIAR

Mansfield Cut

Port Mansfield

Brazos Santiago
Pass

TEXAS

Brownsville

MEXICO

N

0   10 Mls
0   15 Km

The Padre Island Wrecks

9   (*left*) The location of the three ships which ran aground off Padre Island in 1554.

10, 11   The role of conservation is as important as the role of excavation in the study of shipwrecks. Metal artifacts from the 1554 fleet lost off Padre Island are only amorphous lumps (*top*) before years of treatment, including mechanical removal of concretion, electrolysis to remove corrosive chlorides, and boiling in microcrystalline wax to seal the metal against further oxidation. The results (*above*) are a unique group of sixteenth-century armaments, fittings, anchors, and navigational instruments.

Island, while the fourth vessel made it only as far as Havana before being abandoned. Perhaps half of the 300 people on the wrecked ships drowned, and the remainder faced the prolonged misery of starvation and Indian attack during an overland trek toward Mexico that few survived.

Although half the treasure was salvaged shortly thereafter by an expedition mounted by a few who had reached Mexico in a ship's boat, the ships themselves settled into the deep sand that partially protected them for nearly 400 years. One of the wrecks, probably that of *Santa María de Yciar*, which may first have sailed to the New World in 1540, was destroyed in the 1940s by the modern dredging of Mansfield Cut through Padre Island. The site of what is thought to have been *Espíritu Santo,* apparently lost on the return leg of her maiden voyage, was destroyed in 1967 by a treasure-hunting company, although its artifacts were conserved and studied at TARL during litigation between the state and the finders over ownership. The third site, excavated by Texas Antiquities Committee archaeologists Carl Clausen and J. Barto Arnold III, between 1972 and 1976, is believed to represent *San Estebán*, which had previously voyaged to the New World in 1550. Artifacts belonging to the last were found scattered on top of a hard clay layer covered by 0.6 to 1.2 m (2 to 4 ft) of sand and shell.

The second and third Padre Island wrecks were securely identified by markings on coins, bullion and navigational instruments as two of the three vessels lost in the 1554 disaster. Thus the artifact assemblage from the ships, which had left Spain in 1552, comprises an early benchmark in time against which other discoveries may be compared. Although the ships were post-conquest galleons, many of their features, particularly ordnance, were probably not markedly different from those of the slightly earlier exploratory period.

Until about the middle of the sixteenth century most European ordnance was made of wrought iron, for the technique of casting iron in quantities sufficient to make large guns had not yet been mastered. A few guns were cast in bronze, but the first cast-iron cannons did not appear until about 1543. Archival sources reveal that at least some of the ships in the 1554 New Spain fleet carried cast-bronze artillery, but this must have been salvaged in antiquity since the excavators found only wrought-iron breech-loaders. The heaviest of these wrought-iron guns were ship-killing and siege cannons called *bombardetas*. A *bombardeta* was made from many small pieces of iron intricately worked to form a long, parallel-sided gun tube open at both ends. The bore of the tube usually was made up of several 'staves', like those of a wooden barrel, which were reinforced by the addition of iron 'sleeves' and thicker 'bands' more-or-less analogous to a barrel's hoops. The sleeves and bands were fitted alternately down the length of the bore assembly. Lengths of typical tubes varied between 64 cm (2 ft 1 in) and 2.65 m (8 ft 8 in), and bores ranged from about 7 cm (2.8 in) to 11 cm (4.3 in) for a caliber (bore length divided by bore diameter) of 15 to 30. The *bombardeta* and its breech chamber, which contained the powder charge, were mounted in a massive oak carriage having two small wheels near the muzzle end.

Each *bombardeta* had several interchangeable breech chambers which enabled a high rate of fire. These chambers were constructed in the same manner as the gun tube and were usually quite heavy; lifting rings were attached to their upper surfaces. The gunner's rule of thumb was to fill a chamber three-fifths full of powder, after which its open end was sealed with a wooden plug before it was inserted in the breech of the cannon. The charge was touched off by applying an open flame or hot iron to a touch hole near the butt end of the chamber. Breech-loading guns were convenient for use aboard ship since, unlike muzzle-loaders, they could be reloaded without being hauled away from their ports.

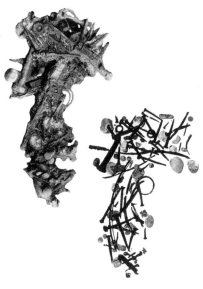

12–14 One method of conservation is illustrated by the various stages through which seabed concretion is removed from a group of 1554 shipwreck artifacts. The interior of a shapeless lump of calcium carbonate is revealed by a radiograph (*far left*) to help guide conservator D. L. Hamilton in the removal of concretion from the metal objects inside. The relative positions of the artifacts are preserved until a photograph (*center left*) and drawing (*left*) can be made of the assemblage, which contains more than a hundred artifacts, including iron spikes, a polished iron pyrite native American mirror, a silver disc, ballast stones, leather and brass.

Highborn Cay

Just off the northern shore of Highborn Cay in the Bahamas, the wreck of an early discovery-period ship has been examined by Institute of Nautical Archaeology (INA) researchers. The work forms part of a Caribbean survey that includes the Bahía Mujeres and Molasses Reef wrecksites.

15 (*left*) Archaeologists begin cutting a test trench across the Highborn Cay ballast mound, September 1986. The relationship of the anchors to the mound implies that the ship sank on her moorings, a theory bolstered by the original appearance of the mound, which to a large extent preserved the shape of the hull that carried the ballast.

Bahía Mujeres

Discovered in 1958 off the northeast tip of Mexico's Yucatan peninsula, this wreck has yielded cannons and two anchors but awaits full excavation.

16 (*below*) Heavily camouflaged by elkhorn corals, the Bahía Mujeres wreck crowns the top of a shallow reef just inside a bay. Here an INA archaeologist explores the site with a metal detector.

Molasses Reef

An INA excavation in the Turks and Caicos Islands is revealing evidence for the oldest known shipwreck so far discovered in the New World.

17 (*right*) Certain head corals, such as this colony of *Montastraea annularis* growing on the ballast mound of the Molasses Reef wreck, can be dated by counting annually formed growth rings. Here the head is cored for dating with the technique called schlerochronology.

18 (*below*) Archaeologists carry a heavily encrusted *bombardeta* off the Molasses Reef wrecksite. Air-filled balloons provide buoyancy, reducing the weight of the cannon.

The most common weapon at Padre Island was the *verso*, or swivel gun, a smaller wrought-iron breech-loader. The body of a typical *verso* consisted of four distinct parts: barrel, swivel, breech and tiller. The guns were generally light enough to be portable and, with their Y-shaped swivels mounted in sockets on the rail, could be trained and fired quickly. Swivel guns ranged from around 2 to 3 m (6 ft 7 in to 9 ft 10 in) in length, about half of which was the aiming tail, or tiller, a long iron rod, usually square in cross-section, which ended in a knob or, more commonly, a loop which may have served for securing lines. Typical bore diameters were in the vicinity of 4.5 cm. The most common type of projectile seems to have been an iron cube covered in lead, but solid cast iron shot and loose 'dice', or iron cubes, were also used.

With their slightly tapering, rounded open ends and loop handles, *verso* breech chambers resemble beer steins. There appears to have been little or no standardization, and simple rectilinear marks on the chambers seem to indicate which gun they belonged to.

Crossbows, which continued to be used well into the sixteenth century, were also found at Padre Island. They are somewhat smaller than typical military crossbows of the period, perhaps reflecting a marine adaptation which favored ease of use in confined spaces over range.

The 'spindliness' of the Padre Island anchor shanks, the shortness of their arms in proportion to the lengths of their shanks, the shape of their palms and the location of 'stock keys' on the same plane as the arms comprised a set of features diagnostic of early sixteenth-century Spanish anchors used in the New World. Sherds of 'Early Style' olive jars provide another sign of early date.

A section of the stern of the ship thought to be *San Esteban* was found preserved in the sand (Chapter Five), but the design and dimensions of this vessel were different from those of discovery ships half a century earlier.

Caribbean Survey

In 1982 the Institute of Nautical Archaeology (INA) implemented a carefully planned, sustained effort to locate, survey and excavate wreck sites of discovery-period ships in the Caribbean. Our objective is to shed new light on the quintessential vessel of exploration, the caravel. Three early shipwreck sites, all appearing to belong to the first half of the sixteenth century or end of the fifteenth century, have already been identified as potential candidates for this research, though not one has been securely dated.

Each of these sites lay in exposed reef environments and the preservation of organic materials such as wood was correspondingly poor. On the other hand, the marine encrustation which typically forms on metal objects in tropical water preserved virtually every metal fastener, tool, weapon and other hardware item that was not carried off the site by floating wreckage. Additionally, each of the sites is located in shallow water with excellent visibility, simplifying mapping and recording.

The Bahía Mujeres wreck. The wreck at Bahía Mujeres, off the northeastern tip of Mexico's Yucatan peninsula, was discovered accidentally by lawyer José de Jesús Lima and his sons in 1958. They salvaged at least one of its small, wrought-iron breech-loading cannons, which they donated to the Isla Mujeres school. Inventor and underwater explorer Edwin Link visited the site in 1959, when at least one cannon was raised aboard his salvage vessel *Sea Diver*, but details of this work are sketchy. The following year the Mexican underwater exploration club CEDAM explored the site more thoroughly by mooring a barge over it for three days' work. Two or three cannons were raised in 1960 and one cannon and two anchors were lifted in 1961. After that, interest in the Bahía Mujeres site waned, probably because it was believed that the wreck had been completely salvaged.

The Bahía Mujeres wreck lies on top of a shallow coral patch just inside the reef line running northeast from Punta Cancún. The site is marked by a low mound of ballast stones less than 3 m (10 ft) below the surface and almost completely obscured by a forest of elkhorn coral. The axis of the irregularly shaped mound has an almost perfect north-south orientation and is contiguous for more than 20 m (66 ft). North of the mound, scattered ballast stones lie individually and in small clusters on top of the reef.

The only extant clues to the identity of the Bahía Mujeres wreck are the ordnance and two anchors raised more than two decades ago. Other than the fragmentary cannon in the Isla Mujeres school, these artifacts now reside in a CEDAM-sponsored museum in Xelha. The most unusual cannon is a *falconete grande* in the CEDAM collection. This is a wrought-iron, breech-loading weapon similar to the *verso* except for its extremely long barrel made up of alternating sleeves and bands. The gunsmith was careful to stagger nine of the ten surviving forge-welded sleeve seams along the bottom of the barrel, presumably to decrease the chances of bursting. The trunnions are set into a special reinforcing ring between the ninth and tenth sleeves (the muzzle sleeve is missing). The muzzle, tiller and swivel mount were not present when the piece was salvaged, or have fallen off since, but the original overall length must have been in excess of 3 m (10 ft). The bore diameter is difficult to estimate, owing to poor preservation, but probably was in the neighborhood of 3 cm (1.2 in). Photographs taken during the salvage show a breech chamber with an intact straight handle lying next to the piece, but it has since been lost.

The other swivel gun in the CEDAM collection is a *verso liso*, a kind of small *verso*. Only the barrel and forward portion of the breech survive, but one of the original salvors, Alfonso Arnold, recalled that when discovered the gun had a tiller that angled up from the axis of the barrel and terminated in a knob. No breech chambers or shot for the piece were found.

The CEDAM collection also contains a small, poorly preserved *bombardeta*, and two probably compatible breech chambers. The *bombardeta* was made by forge-welding alternating sleeves and bands over a barrel made of five iron staves; reinforcing bands were set between the third and fourth, and tenth and eleventh sleeves where lugs for the lifting rings, now missing, were attached. Bore diameter is approximately 7 cm (2.8 in) and the length of the barrel is 2.07 m (81.5 in) for a caliber of 30. The fragmentary, 2.14-m (7-ft) gun tube in the Isla Mujeres school may represent another, longer *bombardeta*, or some other type of gun.

The proportions and configuration of a large iron anchor in the CEDAM collection are characteristic of early sixteenth-century anchors, but it is smaller and lighter than the ships' anchors recovered from other early sites, possibly indicating that the Bahía Mujeres ship was smaller than the others. The long, spindly shank of this anchor, now broken, was at least 3.0 m (10 ft) in length. Arm length is short in proportion to shank length (1:2.6), and the palms are triangular and nearly equilateral. The crown is pointed, the shank and arms are squarish in section, and the stock keys are on the same plane as the arms.

Also in the CEDAM collection is a five-tined grapnel anchor in surprisingly good condition. It is complete except for the ends of the tines and the eye in the head of the shank. Its original length would have been about

1.45 m (4 ft 9 in) and it would have weighed less than 20 kg (44 lb). This anchor probably belonged to one of the ship's boats, and its presence on the site may be an important clue to understanding the wrecking event.

INA combined forces with the Underwater Archaeology Branch of Mexico's National Institute of Anthropology and History (INAH) in 1983 to record the artifacts raised during the salvage of 1958–61. In 1984 another INA/INAH team relocated and surveyed the site with the assistance of several of the original salvors and the Mexican Navy.

Neither date nor nationality have yet been established for the Bahía Mujeres wreck. The earliest known European shipwreck in this area was a vessel identified with the Valdevia expedition lost near the coast of the Yucatan, perhaps on Alacranes Reef or Pedro Shoals, in about 1511. In 1518 Juan de Grijalva encountered on the coast of Quintana Roo two survivors, Gonzalo Guerrero and Gerónimo de Aguilar, who had been living with the Indians for eight years. Hernán Cortés, following de Grijalva's lead, stopped at Isla Mujeres in 1519 on his way to the conquest of Mexico and persuaded de Aguilar to accompany him as interpreter.

The Conquistador of the Yucatan, Francisco de Montejo the Elder, maintained a presence on the Quintana Roo coast of the Yucatan from 1527 to 1529. CEDAM advanced the hypothesis that the Bahía Mujeres wreck was one of Montejo's ships, *La Nicolasa*, but this identification seems doubtful. Captained by a man named Ochoa, *La Nicolasa* was one of four ships Montejo obtained in Spain. Historians list the others as *San Jerónimo*, a large *nao*, and *La Gavarra*, a *bergantín*; the fourth vessel is unnamed. *La Gavarra* was left in Santo Domingo, but the other three vessels proceeded to Cozumel and then to a location near the Maya center of Xelha. According to the testimony of her owner, Martín de Ibiacebal, *La Nicolasa* was dispatched to Veracruz to bring much-

19 (*above*) A crowd gathers to inspect a *falconete grande*, a *verso* and *bombardeta* breech chambers raised from the Bahía Mujeres wreck in 1960. The complete encrusted cannon at right is from another site.

20 (*right*) Ordnance and anchor from the Bahía Mujeres wreck displayed in the old CEDAM Museum in Mexico suffer from lack of conservation by the divers who salvaged them before underwater archaeology had become a fully fledged discipline.

Excavations at Highborn Cay

Test excavation by INA in 1986 followed on from a brief reconnaissance three years earlier.

21 (*above left*) The mast step and central portion of the wreck are revealed in the test trench dug in 1986. Buttress timbers are visible on either side of the step. The wooden chock remains in the mast mortise, but all traces of the mast have vanished.

22 (*above*) Artillery and other artifacts recovered from the Highborn Cay wreck during the 1967 salvage, undertaken by skin divers who discovered the site.

23 (*center left*) The 1986 excavation plan showing the remains of the ship's hull, including the mast step visible in ill. 21. The ship seems to have been carrying about 70 metric tons of ballast, about twice the amount borne by the Molasses Reef vessel.

24 (*left*) The location of Highborn Cay in the Bahamas.

needed supplies back to the colony, but ended up in Cuba instead and never returned to the Yucatan.

The armaments from the Bahía Mujeres wreck appear to be characteristic of those used in the first half of the sixteenth century, but without further archaeological research on the site it is not possible to identify the wreck more precisely. Perhaps it is one of the other vessels used by Montejo; or perhaps it is from another, unrecorded voyage.

It is important to note that only a few of the largest, most easily recognizable artifacts were recovered from the site during the salvage efforts of 1958–61: no ceramics, fasteners, fittings, wood, rigging components, tools, personal effects or even shot. These categories of artifacts, when excavated, will tell us more about the ship than the few objects so far recovered.

The Highborn Cay wreck. In 1965 three skin divers discovered a shipwreck site in Highborn Cut just off the northern shore of Highborn Cay in the Bahamas. Lying in about 6 m (20 ft) of water, the site consisted of a low mound of ballast stones, an assortment of cannons, and an anchor – all nearly obscured by an overgrowth of coral.

With permission from the government of the Bahamas, the discoverers began to salvage the site in March 1966. The project was discontinued in May 1967 and all recovered artifacts were taken to the United States. A portion of the collection, including a *bombardeta*, a *verso*, breech chambers, shot, iron fasteners and a few sherds, was subsequently acquired by the Mariners' Museum in Newport News, Virginia, following conservation treatment by Florida's Bureau of Historic Sites and Properties. The Smithsonian Institution ended up with a second *bombardeta*, another *verso* and a few other ancillary pieces of equipment.

The Highborn Cay wreck was virtually forgotten for fifteen years until INA began excavation of a wreck on Molasses Reef in the Turks and Caicos Islands. Recognizing similarities between the two sites, we obtained authorization from the Bahamas Ministry of External Affairs to make a brief site reconnaissance in April 1983. Three years later, in September 1986, we conducted a test excavation to determine the extent of the ship's hull remains. The opportunity to make direct comparisons between artifacts from the two sites arose when the Mariners' Museum and one of the original salvors made their collections available for study.

Ordnance raised from the site during 1967 included two large *bombardetas* and two compatible breech chambers. At least thirteen smaller swivel guns, also of wrought iron, were found. Most of the latter were *versos* about 2 m (6 ft 6 in) long, but at least two were higher caliber *versos dobles* 2.7 m (8 ft 10 in) long. As many as eighteen breech chambers for the swivel guns were recovered, as well as iron wedges used to lock the chambers in the breeches. One breech chamber was still loaded with powder and sealed by a wooden plug. Shot recovered was exclusively of the iron-cored, lead-covered variety. Unique among the finds was a wrought-iron barbed harpoon or spear with a 2-m-long (6-ft-7-in) shaft.

Elements of the ship's standing rigging were recovered, including three groups of iron rigging components. Numerous wrought-iron hull fastenings lay scattered about the site. Forelock bolts with washers and small key-wedges were common, as were eye-bolts and square-section iron nails. At least three rudder pintles, one still attached to a gudgeon, were discovered.

No coins, navigational instruments or other precisely datable artifacts were found, and only a gold-inlaid wooden knife handle could be classified as a personal possession. No complete ceramic vessels were discovered, although an earthenware bowl, probably an *escudilla,* was reconstructed from fragments. A small pitcher handle, possibly from a *cantaro,* or water jar, was also recovered.

A wrought-iron anchor lay atop the ballast mound when the site was first discovered. Two other anchors were located approximately 100–150 m (328–492 ft) from the northeastern end of the ballast mound. The heaviest anchor, estimated to weigh 270–300 kg (595–660 lb), seems to have been rigged as a bower since it was one of the two found directly off the 'bow' end of the site. The other two anchors were estimated to weigh about 180 kg (397 lb) each. Ordinarily, the largest, heaviest anchor – the sheet anchor – would have been deployed only when the other anchors were lost or would not hold.

The salvors removed ballast stones from both ends of the mound, exposing the bow and stern timbers of the vessel. Hypothetical reconstructions of sections of the hull were attempted, but no records of the actual remains seem to have been made. Our 1986 test excavation revealed that the bottom of the ship was preserved under the ballast mound and that, although the timbers at the bow and stern had suffered much damage during and subsequent to the original salvage in 1966 and 1967, sufficient evidence remained to give us keel length, keelson length, breadth amidships, total number of frames and many fascinating construction details.

We began by re-excavating the western end of the ballast mound, which the salvors thought had been the ship's stern. Although the sternpost, deadwood, hull planking and aftermost frames had vanished, a 'ghost' image of the keel was preserved in the form of a trough, from 6 to 30 cm (2.4 to 12 in) deep, gouged by the keel into the hardpan. The aftermost end of the keel was indicated by an abrupt termination of this trough, which we followed forward for a distance of 5.5 m (18 ft) before it disappeared beneath undisturbed ballast. The keel averaged 15 cm (6 in) wide beneath the frames. It was impossible to determine precisely the depth of the keel since its lowermost portion had been badly eroded in the process of forming the trough, but it appears to have been of the order of 15 cm deep as well. The aftermost end of the keelson was tapered and affixed to the top of the fourth-from-last frame by a treenail and an iron bolt.

Even more informative was our re-examination of the bow. The keel trough was present here, too, running more than 3 m (9.8 ft) beyond the forward limit of the ballast mound. The actual keel and part of the stempost were preserved in the trough, as was the intricate scarf used to join them. Measurements in several locations indicated that the keel had a 10–12 degree list to port. The hardpan on the port side retained the impressions of square-headed iron nails used to fasten the hull planks to the frames. Here also survived portions of five runs of planking, floor timbers and a first futtock more than 2 m (6.6 ft) long. Frames averaged 16 cm (6.3 in) in width. Hull planking was attached to the frames by two treenails and three square iron nails per plank. Hull planks were a minimum of 6 cm (2.4 in) thick, preserved examples ranging from 12 to 25 cm (4.7 to 9.8 in) in width.

Having determined the locations of the bow and stern ends of the keel, we cut a trench 2 m (6.6 ft) wide across the central portion of the ballast mound to find the main mast step. The trench came down on the step, a large mortise cut into an expanded part of the keelson. A wooden chock that held the squared-off bottom of the main mast in the mortise was still in place, although no trace of the mast remained. The step was braced on either side by three tapering buttressing timbers resting on the floor timbers below them. Inboard ends of the buttresses fitted into shallow grooves cut into the sides of the step while their outboard ends were set in notches in floor stringers running parallel to the keelson.

Ceiling planking ran up to the forwardmost and aftermost buttresses, and the space between the buttresses had been covered by limber boards which could have been removed to provide access to the bottom of the ship. Filler planks installed between the first futtocks outboard of the stringers kept trash from finding its way into the bilge. A semi-circular notch in the keelson just aft of the last buttress on the port side was probably the bottom of the pump well. A jumble of thin boards in this vicinity may represent the remains of the pump box, crushed by shifting ballast as the ship rolled over on her port side.

The floor timber beneath the forward end of the step was joined to futtocks on both its forward and after sides, indicating that it was the mastercouple – the widest part of the hull. We noted that the first futtocks were attached to their floors by a peculiar shallow mortise-and-tenon joint which apparently is characteristic of sixteenth-century ship construction, as it appears also in the Basque whaling 'galleon' *San Juan*, under excavation in Red Bay, Labrador (see Chapter Four); the *Mary Rose*, which sank in 1545 off Portsmouth, England, and was raised in the 1980s; the early sixteenth-century shipwreck of uncertain nationality at Cattewater, Portsmouth; and the Molasses Reef wreck.

Historian Mendel Peterson, who participated in the original salvage of the Highborn Cay shipwreck, offered a generalized interpretation of the site based on his observations. The presence of two anchors 100 m (328 ft) or more to the northeast of the site indicated to him that

the ship had been at anchor when she sank, and that her bow pointed to the northeast. The fact that the sheet anchor seems to have been in use led Peterson to conclude that the ship was in peril and her crew were trying to save her when she sank. The main deposit of ordnance and a third anchor were situated at the northeastern end of the ballast, leading to the conclusion that they had been stowed in the hold. Does this indicate that the crew were attempting to increase the stability of their vessel in anticipation of strong winds and high seas?

Scarcity of personal effects implied that the ship did not sink suddenly, since the crew seem to have had time to gather their belongings. Peterson even suggested that the ship might have been scuttled while at anchor. On the evidence of the type of iron-cored lead-covered shot found, he dated the ship to between 1500 and about 1570.

Like the Bahía Mujeres wreck, the Highborn Cay wreck was never identified. The large quantity of ordnance and the ship's location in the remote northern Exumas were difficult to explain. The sum of the evidence led Peterson to conclude that the ship was a pirate or privateer that sank at anchor from an undetermined cause; but he mentioned another possible identification: perhaps the ship was one of the two caravels lost by Vicente Yañez Pinzón in 1500. If so, the wreck of the second caravel must lie nearby. To date, no comprehensive archaeological survey of the sea floor in the vicinity of Highborn Cut has been made. If a contemporaneous wrecksite is discovered there, it will greatly reinforce the association with Pinzón.

The Molasses Reef wreck. In 1982, at the invitation of the government of the Turks and Caicos Islands, a West Indian British Crown Colony, INA initiated excavation of what appears to be the oldest shipwreck so far discovered in the New World. The wreck lies in water only 6 m (20 ft) deep on Molasses Reef. Although three phases of field work and three years of laboratory analysis were completed by 1986, the project was far from over.

The Molasses Reef wreck project is an inductive archaeological investigation: i.e., an attempt to identify as precisely as possible a ship from bits and pieces of material culture recovered through controlled excavation. The inductive method requires that the site be excavated completely in order to produce a complete inventory of artifacts, all of which must be cleaned and studied. An accurate estimate of vessel type, size and rig must be derived from the artifact assemblage, ballast and hull studies. Finally, a team of researchers will search European repositories and archives for references to a vessel matching the date and physical description of the Molasses Reef wreck as determined from the archaeological analysis.

One of the best indicators of the early date of the site is the spectrum of armaments on board – crossbows, *arquebuzes, haquebuts,* hand grenades, at least three types of *versos,* a matched pair of *bombardetas* and a *cerbatana* (a carriage-mounted, medium-size, wrought-iron breech-

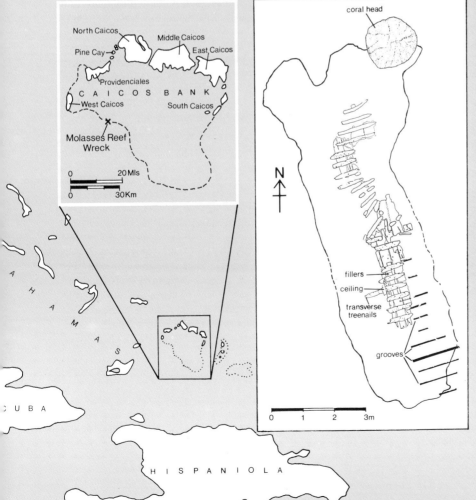

Excavations on Molasses Reef

By 1986 three phases of fieldwork on the wrecksite and three years of laboratory analysis had been completed by INA archaeologists.

25 (*above left*) Thomas Oertling (foreground) discusses hull remnants from the wreck with Donald Keith. Every surviving fragment of wood has been drawn at full scale, providing some of the first evidence of how ships of exploration were constructed.

26 (*above*) Donald Keith inspects wooden hull remains of the ship on the sea bed 6 m (20 ft) down.

27 (*center left*) Plan of the hull timbers of the Molasses Reef wreck. A separate plan (ill. 34) was made of the distribution of armaments on and around the wreck.

28 (*far left*) The location of Molasses Reef in the Turks and Caicos island group.

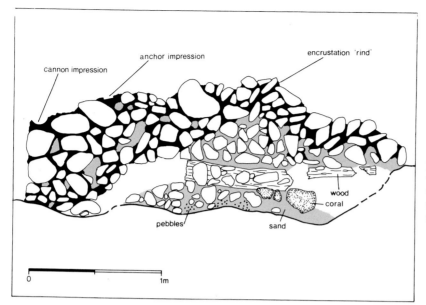

cannon impression   anchor impression   encrustation 'rind'

wood
coral

pebbles   sand

0   1m

29 Many different rock types are included in the approximately 1,000 samples collected from profiles, such as this one, cut through the Molasses Reef ballast mound. Certain rocks, particularly those of igneous origin, have petrological 'signatures' in the form of distinct detectable trace element or mineralogical composition. If the source areas for some of the Molasses Reef samples can be identified, they may provide clues to the course followed on the ship's last voyage. The wrecksites of all discovery ships will likely contain stone ballast, providing the potential for comparative studies.

loader). Such an arsenal seems more typical of the last half of the fifteenth than the first half of the sixteenth century. Dimensions of the fragmentary barrels of two small gun tubes match those quoted for a standard *arquebuz*, a type of shoulder arm fired by a lever or trigger, that gave way to the *mosquete* (musket) around the middle of the sixteenth century. A pair of *haquebuts*, or 'hand cannons', with octagonal barrels, had been fitted after manufacture with Y-shaped swivels. These muzzle-loading guns commonly were used in the fifteenth century, although a few may have been made in the very early sixteenth century. The closest parallels to the *haquebuts* from the Molasses Reef wreck are two almost identical guns on display in the town hall of Hasselt in the Netherlands. The Hasselt guns are believed to have been made in the fifteenth century, but the exact date and place of manufacture is not known.

The two *bombardetas* are a matched pair probably made by the same artisan, or at least in the same workshop. Muzzle bands of both were decorated with patterns of triangles and lines punched into the metal, and the front surface of their muzzle 'sights' was stamped with vertical lines. Perhaps these distinctive markings will eventually provide a clue to their manufacturer. The best parallel for the Molasses Reef wreck pair is a *bombardeta* in Madrid's Museo del Ejército (no. 5957 group 10) that came to the museum from Puerto de Santander and is thought to have been made in the late fifteenth century.

The types of shot found on the site were nearly as diverse as the types of ordnance. Most of the shot were solid cast iron, but 20 wrought iron, 9 hollow cast iron, 69 'composite' (lead-covered iron cubes) and 15 solid lead shot were also found. The solid lead shot were of diameters exclusively appropriate for the smaller firearms – *haquebuts* and *arquebuzes* – while the other types of shot were of diameters appropriate for the *bombardetas*, *cerbatana*, *versos dobles*, *versos*, and *versos lisos*. Of the 137

cast-iron shot found to date, differences in diameters and location of the sprue mark with respect to mold mark indicate the shot were made in at least five different molds. One of these molds was discovered intact on the wreck. Made of cast bronze, it had an iron shot inside, but the shot had not been cast in it, being much smaller in diameter than the mold and with entirely different mold marks. Half of a small bronze mold was also recovered, but, curiously, none of the shot from the Molasses Reef wreck appear to have been cast in it. Both molds retained fragments of the wrought-iron tongs used to handle them when hot. *Pirotechnia*, a treatise on metallurgical technology published by Vannoccio Biringuccio in 1540, states that cast-iron shot first appeared in Italy in 1495. According to *Pirotechnia*, the molds in which the iron was cast at first were made of bronze, but founders switched to iron molds some time prior to 1540 in order to save expense.

One of the hollow cast-iron shot, or 'grenades', broke open during cleaning, revealing a granular substance – probably gunpowder – still dry after centuries under the sea. The technique for casting hollow shot, or grenades, is described at length in *Pirotechnia*. Undoubtedly, the technique was known and used much earlier.

The range of diameters of the shot is astonishing. Apparently fifteenth- and sixteenth-century gunners preferred undersize shot (probably for safety reasons) and were not opposed to a centimeter or two of windage. The shot appear to cluster around 1.4 cm (0.55 in) for the *arquebuzes*, 4.1 cm (1.6 in) for the *versos*, 6.0 cm (2.4 in) for the *cerbatana*, and 7.7 cm (3.0 in) for the *bombardetas*.

A more precise date cannot be reached through a study of the ordnance alone because no chronology has been established for wrought-iron, breech-loading artillery, and individual pieces are seldom, if ever, dated. The *bombardetas* and *versos* which have been cleaned bear a

30 Two sets of leg irons, or *grillos*, were discovered on the Molasses Reef wreck. A radiograph taken before cleaning aids the conservator in the removal of concretion. Careful inspection during conservation revealed that both sets were 'locked', probably indicating that they were fastened around someone's ankles when the ship sank. Was the ship carrying slaves or prisoners?

generic resemblance to pieces from the three ships lost on Padre Island in 1554. At the same time, the battery of the Molasses Reef wreck appears technically inferior to, and therefore earlier than, that of the *Mary Rose*, which sank in 1545. Comparisons with the *Mary Rose* are apt to be misleading since she was the flagship of the English fleet and consequently her battery was composed of the most up-to-date ordnance, including muzzle-loading cast bronze and iron cannon.

Without benefit of complete analysis it is not possible to determine what type of vessel the Molasses Reef wreck was, but given the relatively small size of its ballast mound (11 × 3 m [36 × 10 ft] containing 35 metric tons of stone), the nationality suggested by Iberian ceramics discovered, and the early date suggested by its complement of ordnance, the vessel is most likely to have been a *caravela* or *nao*. Unlike the carrack and galleon, no archaeological example of these types has yet been discovered, and even their progenitors remain largely unknown.

Although hull remains of the Molasses Reef wreck are minimal, ballast, artifacts and their distributions on the seafloor provide clues to vessel size and rig. They suggest a medium-size ship of the period, with perhaps 18–21 m (59–69 ft) of length on deck. The vessel carried slightly more than 35 tons of stone ballast in addition to cargo, crew and armaments. Iron rigging components identified may, when cleaned, indicate the number of masts the vessel carried and how she was rigged. She must have had sufficient deck space to permit the stationing of two *bombardetas*, one *cerbatana* and at least eighteen swivel guns of various sizes; two of the swivel guns, muzzle-loading *haquebuts*, were sufficiently small and light to have been mounted in a main mast fighting top, or on the ship's boat. The projected length of the *bombardetas* when mounted in naval carriages is about 4.5 m (15 ft). If these guns were mounted athwartships in the waist of the vessel,

they provide us with a clue to her minimum beam.

The presence of 'fillers' between frames at the top of the ceiling planking, floor-to-futtock 'tenons', and the use of transverse treenails to join floor timbers to the first futtocks were techniques used in Basque shipbuilding in the mid-sixteenth century, as evidenced by the well-preserved hull remains of the *San Juan* (see Chapter Four). The hull of the early sixteenth-century Cattewater wreck off Portsmouth also possessed these characteristics. Although no absolutely datable artifact, e.g. coin or dated navigational instrument, has come to light among the heavily encrusted artifacts, many concretions remain to be 'excavated' in the laboratory, and a temporally diagnostic artifact may yet be found. The reconstructed shapes of the fragmentary ceramic vessels recovered are Iberian forms of the sixteenth century – *orzas* (storage pots), *jarros* (jars), *escudillas* (small bowls), *lebrillos* (basins) and olive jars. A fragment of an olive jar mouth from the site is very similar to that of a jar found in a 1508–14 context during excavation of the ruins of El Convento de San Francisco in the Dominican Republic, and the base of an *escudilla* has a form which is thought to have disappeared by the end of the third quarter of the sixteenth century. With the exception of the *haquebuts*, the best parallels for which are found in the Low Countries, the artillery suggests a Spanish origin, although this evidence is circumstantial.

Perhaps the ship was exploring the islands of the eastern Caribbean when she was wrecked. The absence of fine artifacts and the general 'utilitarian', early sixteenth-century aspect of the artifacts recovered lend credence to this hypothesis. The geographical location of Molasses Reef in waters traversed frequently during the earliest phase of Caribbean exploration and discovery and its close proximity to the earliest New World Spanish colonies implies an early date for the wreck, and perhaps Spanish nationality, but does not constitute proof.

31 Two curiously shaped lead objects were discovered on the Molasses Reef wreck. They have been identified as one-way pump valves similar to those depicted in Agricola's treatise on mining and metal-working, *De re metallica*, first published in 1556. That two such valves were found on the site suggests that the ship had two bilge pumps, or at least a spare valve.

Could the Molasses Reef wreck be the remains of a recorded explorer's ship? Numerous exploratory vessels were lost in the vicinity of Hispaniola and on the north coast of South America, but not many ships are known to have been lost in the Bahamas. Possibilities include the two ships lost by Vicente Yañez Pinzón on his return to Spain in 1500, and one lost by Ponce de León in 1513.

Perhaps the ship was engaged in capturing Indians to provide slave labor for the early Spanish colonies in Hispaniola and Cuba, and wrecked on Molasses Reef while slaving in the Caicos Islands or en route between Hispaniola and the Bahamas. This hypothesis would conform to the apparently early date of the site as well as explain the presence of armaments. It would seem, however, that if the vessel had been slaving among the Lucayan Arawaks, small arms and crossbows would have been of more use than *versos* and *bombardetas* (although the fragments of two *arquebuzes* were recovered, no edged weapons were found). Parts of two sets of *grillos*, or leg irons, identified among the artifacts probably represent normal ship's hardware rather than specialized slaving equipment.

Little is known about Spanish slaving activities in the Turks and Caicos Islands, but at least one researcher has stated that Middle Caicos had the largest Arawak population in the Bahamas. Given their proximity to the north coast of Hispaniola, the Caicos Islands must have been quickly depopulated; in 1513 Ponce de León sailed the length of the Bahamas without sighting a single village.

Any hypothesis designed to explain the nature of the ship's last voyage will have to accommodate these basic facts: Sometime in the first quarter of the sixteenth century a seagoing Spanish vessel of medium size went aground on Molasses Reef. Heavily armed with crossbows, shoulder arms, swivel guns and *bombardetas*, she appears to have been carrying very little else. Most, if not all, ordnance on board was secured, rather than at the ready. Some of the crew probably survived the wreck and escaped to the islands of the Caicos Bank, although there is no indication whether they eventually succeeded in returning to civilization, were killed by local Indians or remained marooned for the rest of their days.

The historical significance of the Molasses Reef wreck is still unresolved. The archaeological window through which we view the ship is cracked and hazy, but discoveries in the laboratory continue to sharpen the image.

The Emerging Picture

What secrets has the nautical archaeology of exploratory vessels revealed? Before answering we must reiterate that not one of the early shipwreck sites investigated to date has been identified, or even securely dated. Our observations are a little like the story of the seven blind men and the elephant. What we have learned about the ships themselves is mostly details – the big picture is still indistinct.

The ships were relatively small – on the order of 20 m (66 ft) length overall – and they carried between 25 and 70 tons of stone ballast in addition to stores, cargo and ordnance. Their carvel-planked hulls were built entirely of oak fastened with iron bolts and nails, and oak treenails. Planking seams were caulked with thin lead strips driven in between the strakes. Although hull remnants available for study are extremely limited, two rudder gudgeons from the Molasses Reef wreck faithfully define the shape of its now-vanished stern. Re-excavation of the Highborn Cay wreck's hull, protected beneath its ballast mound, may provide critical information on the design parameters and construction features used in exploratory ships.

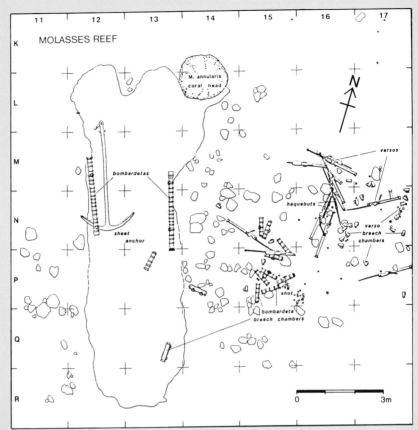

Guns of the Explorers

32, 33   Reconstruction paintings of a sixteenth-century swivel gun or *verso* (*top*) and a cannon or *bombardeta* (*above*) in action.

34   (*above right*) The distribution of artifacts within the Molasses Reef wreck indicates that the ship ran aground and sank more or less intact. The *bombardetas* were found lying directly atop and on either side of the ballast mound, indicating that they had been carried either as cargo or as functional artillery in storage, but were not ready for use. Ten of the swivel guns seem to have been lashed together in pairs; only four were loaded.

35   (*right*) Ordnance from the Molasses Reef, Bahía Mujeres and Highborn Cay wrecks. All three ships carried *bombardetas* of different sizes and calibers, and surprisingly uniformly made *versos*. The Molasses Reef wreck was the most heavily armed vessel. Its *haquebuts* are unique, and suggest an earlier date for this site.

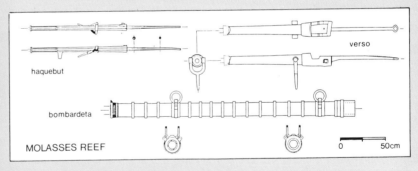

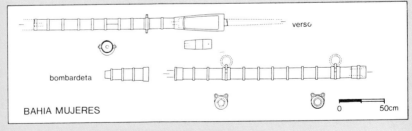

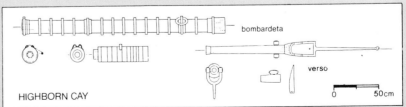

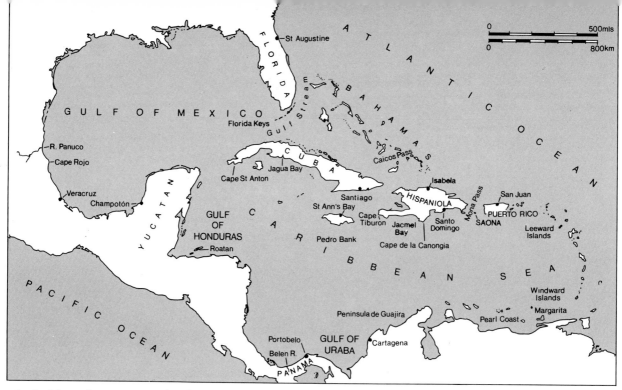

36 Caribbean place-names mentioned in the accompanying table.

Vessels Lost in the New World 1492–1520

Date	Explorer	Ship Type	Ship Name	Location[1]
1492	Columbus	*nao*	*Santa María*	Bay of Caracol, Hispaniola
1494	Columbus	caravel caravel	*Mariagalante* *La Gallega*	Isabela Bay, Hispaniola
1495	Columbus	caravel caravel	*San Juan* *Cardera*	Isabela Bay
1495	Juan de Aguado[2]	4 ships	unknown	Isabela Bay
1498	John Cabot	4 ships	unknown	North America
1499	Alonso de Hojeda	caravel	unknown	Jacmel Bay, Hispaniola
1500	Vicente Yañez Pinzón	2 caravels	unknown	Bahamas
1501	Gaspar Corte Real	caravel	unknown	unknown
1501	Cristobal Guerra	caravel	unknown	Pearl Coast, Venezuela
1502	Miguel Corte Real	caravel	unknown	unknown
1502	Rodrigo de Bastidas and Juan de la Cosa	caravel *nao* pinnace *chinchorro*	*San Antón* *Sta. María de Gracia* unknown unknown	Cape Tiburon, Hispaniola Cape de la Canongia, Hispaniola
1502	Fleet of Bobadilla	*c.*19 ships[3]		Saona I. and Mona Pass
1502	Alonso de Hojeda	caravel	*Santa Ana*	Margarita I.
1503	Alonso de Hojeda	caravel	*Magdalena*	S.E. Caribbean
1503	Columbus	caravel caravel	*Gallega* *Vizcaina*	Belén R., Panama Portobelo, Panama

Date	Explorer	Ship Type	Ship Name	Location[1]
1503	Coelho-Vespucci	ship 3 ships	unknown unknown	Ascención Is? Brazil?
1504	Columbus	caravel caravel	*Santiago de Palos* *Capitana*	St Ann's Bay, Jamaica?
1504	Cristobal Guerra	caravel	unknown	East of Cartagena, Colombia
1504	Luís Guerra	caravel	unknown	Gulf of Urabá, Colombia
1505	Luís Guerra	unknown	unknown	unknown
1505	Juan de la Cosa	4 ships pinnace	unknown unknown	Urabá, Colombia S. coast of Jamaica
1508		more than 20 ships		Santo Domingo, Hispaniola
1509	Bernaldino Talavera	unknown	unknown	Jagua Bay, Cuba
1509		several ships		Santo Domingo, Hispaniola
1510	Francisco Pizarro	pinnace	unknown	Cape St Antón, Cuba
1510	Sebastian de Ocampo	unknown	unknown	Jagua Bay, Cuba
1511	Juan de Valdevia	caravel	unknown	Pedro Bank, S. of Jamaica?
1511	Rodrigo Colmenares	unknown	unknown	W. Cape of Cuba
1511	Diego de Nicuesa	pinnace	unknown	W. Caribbean
1515	Hijacked by Bay I. Indians	ship	unknown	Roatan, Honduras?
1516	Juan Díaz de Solis	ship	unknown	Messiambu, Brazil
1517	Hernandez de Cordoba	*bergantín*	unknown	Champotón, Mexico?
1519	Hernán Cortés	3 caravels 7 smaller vessels	unknown unknown	Veracruz, Mexico
1520	Diego de Camargo	caravel caravel	unknown unknown	Four leagues S. of Veracruz Veracruz
1520	Miguel Díaz de Aux	ship	unknown	Nr Veracruz
1520	Alvarez de Pineda	2 ships	unknown unknown	Panuco R., Mexico
1520	Panfilo de Narvaez	unknown	unknown	S. of Veracruz
1520	Hernán Cortés	3 ships	unknown	Veracruz
1520	Magellan	ship	*Santiago*	Río de Santa Cruz

[1]The places of loss are approximate. Modern names are used whenever possible. There are few reliable 'bench marks' in the study of early Spanish place-name geography in the New World.

[2]Not all the vessels mentioned in this table were engaged in exploratory missions when they were lost. Those such as the four ships of Juan de Aguado, wrecked in Isabela Bay in 1495, were bringing colonists and supplies to the newly founded colony there.

[3]The fact that the Santo Domingo fleet of 1502 numbered almost twenty ships clearly indicates that there was a great deal of ship traffic between Spain and the New World at this early date. There is no way to determine how many ships were scrapped, broken up in harbor or left to disintegrate in early New World ports such as Santo Domingo, Santiago de Cuba, Nueva Cadiz, etc.

In contrast to what many historians have believed, these vessels were heavily armed. The theory that New World discovery vessels had no need of artillery, since the peoples they encountered possessed only a Stone Age technology, is counterbalanced by the observation that, at least in the early years, explorers fully expected to arrive in China or some other advanced Far Eastern country. Further, an explorer's ultimate goal was to find something valuable, and the most hazardous part of any voyage was the return trip. European pirates, freebooters and privateers of every seafaring nationality could be deterred only with superior firepower.

A typical main battery consisted of two *bombardetas,* two *versos dobles,* and up to fourteen *versos.* There are strong indications that the vessels themselves were not designed to accommodate ordnance, and that a great deal of preparation was required to ready the big guns for action. The heavy *bombardetas* on the Highborn Cay and Molasses Reef wrecks were stored below decks probably owing to the fact that captains did not want their weight and encumbrance on deck. Few of the swivel guns from these two wrecksites were loaded and ready for action, although they seem to have been carried on deck. Ten of the Molasses Reef wreck's *versos* appear to have been lashed together in pairs of equivalent gun types.

The ships typically carried a large sheet anchor belowdecks, at least two bowers ready for use, and grapnels or small boat anchors for the ship's boats. No stock was found with the wrought-iron small boat anchor associated with the Molasses Reef wreck, but a hole in the anchor shank just below the ring hole strongly suggests it once possessed a sliding iron stock. Stylistic characteristics of large anchors are present in this anchor as well: long, spindly shank, short arms and triangular palms.

Standing rigging was firmly fixed to the hull by iron eyebolts. Typically, three links of pinch-waisted chain ran from each eyebolt up to keyhole-shaped deadeye straps. Differences in deadeye strap size probably indicate distinctions between masts. When analysis of the Molasses Reef wreck rigging components is completed, it may be possible to extrapolate the number of masts and type of rig from clues provided by this seemingly inconsequential class of artifacts.

Provisions appear to have been stored in wooden casks, rather than in ceramic jars, and ceramics and glass in general were not commonly used. The officers and crew did not possess much in the way of valuables, and the ships did not carry treasure. Virtually everything on board was purely functional. The absence of edged weapons and navigational instruments may reflect selective preference by survivors. With the exception of a single glass bead recovered from the Molasses Reef wreck, no trade goods have come to light.

The Highborn Cay wreck harpoon is anomalous. Nothing like it is known. That at least some exploratory vessels carried harpoons can be inferred from Ferdinand Columbus' account of his father's fourth voyage in which he mentions that the crew of the caravel *Vizcaina* harpooned a giant ray in 1502 off the south coast of Hispaniola.

Our goal is the successful identification of one or more early wrecksites with recorded ships of discovery, or the discovery of a recorded ship. This would provide us with a 'benchmark' around which the geography of fifteenth- and sixteenth-century Iberian explorers could be reconstructed. If, for instance, the Highborn Cay wreck could be identified conclusively as one of two caravels lost by Pinzón in 1499, then we would know that what Pinzón called the 'Shoals of Baburca' are, in fact, the Northern Exuma Islands.

Many early shipwreck sites have land components which should be located and investigated in conjunction with the underwater work. Archaeologists of Parks Canada have demonstrated the value of this approach at Red Bay, Labrador, as described in Chapter Four. Similar situations exist in the Caribbean. *Santa María* was at least partially disassembled for materials with which to build a stockade for her marooned crew. Columbus abandoned at the mouth of the Río Belén in Panama a caravel which was to be used as a store ship for the garrison of Santa María de Belén. Accounts of the early explorers often mention shipwreck survivors moving their base of operations to land to repair their ship, to await rescue or to regroup before setting out again in small boats.

Archaeology is a newcomer to the Caribbean, which has been for decades a stronghold of the professional treasure-hunter. Faced with a rapidly dwindling supply of known gold- and silver-carrying wrecks, professional and amateur salvors have begun to eye historically unique shipwreck sites as potentially exploitable resources. A Florida treasure-hunting company distributed an investment prospectus predicting a $100 million profit to be made from books, movies, video games, museum displays, replicas and sundry memorabilia manufactured to commemorate their salvage of Columbus' *Pinta* – a project which never actually took place. Another treasure-hunting company contracted with the government of the Dominican Republic to search for shipwrecks from the fleet of Governor Bobadilla, lost in the vicinity of Saona and Mona Pass during the hurricane of 1502. The company found wrought-iron, breech-loading ordnance, but no shipwrecks or treasure. A potentially early shipwreck site on Little Inagua containing only wrought-iron ordnance – a sure sign of an early date – was picked clean by treasure-hunters. Later, the purloined artifacts surfaced in a Miami curio shop. They had never received conservation treatment and their deteriorated shapes were scarcely recognizable.

It is a sad fact that of the three oldest shipwrecks discovered in the Caribbean, only one, the Molasses Reef wreck, has been scientifically excavated, but even this example was being actively ravaged by treasure hunters when archaeologists arrived to save it.

CHAPTER FOUR

Basque Whalers in the New World: The Red Bay Wrecks

Robert Grenier

Whales were hunted for their meat by Europeans in the Middle Ages up to the fifteenth century, but it was the oil of the whale that eventually commanded the prices for which whalers risked their lives in icy waters far from home. Whale oil gave a better light and was slower burning than vegetable oils, putting it in increasing demand as fuel for lighting churches, public buildings and eventually streets. Whale oil was also used in the manufacture of more than two dozen different products, including soap, protective coatings for ships, fabric treatments and various pharmaceutical mixes. So rare yet so useful was it that the oil from an average whale was, in the sixteenth century, worth approximately a quarter of a million U.S. dollars in today's money.

For decades the largest supplies of whale oil for all of Europe came from a stretch of coastline barely over 100 miles long on the northeast corner of Spain and the southwest shore of France. This was the home of the Basques, probably the oldest ethnic group in Europe. Originally shepherds and mountain dwellers, the Basques had by the sixteenth century gained fame for the high productivity and quality of two complementary industries: iron-working and shipbuilding. Excellent fishermen and seafarers, they had over the previous centuries developed sophisticated techniques for chasing and killing whales on the open sea in small boats, and for towing them ashore where the fat was rendered into oil in large boiling caldrons. They were in this sense the inventors of modern whaling, from whom the seventeenth-century whalers of England, Holland and Denmark were to learn their techniques. Although whaling ranked behind wool exportation as the Basques' main source of income, it played a major role in their culture, as reflected in art, folklore and heraldic emblems.

When prey closer to home began to vanish, the Basques extended their hunt to the neighboring coast of Asturias and Galicias. Later, with the discovery of the Americas, the Basques – already noted for building some of the best ships of Spain – were well equipped to organize complex whaling expeditions to the newly discovered fishing grounds around Terranova – the New Land. At home

they had rich oak forests for building solid hulls, and an iron industry famous for fasteners, anchors and armaments. A large insurance industry centered in Burgos provided protection for investors, and sometimes capital for shipbuilding and for outfitting expensive overseas undertakings.

No one knows just when Basque sailors first reached Labrador. By the mid-sixteenth century the whalers had established over a dozen ports there, mostly on the shores of the Strait of Belle Isle. Seeing the large number of right whales that swam slowly along the north shore of the Strait between July and October, the first Basque fishermen must have felt at home, as if on the shores of the Bay of Biscay. They had been hunting these whales along their country's shores since at least the twelfth century, so much so that the right whale was nicknamed the Basque whale.

Archival research in Spain combined with both terrestrial and underwater archaeology at Red Bay, Labrador, on the north shore of the Strait of Belle Isle, is beginning to provide a detailed picture of sixteenth-century Basque whaling. In 1977, prompted by archivist Selma Huxley Barkham's discovery that Red Bay had been an important Basque whaling center, James A. Tuck of Memorial University in Newfoundland began an excavation on the island closing Red Bay harbor, where he unearthed tryworks for rendering blubber into whale oil. The following year, informed by Barkham that a whaler called *San Juan* had sunk in the harbor of Red Bay in 1565, I extended Tuck's work beneath the waters of the bay by leading a Parks Canada archaeology team that has now discovered three galleons and excavated one of them – probably the *San Juan* – and explored small boats and other sunken remains of the once-thriving Basque whaling industry.

Vessels and Wrecks

Basque ships. It seems that as early as the 1540s 'galleon' was the preferred term used by Basque shipowners when ordering a ship, although the term *nao* was still employed as a generic one, just as the word 'ship' is today. Used as a whaler, the galleon of the time was just another large cargo vessel, and not an ornate man-of-war as is generally believed. Once in the New World, the whaler was to be moored in harbor to serve as a floating warehouse before the fall homeward voyage. Contracts reveal that these ships were sometimes built in the Basque country just before a whaling expedition to Terranova, with wood cut by Christmas for ships that had to be ready in late spring or early summer. The cost was from 1,500 to 3,000 ducats depending on size, which ranged from 200 to 650 tons. Such ships were capable of bringing back from 600 to 2,000 barrels of whale oil.

Plans of Basque whaling ships were not made, but contemporary building contracts preserve valuable information. Contracts usually specified keel length versus beam versus depth in the hold up to the main deck, the keel most often being slightly shorter than double the beam. As on modern container ships, the size and shape of the common container of the period, the *barrica* or barrel, dictated the spacing between decks: the space of around 3 cubits (1.7 m or $5\frac{1}{2}$ ft) was designed to accommodate three rows of barrels or two rows of *pipas* or double barrels. The contracts are often more specific about unusual spacings between decks, the number of knees in certain areas, the size and shape of the castles, and the location and number of capstans. The number and size of anchors, usually four, seem to have been standardized in relation to tonnage. On average, the life expectancy of ships was about thirteen years.

The 'San Juan'. The remains of what we subsequently came to believe to be those of the *San Juan* were spotted on Labor Day 1978 by Bruce Bennett, our best wreck finder, while he was being towed behind a small boat. Soon after I dived on the wreck myself and came upon loose timbers partly covered with silt. I could tell, from the extent of the solid wreckage, and especially from the size of the frames, that the wreck was substantial. But was it the remnants of a sixteenth-century Basque whaling ship? A later dive revealed part of a cargo of wooden whale oil casks. Further investigations led us to conclude that we had indeed found a Basque ship, probably the vessel described by archivist Barkham as having sunk in Red Bay in 1565 with 900 to 1,000 barrels of whale oil.

Barkham's documentation indicated that two highly paid harpooners of the time, the Echaniz brothers, had complained to a notary about not having received their proper share of the salvage of the *San Juan*'s cargo lost just before its departure for Spain, when it was moored with a full load of whale oil. The archival information was limited, but precise enough for us to deduce that the ship had probably sunk in late fall, in 6 to 12 m (20 to 40 ft) of water, on the north shore of Saddle Island.

Our wreck, covered with oily cask remains, lay 30 m (100 ft) from the north shore of Saddle Island, its stern near the shore in 6 m of water, its bow pointing north at the bottom of a slope in 12 m of water.

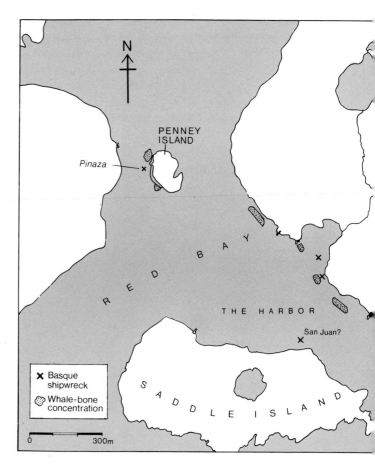

This discovery, combined with the finding of rendering ovens for turning blubber into oil on the adjacent shore by Dr Tuck that summer, led to the largest combined land-underwater excavation ever undertaken in Canada. The National Historic Sites and Monuments Board declared the site of national historic importance, and Parks Canada agreed with the Province of Newfoundland and Labrador to properly investigate the underwater site and to reconstruct the whaling and seafaring activities of the sixteenth-century Basques in Labrador.

A feasibility study season in 1979 confirmed the probable age, identity and wealth of the underwater site, and from 1980 to 1984 Parks Canada undertook an excavation and survey program that employed up to 15 marine archaeologists, assisted by a team of 15 to 25 support staff, including conservators, draftspersons, photographers, mechanics and others. In 1983, a second galleon was found nearby and a third one was located in 1984. During these years, what we believe is the *San Juan* was excavated, mapped, dismantled, raised in pieces to the surface for precise recording, and then reburied on the site. Of special interest in our techniques is a method devised as an experiment by Parks Canada conservators Lorne Murdock and Tom Daly to mold large sections of wreckage under water with latex, supported by a rigid backing, reproducing accurately both the overall shapes

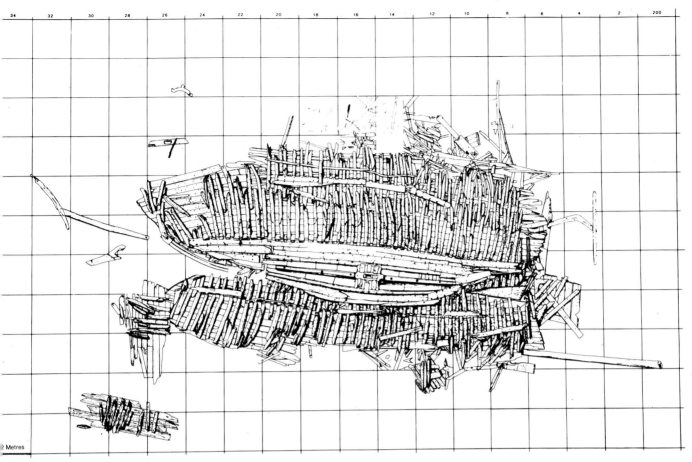

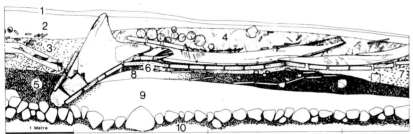

Is this the 'San Juan'?

Plans and profiles provide vital evidence of the Basque whaler's last moments as she sank in Red Bay, Labrador, in 1565.

1 (*facing page*) Red Bay harbor, with shipwrecks, and whale-bone concentrations indicating onshore Basque whaling activity.

2 (*above*) The 'as found' structural plan of what may be the *San Juan*. The wreck lies relatively flat on the harbor bottom, both sides having collapsed away from the ship's centerline.

3 (*center left*) Profile through the stern quarter of the galleon, looking towards the bow. It is evident from the build-up of sand (layer 9) that the ship was moving in a left-to-right direction before grounding on the rock substrata (layer 10). Note the small boat (keel and planking) below the starboard hull.

4 (*left*) A full-size section of the *San Juan* cast from a rubber mold.

and dimensions of a submerged hull, while retaining the fine details of toolmarks and even wood grain. This casting procedure allows the study of the hull in the laboratory with its curvatures, fastening details, construction and wear marks. It eliminates the need for costly preservation and conservation of the original timbers.

The excavation was conducted from a 20 by 8 m (66 by 26 ft) steel barge with 2.5 m (8 ft) hold, in which lay a 100 kWh power plant; a 650 cu/ft/min compressor able to activate up to twelve airlifts at a time for removing silt; a powerful automatic filling station for scuba tanks; a workshop and a large changing room for up to sixteen diving archaeologists. The hold also had watertight compartments for general storage. On deck were a recompression chamber, three large baths for the temporary storage of timbers and artifacts, and an invaluable 13-ton hydraulic crane with 20-m boom, for lifting heavy structural timbers in and out of the water.

Over the years, there were days and sometimes weeks in Red Bay when winds would blow continuously from the northern hills down into the harbor. Waves would break over the stern of the barge, and the docking platform would become useless. Divers would have trouble getting in or out of the water, and had to grab the railing of the diving platform to avoid being carried away by the breaking waves. But even when the winds gusted at over 60 mph, diving never stopped. Thanks to the support barge and the courage and tenacity of the crew, not a single hour of diving was lost in Red Bay because of bad weather during the course of eight years.

The one area where marine archaeology in Labrador faced a considerable challenge was in the temperature of the water. In many ways conditions at the site were ideal for diving – good visibility, light currents and a shallow depth of around 10 m (33 ft). But with the water temperature staying near 0 degrees C even in July and August, it proved impossible for us to perform competently as archaeologists for more than an hour or two at a time, even with the best dry suits available and with a new type of thermal underwear using space-age insulation material.

The second in command and chief of technical operations, Peter Waddell, found the solution in 1979 by adapting the hot-water systems used for deep-water diving off oil rigs. Salt water was heated by oil-fired units on the barge and reached the divers through hoses connected to their suits. The divers remained comfortable for three to four hours while performing more or less stationary tasks like drawing and writing notes. With this system and a slight increase in the size of the diving crew and in the length of the field season, our work rate increased from 1,300 hours spent underwater on the site in 1979 to over 3,500 hours in 1984.

Description of the ship. After eight years of fieldwork, although research is far from complete, we can state that our vessel was a three-masted ship of close to 250 tons cargo capacity, with a length of 22 m (72 ft) at the weather-deck level. It seems to have had three full decks, including the false deck, or the deck located in the hold below the waterline. We estimate that the vessel drew 3 to 3.5 m (c. 10 to 11½ ft) of water.

The ship's breadth – 7.5 m (24 ft 6 in) – is slightly greater than half the length of the keel, which measures 14.75 m (48 ft) from the stern post to the forward scarf. But this ratio on a sixteenth-century vessel can be misleading. To begin with, the keel is shorter than the keel of an equivalent vessel from a later century, that is a vessel of similar length at waterline level; the extreme rake of a sixteenth-century ship, at the bow especially, accounts for the difference. Also, the preliminary lines taken from our research model show a vessel with surprisingly fine lines, especially at the bow, far removed from the round, tubby shape commonly thought of as typical of sixteenth-century merchant vessels. The ship excavated in Red Bay, although not built on the fine lines of a tea clipper, would have been a good sailing ship.

Could these lines be indicative of a type of ship? Could they help clarify the still unclear differences between galleons and *naos*? While most people refer to sixteenth-century merchant vessels as *naos*, and faster war vessels as galleons, we know from our documentation that the majority of Basque shipowners in the early part of the century asked shipwrights to build galleons; very few asked for *naos*. Were they in fact commissioning a new type of vessel with finer hull lines and better sailing capabilities? More archaeological finds and research are needed to answer this question.

We believe that the Red Bay vessel had a sterncastle extending forward to the main mast. We do not yet have evidence of a second level on the castle, although it can be assumed that there was one. Ours would have been quite an elegant vessel, with the sheer lines or deck lines at the stern rising rather sharply, as on most representations of sixteenth-century ships.

The ship had the flat transom, called square tuck, typical of ships of the period, with the transom planking fixed in a chevron pattern up to the top of the rudder. The rudder was made from a single piece of oak, an unusual feature for such a large vessel. The transom was pierced with a single gun or loading port.

Above the rudder was a counter with a large opening for the tiller and two small square hawse-holes, carved through a very heavy transverse beam.

So far, we know very little of the bow and of the forecastle, except that we have a large oak reinforcing piece, pierced with the hawse-hole of the port side. Some evidence would point to the presence of a beakhead, but it has not yet been put together.

The two castles seem to have been built of soft wood planks, and pierced with small semi-circular gun ports.

The rest of the ship's structure, planks and beams were made of white oak, except for the beech keel. The keel has a unique design for a ship of this size. Instead of the usual

LA TERRE DV LABOVREVR.

Whaling Stations

Contemporary maps and paintings shed light on whaling activities in Red Bay.

5 (*above*) A detail of Labrador from a map of the world, 1546, by Pierre Desceliers (south to the top), shows whaling in progress and a galleon probably similar to that excavated at Red Bay. Red Bay is located near the 'L' of 'Le butes', seen above the head of a bow-carrying native.

6 (*right*) This 1634 painting of a whaling station on Jan Mayen Island or Spitsbergen reflects broadly what the scene would have been like in Red Bay almost a century before. Whaling ships are moored in the harbor while onshore a beached whale is butchered and different parts carried off to be cut up and boiled in vats. Barrels filled with whale oil wait to be loaded aboard ship.

'San Juan' Timbers

7 (*left*) The keel of the probable *San Juan*. Looking down, one can see how the raised sides (garboard strakes) at either end are carved from the same beech trunk as the keel, a technique found here for the first time on a large oceangoing ship. It required the shipwright to have a perfect idea at the outset of the final shape and size of his vessel.

8, 9 (*right*) A surprising discovery was this detailed depiction of a ship at anchor. It had been incised on a softwood plank, complete with masts, rigging and anchor lines.

10 (*below*) Robert Grenier (left) and his second-in-command, Peter Waddell, examine the ship's stern-post knee (foreground), a critical element linking keel, heel knee and stern post.

square or rectangular cross-section with rabbets for the garboards, it has a T-shape in the middle and a somewhat open U-shape at the bow and stern. In reality, the Basque shipwright seems to have followed an ancient tradition of carving the keel and the two garboard strakes from a single tree, eliminating the joints and their leakage problems. This unusual keel looks like a dug-out canoe, viewed from bow or from the stern, with the two sides of the 'canoe' flattening out in the middle. It makes for an impressive piece of carving and engineering. One can realize that in the process of making this keel, the shipwright was carving out the exact shape of the entire ship from the very first timber installed and shaped. The use of beech – easier to carve than oak – may be explained by this complex shape. The keels of the other two galleons found in Red Bay, on the other hand, seem to have the traditional square shape and to have been made of oak.

The keel did not extend to the stern post, but was scarfed to a large knee-shaped piece which continued the keel up to the rudder, where it extended upward to become the bottom end of the stern post. So the stern post, instead of being inserted with a tenon into a mortise on the upper face of the keel, was scarfed to this knee-keel piece. This assemblage seems to be a trademark of vessels of the Middle Ages. The famous Bremen cog in Germany, built in 1380, had a similar assemblage, as did several cogs found in Holland. The author has observed a similar construction on a small harbor vessel built in Lisbon in

the early 1960s, indicating a technology in use for at least six centuries.

On our ship, the frames are made on each side of three rows of free-standing timbers or futtocks, not directly linked to one another. The framing of the vessel is held in place by the exterior planking and wales, and by the assemblages of beam shelves and waterways inside the vessel. Exceptionally, only fourteen framing assemblages are joined together laterally in this ship: these are made of fourteen central floor timbers joined laterally with dovetail scarfing, treenails and spikes to the adjoining first futtocks. This type of construction announces a more efficient and modern technique of building ships. It implies that these frames had already been drawn, shaped and assembled before being placed on the keel in sequence, starting with the mid-ship frame and moving fore and aft from it. The two other galleons found in Red Bay show a similar construction of free-floating futtocks above, fore and aft of the central series of pre-shaped, pre-assembled frames of floor timbers with adjoining first futtocks. This construction technique is rather well illustrated in the *Album de Colbert*, preserved by the Service Hydrographique de la Marine, Paris.

The keelson was made of a single piece of oak, with notches cut on its lower face to lock over the floor timbers. These notches clearly indicate that all the floor timbers for some unknown reason were placed slightly diagonally to the keel, and not at right angles to it. The

Assembly Techniques

11, 12 *(left)* Two engravings from the seventeenth-century *Album de Colbert* illustrate vessels in course of construction, with pre-designed central frames in place. The Red Bay ships were built using a similar method.

13 *(below)* A reconstruction of the middle frames from the Red Bay galleon. The floor timbers and first futtocks were joined with dovetail scarfs, treenails and spikes. Note the groove cut in the bottom of each floor timber to allow water to flow to the sumps for pumping. The timbers were hewn from naturally curved pieces of oak.

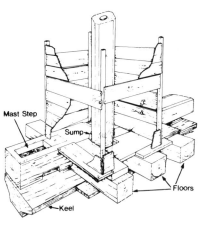

14 (*far left*) In addition to the initial wreck discovery, two other sixteenth-century Basque galleons were found in Red Bay. Shown here are the partially excavated remains of the mast step from one of those two ships. Also evident are the main mast mortise and one of two sump holes, from which the ship's double pump system would have operated. This is in contrast to the first wreck, which had only one pump.

15 (*left*) The restored pump and pump well from the *San Juan*.

central section of the keelson was enlarged, cut off the same timber, to house the large mortise needed to receive the heel of the main mast. A semi-circular cut was made on the port aft side of the mast step to receive the heel of the single bilge pump. The foot valve of this pump was detachable, under the foot of the long beech tube of the pump, like those illustrated in the sixteenth century in Agricola's *De Re Metallica*.

The more-or-less straight beams of the orlop deck were hooked into the beam shelves with a dovetailed joint, as in later centuries, giving the walls of the ship support against not only inward pressure, but also outward stress, especially in cases of grounding. They were braced in the hold with standard knees placed above the beams.

Strakes were usually fixed to each frame with at least one treenail and two large iron nails. The heads of these fasteners were sunk into triangular recesses filled with pitch to protect them against wood borers or corrosion.

The spacing between decks seemed to correspond with the contract specifications of more or less 1.7 m (5 ft 6 in) between decks. These decks also seem to follow faithfully the sheer lines of the hull, however steep they are, with no obvious corrective action to make the stern end of decks closer to the horizontal.

A five-whelp capstan, with a one-piece drum and spindle, was located, to judge from the evidence, on the upper deck behind the main mast. The main partner of the capstan was found with the lower socket, which housed the pivoting end of the spindle.

The main mast, of which we believe we have a cut-off section, shown at the port stern of the site plan, was held in place with seven shrouds on each side. The foremast had three shrouds on each side. There is no evidence of shrouds for the mizzen mast. The shrouds, of which we found long sections still linked with rat lines on the port side, were tightened with triangular-shaped heart blocks, in lieu of dead eyes. The channels for the main mast were, as on the *Mary Rose*, very long, heavy oak planks, extending from the main mast up to almost the aft end of

the ship, thus greatly reinforcing the structure of the half-deck.

The hold of the ship was full of oak barrels or *barricas*, 225-liter wooden containers with wooden hoops. These had been set directly on the ceiling planking with ballast stones neatly placed between them.

This review of a sixteenth-century whaling ship, although fragmentary and superficial, nevertheless provides us with a unique glimpse of how these humble workhorses of the Renaissance were designed and built. With this whaling ship and the two others found in Red Bay, we now have a much better knowledge of the early transatlantic merchantmen which helped an expanding Europe find new territories and exploit their wealth. We also get a much better perception of the ship design and building techniques of the famous but rather obscure Basque shipwrights.

Small craft. The archaeology of Red Bay harbor has provided three different types of small craft, representing quite likely the three basic boats used for servicing moored ships and the shore station, for bringing supplies to and from other stations, and, especially, to chase, kill and tow whales to onshore rendering facilities or, later, to a whaling ship.

Each whaling ship had at least one service boat, often called a *batel* by the Basques, that varied in size according to the vessel it serviced. Many sixteenth-century shipbuilding contracts specified that the *batel* had to be built or provided with the large ship. Several contracts even specified that the *batel* had to fit between the forecastle and the stern castle, often called the half deck, on the port side of the vessel, and that the main hatch on the upper deck had to be on the same side.

The 3-m section from the center of a small boat we tentatively call a *batel* was found astern and mixed with the wreckage of a ship. Its hull was carvel built on the bottom and lapstraked on the sides. Extremely crude woodworking necessitated extensive caulking between the roughly

On Site in Red Bay

Working from a support barge in icy and often dangerous conditions, Robert Grenier and his team have spent eight field seasons excavating Canada's oldest known shipwrecks.

16 (*above*) An archaeologist studies the remains of a sixteenth-century binnacle discovered on the *San Juan* wrecksite. This box-like cupboard, used for housing navigational instruments, was found embedded in a layer of barnacle shells. The wooden frame of a sandglass was lying next to the binnacle, with the ship's compass a short distance away. See also ills. 21–23.

17 (*above right*) Persistent spring ice and the occasional iceberg are some of the hazards marine archaeologists face in Red Bay harbor. Saddle Island, at the harbor entrance, was the site of numerous Basque try-works, primarily because of its proximity to the Strait of Belle Isle. The Strait, then a migration route for the right and bowhead whales, is seen in the background blocked by Arctic ice.

18 (*right*) The temperature in Labrador waters is often below 0 degrees C. While this makes for excellent visibility, it severely restricts dive times. Here divers in hot-water suits descend onto the hull of a Red Bay galleon. Using airlifts and aluminum grids they carefully uncover and record every timber and artifact.

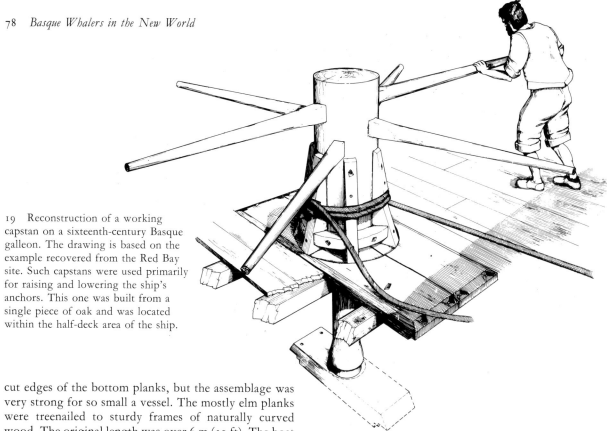

19   Reconstruction of a working capstan on a sixteenth-century Basque galleon. The drawing is based on the example recovered from the Red Bay site. Such capstans were used primarily for raising and lowering the ship's anchors. This one was built from a single piece of oak and was located within the half-deck area of the ship.

cut edges of the bottom planks, but the assemblage was very strong for so small a vessel. The mostly elm planks were treenailed to sturdy frames of naturally curved wood. The original length was over 6 m (20 ft). The boat seems to have been designed to take the abuse expected for the service boat of a galleon moored in a harbor like Red Bay or in a river estuary or close to a seashore.

In 1984 I investigated the remains of another small craft, located a few years earlier in less than 2 m (6 ft) of water behind a small island (Penney Island), not far from what is believed to be a Basque wharf and a whaling oven. The remains of the bottom of a medium-size boat turned upside down were spread over 11 m (36 ft). The keel, garboard strakes and a few bottom planks had been taken away, probably by the ice, but the floor timbers, much larger than on the *batel*, were still in place with the futtocks on each side. The hull was carvel built on the bottom and lapstraked on the sides near the gunnels. The remains of a simple step for the foremast was fixed to the base of the stem. More or less in the center was evidence of a second mast step assembly, although the step itself was not found.

This vessel probably had two square sails, and was used to assist and supply lighter whaleboats in the killing of whales, to carry supplies and people between the whaling stations along the coast, or as a lighter or large service boat in the harbor. Some of its features and its heavy mast support system remind me of an antique fishing vessel in the Maritime Museum of Bermeo, a famous seafaring town in the Basque country. The Red Bay boat was possibly a *pinaza*, a two-masted vessel used for fishing offshore, but not in the open sea, during the sixteenth century. It had grown into a vessel capable of holding twelve or more men from the earlier *pinaza*, a common term used for small fishing boats throughout the Middle

Ages. The word *pinaza*, however, was for a long time to become used interchangeably with the term *chalupa* and sometimes *batel*.

The prize of our small boat flotilla is what we call a *chalupa*, the whaleboat itself, the one used for the chase and the killing. The small boat was possibly attached to the starboard side of the ship when it went down. In any case, it was trapped and slowly flattened as the large ship collapsed over the years. Preliminary analysis has revealed a boat 8 m (26 ft) long, 1.8 m (6 ft) wide, 1.2 m (4 ft) high at the bow, and a few centimeters lower at the stern. It shows evidence of six benches or thwarts, and of a central mast step under a bench used as mast support. Two lateral longitudinal supports run aft to the next bench to complete the bracing of the mast.

This boat was finely made of hardwood. The keel curves upward slightly at both ends and has short rabbets for the garboard strakes only at the ends. The last two upper strakes are lapstraked, while the bottom ones are fitted edge to edge. The whole assemblage was nailed together, without the use of treenails. The gunnels were very light, L-shaped, and had holes for single thole pins. Heavy wear on one gunnel indicates that there was no thole board to protect the gunnel and that the oar pulled on the strope, or small rope which linked the oar and wooden thole pin.

With its fine lines at the bow and stern, this double-ended boat was obviously designed for lightness and speed. Although sturdy and seaworthy, it would not have

Basque Navigation

20 (*left*) Robert Grenier examines the remains of an astrolabe recovered from one of the Red Bay galleons.

21 (*below, far left*) Hypothetical reconstruction of a sandglass from the Red Bay galleon. The two wooden disc ends and five spindles are represented as found. The glass globes and rope suspension system have been added based on illustrations of similar sandglasses. This was probably a watch glass.

22 (*center left*) A reconstruction of the binnacle used for storing navigational instruments, one of the earliest known. The compass could be continuously observed through the viewing port, as shown. Interesting features include a lubber's point or notch located on the viewing port, a burn mark inside from a candle, and an incised checkerboard pattern on the top.

23 (*below*) The complete Red Bay compass, a reconstruction extrapolated from archaeologically recovered components. The design of the card, which was not found, is based on typical mid-sixteenth-century compass card illustrations.

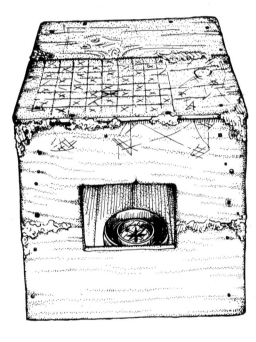

been able to sustain the tremendous stress created by the later technique of letting the boat down from the side of a rocking ship; it had no ceiling or inner planking and no wale on the side to sustain the shocks associated with such raising or lowering.

Lack of any signs of reinforcement at the bow or of a bit near the sternpost suggest that the whaleboat in Red Bay was not designed to be towed by the whale as were nineteenth-century whaleboats in both the Basque country and New England. This negative evidence combined with documentation concerning the shorter lengths of sixteenth-century Basque harpoon lines give weight to the hypothesis that the Basques in Terranova simply used a float at the end of the harpoon line so that they could follow the whale as it tired and bled to death.

All three boat types show that what have often been perceived as lapstraked boats on older paintings and sketches may have been carvel-built boats with lapstraked side planking.

The Organization of Voyages

Outfitting. The outfitting of a whaling ship often exceeded the value of the hull; for the large *San Nicolas,* outfitting cost over 2,000 ducats in 1566. The contract specified even the material for proper recaulking of the vessel in Terranova before its return voyage. The outfitter, often the captain, had to provide food and drink as well as all of the whaling equipment and supplies. Food included

bread, meat, beans, biscuits, cod, sardines, olive oil, cider and wine. Food portions might include close to 1½ lbs of biscuits a day, and possibly ½ lb or more of meat or cod; the allotment for cider or wine could reach the equivalent of three bottles a day per man.

The ship had to be armed, usually with six to eight medium-size guns and a dozen or more anti-personnel weapons called *versos*. All of the ship's preparation was the responsibility of the owner. The staff included the captain or master, the pilot, the guardian and sometimes one or a few more ship-hands such as carpenters, a gunner and a caulker.

Insurance. The high value of whale oil and the share system, described below, ensured participants of excellent benefits on successful voyages, while insurance contracts offered investors and shipowners some safeguards.

In England insurance contracts became available only in the early 1600s, but Basque whalers and seafarers had been able to insure their ships and their cargoes at home before the beginning of the Terranova voyages. The Consulado de Burgos had registered insurance policies long before the sixteenth century, and people came for insurance services to Burgos, just outside the Basque country, from all over Spain and even from France, Italy and, later, England.

Spanish insurers in Burgos covered all sorts of businesses and cargoes, including fish, wool, spices, iron and even slaves. Coverage could be obtained for the outgoing trip, the long stay overseas, or the return trip, or for the three combined; one could insure the hull of the ship, the rigging, the whaling or fishing gear, and the cargo. Contracts show that a famous Burgos insurance broker, Juan Lopez de Soto, asked a premium of 3 to 4 percent for the trip along the Spanish coast, and up to 15 percent for voyages to Terranova. Several contracts were usually signed for one expedition.

Parks Canada historian Jean-Pierre Proulx has studied a total of 407 contracts for 197 trips to Terranova between 1565 and 1573. Of these expeditions, 72 were whaling enterprises, 8 were for cod fishing and whaling, and the remaining 105 were for cod fishing and other voyages. From 1566 on, premiums almost doubled, and stayed around 14 percent for whaling trips to Terranova, which were usually insured for the round trip and for the stay overseas. Cod-fishing trips were usually insured for the return trip only at around 6 to 7 percent.

Insurers, as today, were prepared for questionable claims. In 1566, two large ships had to leave their whaling harbors in Labrador hastily, and Juan Lopez de Soto refused to cover certain items in the claims. In the first claim, outfitter Miguel de Cerain had taken one insurance

Model of the 'San Juan'

24 (*left*) A 1:10 scale model of the sixteenth-century Basque galleon found in Red Bay is being meticulously constructed, piece by piece, on the evidence of archaeological drawings and other on-site records. Through the process of modeling, the marine archaeologist is able to see the ship through the eyes of the shipbuilder.

The Small Whaleboat

25, 26 (*right*) Plan as found, and view towards bow of reconstructed model, of a double-ended whaleboat. Built of hardwood, mostly oak, she had one set of futtocks or frames on each side, a central mast step and seats for six rowers plus a steersman. This boat is believed to be the oldest and most complete example of an early whaleboat used to hunt whales.

policy from de Soto for 1,000 ducats to cover the outfitting, including food, for the whole return trip, including the stay in Terranova, and for the cargo of whale oil to be carried on the 450-ton galleon *Nuestra Señora de la Guadelupe* with a capacity for 1,500 barrels.

De Cerain stated that because of a sudden freeze his party had had to leave Puerto Nuevo near Chateau Bay suddenly. He claimed for the value of four dead whales they had had to leave in the harbor, of 400 empty *barricas* (barrels), 10 *chalupas* (whaleboats), 16,000 roofing tiles, 70 barrels of whale oil thrown overboard during a storm to save the ship, and of various costs to repair the ship. He even claimed for a pilgrimage of thanksgiving! The total claim amounted to 2,775 ducats, almost three times the amount insured by de Cerain through de Soto.

The insurer refused to pay for the abandoned whales, claiming that they were not on the ship, hence not insured. The claim indicates that three whales were tied to the ship while the fourth was cut apart and ready to be processed ashore. This revelation that a whale was being chopped along the shore supports the archaeological evidence found in Red Bay, where parts of whales were found butchered along the shore, near the ovens. The document gives the price of whale oil at 6 ducats a barrel; it also states that, as usual, the four whales would have given 200 barrels, or 50 barrels per whale.

In the second claim, de Soto had insured Martin Lopez de Ysasi, half-owner of the *Nuestra Señora de la Concecion*. The contract covered the hull for 2,000 ducats at 15 percent, and the cargo/outfitting for 1,600 ducats at 14 percent (the actual value of the outfitting alone was 2,441 ducats).

De Ysasi's ship was also caught by early freezing in November 1566 in the harbor of Chateau, forcing the crew to abandon a large quantity of equipment and goods on the shore and, as had de Cerain, several dead whales tied to the ship. De Ysasi claimed for the loss of cables, an anchor, two *chalupas*, empty barrels, ten full barrels of whale oil at 6½ ducats each, five smaller barrels at 4 ducats each, and various other items. Besides interesting details about ship's mooring, with the bow tied to the shore and three anchors, and about the claim of the *chalupas* at nearly double the price claimed by de Cerain, the document also indicates the sharing system and the latitude of the return trip (at the 50 degree latitude).

Whaling

The crossing. Although several contracts stipulated that the ships had to be ready in April, statistics compiled by historian Proulx from the insurance contracts indicate that the average departure date from Spain was around the middle of June, while the return from Terranova was around the middle of October (for cod-fishing, departures took place around the middle of April). Construction delays were often costly. In one case the death of a master builder delayed the completion of a hull to the point that the ship could not leave before the latest accepted departure date, 24 June. Such a ship would miss part of the early season and have to stay for the so-called second season, up to early January, a costly and more risky business.

Some sailed in small convoys of three to four ships with one pilot. And some of these, it is believed, took the southern or Basque route, crossing west near the Azores and then following the Gulf Stream northward to Newfoundland and the Strait of Belle Isle. Others could have taken the more difficult Breton's route by leaving from les Sables d'Olonne at Parallel 46°30, counting on favorable winds.

Crossing westward could take up to two months in conditions that were hard, but somewhat healthier and easier than those faced on the road to the West Indies. The northern climate offered fresh supplies of rainwater and cod fish besides keeping existing supplies cooler.

Captains did not seem to have clear instructions about their destinations; they aimed for the Grand Bay or the Strait of Belle Isle and chose whatever harbor they found fit and free. Documents indicate that they made agreements with other ships in the same harbor to join forces in the hunt and to share in the catches. We know that in 1575 three ships in the small harbor of Breton, now Carrol's Cove near Red Bay, shared their catches equally. The same year in Red Bay, nine ships were sharing catches according to tonnage and crew sizes.

The ships, anchored safely near a shore station, served as living quarters and warehouses for the products to come. Ovens, like those excavated by Dr Tuck on Saddle Island, were built ashore by the construction of a large stone wall behind a series of circular hearths. A roof of red tiles resting on an open wooden structure sheltered the caldrons and the operating crew.

The prey. The right whale (*Balaena glacialis*), as its name indicates, was the right whale to hunt because it was easy to kill and it gave a high commercial output in oil. Averaging 15 m (50 ft) in length and 50 to 60 tons in weight, the right whale was very fat and gave a high ratio of nearly 40 percent of its weight in blubber. Since it migrated along the shores at a speed of only 1 to 2 knots, it was an easy prey for the early whalers. The short distances involved made it relatively simple for the whalers to spot their prey in time to race out and spear them. When killed, the right whale usually floated to the surface and was thus easy to retrieve and tow back to the shore station. This species of whale also often traveled in packs. No wonder that this gentle, slow and fat giant was called '*la bonne baleine*' by the French.

But the Basques who stayed late, past October, after the departure of the right whales for the south, could also

witness in the Strait of Belle Isle the coming of similar-looking, but slightly larger, longer and fatter whales. Zooarchaeologist Steve Cumbaa has been able to identify a large quantity of bones from bowhead whales (*Balaena mysticetus*), to the surprise of many whale specialists, historians and archaeologists who had assumed that mostly right whales were the prey. The sampling available so far indicates that the Basques killed as many bowheads as right whales. This Arctic whale is known to stay near the ice floes and is not expected today to be found as far south as the Strait of Belle Isle. This late-season visitor must have been a bonus to the whalers who had not managed to complete their catch by late September or October, and may help explain references in documents to a second or late whaling season, and certainly can explain why whaling ships could still be anchored in small harbors near Red Bay as late as Christmas Eve, up until the harbors froze.

The hardship associated with stronger and more frequent winds, bitter cold and very short days must have been alleviated slightly by the bowheads, which, because of their larger size and higher blubber content, provided five to ten more barrels of oil apiece than right whales.

The thought of these extra barrels, worth the annual salaries of two skilled laborers of the period, must have helped the rowers and the harpooners face the bitter cold of the winds and the freezing water while chasing and towing these monsters in November and December, the towing sometimes lasting well into the middle of the night.

It must have been heartbreaking for Miguel de Cerain and his rowers and harpooners when they had to abandon four such large whales late in the 1566 season because an early freeze forced them to leave in a hurry and return home. Abandoning four whales meant a loss of more than 200 barrels of whale oil, which can be estimated to have been worth more than $1 million at today's prices, based on estimated relative purchasing power then and now.

Most of the whale remains found in the silt of Red Bay harbor seem to belong to adult individuals, although a few were not full adults. The age estimations are based on maturation of the bones. At least one baby whale was present among the sample of the catch we have investigated so far. The nearly complete maxilla seems to belong to an approximately 6-m (19-ft) right whale. Since right whales are already around 5 m (16 ft) long at birth in February or March, this one must have been five to six months old, in the middle of the summer, when it was killed by the whalers on its first northward migration. We cannot tell if this single whale calf relates to reports of Basques killing calves to attract their mothers.

Whaling technology. Whale bones found in Red Bay, although numbering more than 3,000, form too limited a sample to help us determine the size of the population killed around the bay. The study of their distribution on the site, of cut marks, and of the presence or absence of particular bones, however, has helped us understand Basque techniques of towing and cutting whales, and of disposing of their remains.

It is clear that the whales were towed into the harbor and to the flensing sites along the north shore of Saddle Island with their tails and flippers still attached. The archaeological evidence so far indicates that tails and flippers were cut away along the shore, in less than a meter of water, off slipways and wharves. In depths from 1 m to 5 m (3 to 16 ft), we found bones representing virtually entire flipper and tail sections, often in articulated and anatomical position, as if they had rotted on the spot where they had been dropped. Marks on certain caudal vertebrae, a meter or so ahead of the flukes, indicated where the tail had been severed. The most striking of the bones, and often the best preserved and most diagnostic, is the large bone (humerus) of the flipper, often found with the lower part of the limb, the distal radius, ulna and even, sometimes, with the carpals, metacarpals and phalanges. These giant flippers were often found close to or overlapping each other in the water. More than 20

percent showed chop marks from all directions, not consistent with regular fleshing operations. The marks suggest the use of flippers as onshore chopping mats, as known from seventeenth-century Spitsbergen. These thick, wide rubber-like pads were ideal to protect the cutting tools used to chop the blubber into portions about 30 cm (12 in) square.

Although a few lower jaw bones or mandibles were found along the shore with the odd rib, trunk vertebra or skull fragment, it seems that the larger, forward parts of the carcasses were towed away from the shore station areas once the flippers and flukes had been cut off and the thick blubber removed.

The Financial Rewards

The share system. Seamen received an average of one share, worth between 4 and 6 barrels (*barricas*), for a five- to nine-month expedition, far exceeding the annual average income of Basque laborers. But specialists like harpooners could earn up to 14 to 15 barrels for their shares, and sometimes as many as the pilot, one of the two highest paid members of a voyage.

Whales and Whale Bones

27 A zooarchaeologist examines the bones of a whale flipper excavated from Red Bay harbor. Zooarchaeological research has concentrated on species identification, carcass disposal patterns and butchering techniques. As a result, it is now known that the Basques hunted the right and bowhead whales, both of which no longer inhabit Labrador waters.

28 The semi-articulated remains of a tail from one of the many whales killed in Red Bay during the sixteenth century. Such faunal remains are abundant throughout Red Bay harbor, making it a unique repository of right and bowhead whale elements.

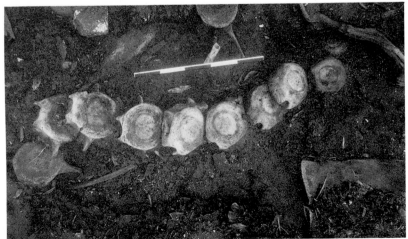

The share system was the rule and it was a rare exception that a crew went to Terranova for straight remuneration, as on a 1564 trip for which regular crew members were to receive salaries of 26 ducats. More representative was the case of the *San Nicolas*, a 453-ton galleon which returned from Terranova in 1566 with a cargo of 1,194 barrels of whale oil. If we assume that its crew totaled 79 or more, as on another expedition, and using the list published by Ciriquiain-Gaizarro, we come to the following share distribution:

Out of 1,194 barrels, one third or 398 were generally divided into equal shares for each of the persons on board except the grumetes, young lads on sort of apprenticeships; one quarter or 298.5 barrels would have gone to the owner of the ship; the rest or 497 barrels to the outfitter. From this gross breakdown (although each trip was a special case), the three subdivisions were treated as follows: the outfitter's share was raised to 509.5 by charging shares to the whaleboat crews and to the oven processors for using equipment provided by him. But from his 509.5 barrels, the outfitter had to provide 113 extra barrels to specialized participants (pilot, captain, harpooners, etc.) for their skilled trades, these barrels being added to the 5-barrel share of each participant. Finally, the shipowner also had to provide extra shares or barrels to the ship's personnel, being left himself with 272 barrels.

While the basic mariners on board seem to have received one share or 5 barrels each, the captain, with his extra shares from the outfitter and from the shipowner, received a total of 30 barrels, 5 more than the pilot. The four best-paid harpooners received 15 barrels each.

Among the whaling crews, experienced harpooners were the highest paid, followed by the coopers. But even the simple mariner on the *San Nicolas*, with his 5-barrel share, worth over 30 ducats, was still better off than the mariner on the 1564 expedition with a fixed 26-ducat salary. With a share of more or less 15 barrels, harpooners like the Echaniz brothers on the *San Juan* could have earned in seven to nine months the equivalent of three times the maximum annual ship-carpenter's salary.

More eloquently, we can state that a first-class harpooner on the *San Juan* could have earned, in less than a year, fifteen times the annual salary of a Brittany sailor in 1539, whose annual wages are given by French maritime historian Jacques Bernard in *Navires et gens de mer à Bordeaux*.

Market and production. An estimated ten galleons could have been moored in Red Bay for whaling. In 1575, Juan Lopez de Recu reported at least nine whaling ships there. Taking the *San Juan* as an average whaling ship with a cargo of around 1,000 barrels, we can estimate that about 10,000 barrels came out of the harbor of Red Bay in a good year. Such a production meant the killing of at least 200 whales a season, not counting the losses, far exceeding the few individual whales that Basques were still killing along their home shores during the sixteenth century. By extending the number of whaling ships to an estimated thirty in Terranova, we reach a conservative estimated output of 30,000 barrels a year, at least valid for some seasons.

This huge production was mostly unloaded back in home ports, whence it was exported to outside markets. Whereas freedom was given to captains to go wherever they wished in Terranova for whaling, most charter parties are specific on the need to return to the Basque country, directly to a home port if possible.

Whalers in Red Bay and Chateau seem to have used baleens on shore for various purposes, including construction, but commercial demand for this strong, flexible bone which grows from the upper jaws of some whales was not constant. Although used in the thirteenth century, baleens do not often appear as part of the share distribution at the time of the *San Juan*. They are absent from the shares of the *San Nicolas* in 1566, and not mentioned for the *Concecion* of 1566, although they are an important part of the shares from a trip of 1580. The captain of the small ship was originally assigned 28 barrels of oil and 200 baleens, the pilot 14 barrels and 40 baleens, one cooper $7\frac{1}{2}$ barrels and 7 baleens.

In later centuries, baleens became so valuable that whalers killed just to retrieve these long, thin bones; carcasses were abandoned and the blubber became a complete loss.

Value. Whale oil was a rare commodity, very expensive to produce and, as a result, it commanded high prices. The price of 1 barrel of whale oil was worth a quarter of a good annual salary in the 1560s. The gross value of the *San Juan*'s 1,000 barrels of oil was more than 6,000 ducats, sufficient to have allowed the purchase in 1571 of a larger, two-year-old vessel of 500 tons which could be bought completely equipped, armed and outfitted for 5,500 ducats. In fact, the cargo of the *San Juan* was more than sufficient to purchase two medium-size galleons, excluding the outfitting. In 1566 only 1 or 2 barrels of whale oil were needed to purchase a new whaleboat or hunting chalupa for Terranova.

One can understand why the Echaniz brothers, harpooners on the *San Juan* in 1565, were still trying to get their fair share of the salvaged cargo when they complained to the notary in 1575, ten years after the sinking. Even a few barrels of whale oil meant a lot back home.

Recent documentary evidence indicates that the waters around Newfoundland and the Gulf of St Lawrence were host to more ships and to a larger tonnage in the sixteenth century than the waters of the West Indies and the Gulf of Mexico. Maritime archaeology as practiced in Red Bay, by archaeologists from Parks Canada and Memorial University, has been instrumental in opening up a few pages of that neglected northern saga.

CHAPTER FIVE

Treasure Ships of the Spanish Main: The Iberian-American Maritime Empires

Roger C. Smith

Three decades after the discovery of the New World, almost all the Caribbean, Gulf and Atlantic coasts had been explored and charted by European navigators. Columbus and his followers had found that sea and air currents of the North Atlantic Basin rotated in a clockwise direction, and could be followed to and from America. This wind and current pattern would dictate maritime sailing routes until the Age of Steam, carrying countless people and products between two hemispheres.

Sometimes referred to as the American Mediterranean, the Caribbean Sea to a lesser degree is also a closed system. Entering the basin through the Windward or Leeward Islands, Spanish navigators discovered that prevailing winds and currents flow from east to west, making it extremely difficult to leave the system by the same route. Instead, three major paths – the Anegada, Mona and Windward Passages – required ships to beat northward between the Greater Antilles to return to the Atlantic. With the circumnavigation of Cuba, another exit, the Yucatan Channel, was found. This led ships into the Gulf of Mexico, from which the Gulf Stream ran northward through the Straits of Florida and into the Atlantic. While this Leeward Passage became essential with the conquest of Mexico, merchant fleets soon learned the dangers of the route between Florida and the Bahamas, bordered by treacherous reefs along each side of the Bahama Channel.

In the wake of discoveries, cartographers noted nautical landmarks useful for charting courses and reckoning distances in the New World. With the process of conquest and colonization, natural harbors, convenient roadsteads and river estuaries were incorporated into a growing network of New World nautical knowledge. But while the entrances and exits to the Caribbean Basin had been identified, and islands and their relationships to the mainland mapped, charting their exact locations was a difficult proposition. Medieval mariners had learned to acquire celestial measurements with the use of the quadrant, astrolabe and cross-staff, which, when applied to German or Italian astronomical tables, gave them a fair determination of latitude. Longitude, on the other hand, could only be roughly estimated by reckoning elapsed sailing time and adding or subtracting for ocean currents to deduce how far east or west a ship had progressed. Precise timepieces, adapted for shipboard use, became common at sea only centuries later. Consequently, most early nautical charts placed islands and shoals in their correct latitudes, but rarely according to longitude. Yet, while such navigational errors often caused catastrophes, they did not prevent the creation of sophisticated transatlantic lifelines to and from the New World by the Iberian peoples of Spain and Portugal. For more than 300 years their ships supported their colonial empires. The numbers of men and the amount of materials moved across the ocean were enormous; not until World War II would so many vessels assemble routinely in convoys to sail back and forth across the Atlantic. The degree of preparation, provisioning and protection required to support this seafaring enterprise was staggering.

The 1494 Treaty of Tordesillas had divided the nautical sphere between Spain and Portugal, inadvertently giving the latter a portion of eastern South America. Spain had received by far the greater part of the New World, its extent still unknown. But, with the colonization of the Caribbean islands, and the discovery of wealth in Mexico and Peru, Spain's jealous European rivals, France and England, began to venture into her overseas realm. As increasingly vast cargoes of American gold and silver, ultimately sufficient to alter the economy of Europe, began to flow from the mines to the ships, and eventually into the coffers of Spain's creditors, predators lurked on both sides of the Atlantic to seize their share. Armed caravels and *naos*, sailing on solitary runs early in the sixteenth century, became prey to groups of foreign corsairs, and even small fleets of merchantmen came under attack by nimble privateers.

To counter this threat, Spain devised a formal convoy system as early as 1537, which became a successful pattern of maritime defense for over three centuries. At least two armed escorts – a *capitana*, or flagship, sailing in the vanguard, and an *almiranta*, or vice-flagship, sailing in the rear – accompanied merchant vessels across the ocean. Occasionally another armed vessel, or *gobiernador*, filled

Spanish Convoys

1 (*left*) Spain devised a convoy system as early as 1537 to protect her treasure fleets and, by the time of this seventeenth-century engraving of Spanish vessels in the Caribbean, her captains were well used to sailing in tight formation. A royal decree pronounced that 'no ship may leave the convoy for any reason, not even to pursue an enemy sail'.

2 (*right*) A 1541 map hints at what became a regular pattern of outward and homeward voyages. Two separate fleets departing from Spain sailed together via the Canary Islands to Trinidad or the Windward Islands where they diverged, the Tierra Firme fleet making for Cartagena in what is now Colombia, the New Spain fleet for Veracruz, Mexico. The two fleets joined together again in Cuba for the return voyage via the Straits of Florida.

with soldiers, took overall charge of defense at sea. Often larger *armadas* escorted the convoy along the first leg of the outward-bound journey to defend it against attack by French or North African corsairs. To pay for this protection, merchants whose cargoes were carried in the fleet paid to the Crown an *avería* tax on their merchandise, which increased from 2 percent in the sixteenth century to 12 percent by the seventeenth century.

Two separate fleets departing Spain for America each year normally sailed down the coast of Africa to the Canary Islands, where they re-provisioned and took leave of coastal escorts as soon as they were safely out to sea. The fleets rode the trade winds to a landfall near Trinidad or the Windward Islands, then entered the Caribbean Basin, where their routes diverged. The New Spain fleet, or *flota*, sailed on to the port of Veracruz for products brought down from Mexico City by mule train, and for Chinese trade goods shipped across the Pacific from the Philippines in Manila galleons to Acapulco and then also transported overland to Veracruz. Cargoes loaded and supplies stowed, the New Spain *flota* departed Veracruz and proceeded on a northeasterly course into the northern part of the Gulf and down the west coast of Florida, past the Dry Tortugas and into Havana.

The *galeones* of Tierra Firme, on the other hand, proceeded towards Cartagena, in what is now Colombia, to load South American goods. Word of the impending arrival having been sent ahead by swift dispatch vessels called *pataches*, the Governor of Panama would have

arranged for the transport of Peruvian treasure across the Isthmus from Panama City to the Caribbean town of Portobelo. From Cartagena, the captain-general of the convoy sent vessels to Panama to collect the goods at Portobelo and deliver them back to the Tierra Firme fleet, to be loaded along with those of New Granada. At the same time, another ship was sent to the island of Margarita to pick up the year's production of pearls from the offshore beds. Having registered and loaded the combined products of South America, the *galeones* sailed for Havana following a course through the Yucatan Channel around the western tip of Cuba. As this fleet sailed up the coast of Central America, it was joined by ships bearing the outputs of Guatemalan mines and plantations.

At Havana the *flota* joined the *galeones*; as soon as preparations were completed for the return voyage to Spain and the commanding officers judged the weather to be right, the combined fleet set sail into the Straits of Florida, pushed northward by the Gulf Stream. After the pilots determined that the northern part of the Bahamas archipelago had been cleared, the course was altered to the northeast to Bermuda, then east to catch westerly tradewinds which carried the ships towards Spain.

For the most part, this armed convoy system worked well against depredations of other nations, but the Spaniards were plagued by other, equally treacherous factors. Despite the establishment of a school for navigators at Seville, the convoys often lacked experi-

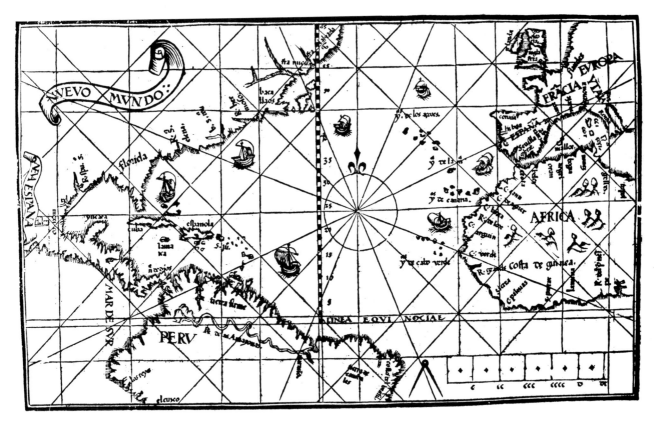

enced pilots and skilled seamen. Shipboard crews were recruited from men of every sort, often with little nautical knowledge. The design of merchant vessels lagged far behind the need for increased tonnage, resulting in ships that were top-heavy and unmanageable at sea. Specifications in construction contracts for new ships were often compromised in favor of increased profit. Similarly, worn-out vessels were sent back to the West Indies in attempts to squeeze from them one last voyage. Imperial decrees on shipping were routinely ignored, as maintenance in port was postponed and contraband overloaded the vessels at sea. Despite attempts at sheathing the lower hulls of merchantmen, shipworm damage from *Teredo navalis* quickly weakened planks and timbers in the tropics. Shipboard conditions robbed sailors of their health and spirit, especially on the long Pacific run between Manila and Acapulco, where the specter of scurvy accompanied the dawning of each day at sea.

Shoals and unfamiliar but deadly weather proved still more costly to Spanish shipping. Columbus lost his flagship to the former on his initial voyage, and learned the meaning of the Indian word *huracán* when several of his ships sank on the second voyage. Tropical hurricanes, forming in the Atlantic, threaten the Caribbean between August and October; and between November and March a sudden intense pressure system, called '*el norte*', descends into the Gulf of Mexico. While lookouts learned to distinguish dark water during the day and listen for breakers at night, and while pilots learned to watch for a thin line of clouds on the northeastern horizon and monitor the color of the sky at sunset, these were virtually the only warnings available of such impending dangers.

Shoals and storms – and their combination – left the remains of countless vessels along the maritime routes pioneered by Iberians. Although the political and economic history of Iberian-American seafaring systems is well known, the wrecks of ships that never completed the circuit are just beginning to tell their side of the story. It is a complicated tale of imperial enterprise, royal and private fortunes, as well as technological achievements. But it also is a tale of greed and avarice, nautical ignorance and misfortune. Aside from material wealth swallowed by the sea, the sites of wrecked ships represent the historical wealth that can be pieced together through careful study of their waterlogged remains.

The Cayo Nuevo Shipwreck

An enigmatic Spanish vessel lost sometime in the mid-sixteenth century was likely en route to Veracruz when she encountered an uncharted shoal at Cayo Nuevo, some 100 miles from the Mexican coast, barely protruding from the Bay of Campeche. Her crew attempted to secure the vessel, but the anchor failed to hold and the ship was driven some 200 m (650 ft) across the ragged coral before she sank.

There, in 1979, two sport divers from Louisiana spotted a large bronze cannon in the sand and coral rubble, with two iron cannons and an anchor wedged into

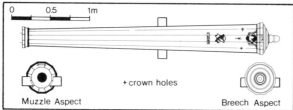

0   0.5   1m

+ crown holes

Muzzle Aspect   Breech Aspect

the reef nearby. The divers attempted to raise the bronze cannon, but succeeded only in uncovering the length of its tube. The twelve-sided barrel bore a date – 15?2, possibly 1552 – and a curious escutcheon in bas relief composed of a calvary cross, crescent moon and a five-pointed star or rowel. In addition, the raised design of a winged seashell and crowned dolphin decorated the cannon's touch hole.

Realizing the uniqueness of their find, the site's discoverers contacted the Institute of Nautical Archaeology and, in turn, the Mexican National Institute of Anthropology and History (INAH). Later that year, the first of three joint INA/INAH expeditions to the shoal was directed by archaeologist Pilar Luna. Aboard a Mexican Navy minesweeper, two of the site's discoverers, Farley Sonnier and Ned Weeks, led the team back to the bronze cannon – a long-range, large caliber *media culebrina* or demi-culverine, a medium-sized, front-line cannon. The two early cast-iron guns each bore a crudely etched identification mark, possibly a founder's or gunner's imprint, also found on the bronze culverine, suggesting that the three guns were in use together when they were lost.

These sixteenth-century finds – among the oldest documented artillery of their type in the New World – along with numerous ballast stones, ship's fittings and fragments of lead hull sheathing, confirmed the site to be a wreck and not mere jetsam. Test excavations produced fragments of Spanish olive jars, suggesting a Spanish carrier, and globules of mercury adhering to brass pins, suggesting in-bound cargo from Europe. Three additional cast-iron cannons and another anchor were found.

Although her identity has yet to be ascertained, this valuable, early ship can be studied because her remains were discovered by responsible sport divers who chose to seek assistance from archaeologists and government officials to ensure that their find was given the attention it

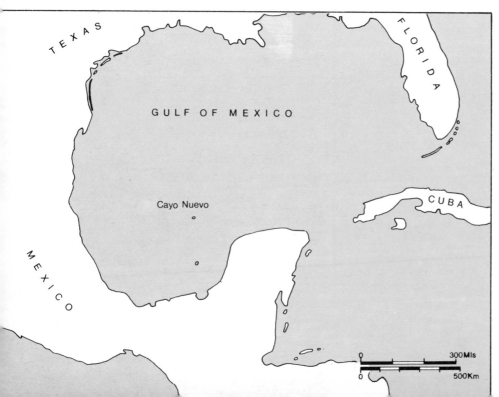

The Cayo Nuevo Wreck

3, 4   The discovery in 1979 of this bronze demi-culverine, protruding (*top left*) from the sand and coral rubble at Cayo Nuevo in the Bay of Campeche, led to a joint Mexican-American investigation of the sixteenth-century shipwreck it marked. The drawing (*above left*) shows the cannon after conservation.

5   (*left*) The location of the wrecksite.

deserved. While further investigations are planned, the distinctive bronze cannon that pinpointed the site now occupies a prominent position in the Museo Regional in Campeche.

The 1554 Fleet

Contemporary with the Cayo Nuevo calamity was the disaster at 'Isla Blanca', now Padre Island, Texas (see Chapter Three). The fleet of four ships was loaded with New World products: gold and silver; cochineal and cowhides; sugar, silk and wool; liquidamber (a resinous medicinal); and sarsaparilla root (a new drug obtained from the Aztecs and used for respiratory diseases). In addition to the ordnance described in Chapter Three, modern salvage and excavation of two of the ships have brought to light swords and chain mail; silver coins of various mints; silver disks and gold ingots; pewter plates and porringers; multicolored majolica ceramics and German stoneware; brass shoe buckles; obsidian blades and an iron pyrite mirror of aboriginal manufacture; a gold crucifix and gold-trimmed wooden cross; brass astrolabes and navigational dividers; and hammers, pincers, a pick adze, an awl, an auger and caulking irons.

The archaeology of the 1554 vessels as conducted by the Texas Antiquities Committee demonstrated that proper scientific excavation and treatment of 'Spanish treasure ships' can tell us far more than simple salvage for commercial profit. During systematic laboratory procedures, each shred of rope and cloth, each splinter of wood, and each bone and seed was studied and conserved for its contribution to knowledge of Iberian-American trade. Even sixteen stowaway cockroaches and their egg cases were identified in the debris.

Apart from their weapons and cargoes, what can we learn about these merchant vessels? Fortunately a telltale fragment of *San Esteban*'s keel assemblage survived to give us clues to her dimensions. Studies by Edwin and

Michael Doran, and William Baker, permitted reconstruction drawings and a scale model to be made by Jay Rosloff. A large notch had been cut from the stern-most port side of the keel in order to fit the similarly notched lower end of the sternpost. Rabbets for the garboard planking were carved into both sides of the keel and the sternpost. The stern knee was cut from naturally curved timber, which was bolted to both keel and sternpost. A layer of pitch or resin was daubed between the joining surfaces of these three timbers. Apparently every fourth frame had been bolted to the keelson, but intermediate frames only lightly nailed in position. Remains of one garboard plank and a fragmentary upper plank on the port side of the structure narrowed slightly and slanted progressively outward toward the forward part of the hull, indicating a wide-bottomed vessel. The garboard strake appeared to have been cut to this curved shape, rather than bent over the hull frames as upper strakes presumably would have been. Planks had been caulked with a mixture of oakum and animal hair held in the seams by parceling of resin-soaked fabric covered by thin strips of lead to prevent *Teredo* infestation. The lead strips were fastened with rows of iron tacks that had been forced into the caulked seams, rather than nailed into the planks themselves. Such details help us to understand the characteristics of a small but typical Spanish merchantman, in this case a *nao* of under 200 tons, that carried early commerce along the Spanish mercantile lifeline.

The Bermuda Wrecks

In 1950, on Bermuda's inner reefs, local salvor Teddy Tucker discovered late sixteenth-century materials thought to represent the remains of the *San Pedro*, a 350-ton merchant *nao* of the 1596 New Spain fleet.

The ship's defensive weapons consisted of a main battery of cast-iron, muzzle-loading cannons, descendants of the type found at Cayo Nuevo, but also included

Studying the 'San Esteban'

6, 7 The only surviving hull remains from the 1554 fleet to be examined archaeologically are these stern fragments of the *San Esteban*. The photograph (*far right*) shows centuries of mud and concretion being cleaned from the timbers at the Texas Archaeological Research Laboratory of the University of Texas at Austin. Subsequently Jay Rosloff studied the fragments in detail and produced a 1:10 scale model, enabling this accurate drawing to be made (*right*) of the vessel's keel, stern post, stern knee and several hull planks. The reconstruction allows an estimated length overall for the ship of just over 20 m (65 ft 6 in).

secondary wrought-iron, breech-loading *versos*, similar to those of the 1554 fleet (see Chapter Three). As shipboard ordnance evolved from wrought-iron to cast-iron artillery, a sophistication in projectile forms also seems to have occurred. While wrought-iron cannons continued to fire iron and lead shot or a handful of sharp flint pebbles, the new high-velocity, larger caliber cast-iron guns could be loaded with solid iron shot or a type of spiked shot wrapped in hemp and soaked with tar. When fired, the latter was ignited by the powder charge to fly flaming toward an enemy ship where it would embed itself.

San Pedro also carried expanding bar shot of hemispherical lead weights joined by two sliding wrought-iron bars. During trajectory, the bars were pulled apart by centrifugal force to a length of 75 cm (2 ft 6 in); the spinning projectile could take down masts and sails. Brass hand grenades with threaded fuses and small iron axes were available for defense against boarding. Soldiers on the ship were equipped with matchlock muskets – which fired lead balls 20 mm in diameter that sometimes were wired together like miniature bar shot – and were armed with Spanish long swords and left-hand daggers; a steel helmet and breastplate may have belonged to an officer.

The homeward-bound *San Pedro* had been laden with gold bullion, silver coins and jewelry from the Americas, and has yielded one of the most valuable pieces of jewelry recovered from a Spanish shipwreck in modern times: a gold pectoral cross set with seven emeralds from the mines of New Grenada. The cross was put on display at the Bermuda Maritime Museum, but on the occasion of a royal visit in 1975 it was discovered that the cross had

been replaced by a plastic replica. The real cross has never been found.

While common mariners aboard *San Pedro* ate from coarse redware bowls, passengers were served on fine silver and French pewter plates, taking wine from gilded silver ewers. Aboriginal souvenirs, including a unique Carib Indian staff of office carved from black palmwood, and bows and arrows, are now displayed at the Bermuda Maritime Museum.

Although flint ballast and fittings were present, no remains of the ship's hull were found. Tucker hypothesized that a storm had carried the vessel over the outer reefs. The weight of heavy guns, cargo and ballast had snapped the center of the ship, spilling her contents onto the seabed 10 m (33 ft) below, before carrying her shoreward to some yet undiscovered location.

Tucker later discovered the wreck of another Spanish *nao*, driven ashore in Bermuda in 1621. Part of a combined fleet sailing homeward from Havana, the 300-ton *San Antonio* had struck a southwestern fringing reef and quickly bilged. The crew mutinied and took the only boat, abandoning officers and passengers on the stern, which was still above water. Next day a raft built from ship timbers carried the remainder of the ship's complement to shore. Bermudians soon salvaged much of her ordnance and precious cargo, including gold and silver.

Weapons aboard the *San Antonio* were similar to those found at the site of *San Pedro*: a main battery of cast-iron, muzzle-loading cannon, a secondary battery of breech-loading swivel guns and shoulder arms. Corresponding stone and iron round shot, incendiary spike shot, expanding bar shot and musket balls were found. Several

8, 9 During the summer of 1987, archaeologists from the Institute of Maritime History and Archaeology at the Bermuda Maritime Museum began new test excavations (*left*) on the site of a late sixteenth-century wreck in Bermuda, possibly that of the *San Pedro* (1596). The site was originally investigated by local salvor Teddy Tucker and Mendel Peterson of the Smithsonian Institution. One of Tucker's major discoveries was this magnificent gold pectoral cross (*below*) set with seven emeralds.

new types of projectiles were uncovered and subsequently studied by Mendel Peterson of the Smithsonian Institution: wooden case shot charged with langrel for the larger cannons was fashioned from a lathe-turned wooden cylinder split longitudinally, filled with fragments of scrap cast iron and lead balls, then wired back together. Three types of small arms shot had been designed like miniature chain shot and sliding bar shot: two lead balls connected by a coiled brass spring, a single split ball on twisted brass wires hinged together (corresponding to split chain shot for heavier guns), and two lead balls joined by twisted brass wires forming a sliding bar. That this ammunition could be manufactured at sea by the ship's armorer was demonstrated by the discovery of sections of lead bar, a musket ball mold, balls with sprues still attached and hanks of coiled brass wire.

New World natural products, not salvaged at the time of *San Antonio*'s wrecking, remained surprisingly preserved beneath the sand. Tobacco leaves rolled into cones around wooden sticks had been harvested under a strict Crown monopoly. Tanned red hides represented Mexico's third most valuable export at the time; since Spain also produced hides, most from the New World were sold to Northern European countries. A wooden chest packed with balls of pressed indigo dyestuff turned the surrounding water a deep blue when excavated. Billets of *lignum vitae* hardwood, cut from the forested shores of Yucatan and Central America, had been destined for the shipbuilding industry, where 'ironwood' was fashioned into blocks and sheaves for running rigging. Fragments of tortoise shell from the carapace of the Caribbean hawksbill sea turtle told of the early trade in a fashionable but limited resource. Red cochineal dye, a rare product of crushed insects collected from Mexico, had been packed in earthenware jars. Other exotic products of the Indies included cocoa beans to satisfy the growing thirst for hot chocolate among wealthy elites, and cassia beanpods for a new-found preparation to purge the results of dietary indulgence.

Thousands of Indo-Pacific cowry shells (*Cyprea moneta*), shipped to Mexico in Manila galleons and carried overland by mule train to Veracruz, were found mixed with small billets of copper. Both the shells and raw metal were highly prized in the barter for West African slaves.

Spanish ceramics included Mexican tin-enameled majolica wares, utilitarian earthenwares, and intact olive jars. Although precious metals had been salvaged after the ship sank, some gold (in cakes, nuggets and dust) and silver coins were found; the latter helped to identify the *San Antonio*. Amerindian skills were reflected in jewelry which, as personal items, had been exempt from the King's tax on gold. Many of the artifacts are on display at the Smithsonian Institution and the Bermuda Maritime Museum.

Beneath the cargo, some 30 m (98 ft) of ship timbers were uncovered, providing evidence for the construction of Spanish merchantmen of the early seventeenth century.

The vessel's large keel featured a grooved water course cut along its upper surface, where stout floor timbers were fastened. Planking, framing and keel were of oak, but mahogany patching of some of the strakes suggested that the vessel had been repaired in the Caribbean. Curiously, no trace of a keelson was found among the wreckage. Although no drawings or plans of the site have been published, the size and arrangement of *San Antonio*'s timbers suggest a relatively large armed Spanish *nao* of the type that played such an important role in early Spanish-American trade.

Wrecks of Spanish Galleons

The *San Esteban*, *San Pedro* and *San Antonio* were all armed merchant *naos*, but during the sixteenth century the short, deep, tub-shaped *nao* was evolving into a longer vessel of lighter draft, lower freeboard and finer lines: the galleon. The earliest galleons were simply enlarged merchantmen fitted with heavy artillery to guard their cargoes against French and English predators. Greater carrying capacity was obtained by increasing beams, and raising bulwarks into high castles fore and aft to accommodate more cannons. These developments were promoted by Admiral Alvaro de Bazán and his brother Alonso, who ordered the construction of large galleons for the Indies trade, borrowing features of Genoese and Venetian armed ships. The Bazáns combined the bulkiness of carracks with the slim lines of galleys and the rigging of caravels to produce the *galeón*. But these new 'castles of the sea', often fitted with three and four decks of artillery, were top-heavy and, when fully laden, extremely unseaworthy.

The mid-sixteenth-century increase in size and tonnage soon prompted a change in the theory of ship construction. Encouraged by the Bazáns, but opposed by older builders, Admiral Pedro Menéndez de Avilés urged adoption of a longer keel to overcome the poor sailing qualities of armed galleons. Charged with designing a naval defense of the Indies in the 1560s, Menéndez promoted the construction of colonial-built prototypes called *galeoncetes*. Much lighter and longer than the clumsy galleons, these vessels proved to be good sailors and promised to elude attacks by pirates, especially in calm waters, since their lower decks had been fitted with oars. When laden with valuable merchandise, however, the vessels' oar ports tended to be too close to the waterline to risk rowing in moderate seas. Despite design faults, *galeoncetes* represented the first step in the evolution of fast armed frigates that would become accepted in all navies by the end of the seventeenth century. And in their time, they prompted a change in construction from broad-beamed ships to sleeker and faster galleons.

With the adoption of an increased length-to-beam ratio of three-to-one, the galleon was further streamlined by diminishing the size of the forecastle and setting it back from the stem, making it less apt to catch the wind and force the ship's bow to leeward. Accentuated tumble-home, whereby the top gundeck was much narrower than the hull at the waterline, helped to concentrate the weight of the ordnance nearer the ship's center of gravity. Galleons were 'ship-rigged' with fore, main, mizzen and bonaventure masts carrying a square and lateen combination of seven to nine sails. Fighting tops, from which shoulder arms and hand-held projectiles could be deployed, were mounted at the bases of fore and main topmasts. With clean hulls and normal cargo loads, galleons could average 4 to 5 knots; in a following wind they might reach 8 knots.

By the early seventeenth century, the Spanish Crown maintained a growing fleet of war galleons, financed by tax revenues from the Indies trade, to escort convoys of merchantmen to and from the Americas. Because of their heavier artillery and better sailing qualities, these escort galleons usually carried the Crown's treasure, while private valuables and general cargo were transported by *naos* and flat-bottomed, bulky storeships called *urcas*. At the head of the convoy, the *capitana* carried the captain-general, who was senior in command and responsible for navigation, provisions and the general welfare of all the ships. The *almiranta* carried the admiral, who was second in command and usually assumed military leadership if the fleet was attacked.

The 'Atocha'. Mention of the *Atocha* today elicits a variety of responses from those concerned with shipwrecks. Aside from sensational newspaper stories of silver bars and gold doubloons, the legal and political ramifications created by the recovery of materials from this full-blown Spanish galleon of the early seventeenth century have overshadowed its significance as an archaeological site. Fortunately, commercial aspects of the *Atocha*'s modern-day salvage have been tempered with archaeological guidance from Duncan Mathewson.

The *Nuestra Señora de Atocha* was a seagoing fortress built for King Philip IV in Havana. Commanded by Vice-Admiral Pedro Pasquier de Espanza, the 550-ton galleon carried 20 bronze cannons manned by 18 trained gunners. She also carried 115 other crewmen and boys, 82 soldiers and 48 passengers when she left Havana for Spain, on 4 September 1622, as vice-flagship of a fleet of 28 vessels.

One of seven large galleons in the convoy, the *almiranta*'s holds were filled with gold and silver bullion and specie – part of the Crown's 20 percent revenue from the mines of Potosí and New Granada, and financial returns from numerous commercial transactions. The *Atocha* also carried indigo, tobacco, cochineal and rosewood, and tons of Cuban copper ingots were stowed atop her ballast.

The convoy was struck by a hurricane as it headed into the Straits of Florida. Eight vessels were separated from the others and driven toward the lower Florida Keys where all were lost, including the *Atocha*. Soon located by salvors from Havana, she had settled intact with her mizzen mast projecting above the surface of the water. Five survivors – two ship's boys, a seaman and two slaves – told how the galleon had struck a reef and sunk.

Divers had recovered only two bronze cannons before a second storm broke up the ship and dispersed the surface buoys which marked her grave. Efforts over the years to relocate the wreckage with a diving bell, slave divers from Acapulco, and Indians from the Caribbean pearl beds, were all fruitless. The Marquis of Cadereite, convoy commander, came himself to supervise; an island salvage camp was referred to as 'el cayo del Marquez'.

Modern attempts to locate the *Atocha* began in the mid-1960s, mostly centered in the middle Florida Keys, since documents cited 'Matecumbe', corresponding to the modern 'Matecumbe Key', as the area where the ship sank. Treasure-hunter Mel Fisher and his group, Treasure Salvors, Inc., led the most comprehensive search. After covering the middle keys, Fisher concentrated on the northern keys, with no better luck.

Then, in 1970, historian Eugene Lyon located Spanish salvage records of the 1622 fleet in Seville's Archive of the

ORIZONTE

10, 11 Mariner's astrolabe (*far left*) discovered on the wrecksite of the *Atocha*, which went down off the Florida Keys in 1622. A contemporary engraving (*above*) suggests the way in which the instrument was suspended from the navigator's thumb; it could then be adjusted so that the angle of the sun or stars relative to the ship could be measured.

12 An artist's impression of a Spanish galleon of about 1600.

FOREMAST

MAINMAST

MIZZENMAST

BONAVENTURE MAST

2-POUND CULVERIN

FORECASTLE

1-POUND SWIVEL GUN

SHIP'S BOATS

4-POUND GUN

BOWSPRIT

CAPSTAN

POOP

ADMIRAL'S CABIN

CAPTAIN'S CABIN

9-POUND GUN

RUDDER

GUN DECK & CREW'S QUARTERS

ANCHOR CABLES   SHOT   BILGE PUMP   POWDER   WATER CASKS   SMALL ARMS

SHIP'S STORES   TREASURE STORE ROOM

Indies. Lyon found a reference to the *Atocha*'s location as being near the 'Cayos del Marquez'. Old maps of the region showed that 'Matecumbe' actually applied to the entire Florida Keys area, but that the salvage site was in the remote Marquesas Keys, some 70 miles from the Florida mainland. Fisher moved his operation and after a year of intensive magnetic searching located a large anchor. A gold chain, musket shot, ballast, a sword, a few coins and two unnumbered gold bars thought to be contraband were uncovered nearby.

By 1973 the salvors had followed an artifact trail from the galleon anchor to an area containing thousands of silver coins. Discovery of a mariner's astrolabe followed, then three large silver bars which bore registry marks that historian Lyon was able to match with listings on the original cargo manifest of the *Atocha*. Study of their distribution pattern convinced archaeologist Mathewson that these materials were from the vessel's sterncastle, and that the primary deposit would be found in deeper water.

In 1975 five bronze cannons were encountered lying exposed on the seabed, and four more were found a few days later. Four of these matched ordnance weight registries on the *Atocha*'s manifest. The alignment of the guns suggested that the galleon's superstructure and gundeck had become separated from the hull during the second storm. Digging along a vector between the guns and the rich area of silver coins yielded two silver ingots, a gold bar, a gold chain and a copper ingot.

Finally, in 1985, the main deposit of the *Atocha*'s lower hull was found in 19 m (62 ft) of water. An enormous mound of encrusted silver bars formed an artificial reef of treasure. Within a week, over 500 silver bars, each weighing 70 pounds, and numerous wooden chests containing silver coins were recovered. One chest was filled with gold bars.

The wreckage had been strewn along the seabed some 7 miles from the spot where the sinking originally occurred. Beneath cargo, ballast stones and dunnage, massive timbers, consisting of the vessel's lower floors, futtocks and bottom strakes, marked the *Atocha*'s final resting place; there was no evidence of keel and keelson, which were perhaps wrenched from the ship as she ground along the seafloor during the second storm. Clues to colonial construction practices at the Havana shipyard should emerge from careful study of the *Atocha*'s remnants, especially when compared with her original builder's contract, which survives in the archives.

'*La Concepción*'. In 1640, the 600-ton *nao*, *Nuestra Señora de la Pura y Limpia Concepción*, was one of two elderly merchantmen that had been converted and armed to serve as escorts for a convoy to Mexico; major alterations to her structure enabled this fleet *capitana* to mount forty bronze cannons supplied by the royal arsenal.

Once in Veracruz, the ships spent over a year rotting in tropical waters. Finally, in June 1641, the reassembled convoy laden with precious cargoes embarked for Havana and home, with *Concepción* serving as *almiranta*. More than twenty years old, her hull had not been careened properly or re-sheathed with lead for eighteen months, and many of her seams had opened. Probably the captain-general realized her unseaworthiness, for at the last moment he shifted his flag to the other converted ship, making it the *capitana*. Admiral Juan de Villavicencio, now in command of the *Concepción*, complained at Havana of her condition, to no avail. Just seventeen days later the fleet sailed, but the vice-flagship soon developed a serious leak. The ships turned back to Havana, where one of *Concepción*'s stern planks was replaced by divers.

At sea again, dangerously late in the season, the convoy had passed the Florida reefs when it was struck at night by a September hurricane and dispersed. The flagship made it back to Spain – only to sink at the entrance to the Guadalquivir River – but the *Concepción*, her main and foremasts broken, drifted out of control. Part of her crew, two bower anchors, and three lifeboats had been swept from her decks by enormous waves.

Finally, after wet powder, several of the ship's cannons and less valuable cargo had been cast overboard, steerage was regained. Admiral Villavicencio and his senior officials decided to attempt a course for Puerto Rico. During the following weeks the pilots changed course several times, finally settling on a heading of due south. Familiar with the waters, Villavicencio insisted the course would lead them onto coral banks north of Hispaniola. Under regulations then current, however, the pilots' decisions were supreme. The Admiral called for a silver bowl of water and, before the assembled crew and passengers, washed his hands of responsibility.

On the night of 31 October, *Concepción* hit a series of submerged reefs. Despite efforts to hold her with anchors, the vessel was blown farther into the labyrinth of shoals until, on the third day, she filled with water, her stern held between two coral heads. The pilots determined the reefs to be those of Anegada to the east of Puerto Rico, but the Admiral knew that they had sailed into the Abrojos shoals north of Hispaniola. Passengers and crew took refuge on the poop deck, which remained above the water, but there was not enough room for all. When daylight came, the Admiral ordered rafts built from beams and planks, while he and thirty-two of the passengers embarked in the sole surviving ship's boat for Hispaniola. In the following days, eight rafts were completed as the ship gradually sank. The pilots loaded two of them and set a course for where they thought Puerto Rico lay; the remainder of the people headed southwards. The Admiral's boat and some of the rafts reached the north shore of Hispaniola, but the others were never heard from again. Of 532 souls on the *Concepción*, only 194 survived. From Santo Domingo, Villavicencio attempted two separate salvage expeditions to the wrecked *almiranta*, but was foiled by weather, corsairs and shipwreck. Eventually the Admiral gave up, but the treasure lost under his command was not forgotten. Private expeditions, none successful, were attempted in 1650, 1652, 1667 and 1673.

A Boston sea captain, William Phips, found the coral-covered wreck of the *Concepción* in 1687. He never knew her name, only that she was a Spanish *almiranta*. Phips salvaged a quarter of a million pounds sterling worth of treasure, which he brought to England, receiving a knighthood and the post of Governor of Massachusetts.

Modern searches for 'Phips' Wreck' (by Alexandre Korganoff, Edwin Link and Jacques Cousteau in the 1950s and 1960s) were unsuccessful until American treasure-hunter Burt Webber took up the quest. Webber, too, failed at first, although he discovered thirteen different wrecksites in the remote shoals during his initial survey in 1977. Meanwhile, English historian Peter Earle, writing a book about the *Concepción*, discovered the logbook of Phips' salvage ship *Henry* in the Kent archives, providing the precise locational bearings needed by Webber. With Earle's assistance, Webber narrowed his search area to an eighth of a square mile and returned to the 'Silver Bank' in November 1978. A newly devised, hand-held cesium magnetometer led him and his divers through the maze of coral heads comprising 'ye Wracke Reefe' on English salvage charts. Only 150 m (c. 500 ft)

Spanish Salvage

13   The Spanish were often as keen to salvage wrecked ships from their treasure fleets as modern archaeologists. They used specially equipped vessels and free-diving Indians and Africans for the purpose, as shown in this illustration of 1626.

from the spot indicated on *Henry*'s log, they found silver coins cast between 1600 and 1641, silver ingots, plates, candlesticks and Chinese Ming porcelain.

The galleon had broken its back on a steep coral promontory and spilled its contents. Phips had found the stern deposit, but Webber soon located the remainder of the wreckage. Cutting through centuries of coral with hydraulic chain-saws, divers penetrated to deep cavities containing the *Concepción*'s cargo. Silver, ceramics, glass beads, wooden cups, an astrolabe dated 1632, a marble statue and gold chains appeared. The wooden trunk of a wealthy passenger contained porcelain cups and silver tablewares as originally packed by their owner. The trunk had a false floor, under which were found 1,440 contraband coins.

The variety and quality of the artifacts recovered by Webber's thorough excavation, conducted under a Dominican license, constituted a major museum collection of archaeological and numismatic value. Much of the bullion was found without assessment and tax markings, suggesting that it was private contraband (copies of the *Concepción*'s manifest, signed in triplicate, no

longer exist; one sank with the ship, another with the returned *capitana*, and the third burned with the archives of Havana). Over 60,000 coins were found. The vast majority were minted in Mexico City, but others in such diverse places as Cartagena, Bogotá, Cuenca, Madrid, Seville and Valladolid. The most significant were those minted at Cartagena and Santa Fé de Bogotá: numismatists believed that both mints had started in 1623, but the galleon carried coins from them dated 1621 and 1622.

The Plate Fleets

The 1715 fleet. For years pieces-of-eight were found washed up on the beach near Sebastian Inlet, Florida. In the late 1950s, beachcomber Kip Wagner wondered whether they might be from an offshore shipwreck being eroded by storms. Floating on an inner tube in shallow water, the retired building contractor came across the remains of a ship that changed his life and began a modern gold rush. He learned from the Spanish Archive of the Indies that an entire convoy of treasure ships had been wrecked in the area – one of the worst losses of shipping in the history of Spain's maritime empire.

A combined fleet of eleven ships of the Tierra Firme squadron and the New Spain *flota* embarked from their rendezvous at Havana on 24 July 1715 to begin a homeward voyage. Registered cargoes of gold and silver amounted to almost seven million pieces-of-eight; an additional fortune in contraband bullion was probably on board. Sailing with the Spanish ships was a French merchantman, *Grifon*, detained at Havana so as not to fall prey to corsairs who might learn of the impending fleet departure, which had been delayed by lading and paperwork well into the hurricane season.

On 31 July, borne northward through the Florida Straits by the Gulf Stream, the ships were struck by a hurricane and driven one after another over the shoals and onto the sand, splintering in the darkness. Nearly half the 2,500 people on board were lost. Only the *Grifon* managed to stay clear of the reefs; ironically, her captain had disobeyed fleet orders by heading a half-point farther to the northeast.

Wagner organized the Real Eight Corporation to search for and recover the treasures of the 1715 fleet. A stupendous amount of precious metals was extracted from the shallow sands along the disaster zone over a period of twenty-five years of seasonal salvage activity, but only five of the shipwrecks were located, and their individual identities have never been positively determined due to inadequate archival documentation and artifact cataloging procedures.

The salvors nicknamed the wrecks, sometimes after the closest shore features. The 'Cabin Wreck' yielded the majority of silver coinage recovered from the vessels. Dug initially with a dragline from a temporary pier built out into the water, its timbers and other debris were scooped up, dumped on the beach, and combed with a metal detector. The site also yielded twenty cannons, located in 1966.

The amount of gold and silver artifacts on another site, the 'Gold Wreck', suggested that, despite lengthy Spanish salvage efforts in shallow water, little of the ship's cargo had been recovered, perhaps because it had been scattered over four submerged acres.

Only 3 m (10 ft) deep, and extensively salvaged by the Spaniards, the 'Wedge Wreck' was named after crudely cast silver wedges that originally fit together to form a pie-shaped assemblage which could have been concealed at the bottom of a barrel. 'Corrigan's Wreck' showed that the disabled vessels seem to have been pushed shoreward from a southeasterly direction, striking the shallow reefs and spilling the contents of their lower hulls, while their superstructures and upper decks piled up on the beach, and debris drifted northward with the prevailing current along the shore. A fifth site, 'Sandy Point Wreck', was found with clusters of cannons, the familiar silver and gold coinage and Mexican pottery, and a brass ship's bell.

Other wrecks in the vicinity were initially considered part of the 1715 fleet, but finds from the 'Green Cabin Wreck' suggest it is the lost *almiranta* of the 1618

Honduras fleet. The 'Rio Mar Wreck' contained precious artifacts, bullion and specie, but five cannons piled together with muzzles placed against breeches in an alternating pattern, along with fragments of manila line around the gun tubes, suggest that they were bound prior to being lost; thus the wreck could be that of the *Jesus María*, a salvage ship which rolled over in 1716 while loading materials from the sunken fleet.

Modern salvage of treasure from the 1715 fleet was at first exclusively conducted by Real Eight Corporation under a lease from the State of Florida, which retained 25 percent of the salvaged materials. Other treasure-hunters soon demanded similar permits, and an administrative program was established to supervise recovery operations. Nevertheless, although many of the finds were unique archaeological discoveries, the absence of their precise proveniences and their subsequent dispersal into private collections undermined the significance of the wrecksites from the start. The largest collection of materials, displayed in Real Eight's museum at Cape Canaveral, suffered from a massive burglary which caused the closing of the building. Some of the finds are now in the state's museum at Tallahassee.

Recently, the site of the 'Wedge Wreck', which was a large *urca* (storeship) belonging to Miguel de Lima, was opened to the public as Florida's first Underwater Archaeological Preserve. Also known as the *Nao de Refuerzo*, the flat-bottomed *Urca de Lima* had been reinforced for the Atlantic trade routes. Her double-planked hull grounded in shallow water near present-day Ft Pierce, and supplied survivors of other less fortunate ships with food and shelter until rescuers arrived from Havana. Today, her resting place can be recognized by heavy frames, planking and ballast that protrude from the sand. Concrete cannons have replaced those salvaged years ago, and a special underwater plaque marks her grave. By placing one of Florida's most famous shipwreck sites in the public's trust, it is hoped that the remains of the *Urca de Lima* will survive for future generations of visitors to witness a wrecked Spanish galleon on the sea bed.

The 1733 fleet. On 13 July 1733 the New Spain fleet left Havana on its return voyage to Spain. With the newly built *capitana*, *El Rubi Segundo*, the convoy consisted of three other armed galleons and eighteen merchant *naos* and smaller ships carrying the products of Mexico.

Next day, when the vessels sighted the Florida Keys, Captain-General Rodrigo de Torres sensed an approaching hurricane and ordered his captains to turn back to Havana. Already it was too late. By nightfall, most of the ships had been scattered 80 miles up and down the Florida Keys, sunk and swamped, their survivors gathered in small groups throughout the low islands. Only the 500-ton *Nuestra Señora de Rosario* returned safely to Havana.

Admiralty officials in Havana sent a sloop to search for wrecks, but before the sloop returned another vessel

The Wreck of the 'Concepción'

On the night of 31 October 1641 the 600-ton Spanish galleon, *La Concepción* – vice-flagship of a Europe-bound convoy laden with precious cargoes – struck reefs north of Hispaniola (Dominican Republic) and foundered. Of 532 souls on board, only 194 survived. The stern deposit was salvaged in 1687 by a Boston sea captain, but when wreck-hunter Burt Webber relocated the ship in 1978, he found silver coins, ingots and Chinese Ming porcelain.

14 (*right*) The wooden trunk belonging to a wealthy passenger contained silver tableware like these forks and spoons, plates and a candlestick, here set out as their owner might once have enjoyed them.

15 (*below*) A diver raises part of the coral overburden which helped preserve the *Concepción's* cargo for more than three centuries.

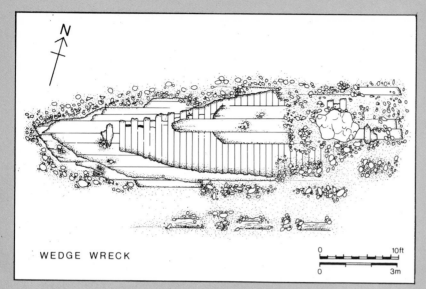

WEDGE WRECK

N

0 ——— 10ft
0 ——— 3m

The 1715 Fleet: A Florida Tragedy

16 (*left*) Plan of the remaining Wedge Wreck, so-called because of the silver wedges found at the site. This galleon was one of the vessels in the plate fleet that went down off the east coast of Florida in 1715. In 1987 the site was opened to the public as Florida's first Underwater Archaeological Preserve.

17 (*below left*) An eighteenth-century chart of eastern Florida indicates where the 1715 fleet was wrecked off the mouth of the St Sebastian River.

18 (*below*) Silver wedges and quoits of the type discovered on the Wedge Wreck. Crudely cast, the wedges were made to fit together in a pie-shaped assemblage which could be concealed as contraband at the bottom of a barrel.

19 (*bottom*) A steel-mounted cavalry-type pistol recovered from a 1715 fleet wreck.

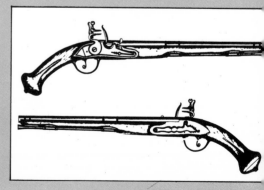

arrived in Havana and reported many large ships grounded near a place called 'Head of the Martyrs'. Nine salvage vessels loaded with supplies, food, soldiers, divers and salvage equipment immediately sailed for the scene of the disaster.

The Spaniards marked the location of each wreck on a map, and continued their salvage for years. Vessels that could not be refloated were burned to the waterline so that divers could descend into their cargo holds, and to conceal them from freebooters. A calculation of salvaged materials showed that more gold and silver was recovered than had been listed on the original manifests, a result of inevitable contraband.

In recent decades, most of the wrecks of the 1733 fleet have been relocated by modern salvors. None has been excavated or published in an archaeological manner. Thus, the historical and archaeological value of the wrecks, owing to their relatively intact deposition and stable environment, has suffered from repeated looting and destruction during attempts to find mostly non-existent treasure. In 1977, archaeologists from the State of Florida relocated eight of the wrecks to establish their potential for future research. They found a great deal of hull structure remaining. Since the fleet consisted of ships built in several different European nations, an archaeological comparison of contemporary building techniques among early eighteenth-century ship-yards of varying nationalities would add much to the history of naval architecture.

The first 1733 wreck discovered is believed to be that of General Torres' *capitana*, *El Rubí Segundo*. Found in the 1930s on an offshore reef by a fisherman, the site was shown to Arthur McKee, a local helmet diver. McKee brought up several badly sulfided coins, including a gold *escudo* dated 1721. From the Archive of the Indies he obtained copies of documents concerning the lost fleet and a photograph of an old chart depicting the locations of the salvaged wrecks, one of which was the site he had been investigating. For over a decade, McKee and his associates worked on the massive mound of ballast, timbers and debris in 10 m (33 ft) of water, recovering over twenty cannons of various sizes, more than 1,000 silver coins, statues and religious medals, small arms and edged weapons, jewelry, navigational instruments, ship's gear and galley wares. Realizing the historical importance of these items, McKee built in 1949, at Tavernier in the Florida Keys, the nation's first museum devoted to shipwreck materials. Publicity and the increased popu-larity of skin diving in Florida waters prompted McKee to apply to the state for a ten-year lease for much of the shallow water seaward of the Florida Keys, but he eventually learned that he could not rely on the protection of the state, since his site was beyond its jurisdiction. Consequently it has been and is continuing to be worked by every weekend wreck explorer who can find it.

The foreign-built galleon *Nuestra Señora de Balvaneda* (alias *El Infante*), purchased at Genoa in 1724, went aground in only 4 m (13 ft) of water, allowing most of her passengers to reach shore safely. The Spaniards salvaged her registered treasure of six million pesos, as well as a large portion of her general cargo, which included ceramic jars, jugs and plates. One of the first wrecks rediscovered as a result of McKee's map, she has been worked continuously by different salvors since 1955. Among reported finds are *Dos Mundos* pillar dollars, dating from 1732 and 1733. These silver coins were the first minted in the New World by a screw press; their unique milled edge was designed to discourage the shaving of metal from the coins. Chinese porcelain, jewelry, ivory fans and a silver helmet are among other finds mentioned in published accounts.

Another wreck, accidentally discovered in the early 1960s, was subsequently thought to be the *almiranta* of the fleet, *El Gallo Indiana* ('Cock of the Indies'), but its location corresponded more closely with that listed on the Spanish salvage chart for the 264⅔-ton, English-built merchantman *San Francisco de Asís*. Archaeological evidence is insufficient to clarify the wreck's identity since diagnostic cargoes have been removed, features of the site altered and no systematic excavation records kept.

The 220⅜-ton Genoese-built freighter *Nuestra Señora del Carmen, San Antonio de Padua y las Animas*, also called the *Chaves* after her owner, Antonio de Chaves, carried no registered treasure when she ran aground near 'el Cayo de Matecumbe el Viejo', now known as Upper Matecumbe Key. Extensively salvaged after the disaster, she was relocated in modern times by an aerial search and promptly picked apart by divers.

Commonly referred to by the name of her owner and captain, Luís de Herrera, a 242½-ton, English-built merchant *nao* was stranded near her consort *Chaves*. Listed as carrying 12,000 pesos in silver specie and bullion and 359 *marcos* in worked silver, most of which were probably salvaged by the Spaniards, the *Herrera* became known to modern salvors as the 'Figurine Wreck' after hundreds of small Mexican ceramic statuettes in fish, animal and human shapes. These unique objects have never been adequately recorded or interpreted; like other artifacts recovered in the last two decades from this fleet, most reside in private collections. Of other materials from this wrecksite, only a few are mentioned in print: ceramic bowls and jugs, numerous animal hides, Chinese porcelain, and at least one large anchor and cannon.

The shipwreck known as 'El Lerri' has never been identified, nor even proven to be from the New Spain fleet. Divers removed an anchor and several cannons as trophies, and began dismantling the large ballast mound in anticipation of finding valuable cargo, before moving on to more lucrative wrecksites.

Spanish documents stated that a 287¼-ton Dutch-built ship, *San Pedro*, was carrying 16,000 pesos in Mexican silver and numerous crates of Chinese porcelain when she was wrecked near an island known today as Indian Key. Her discovery in recent times was rewarded by thousands

The Quicksilver Wrecks

Mercury (quicksilver) was crucial in the extraction of silver from ore in the New World. In 1724 the Spanish Crown suffered a terrible loss: two great galleons, the *Tolosa* and *Guadalupe*, carrying enough mercury to supply the Mexican mines for a year, sank during a hurricane off the coast of Hispaniola.

20, 21   In addition to the main cargo of mercury, the *Guadalupe* and *Tolosa* were laden with expensive European-manufactured wares for the colonies, such as tableware (*left*), including superb crystal wine goblets (*below*). Hundreds of these drinking glasses survived intact, some coral encrusted but others virtually like new.

22   (*right*) A diver examines mercury from one of the cases low down in the hold of the wrecked *Tolosa*.

of silver coins in small denominations, dated 1731 to 1733. Few of the 1733 sites proved financially profitable to wreck hunters, since those in shallow water had been thoroughly salvaged by the Spaniards. Consequently, the *San Pedro* was dug repeatedly over a period of years by weekend treasure-seekers; remains of her timbers and ballast today lie strewn across the seabed, mixed with modern litter and discarded digging tools. Flat red bricks mark the remains of her galley stove.

A shipwreck most likely matching the location of a 1733 vessel named *El Sueco de Arizón* ('The Swedish ship belonging to Arizón'), found in 3 m (10 ft) of water on the edge of one of the smaller cays, reportedly yielded Mexican four- and eight-*reales* silver cobs dated 1720 to 1733, and newly minted pillar dollars.

Another foreign-built ship, the 212⅜-ton *Nuestra Señora de Belén y San Juan Bautista*, stranded inshore of the reefs with her decks awash, was salvaged of all valuable goods soon after the disaster. Her wreck, lying 6 m (20 ft) deep, was relocated in the 1960s by aerial reconnaissance. Little is known of the recoveries that ensued, but a large conglomerate of sand-cast silver ingots, apparently poured from clipped edges of cob coins, was probably contraband, since the ship had no treasure listed on her manifest.

Remains of the *San José de las Animas*, an English-built ship of 326½ tons, laden with over 30,000 pesos in silver bullion and specie and an assortment of export luxury cargo, were discovered with a magnetometer in 1968 by Tom Gurr. Mendel Peterson, and George Fischer of the National Park Service, joined the initial salvage operations to plot wreckage and evaluate artifacts. In less than a month, salvors had recovered thousands of coins, thirty-three gold rings, hundreds of rosary beads, assorted fine jewelry, eighteen large silver chargers, brass candlesticks, pewter tablewares, porcelain, pistols and swords, and an enormous collection of pottery unparalleled on any other 1733 wreck. Twenty-three cannons were scattered over the site. Relatively free of shipworm infestation, the massive timbers of *San José*'s lower hull were partially mapped by photography. Some 200 m (650 ft) from the main ballast pile, salvors located the ship's 8-m-high (26-ft) rudder assembly, lined with lead and still fastened with pintles. Four additional cannons were encountered under the rudder.

Despite years of salvage, and initial archaeological consultation and supervision by Florida officials, scholarly data generated from this well-preserved galleon site were minimal. Recent video recordings of her timbers may provide much-needed comparative information on ship construction during the decline of Spain's great fleet organization.

Another English-built ship of the 1733 fleet, *Nuestra Señora de las Angustias y San Rafael*, nicknamed '*El Charanguero Grande*' (the Great Coastal Trader), long eluded modern salvors who incorrectly believed that she

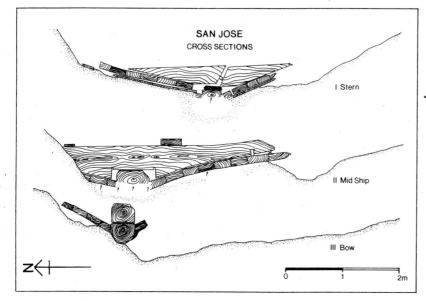

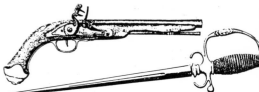

The 'San José': Disaster of 1733

23, 26 Cross-sections (*left*) taken at three different points of the remaining *San José* hull timbers (*below*). This is one of the few published plans of a wreck from the plate fleet destroyed by a hurricane off the Florida Keys.

24, 25 (*above*) Reconstruction of an English-made flintlock pistol from the *San José*, and a gentleman's short sword from another 1733 wreck.

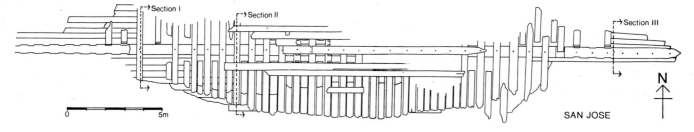

had been refloated and towed back to Havana. Research in the Spanish archives by historian Jack Haskins, however, turned up a poem written by a survivor of the *Angustias* that refers to her keel being broken, suggesting that the ship could not have been saved. Subsequently, Haskins and Dick MacAllister obtained an exploration permit from the State of Florida in 1972. Using six Spanish charts of the area, and a magnetometer, they discovered *Angustias*' ballast mound, with three anchors and two cannons resting on top, under 1.2 m (4 ft) of murky water. Test trenches dug at the bow, amidships and stern of the wrecksite produced rosary beads, pottery sherds and a gold two-*escudo* coin dating between 1724 and 1727, but wooden remains were almost nonexistent. After receipt of a salvage permit, the wrecksite was excavated under close supervision of state field agents, who mapped and recorded the finds, mostly religious objects such as crucifixes and reliquaries, but including a jade Buddha figurine and a rare gold four-*escudo* 'Royal' coin, minted as a proof for the King of Spain.

The 1733 fleet would have been a major financial disaster for the Spanish Crown had not salvors recouped much of the loss. The same wrecks represented a modern experiment in private enterprise under the administration of state supervision. Although archaeological priorities were secondary, and many of the artifacts ultimately found their way into private hands, archival research and field records have given us new perspectives on a composite fleet of vessels employed in the eighteenth-century maritime lifeline between Spain and the Americas.

The Quicksilver Transports

In spring 1724 two galleons sailed from Cádiz, bound for Veracruz via Havana on a royal mission. They carried 400 tons of mercury, enough to supply the mines of Mexico for a full year. Used in the amalgamation of silver, mercury had long been a Crown monopoly. It was mixed with salt and added to the mined silver ore, from which it absorbed most of the metal after approximately eight days. The resulting amalgamation was washed, collected in linen sacks, separated and heated, causing the mercury to vaporize from the cleaned silver. Mercury was borne across the Atlantic in specially strengthened galleons called *azogues*.

Nuestra Señora de Guadalupe was an enormous galleon of 1,000 tons and 74 guns, constructed in 1702 in the colonial shipyards of Campeche in the Gulf of Mexico. Two specially designed cargo holds held 250 tons of the heavy liquid metal packed in small boxes on shelves low down in the interior of the ship. Flagship for the voyage from Cádiz, *Guadalupe* also carried iron fittings and wooden rigging hardware for the construction of another galleon in Havana.

The 1,500-ton *Conde de Tolosa* had been built in honor of the Count of Tolosa, illegitimate son of Louis XIV. Although larger, the *Tolosa* was of lighter construction, not specifically built for the transport of mercury. She carried only 150 tons of the heavy metal in her holds. In addition, the two ships were laden with European merchandise bound for sale in the colonies.

Heading for Havana, the armed galleons were struck by a hurricane on the night of 24 August 1724 off Samaná Bay on the northeast coast of Hispaniola. *Guadalupe* was driven into the bay, where she landed upright on a shoal. Throughout the two-day storm the ship held together, allowing 550 of her 650 passengers to reach shore, where many soon succumbed to hunger and exhaustion. Several hundred set out for Santo Domingo, a 200-mile march along the coast; others reached Cap-Haïtien, 240 miles to the west, in *Guadalupe*'s lifeboat.

Separated from her consort, *Tolosa* managed to anchor in the mouth of the bay and ride out the first night. At dawn, however, she was swept into the bay, where she broke up on a coral reef. Fewer than 40 of more than 600 people on board survived. Eight men scrambled onto the mainmast, which was still upright. When Spanish salvage crews from Santo Domingo arrived 32 days later, one of the survivors had perished from exposure, and another had gone mad from the sun.

The salvors found *Guadalupe* intact, listing slightly, but the heavy shipment of iron ship fittings prevented divers from recovering the mercury stored in her lower hold. *Tolosa* was found totally submerged in deeper water, which was infested with sharks attracted by corpses trapped in the wreckage. Again, divers were unable to recover the valuable cargo of mercury, and the galleons were abandoned.

In 1976 the Dominican government assumed control of a shipwreck site in Samaná Bay from which divers were reported selling artifacts to collectors. Dominican Navy divers soon recovered numerous cannons, olive jars, religious objects and fine crystalwares. The Museo de las Casas Reales examined more than 400 Spanish coins minted during the reign of Philip V, and dated the wreck to between 1700 and 1746. Additional research identified the site as that of the *Guadalupe*.

To recover the remainder of the cargo, the government contracted an American firm, Caribe Salvage, and created a Commission for Underwater Salvage to oversee the operation. *Guadalupe*'s remains, marked by potsherds, were mostly buried under sand in 7 m (23 ft) of water. Excavation uncovered the bow section of the ship, where hundreds of olive jars had been stored. Massive deck beams and frames from the sides of the vessel were found in the area of one of the ship's cargo holds. Wooden crates of iron nails and other fittings, part of the consignment for the Havana shipyards, again blocked access to the mercury in the lower hold. Despite this, divers were able to recover one of the largest collections of European luxury materials to come from a shipwreck in the New World. Aside from precious metals, jewelry and religious artifacts, there were fine pewter and silver tablewares, brass lanterns, a London-made clock, scissors, quill pens — everything one would find in a fashionable household of

Treasures of the Plate Fleets

27 (*far left*) One of the gravest disasters to befall Spain's colonial empire was the destruction of a treasure fleet by a hurricane off Florida's east coast in 1715. Gold bullion, doubloons and chains from the wrecks are displayed in the Museum of Florida History.

28 (*left*) This delicate Chinese porcelain case-bottle was en route from Manila to Spain via the Isthmus of Panama when it was lost aboard the *San José* off the Florida Keys in a 1733 hurricane. Despite the violence of the storm and centuries under the seabed, the contents of the bottle were still protected by its threaded pewter cap.

the period, including bottles of wine, some still corked. In the stern of the wreckage were more than 400 intact crystal drinking glasses; crystal decanters were still wrapped in fabric. Bronze swivel guns, muskets, cutlasses, sword handles and shields are thought to have been in use and also part of the cargo. Fifty iron cannons were counted around the periphery of the wreckage; the other twenty-four were lost in the hurricane.

Relocated with a magnetometer, the wreck of the *Tolosa* lay on the edge of a reef in 9 to 15 m (30 to 50 ft) of water; seventeen cannons and part of an anchor fluke were recognizable, but the remainder of the site was covered with encrustation. The vessel's bow section still contained boatswain's stores: pulley blocks, cables, a barrel of iron nails and other small fittings. Jars of black pitch for caulking lay nearby.

Tolosa's cargo of mercury, highly subject to corrosion in the atmosphere, had been poured into sheepskin bags, then sealed in small wooden casks. Each cask held half a *quintal* (hundredweight) of the liquid metal; three such casks were packed into a wooden box padded with thick grass matting. Each box thus held 1½ *quintals* of quicksilver (about a gallon and a half) and was painted on top with the royal arms of the Crown. The boxes had been stacked four deep in the lower hold.

Although *Tolosa* had suffered more damage than *Guadalupe*, her keel and lead-sheathed rudder were found intact, as well as part of her tiller assembly. A sheet anchor, over 4 m (13 ft) in length, was discovered in her hold. Divers in deeper water found a small grapnel that had been deployed in a vain attempt to save the ship. Had the larger anchor been dropped, *Tolosa* might have survived. Thirty-three of the ship's seventy cannons were counted in and around the wreck; a chest of fused hand grenades turned up in the stern. Under one of the iron guns, a patch of discolored sand disclosed the remains of

one of *Tolosa*'s sailors: bones, three bronze buttons and a buckle. Fragments of a pistol lay near the victim's right hand, and the wooden heels of his boots nearby.

Tolosa contained more artifacts than the *Guadalupe*, since she rested in deeper water and had not been previously pirated. These included the ship's bronze bell, cast in Amsterdam in 1710; additional crystalware; and passengers' possessions, including a gold medallion with the cross of the Order of Santiago, framed by twenty-four diamonds.

The unique discovery of two armed *azogues* has provided rare collections from vessels in-bound from Europe rather than out-bound from the Americas, giving us an unparalleled picture of Old World products sought by Spanish colonists.

Portuguese Shipping

After the accidental discovery of Brazil by Pedro Alvares Cabral in 1500, 'the Land of the True Cross' became a Portuguese possession, since it lay to the east of an imaginary line drawn 370 leagues west of the Cape Verde Islands by the Treaty of Tordesillas in 1494. Second in priority to India and Asia, Brazil remained a stepchild of Portugal until late in the sixteenth century, when Philip II of Spain inherited the Lusitanian throne. Its value in the first twenty to thirty years as an overseas colony was primarily for the export of brazilwood, and occasional monkeys and parrots bartered from natives. Traders coasted Brazil's shores in caravels and *naos* of 100 and 150 tons, and small but heavily-built carracks were sometimes employed in the early sixteenth-century trade; all were smaller than ships of the India fleets, to whose construction and arms greater capital resources were directed, but the swifter caravels at least could complete two round-trip voyages a year in the South Atlantic trade.

Frenchmen from Normandy and Rouen also frequented the Brazilian coast for dyewood, which was cut and prepared for shipment by Indian and African slaves. Spanish expansion in South America also threatened Portugal's virgin possession during the first decades of the sixteenth century. Ultimately, in the 1520s, Joaõ III was moved to formally colonize the wild coast. A French Huguenot base at Rio de Janeiro was expelled in the 1560s, and Brazil gradually began to produce sugar, tobacco, cotton and cacao for the mother country.

Like Spain, Portugal attempted to monopolize her American trade, but never managed to achieve absolute control. Illegal contraband increased, even after royal governors had been appointed. Initially friendly with the Portuguese, the English government considered Brazil a fair field for attack from 1580 to 1640, when Spain controlled her Iberian neighbor. Similarly, the Dutch West India Company, created chiefly to attack Brazil, began to send armed fleets into the Americas; one seized the major port of São Salvador de Bahia in 1624.

Finally forced to introduce a convoy system to protect her shipping from pirates, the Brazil Company in 1649 promised a fleet of thirty-six warships in two squadrons to escort merchantmen between Portugal and Brazil. In return, the Company was to receive a monopoly on the transport of the four most essential products in demand by the colony: wine, flour, olive oil and codfish. Two decades later, the Portuguese Crown incorporated the Brazil Company, or Companhia Geral do Comércio do Brasil, for the purpose of providing armed convoys for the annual Brazil fleet, to be paid for by *averia* and other taxes. Often numbering over 100 sail – more vessels than in contemporary Spanish convoys – the Portuguese fleet system resulted in the building of better and larger ships on both sides of the Atlantic for South American trade. Shipyards were established in the seventeenth century at Bahia, Rio de Janeiro and Belém do Pará. Vessels constructed in the colony often cost twice as much as at home, since requirements for labor on the sugar plantations caused a shortage of manpower elsewhere, but ships built of Brazilian hardwoods, being more impervious to shipworms, were considered superior even to those of Indian teak.

The passage from Lisbon to Bahia took an average of two to three months; a late departure sometimes caused the ships to be becalmed along the equator. A royal decree of 1690 ordered that annual fleets depart from Portugal between 15 December and 20 January, and begin their

Last Hours of the 'Sacramento'

29–31 Flagship of a convoy of fifty Portuguese ships bound for Bahia (São Salvador), Brazil in 1668, the *Sacramento* struck a shoal at Bahia's harbor entrance during a storm on the afternoon of 5 May. In worsening weather she was blown into deeper water and finally sank just before midnight. Brazilian excavations (site plan *below*) begun in 1976 have yielded forty-two cannons of English, Dutch and Portuguese manufacture, and many other items carried on the ship.

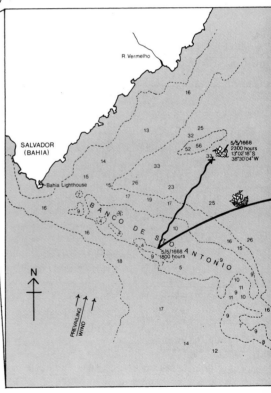

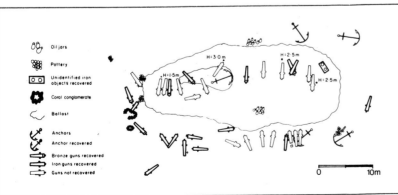

return voyages between the end of May and 20 July, but these schedules were seldom met.

Eighteenth-century fleets were divided into three separate convoys, sailing from Lisbon to Bahia, Rio de Janeiro and Pernambuco. Each returned to Portugal with gold, sugar, tobacco, hides and lumber. Although the Rio fleet transported more gold than the other two, each fleet was escorted by from one to four warships which actually carried the gold.

Portuguese galleons. The 60-gun galleon *Santíssimo Sacramento* began her last voyage from Portugal to Brazil as *capitania* of an armed escort provided by the Companhia Geral do Comércio do Brasil for the annual Atlantic fleet. Commanded by General Francisco Correa da Silva, the 1668 convoy of fifty ships was of great economic importance to Portugal and her overseas colony. In the conflict with the Netherlands over possession of the Brazilian coast, Portugal's ultimate supremacy in Brazil depended on the security of her maritime commerce in sugar and gold.

Bound from Lisbon to Bahia (São Salvador), the armada was laden with European manufactured goods, including arms and ammunition, and foodstuffs for colonial consumption. On the *Sacramento* were 200 civilians, including clergymen and civil servants, and 800 sailors and soldiers.

Late on the afternoon of 5 May the entrance to Bahia's Bay of All Saints was sighted. In spite of storms accompanying the growing darkness, *Sacramento's* pilot decided to attempt the tricky entrance to the bay. A shoal blocking the eastern edge of the channel caught the galleon and held her fast. No captain would leave port in the tempest to assist the stranded vessel. Shortly before midnight *Sacramento* was blown into deeper water, where she foundered and sank. There were but seventy survivors.

In the mid-1970s, several large cannons in a Salvador salvage yard came to the attention of Brazilian naval officers. The unique guns were seized as national treasures, and ultimately traced to an offshore shipwreck. Dates and founder's marks on the cannons indicated that the ship had sunk sometime after 1653, and that her owner was the Brazil Company. Thus began in 1976 a joint archaeological investigation by the Ministry of the Navy and the Ministry of Education and Culture, supervised by Professor Ulysses Pernambuco de Mello.

Cannons, anchors, olive jars and encrusted porcelain were found scattered around granite ballast blocks on a gravel bottom 31 to 33 m (102 to 108 ft) deep. After a detailed survey, the site was divided into grids for excavation. Brass artillery of English, Dutch and Portuguese origin bore dates from the last decade of the sixteenth century to the mid-seventeenth century; many bore the words '*Companhia G¹ do Brasil*'. Portuguese silver coins, mostly from the reign of Dom João IV (1650–1656), had been over-stamped to raise their value in

an attempt to stop the drain of silver, which was badly needed for Portugal's struggle against Spain. Authorization for over-stamping by 25 percent had been given in 1663, providing a more accurate *terminus post quem* for the shipwreck. Positive identification of the site as that of the *Santíssimo Sacramento* was established by several pieces of Portuguese majolica ceramics bearing the coat-of-arms of the da Silva family.

Although a warship, the *Sacramento* had been authorized by the Brazil Company to carry cargo not exceeding one-third of her capacity. Hundreds of brass sewing thimbles, as well as a shipment of wooden-handled razors, may represent this cargo. Evidence of a shipment of textiles was provided by lead baling seals of two varieties. Official Portuguese seals carried the royal arms on one side, the fiscal department's emblem on the other, whereas merchant seals carried the initials of private businessmen; seals from the city of London suggested that English textiles were carried on the galleon as well. Fragments of green case bottles with pewter caps may have constituted part of her lading, along with lead images of Christ, packed without wooden crucifixes. Thousands of lead musket balls, comprising most of the ship's cargo, were packed in olive jars, more normally used for liquids and condiments.

The unlucky pilot's equipment also appeared: two brass astrolabes, brass rules and dividers, and sounding leads of various sizes. Other ship-related objects consisted of ceramic tablewares with the Brazil Company emblem, and pewter candlesticks, bowls and plates.

Forty-two cannons on the site were of various origins. The oldest were of English manufacture: two brass culverines from the middle of the sixteenth century and two demi-cannons inscribed by their founders, John and Richard Phillips, dated respectively 1590 and 1596. Two additional brass quarter-cannons bore the inscription: GEORGE:ELKINE:MADE:THIS:PEECE:1597. All the English guns were inscribed with the Brazil Company's logo. Others were Dutch, including three brass falconets of 1646 from the town of Campen, and a demi-cannon of 1649 from the Hague. Most of the Portuguese cannons had been cast by founder Matias Escartim.

Nearly half the ordnance aboard *Sacramento* was of cast iron; bronze artillery was probably mounted from available foreign pieces, since Portugal suffered from a shortage of weaponry following her independence from Spain in 1640. Examined by military historian John Guilmartin, the early bronze guns displayed manufacturing characteristics much more complicated and labor intensive than previously known. Their presence on a ship of the mid-seventeenth century reflected the longevity of bronze artillery at sea, suggesting that the best bronze cannons of the sixteenth century were still effective and useful weapons almost a century later. The earlier foundry practices that produced fine cast bronze cannons may not have been retained in the inflationary price and wage spirals of the seventeenth century.

CHAPTER SIX

The Thirteen Colonies: English Settlers and Seafarers

J. Richard Steffy

John Cabot, an Italian sailing under the English flag, explored the North American coast from Labrador to the southern end of the Chesapeake Bay in 1497. Thus began the organized campaigns for New World expansion by three competing European maritime powers: England, France and The Netherlands. Cabot (or Giovanni Caboto) was followed by another Italian in 1524, Giovanni da Verrazano, who carried the French flag northward from South Carolina and sailed through the narrows into what is now New York harbor. The Dutch entered the scene in 1609 through the efforts of an Englishman, Henry Hudson, who explored the length of the river that now bears his name, as well as large sections of Canada. A year before, the Chesapeake Bay and the coast from Virginia to Florida had been investigated by John Smith, a remarkable English adventurer who accompanied settlers to Jamestown in 1607; this time an explorer was flying the flag of his own country.

There were others of course, but the aforenamed men reported most accurately the potential of the great new continent. Rocky and hilly in the north, flat and sandy in the south, the vast and undeveloped coast was blessed with most of the attributes that make colonization desirable. Timber, stone, game and fertile soil were plentiful. Climate was varied but tolerable; abundant rainfall provided irrigation, power and nourishment.

But it was not so much what was on the land that promised certain development and expansion – it was the coast itself. Thousands of miles of shoreline wrapped itself around hundreds of sheltered bays and natural harbors. Long, navigable rivers provided easy access to the interior, while much of the coastline was protected by barrier reefs and inshore islands to form intracoastal waterways. The only problem was that all this lay thousands of difficult miles from Europe.

The First Settlements

Colonization followed exploration in a faltering, scattered fashion. England's first efforts toward colonial permanence came in 1585 when Sir Walter Raleigh unsuccessfully attempted to establish a colony at Roanoke Island, in what is now the state of North Carolina. Success followed in 1607 with the settlement at Jamestown, Virginia, which, after severe hardship and uncertain existence, survived and eventually prospered.

In 1610, only one year after Henry Hudson discovered the Hudson River, the Dutch established a post for trading furs with the Indians on what is now Manhattan Island. The colony of New Netherlands was officially started with thirty families in 1624, and New Netherlands was documented as extending from New Amsterdam (Manhattan) to Fort Orange (Albany). Early French attempts at colonization in the south had failed by this time; their efforts were now concentrated in the region around the St Lawrence River. The English quickly expanded their territory up and down the coast, although some of their new communities were immediate failures. Among the more successful were Plymouth in 1620; to the north on Massachusetts Bay where eleven ships landed 1,000 Puritans in 1630, followed by thousands more in the next decade; Lord Baltimore's establishment of Maryland in 1634; the Connecticut area in 1633; and Rhode Island in 1636.

The Dutch surrendered all of New Amsterdam to the British in 1664, who soon named their prize New York. Additional English colonies in North Carolina (about 1653), New Jersey (1664), South Carolina (1670), William Penn's Quaker colony on the Delaware (1681) and Georgia (1733) completed the extent of colonization. In a little more than a century, England had established thirteen colonies – eleven by settlement and two by conquest – and dominated a coastline extending from Maine to Georgia. An English population of less than 5,000 in 1630 had swelled to more than a quarter-million by 1700. And ships were the dominant factor in all of this. They served as the umbilical cord to the motherland, and spun the web that converted isolated settlements into a teeming colonial empire.

The Settlers' Ships

At least one small remnant of seventeenth-century Dutch maritime activity survives in New York City. Late in

1613, Captain Adriaen Block loaded his ship, the *Tyjger* (Tiger), for the return voyage to Holland. Block, apparently an adventurous opportunist, was preparing to complete his fourth voyage to New Amsterdam since 1611. Although the exact dimensions of the *Tyjger* are unknown, she is estimated to have been at least 75 ft (22.9 m) long and capable of carrying in excess of 100 tons of cargo. On her deck were six large cannons. The vessel accidentally burned before embarking, forcing Block and his crew to spend the winter in the New World. Surviving with the help of friendly Indians, they constructed a smaller ship which they named *Onrust* (Restless) and launched the following spring. Block used it to explore Long Island Sound and part of the New England coast before returning to his homeland.

In 1916, while the Interborough Rapid Transit was digging subway tunnels near the southern end of Manhattan Island, the badly charred timbers of the lower bow of a ship were uncovered. A photograph taken shortly thereafter reveals part of a stem scarfed to a keel, several lower planks, frames and a keelson. The oaken timbers were surrounded by a bed of charcoal and a few artifacts, including a Dutch broad-headed axe, trade beads, clay pipes, chain, a cannon ball and blue and white pottery sherds. An 8-ft 6-in (2.6-m) long section of the bow timbers was removed; it is presently housed in the Museum of the City of New York. The disposition of the artifacts is unknown.

Metallurgical studies, carbon dating of the wood, and the arrangement of the bow structure all point to an early seventeenth-century date. The location of the discovery probably coincides with the original shoreline, since the island was extended by landfills more than two centuries ago. Historical records do not list any other ship fires in the early decades of the seventeenth century, strengthening the probability that these were the remains of the *Tyjger*.

Since much of the submerged area of the ship would not have burned, some historians believe that 50 ft (15.2 m) or more of the hull's bottom must have survived. The location of the unexcavated remains were charted in 1916 but were not excavated. Over the years, proposals to raise the ship beneath Globe Square were considered but not implemented. In 1968 the area again was excavated, this time for the erection of the World Trade Center. Attempts to locate the rest of the hull resulted only in the discovery of two unassociated anchors. What happened to the rest of the hull, if indeed much more survived, is a mystery now covered by one of the world's most gigantic buildings.

Rapid colonization required that many ships make the long and dangerous Atlantic crossing, not only to bring settlers and supplies but also to transport merchandise in both directions. For the most part the vessels were rather small and unimpressive, but large vessels were built for other duties. England's *Mary Rose* and Sweden's *Wasa* are extant examples of early European maritime giants. The *Mary Rose*, built in 1511 and sunk off Portsmouth in 1545, carried 91 ship's guns and 200 troops. The 1,400 ton *Wasa* sank in Stockholm harbor during her maiden voyage in 1628. In recent years both ships have been raised, partially restored and displayed along with their thousands of artifacts in shoreside museums nearby. Although such ships were impractical for exploration and colonization because they cost too much to operate and were too large for navigating uncharted bays and rivers, their size and complexity reveal the state of the art in shipbuilding and navigation of the period. Naval architecture, still a young science, was blessed with purists who insisted on its orderly development, while seafarers and influential laymen contributed information and support to the field. Naval architects and shipbuilders were one and the same; designers constructed at least some of their own creations, and thereby had a practical understanding of the correlation between planning and production. Before the mid-point of the sixteenth century, King Henry VIII of England encouraged improvements in the design and construction of the Crown's vessels. But it was his daughter, Queen Elizabeth I, who later in that century fostered the atmosphere which permitted a marked improvement in ship construction and navigation, and which eventually nurtured the expansion of the empire. Matthew Baker, one of her master shipwrights, is believed to have produced, about 1585, some of the earliest

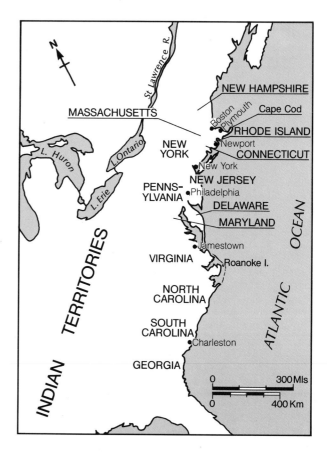

English-language manuscripts on the design and construction of seagoing ships. Her colorful admiral, Sir Walter Raleigh, took it upon himself to criticize existing vessels and make suggestions for their improvement. So did another of her famous admirals, Sir John Hawkins, who is credited with pioneering the lower-profiled (and hence more stable) warships which enhanced England's status as a dominant sea power. Contributions by Raleigh, Hawkins, Sir Francis Drake and other influential seamen were to have a marked effect on English shipbuilding for the next century or so.

A fair amount of geometry went into the design of a proper seagoing craft by the seventeenth century, and drawings were already beginning to resemble twentieth-century architect's lines drawings. Plans were made on smooth boards or parchment, usually to some sort of scale, and frequently the drawings were artistic in style. Some were artfully done in watercolor with fish superimposed over them, or elaborate designs were set into unused corners and borders.

Essentially, new ship designs were the result of combining mathematical ratios and geometric projections with experience and common sense. The shape of a ship's midsection, and often other sectional shapes as well, was derived from the sum of a series of arcs whose radii were established by the intersection of projections based on ratios relating to principal hull dimensions. Large

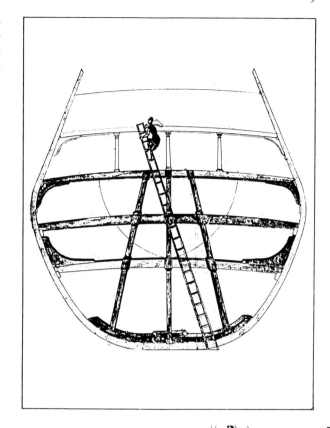

The Early Settlers

1 (*left*) The original thirteen English colonies. Permanent boundaries were not established until the eighteenth century.

2 (*above right*) A draft of the midship section of an Elizabethan ship, showing some of the construction and a cross-sectional shape further aft. The ladder describes the radius of one of the arcs of the section.

3 (*below*) R. Leeman's engraving of seventeenth-century shipyard activities.

4 Naval architect and historian William Avery Baker's replica *Mayflower II*, at Plimouth Plantation. Probably representative of many of the early settlement ships, she measures 106 ft 5 in (32.5 m) from beak to stern. The original *Mayflower* carried 102 pilgrims across the Atlantic in 1620.

compasses, curves and straight edges were employed to determine the curved shapes of the bow; keel length, hull breadth and depth, and the rake of the sternpost were all based on carefully derived mathematical proportions.

Undoubtedly there was a gap between theoretical designs and practical applications, but nevertheless there was a scientific process involved in the construction of seventeenth-century vessels. The more progressive shipyards probably made the most use of such drawings, while smaller yards employed more limited and perhaps, for them, more practical methods of deriving hull shapes. Whether by formal graphic design, the use of simpler body molds, or the copying of hull shapes from a previously constructed vessel, the skeletal structure of each new hull was cut and assembled by a controlled method. Shipwrightery was far more complex and scientific than many historians are willing to concede.

Ship sizes were usually designated by tonnage; dimensions, such as length, breadth and depth as general descriptive terms, were more a concern of later periods. The tonnage of a vessel in seventeenth-century England automatically indicated the hull's approximate dimensions. Tonnage designations, as applied to modern ships, probably originated in the thirteenth century when one of the predominant ship cargoes was wine carried in large casks, called tuns. At that time a ship's capacity was judged by the number of tuns of wine it could carry. In the fifteenth century, English standards set the tun, which held about 250 gallons of wine, at a volume of 57 cubic feet (1.61 cu. m) and a weight of 2,240 pounds (1016 kg). By the time the first settlers reached American shores, wine was no longer a primary cargo. Tun had changed to ton and, although its weight remained the same, the volume of hold space allotted for it was increased to 100 cubic feet (2.8 cu. m) to allow for the lower average cargo weight being carried. In other words, tonnage, or tons burden, was a volume designation and was not directly related to the weight or displacement of the vessel or its cargo. Tonnage ratings were also used to levy port taxes and duties on cargo entering and leaving the ports. Rather than undertake the complicated procedure of measuring hold volumes, ship's tonnages were calculated by simple formulas which were considered fair and generally applicable to all vessels. For most of the seventeenth century, the English formula was:

$$\text{keel length} \times \text{breadth of hull} \times \text{depth of hold}\,/100$$
$$= \text{tons burden}.$$

In 1694 the average volume ton was judged to occupy 94 cubic feet (2.66 cu. m), and so the denominator of the above formula was changed to 94.

Most ship records in the American colonial period indicate only tonnage, but the tonnage formulas and knowledge of contemporary hull designs can be combined to provide approximate hull dimensions. A 20-tonner was a very small vessel, usually 35 to 40 ft (10.7 to 12.2 m) long on deck if a seagoing vessel. Two to four hundred-tonners were the colonial equivalents of our modern ocean freighters. But there were giants, too; Dutch East Indiamen were rated as high as 1,200 tons in the seventeenth century.

The majority of colonial ships were solidly built of white oak, fastened with a combination of wood and iron as experience dictated, and decked in pine or spruce. Naval architect and historian William Avery Baker, who spent much of his adult life researching colonial vessels, has provided us with several excellent reconstructions of ships of the period. His most famous, *Mayflower II*, is probably representative of many of the early settlement ships. Governor Bradford's journal indicated that the original *Mayflower* had a burden of 'nine score tons', and from this Baker calculated a keel length of 58 ft (17.7 m), a hull length of about 90 ft (27.4 m), breadth of 25 ft (7.6 m), and a depth of 12.5 ft (3.8 m). From the extreme tip of her beak to the after end of the stern, the replica spans 106 ft 5 in (32.5 m). It carries six sails on three masts and a bowsprit. The original was probably considered a fairly large vessel; some colonists made the trip in smaller – much smaller – ships than this.

The *Mayflower* brought 102 pilgrims across the Atlantic alone, but that was only because her accompanying vessel, the smaller *Speedwell*, was found unfit and had to be abandoned at Plymouth, England. It was considered wiser to undertake such ventures in two or more vessels to better assure the safety of the passengers (or was it the investment of the charterers?) in the event one of the ships became badly damaged. Probably a typical fleet was the one which carried the original settlers to Jamestown in 1607. It consisted of three ships – the 100-ton *Susan Constant,* the 40-ton *Godspeed* and the 20-ton *Discovery*. Replicas of these vessels were completed recently at Jamestown, and all are smaller than the *Mayflower*. The pinnace *Discovery,* for example, has a length of only 37 ft (11.3 m) on deck.

The 'Sea Venture'. Nautical archaeology has provided us with firsthand information about one early colonial vessel, the *Sea Venture,* or *Sea Adventure* as it is listed in some contemporary documents. This shipwreck was not found along the eastern coast of the United States, but in nearby Bermuda. Its history, however, typifies the problems of colonization.

On 7 June 1609, seven ships and two pinnaces left Plymouth, England, for the new colony at Jamestown, Virginia. They carried 600 settlers, the third such group to embark for Virginia in two years. One of the pinnaces, the *Virginia,* served as consort vessel to the flagship *Sea Venture*. The *Sea Venture* was commanded by Christopher Newport; Sir Thomas Gates, Lieutenant-Governor of the colony under Lord De La Warr and Sir George Somers, Admiral of the fleet, also sailed aboard her. One would suspect that this flagship was the finest, if not the largest, of the seven ships. Six weeks later the fleet ran into the tail of an Atlantic hurricane and *Sea Venture* was separated from her companions. Then began an ordeal which inspired Shakespeare to write *The Tempest*. For four days the ship was buffeted by storms and driven toward Bermuda's treacherous shores. Seams opened and she was leaking badly. With the crew pumping continuously and the ship barely afloat, she became lodged in a reef off the northern tip of the island. There she remained, permitting all 150 persons aboard to reach shore safely.

When all were settled on the island, *Sea Venture*'s longboat was fitted out for sea and, with a crew of eight, set sail for Jamestown to seek rescue of the survivors. The voyagers were never heard from again, nor did help arrive from Virginia. During the months of waiting, whatever could be salvaged from the *Sea Venture* was brought ashore, including timber, pitch, rope and oil. These materials, along with some rather poor cedar found on the island, were used to build a pinnace. Beams and bow planking were made from oak salvaged from the ship, the rest of the hull being fashioned from native cedar. On 30 March 1610, the little vessel was launched as the *Deliverance*. Her keel was 40 ft (12.2 m) long, and her breadth was 19 ft (5.8 m). Late in 1609, a second pinnace had been started, because it was apparent that help would not arrive from Virginia and the *Deliverance* could not carry everyone from the island. This smaller vessel was launched a month later and named *Patience*. On 23 May 1610, after a delay of nine months, the survivors reached Jamestown aboard the Bermuda-built pinnaces.

In 1958, the remains of the *Sea Venture* were discovered between two reefs in about 30 ft (9 m) of water. After preliminary studies and some dispute about the identity and date of the wreck, it remained untouched for two decades. In 1978 the Bermuda Maritime Museum Association launched a full-scale excavation under the direction of Allan J. Wingood, who established positive identification of the wreck.

Dimensions of the *Sea Venture* are not specifically recorded; the only indication of size is one listing her as being 'of 300 tunnes'. Tonnage designations of the period can be fickle but, if based on the 100 cubic foot formula, this one would indicate that the *Sea Venture* was appreciably larger than the *Mayflower*. This may indeed be the case because 52 ft (15.5 m) of keel survive, and Wingood presents evidence in the form of keel bolts and worm casts which suggest an original length as great as 75 ft (22.9 m). There are eighteen floor timbers (parts of the frames [ribs] which crossed the keel) placed at average intervals of 2 ft (61 cm). They were approximately 1 ft (31 cm) square in section and were fastened to the keel with long iron bolts. Layers of inner and outer planking survived, all of it made from oak. The outer skin of planking had its seams caulked with oakum to prevent leakage.

Only one gun has been found by the archaeologists, although others are known to have been salvaged by early Bermudians between 1619 and 1622. The cannon was found to be in a 'stored' condition, with a tompion in the end of its barrel. When the tompion was removed, a cannon ball 3 in (7.6 cm) in diameter rolled out. In all, seventy-seven cannon shot representing four types of guns had been excavated at last report. The weight of the shot ranged from 1½ to 12½ pounds (0.7 to 5.7 kg). Thousands of shot for small arms and gunnery accessories were recovered. Various types of ceramics and cooking pots were excavated, some examples matching those found in the excavations around Jamestown. The pottery was predominantly plain material produced in the sixteenth and seventeenth centuries in Devon. Among the more interesting foreign ceramics were fragments of a Spanish olive jar, salt-glazed stoneware from the Rhineland, and fine Ming porcelain made during the reign of Chinese Emperor Wan Li (1573–1619). Two circular lead weights were stamped with monarch's crowned initials and the

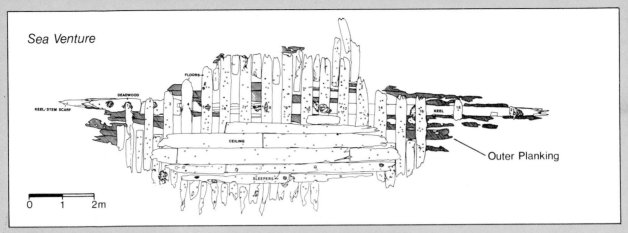

Sea Venture

KEEL/STEM SCARF · DEADWOOD · FLOORS · CEILING · SLEEPERS · KEEL · Outer Planking

0 1 2m

'Sea Venture': An Early Colonial Wreck

The ordeal of the *Sea Venture*, wrecked off Bermuda in 1609, inspired Shakespeare to write *The Tempest* and modern marine archaeologists to investigate her remains for clues to early colonial shipping. En route from Plymouth, England, to Jamestown, Virginia, together with eight other vessels, she caught the tail end of a hurricane. Buffeted by storms for four days and nights she eventually struck a reef – but all her passengers and crew reached safety.

5, 6   Plan (*above*) and underwater view (*left*) of the ship's remaining hull timbers.

7   (*far left*) A baluster jar of west-of-England plain pottery is typical of the type of earthenware found on the wreck of *Sea Venture*. This example stands 12 in (30.5 cm) high.

8   (*lower left*) Map of Bermuda with the wrecksite marked off St George's Island.

9   (*below*) A cannon recovered from the wreck. Known as a 'Finbanker' minion, it fired shot weighing nearly 4 pounds.

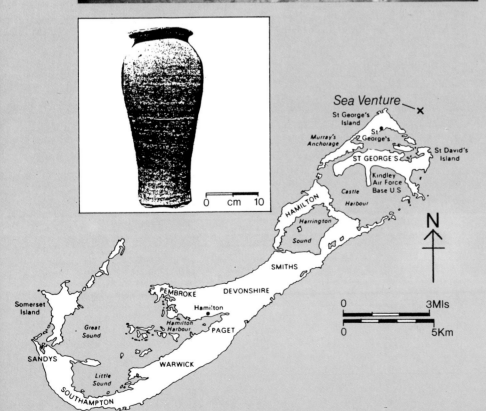

0 cm 10

Sea Venture —×

St George's Island
Murray's Anchorage
St George's
ST GEORGE'S
St David's Island
Kindley Air Force Base U S
Castle Harbour
HAMILTON
Harrington Sound
SMITHS
PEMBROKE · DEVONSHIRE
Hamilton
Hamilton Harbour · PAGET
Somerset Island
Great Sound
SANDYS
WARWICK
Little Sound
SOUTHAMPTON

N

0   3Mls
0   5Km

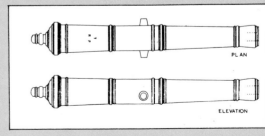

PLAN

ELEVATION

sword of St Paul, a one-pound weight of Elizabeth I and a quarter-pound weight of James I. There was a brass casting counter, or jetton, perhaps brought on board by an optimistic colonist who hoped to use it to calculate the profits from his future holdings. A calcareous concretion produced an accurate replica of a late sixteenth-century ball padlock. Part of a clay pipe, including its tiny bowl, reminded researchers of the high cost of tobacco at the beginning of the seventeenth century; it was also important to them in dating the wreck.

The study of the *Sea Venture* site continues, but already it has provided important information about the voyages of early colonists. The hundreds of artifacts offer a partial inventory of the variety and quality of possessions and equipment carried on such voyages. Because a precise date can be assigned to these materials, they can also be used to establish identification of similar artifacts found on other underwater or terrestrial excavations.

Hull remains, although limited to a small part of the ship's bottom, are equally important to the historical record. This was the period when the earliest English documents on naval architecture were being written and put to use, and the archaeological evidence can be compared to such documents. Contemporary manuscripts and drawings describe ship design and construction in vague, general terms. Details of commonplace methodology were omitted, and yet it is those details which we do not now understand and must learn in order to fully appreciate shipbuilding techniques of that period. Here is where archaeology is most helpful. The details, such as timber shapes and sizes, fastening systems, and the use of tools as evidenced by the marks they left on wood surfaces, can be extracted from the hull remains and added to or compared with contemporary records. The result is a greatly expanded understanding of this period of history. According to archaeologist Jonathan Adams, hull lines are being drawn based on existing timber measurements and the known geometric design rules of the period. Not only do such sparse hull remains confirm and expand our knowledge of shipbuilding of the period; they additionally reveal information about general technology and economics.

The 'Sparrow Hawk'. In the Seventeenth-Century Ship Room in Pilgrim Hall, Plymouth, Massachusetts, are the remains of a vessel uncovered by a storm in 1863 along Pleasant Bay on the east side of Cape Cod. They had been seen infrequently before, one recorded instance occurring in 1782, but this time they were removed and eventually reassembled for display in Boston and later in Pilgrim Hall. Some reputable historians have stated that these are the remains of the *Sparrow Hawk*, a small ketch carrying forty people to Plymouth when she was wrecked on Cape Cod in 1626. The name seems to be an adopted one, for it does not appear on colonial records. Nor are there convincing arguments that this was a ketch-rigged vessel. No artifacts or identifying materials survived to link the timbers with any precise date or vessel. But it is a very old wreck, probably similar in size and construction to the pinnaces and other small oceangoing craft of the colonial period. Only the bottom and lower stern of the vessel survive; bow, topsides, deck and rig have all disappeared. Total hull length could not have exceeded 40 ft (12 m). The keel, which is 28 ft 6 in (8.7 m) long, is made of English elm. All other timbers are of oak.

Thorough historical and geographical research has presented some convincing links between the hull remains in Pilgrim Hall and an unnamed wreck described by

10 (*right*) Interior view of the *Sparrow Hawk* as seen from the stern. The remains of this colonial vessel, wrecked on Cape Cod in 1626, were removed from the beach there in the late nineteenth century, and are now on display in the Seventeenth Century Rooms of Pilgrim Hall in Plymouth, Massachusetts.

Governor Bradford of Plymouth Plantation. In his history *Of Plimoth Plantation 1620–1647* he refers to a ship aground in what is now Pleasant Bay, along the east coast of Cape Cod, in the early part of the winter of 1626. The ship was bound for Virginia with 'many passengers and sundry goods'. The crew apparently were unsure of their location, the captain was sick and lame with scurvy, and the passengers had run out of water and beer. He suggests that they may have become unruly because of more than six weeks at sea, and were fearful of starving or becoming consumed with diseases. They were saved by friendly Indians, who contacted Bradford and advised him of the wreck and the pitiful condition of the survivors. Temporary shelter was provided the travelers by residents of Plymouth during the winter. Repairs were made to the ship, but it was broken up by another storm and abandoned. Whether Bradford is referring to a larger vessel, or the one on display in Plymouth, may continue to be debated. What is important is that the hull remains are representative of the smaller vessels which dared to cross the broad ocean with immigrants, and Bradford's account is awesome testimony to the hardships experienced by these early travelers.

Early Boatbuilding and Navigation

As each band of settlers arrived on this alien shore, the first priority was survival. Although some are known to have held expectations of finding riches, and others were simply adventurers, the basic reality of having to erect shelter, plant crops, fish, hunt and trade with the natives where possible loomed before all of them until each colony was well established. Once survival appeared imminent, they naturally turned to other interests with which to improve their lot. Among these were acquisition of watercraft for fishing and hunting, exploration, trading with natives or other colonies, or merely transporting

their own material requirements from remote areas. Ship carpenters, smiths and other artisans whose expertise was essential to the building of ships and boats were to be found among the colonists, although their number was severely limited. As the intense struggle for survival subsided, some were able to turn their talents to the building of watercraft.

At first there was a shortage of boats in many of the new colonies. In the Virginia colony in particular, dugout canoes, because they were quickly and easily acquired (sometimes by questionable means from the natives), probably served as the leading form of transportation until the colony was secure. The Europeans quickly improved and enlarged these local craft. Sharper ends, flatter bottoms, and keels solved handling and stability problems. The joining of several logs to make broader and deeper hulls, and eventually the addition of decks and rigging, were among the innovations. Descendants of those vessels still survive in the Chesapeake Bay as schooner-rigged bugeyes and racing log canoes, but they bear little resemblance to the simple, hollowed tree trunks which met the settlers.

Another source of watercraft for initial local navigation were the boats of the ships which brought the colonists across the Atlantic. Shallops, barges and longboats acquired in this manner were extremely helpful (*Mayflower* pilgrims lived aboard the first winter, and used a shallop, a small open boat which could be sailed or rowed, to commute to shore), but usually were available only until their ships returned to England.

The first vessel known to have been built in the English colonies was the *Virginia*, a product of the second expedition in 1607 which, under George Popham, briefly established a colony called Sagadahoc at the mouth of the Kennebec River, in what is now Maine but then was considered to be northern Virginia. A shipwright named

11, 12   A nearly completed log canoe found near the mouth of Outland Creek, at the entrance to Waccamaw River in South Carolina. The cypress log was worked with axes and adzes of the historic period and probably dates from the early nineteenth century, although it could be a hundred years older. The canoe weighed about 14,000 pounds. It was probably abandoned before completion because the log began to split

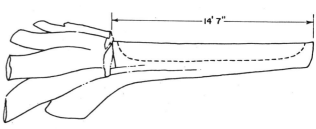

Coastal Craft

Digby was ordered to build a smart vessel for maintaining contact with the colony at Jamestown and for other coastal work. The resulting 30-ton pinnace, named *Virginia*, was used instead to return the settlers, who had become discouraged by the climate and privation, to their native land. This was the same little *Virginia* mentioned previously as the consort vessel to the *Sea Venture* during that ship's fateful voyage of 1609. Although probably less than 50 ft (15 m) in length, and identified from a drawing on Popham's map as having a single headsail and a sprit mainsail, this type of vessel was probably typical of early coastal craft which could, when the need arose, withstand deepwater duties as well.

Colonial records mention all sorts of small craft – barges, flats, skiffs, canoes, punts, frigates, cutters, longboats, sloops, periaguas, bateaux, shallops and pinnaces dominate the listings. Many of the accounts were written by lubberly folks, some of whom obviously applied their own designations. A single type may have been described as a flat, barge, longboat, or simply a boat, depending on the location and whim of the writer. In spite of this confusion, it is obvious that numerous small watercraft served communities and plantations in a variety of ways.

Some historians have contended that there were no boatbuilders among the early colonists. This could not have been the case, because successful craft, including seagoing vessels, were built from the start of colonization. We have already mentioned the two built at Bermuda, which permitted settlers to complete their voyage in 1610, and the 30-ton *Virginia* built a couple of years before. Still, expertise in shipbuilding must have been scarce, since virtually every colony placed requests for experienced boatbuilders and shipwrights during its first years of occupation.

Reports of nearly all explorers and early colonizing expeditions praised the New World as a source of shipbuilding materials. They spoke of oak and walnut, strong and tall; of pines large enough for the tallest masts, and in uncountable numbers; of mulberry, cedar, locust and elm; of iron ore for fastenings, anchors, tools and chandlery; of pitch, tar and resin for caulking; and of fertile soil to produce flax and hemp for sails and rope. News of these resources was received with enthusiasm in England, where far too much costly shipbuilding timber was being imported from Poland and Prussia.

The construction of watercraft in the colonies was limited during the first half of the seventeenth century. Four of the colonies had not yet been settled permanently; Virginia, New Amsterdam and the New England colonies already were thriving, but most construction was directed to working vessels for coastal or riverine duty, with an occasional moderate-sized hull capable of offshore assignments.

As population increased, so did production and the need for more supplies from Europe. Raw materials and farm products made up a large part of the eastbound cargoes, while tools, manufactured goods and the bare necessities of life dominated the holds of westbound ships. Not many luxuries were sold to the colonists in the first few decades of habitation.

Most transatlantic cargoes and passengers were carried in English bottoms, although the Dutch share of this ocean transport was increasing at a rate that alarmed English interests. During the first half of the century, navigation was improving because of frequency but was still somewhat of a hit-or-miss affair. The sextant and chronometer would not be invented for another century; compasses, staffs or astrolabes, and crude charts were the main navigational aids. The exchange of information between mariners, verbal or written, was another important factor to successful voyaging. Broad approximations were normal for long ocean voyages, and exact landfalls were rare or accidental.

Although ships varied widely in size, rig and speed, a typical medium-sized vessel of about 1630 was approximately 80 ft (24 m) long on the waterline and carried a basic ship rig of six sails on three masts – lateen mizzen, mainsail, main topsail, foresail, fore topsail and spritsail. Under ideal conditions such a ship might have moved along at 6 or 7 knots, but on a long voyage that speed was reduced to an average of 5 knots or less. The *Mayflower* took sixty-five days to cross the Atlantic; one could hardly expect to do much better. The hold of our typical ship was filled with an awesome variety of goods, nearly 200 tons of them, ranging from tools and cookware to muskets and Bibles. And always there were the people. Merchants and officials may have enjoyed some small comforts in cabins or segregated areas, but the immigrants – perhaps a hundred or more – were jammed into 'tween deck spaces which might have been high enough only for a child to stand up. After their first few weeks on board, life must have become unbearable; human tolerance and human suffering oppose each other under such demeaning conditions. Raw dampness, darkness, scurrying vermin, the stench of bilges, sickness and unwashed bodies, and the sights of the ill and dying must have demoralized even the stout hearted. But probably the noises were the worst, for these old ships had none of the silent majesty attributed to them by modern films. There were the groans of the suffering, the curses and shouting as tempers became shorter, the crying of babies, the sloshing of sea and bilges, the screaming of wind in rigging, and that intolerable and constant groaning of massive ship's timbers as they resisted movement. Add to all that the endless rolling and pitching of the ship, and there is little wonder that often hostile land looked inviting at first.

The Colonies Take Root

If colonization sputtered and remained rudimentary for the first few decades, that was not the case in the latter half of the century. Coastal voyaging between colonies increased appreciably, and ships from the motherland came and went with accelerated frequency. Not only did these ships carry more supplies from England than ever before, but the nature of the supplies was changing. Signs of wealth and the realization or hope of success were noticeable in many of the settlements. Where originally only essentials made up the cargoes, luxury items began to appear more frequently in manifests. One ship, the *Virginia Merchant*, which sank on the south coast of Bermuda on its way from England to Virginia in 1660, was discovered three centuries later by Teddy Tucker of Bermuda. Although the ship had broken up and disappeared, Tucker discovered part of her cargo strewn on the seabed. There were the usual necessities – tools, guns, ammunition, etc. – but there were ivory combs,

ivory-handled knives and lead settings for window panes as well.

While the sparse remains of one shipwreck do not attest to the improved condition of colonial existence, the abundance of historical records does. Shipbuilding became an industry just before 1650, about the time West Indian trade expanded. Most of it seemed to center in New England, perhaps because of a combination of demand, natural advantages and the influx of shipwrights, ship carpenters and sawyers during the years of the Great Migration. After 1640 the migration temporarily slowed to a trickle, mainly because Oliver Cromwell had seized power in England and there was no need for Puritans to escape from religious persecution. The accompanying shortage of tools and replacements for worn equipment was becoming a problem, too; the New Englanders were forced to take things into their own hands.

In one year, 1641, in excess of 300,000 codfish were hauled into Massachusetts ports and prepared for overseas shipment. Because English ships no longer arrived in sufficient numbers to accommodate such production increases, Governor Winthrop initiated ventures that led to the establishment of shipbuilding as an industry. He established water-powered sawmills, exempted shipbuilders from military service and encouraged the construction of larger vessels. In the first five years (1641–46) at least six ships of more than 200 tons burden and several smaller ones are known to have been built. This in turn created logging centers to the north, while throughout the area businesses developed to produce sailcloth, cordage and chandlery.

During the eighteen years of political strife in England, colonial merchants, especially those of New England, established fishing fleets and expanded trade with the West Indies. The Dutch, who were then the world leaders in commercial shipping, were also expanding their West Indian and colonial routes, prompting passage of the First Navigation Act in 1651. The law required that products shipped into England be transported only in English-built ships manned by English crews. Dutch trade continued nevertheless, since the act was not strictly enforced. The restoration of the Crown in 1660 strengthened the spirit of mercantilism, resulting in the Second Navigation Act which required that most goods imported into the colonies had to pass through England first. A following act in 1672 required goods passing from one colony to another to be routed via England. The laws were opposed by many colonists, but did little to hamper colonial trade. Restrictions were often ignored as smuggling became widespread; shipbuilding naturally benefited since the laws encouraged colonial shipping. Triangular trade routes developed in a variety of patterns. The major ones carried food, lumber and other raw materials to the West Indies, thence to England with foodstuffs, molasses and sugar, and back to the colonies with manufactured goods.

Archaeology is now bringing back to life one of the most famous, or infamous, of the ports in this

A True and Perfect Relation of that most Sad and Terrible

EARTHQUAKE, at Port-Royal in JAMAICA,

Which happened on *Tuesday* the 7th. of *June*, 1692.

Where, in Two Minutes time the Town was Sunk under Ground, and Two Thousand Souls Perished: With the manner of it at Large; in a Letter from thence, Written by Captain *Crocket*: As also of the *Earthquake* which happen'd in *England, Holland, Flanders, France, Germany, Zeland, &c.* And in most Parts of *Europe*: On *Thursday* the 8th of *September*. Being a Dreadful Warning to the Sleepy World: Or, God's heavy Judgments shewed on a Sinful People, as a Fore-runner of the Terrible Day of the Lord.

The EXPLANATION:

A. The Houses Falling. B. The Churches. C. The Sugar-Works. D. The Mills. E. The Bridges in the whole Country. F. The Rock and Mountains. G. Captain Ruden's House Sunk first into the Earth, with his Wife, and Family. H. The Ground rolling under the Minister's Fort. I. The great Church and Tower Falling. K. The Earth Opening and Swallowing Multitudes of People in Morgan's Fort. L. The Minister Kneeling down in a ring with the People in the Street at Prayers. M. The Wharf covered with the Sea. N. Dr. Hearh going from Ship to Ship to Visit the bruised People, and do his last Office to the dead Corpses that lay floating from the Point. O. Thieves Robbing and Breaking open both Dwelling Houses and Ware-Houses during the Earthquake. P. Dr. Trapham, a Doctor of Physick, hanging by the Hands on a Rack of the Chimney, and one of his Children hanging about his Neck seeing his Wife and the rest of his Children a Smoking. Q. A Boat coming to save them. R. The Minister Preaching in a Tent to the People. S. The dead Bodies of some Hundreds floating about the Harbour. T. The Sea washing the dead Carkasses out of their Graves and Tombs, and dashed to pieces by the Earthquake. V. People swallow'd up in the Earth, several as high as their Necks with their Heads above Ground. W. The Dogs eating of Dead Mens Heads. X. Several Ships Cast away and driven into the very Town. Y. A Woman and her two Daughters beat to pieces one against the other. Z. Mr. Beckford his Digging out of the Ground.

15 (*above*) A contemporary London broadside announces the 'most sad and terrible earthquake' at Port Royal, Jamaica, on 7 June 1692. At the time of the disaster, Port Royal was the most active English port in the New World colonies.

16 (*right*) About two-thirds of Port Royal sank into the harbor during the 1692 earthquake. The six-room building (ill. 17) excavated by the Institute of Nautical Archaeology between 1982 and 1985 lies near the southwest edge of the drowned part of the city.

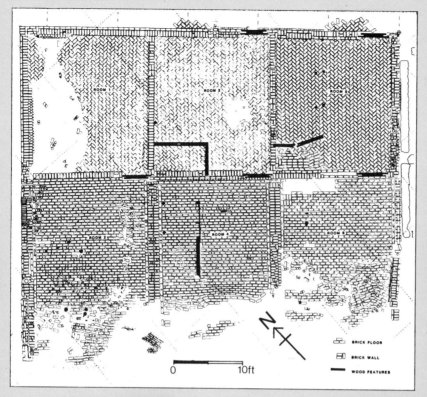

Port Royal: Excavating a Sunken City

17 (*left*) Building One at Port Royal, excavated underwater by the Institute of Nautical Archaeology, exhibits the typical seventeenth-century arrangements of shops within a single structure. The building sank vertically, to a present depth of 9–15 ft (2.7–4.6 m), with little horizontal movement. The thicker walls of the back three rooms (bottom side on the plan) indicate a later, two-story addition to the building.

18 (*below left*) D. L. Hamilton (project director) and Helen DeWolf looking over some of the artifacts recovered from submerged buildings in the 1987 excavations at Port Royal. Pictured are pewter plates or platters, a bowl, two spoons, and a candlestick; brass mortars, two candlesticks, two sieves, a key, two buckles, and a set of dividers; a silver fork; a copper pail; numerous clay smoking pipes; a liquor bottle; an ivory ring; a pearl; a gold ring; and Chinese porcelain. The excavations are conducted jointly by the Institute of Nautical Archaeology and Texas A&M University in cooperation with the Jamaica National Heritage Trust.

19 (*below*) Three slipware mugs from the area along Lime Street in Port Royal show the excellent condition of artifacts lost in the great 1692 earthquake.

seventeenth-century trade. Jamaica's Port Royal, once the richest English colony in the New World, sank beneath the sea during a terrible earthquake in 1692. Mined for centuries for building materials and souvenirs, the sunken parts of the city are being measured, mapped and reconstructed by a team of archaeologists working under a long term plan of collaboration between the Government of Jamaica, the Institute of Nautical Archaeology, and Texas A&M University. Texas A&M's D. L. Hamilton, director of the project, and his associates have recovered more than 20,000 artifacts and produced a detailed reconstruction of the six rooms comprising the first floor of a large building. A second story may have served as the living quarters for owners of the shops below. The building was obviously a busy commercial structure, for there are artifacts belonging to a wood turner in one room while other rooms contained tools and possessions of a cobbler and a butcher. One room seems to have served as a combination wine and pipe shop, another as a tavern; some wine bottles are still filled and corked. Bones of a few of more than 2,000 victims who sank with the city (disease and pestilence claimed another 2,000 or 3,000 within several months) are scattered among the debris.

Decades of work will be required in order to completely document the streets, buildings and artifacts of Port Royal. Each year of excavation, however, increases our understanding of this boisterous city whose streets were crowded with prosperous merchants, artisans, buccaneers and slaves.

Vessels of the Eighteenth Century

By 1700 the American profile that would last for decades had already developed. Northern colonies nurtured fishing and industry, the middle colonies were noted for their fertile farms, while the dominant feature of the south was its plantations of tobacco, rice and eventually cotton. Each area had its trading centers, and shipbuilding had spread southward. Colonial merchants held title to hundreds of seagoing ships, and wealth and prosperity were becoming evident in the form of spacious houses and the finer luxuries arriving in ships from Europe. The Navigation Acts also benefited merchants and shipbuilders in England. Between 1660 and 1690 merchant shipping doubled; Britannia was now the undisputed leader in maritime commerce.

We are fortunate to have actual examples of both seagoing and coastal vessels built in the first half of the eighteenth century. Both were well preserved and were carefully recorded and studied by nautical archaeologists. Although work continues on the vessels, enough is known about them to provide a comprehensive look at eighteenth-century construction.

The Brown's Ferry vessel. On 28 August 1976, people along the banks of the tannin-stained Black River at Brown's Ferry, Georgetown County, South Carolina, witnessed the remains of a small merchant vessel, nestled in a metal lifting frame suspended from a large crane, slowly break the surface of the dark water. It was a triumphant moment for the team of underwater archaeologists from the Institute of Archaeology and Anthropology at the University of South Carolina. Directed by Alan B. Albright, they had spent nearly two months recovering artifacts, including the vessel's cargo of about 25 tons of bricks and numerous hull timbers scattered about the riverbed. Hampered by a severely limited budget, time restraints and near zero visibility in the murky river, they had done a commendable job in saving what was even then suspected of being a colonial vessel dating to around 1740.

The hull was found lying parallel to the river bank, where an abandoned ferry ramp had been cut into a low bluff. It was no more than 25 ft (7.6 m) from the end of the ramp, and lay partly on its starboard side at a depth of 20 to 25 ft (6.1 to 7.6 m). The upstream end of the hull (the stern) rested on a large rock, while the downstream end, except for the top of the stempost, was covered with sand. Because of its easy access to the water, the adjacent shore area was a favorite dumping ground and the wreck was covered not only with mud, sand and trees, but with bricks, gravel, rocks, remnants of a horse and buggy, two automobiles and other relics of human disposal deposited over a period of more than 200 years. The cargo of bricks had broken part of the starboard side away and spilled down the steeply sloping river bottom. These bricks, the sole cargo, numbered 10,000.

Included among other artifacts were a beer mug inscribed with the coat of arms of George II, four millstones, two dozen bottles, three iron pots, loose buckshot, a slipware cup, a straight razor and several gourd smoking pipes. Perhaps the most surprising artifact was a nearly complete Improved Davis Quadrant, a deepsea navigating instrument one would not expect to find on a coastal vessel such as this.

But the most important artifact of all was the hull. More than two-thirds of it survived, nearly half in an assembled state. Historians and archaeologists had not recorded such a hull before, and so steps were taken to insure its thorough study. With visibility limited to 18 in (45 cm), and that only during changes in currents and tides, it could scarcely be recorded extensively under water. Since the hull almost certainly would be lost if it remained on the riverbed for any length of time, it was decided to raise and preserve its remains for later documentation.

After overburden and artifacts, including cargo, had been removed, loose planks and timbers were brought to the surface and kept wet under fresh-water sprays. Time and limited underwater visibility prevented the disassembly of the extant hull section, a process sometimes used by archaeologists to enhance conservation and reduce material breakage. Instead, Albright and his crew hoisted the hull from the water in a specially designed steel frame. Once on land, legs added to the frame allowed it to be transported to a holding site to await conservation. The entire hull assembly then was immersed in a bath of polyethylene glycol, a waxy substance frequently used to treat waterlogged wood, in what is probably the largest treatment tank of this type ever built. When conservation is completed, the hull will be reassembled and displayed in a museum near the wreck site.

Before they were immersed in the holding pond, I made a preliminary study of the hull timbers. They will be investigated more thoroughly when the wood is stable after its five-year treatment, and is unrestricted by cradle, slings and metal frame. But it was possible at least to produce a preliminary set of drawings and a large model demonstrating construction features. Both are illustrated here, although they must be regarded with caution in those areas where there was no hull survival. For instance, the stern did not survive; on the drafting board it was determined that the hull had a pointed stern, but further study may indicate a small square stern or high transom. The location of the masts are accurate, but the sprit rig shown on the model may have taken the configuration of a variety of schooner rigs on the original vessel. Rigging and topsides are based on archival research; so little of them has survived that we may never know the configuration of sails and rigging on this vessel. Yet these areas are not as important as those which have been preserved. What we have learned already from this wreck, our first look at a regional coastal type from this period, is impressive.

The Brown's Ferry vessel was intended for service in southern rivers and for limited duty along the coast. It was not built to withstand ocean voyages. The cargo of bricks on board at the time it sank was probably representative of the types of cargoes carried by such vessels, which included lumber, animals, bales of cotton or tobacco, and other produce. This hull may have carried many such cargoes of bricks, perhaps from a plantation kiln upstream to the sea and along the coast, to the rapidly growing city of Charleston or wherever brick structures were adding permanence to the young colony. Since there were no good roads over most of the southern colonies, vessels such as this also served as passenger carriers between the many barrier islands and coastal settlements.

The Brown's Ferry vessel is believed to have been fully loaded when discovered, and so I have rated her a 25-tonner. The hull was 50 ft 6 in (15.4 m) long on deck, had a maximum breadth of about 14 ft (4.2 m), with a hull depth of about 4 ft (1.8 m) amidships. There was no keel, only a heavy flat bottom which permitted her to operate in shoal waters and load from river banks where piers did not exist. The two masts, whether rigged as a gaff-schooner or as shown in the model, would have required a crew of no more than three or four. The ends of the hull provided shelter for these people; indeed that shelter may have amounted to their permanent home in some cases. There was a galley stove forward of the foremast.

Where this coaster was built may remain a mystery, although it must have been somewhere along the Carolina or Georgia coast; all the species of wood found in the hull are native to that area. The shipwright need not have gone far for the timber that seasoned in his yard. There was yellow pine for planking, oak for framing and for timbers in the ends of the hull, and cypress for strong longitudinal members. Although not as impressive as the store of timber for a large ship, it still required dozens of trees to build a coaster such as this. There must have been a smith nearby, perhaps even within the yard, who forged the nails, bolts and hardware exactly as the shipwright wanted them. These he made from iron stock. There were also suppliers of pitch, cordage, rigging materials, paints, sails or sailcloth, and many other items which went into the finished vessel.

Instead of a keel, three bottom planks 4 in (10 cm) thick were cut from one or more large yellow pine logs. One plank was nearly 50 ft (15 m) long and more than 18 in (46 cm) wide; the other two were slightly smaller. They were probably cut by stage sawing. By this method, staging was laid across scaffolds about as high as a man. The log was placed on the staging, the cut marked on the log and then made by means of a two-man saw. One of the

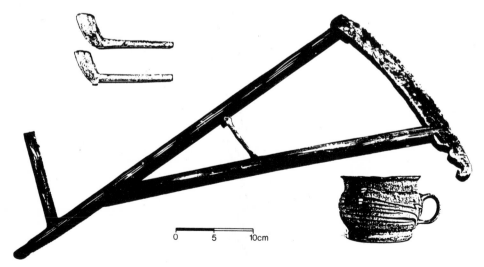

0   5   10cm

20–22 Two clay pipes, a quadrant and a slipware cup from the Brown's Ferry wreck. Why the quadrant – a deepsea navigating instrument – should have been on board is a mystery. Had an oceangoing skipper kept his most valuable tool when he retired to riverine and coastal duties? Was it navigational insurance against the possibility of being blown far off shore?

Raising the Brown's Ferry Vessel

It was a moment of triumph. After nearly two months spent excavating the Brown's Ferry vessel in its watery South Carolina grave, on 28 August 1976 Alan Albright and his team managed to raise the well-preserved hull from the riverbed and hoist it ashore.

23, 24 (*right*) Two drawings of the Brown's Ferry wreck *in situ*, one showing the cargo of bricks still in place, the other the hull after bricks, trash and overburden had been removed.

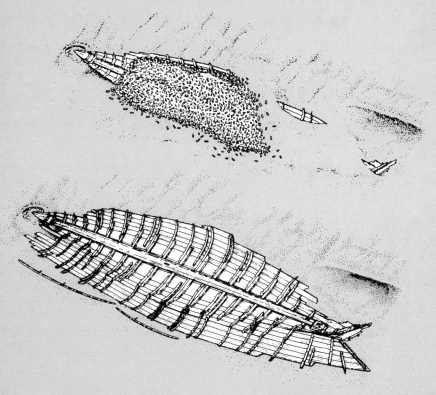

25 (*right*) The intact hull remains of the Brown's Ferry vessel are hoisted from the Black River near Georgetown, South Carolina.

26 (*below*) A lower portside section of the Brown's Ferry hull, showing a plank which had pulled away from a floor timber. Note the void created by the partially extracted treenail.

Ships of the Founding Fathers

John Cabot in 1497 was the first of the early navigators sailing under the English flag to explore the North American coast, but it was not until Sir Walter Raleigh's time that the English attempted serious colonization (1585) – and not until 1607 that the first colony was established which took firm root.

27, 28 Modern replicas have been built of *Susan Constant*, *Godspeed* and *Discovery*, the three vessels that brought 100 men from England to Jamestown, Virginia, in 1607 (*left*, *Godspeed* under sail, *right* the three at anchor).

29 (*below*) A drawing of an English galleon of about 1586, from a manuscript attributed to Matthew Baker, master shipwright. The location of the fish along the underwater portion of the hull perhaps attests to the fact that early architects took some of their ideas from nature's best swimmers.

sawyers stood atop the platform and guided the saw on the downstroke and raised it on the return stroke. Another sawyer at ground level, who probably got a lot of sawdust in his eyes and nose, supplied the cutting power on the downstroke of the saw. A third man shifted the log when necessary so that the saw would not cut into the staging. The work was slow, difficult and required skill. Sawyers were recognized as artisans in the colonies.

A flat surface was cleared near the shore but above tide or flood line for erecting the hull. Logs or sleepers were laid crosswise to provide a level surface for the bottom planks, high enough for the shipbuilders to slide underneath the hull when necessary. Now the three planks were laid edge to edge with the longest one in the center. The shipwright then drew the outline of the bottom of the hull on the planks with an awl or other scribing tool. Along these lines the outer edges of the planks were hewn to their proper curvatures with axes. The center plank required only that its ends were cut to shape; the other two had arced edges over their entire lengths. Next, the center plank was laid flat on the supporting cross-pieces and the two outer planks fitted to it. They were kept in alignment by a series of treenails (large wooden dowels which swelled when wet) drilled into their edges. When assembled, this thick bottom resembled a giant elm leaf. The elliptical outer edges were left rough at this stage; they would be trimmed to perfection only after the hull was planked.

Next, the three pieces of oak comprising the stem were assembled and fastened to the bottom planking. The stem assembly was held together with iron forelock bolts, a made-to-order bolt which used a tapered iron key to hold it in place rather than a threaded nut. Forelock bolts were used to hold thick timbers together on ships at least as far back as the classical periods of history. The sternpost may have been constructed in a similar fashion, although the evidence is limited because only a small part of it survived.

The hull probably was designed by a process called whole molding, a simplified design method often applied to boats and simple larger craft such as this. In this instance I suspect the shipwright was designing a vessel of similar size and characteristics to one he had done previously, perhaps with minor modifications here and there. Hull shapes were scribed full size on a convenient flat surface with two, or perhaps three, standard molds for curvatures, from which the various timber patterns were taken. The model we made was so built; the lines drawings illustrated here were a later addition.

With lofting completed and hull bottom assembled, the shipwright made a mark on the central plank for the location of the midship frame; this was the widest frame in the hull and was located a few feet forward of the middle of the hull. Then he scribed seven locations forward of the midship frame and twelve aft of it for additional frames, each centered 2 ft (61 cm) from its neighbors. Every third or fourth frame, including the midship frame, was

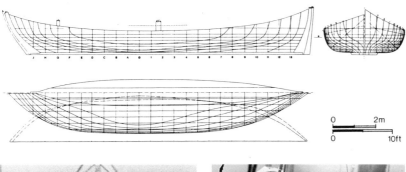

Short-haul Truck of Her Time

30–32 J. Richard Steffy's preliminary lines drawing of the Brown's Ferry vessel's hull (*left*) and his large-scale research model (*below left*, under construction and interior view) are both aids in the interpretation of what this 25-ton cargo vessel might have looked like and how she might have performed. Flat-bottomed and difficult to maneuver, she would have had to float or sail downstream on rivers with the current and upstream with the tide. But under sail at sea, in offshore waters, she may have been quite efficient at beating along the coast.

33 Hampton Shuping (left), discoverer of the Brown's Ferry vessel, examines with J. Richard Steffy the 1:10 scale reconstruction model of the vessel built by Steffy.

assembled on or near the lofting surface. Made of three pieces of timber, each of these main square frames consisted of a floor timber, which spanned the bottom planking, and two side timbers, called futtocks, which lapped over the floor timbers and were fastened to them. Curved frame timbers were hewn and sawn from carefully selected, naturally curved tree trunks and branches.

Temporary cross-pieces were nailed to the tops of the futtocks to keep the whole assembly rigid until the hull was planked. With the three bottom planks still fitted snugly against each other, the midship frame was aligned with its marked location atop the bottom planks and fastened to them with oaken treenails $1\frac{1}{8}$ in (3 cm) thick; these were spaced at intervals of 6 to 8 in (15 to 20 cm). The frame was then leveled and plumbed in all directions, and temporarily braced against the bottom planking.

This procedure was repeated for the half-dozen or so preassembled frames fore and aft of the midship frame. Battens, long thin pieces of wood, were bent around the outer surfaces of the standing frames and their ends nailed to the stem and sternpost. These battens were used to determine the shapes of some of the intermediate frames which had not yet been assembled; a few in the center of the hull and all of the frames in the ends of the vessel were not installed until the sides were planked.

When a sufficient number of frames had been erected, the sides were planked with broad pine boards 1 in (2.5 cm) thick. Next, the keelson, an internal backbone which added considerable longitudinal strength, was treenailed through frames and bottom planks. The keelson housed the steps, or cavities, into which the mast heels were inserted. Near the bow it also bore hundreds of hatchet marks where the cook had cut kindling for the hearth. Other internal timbers, deck beams and decks were added; no signs of a deck could be found on the wreck and so the modern model was decked only in the

ends, although there may have been a full deck with large hatches to provide access to the hold.

Bulwark, caprail and topside joinery completed the hull, during or after which time the planking seams were caulked with oakum and pitch to prevent leakage. The hull seems to have been coated inside and out with pitch or resin. The addition of a rudder, spars, rigging, anchor windlass and a hundred other details would have finished the job. There was no graceful champagne launching for such a hull; probably it was shoved or dragged into the water unceremoniously.

It is impossible to determine when the Brown's Ferry vessel was built, but we know it was repaired and recaulked at least once. Regardless of its age, it must be regarded as an example of early eighteenth-century construction. This was far from a graceful vessel. It seldom, if ever, tied up to docks. It moved along any way it could, floating downstream with the current and upstream with the tide, using the poles and oars which were found to keep clear of banks and snags or to provide propulsion when wind and tide failed. Once clear of the rivers, however, it could probably beat along the coast to its next port at a fair rate. This was the short-haul truck of the day, and there must have been many such vessels. Without good roads, they were vitally important to the survival and growth of the areas they served.

The Ronson ship. I shall never forget the strange sight on a cold day in January 1982. Summoned to 175 Water Street in New York City to give advice on the excavation of a ship, I protested when the cab driver dropped me off in the middle of lower Manhattan. Shipwrecks are supposed to be near water, and we were blocks away. A glance through the boarded fence of a construction site confirmed that the driver was right, however; there, in a hole at least 20 ft (6 m) deep and 100 ft (30 m) long, was a nearly complete ship's hull, and a big one at that. Its construction indicated that it was probably about the age of the Brown's Ferry vessel, an assumption which has since been confirmed. If the Brown's Ferry vessel was the colonial version of a delivery truck, this armed ocean carrier, approximately 100 ft (30.5 m) long with a maximum beam of 26 ft (8 m), was the equivalent of the long-haul eighteen-wheeler. European and American tonnage rules varied somewhat in this period; depending upon where the ship was registered, it would have been rated at least 200 tons burden and possibly in excess of 300 tons.

Known variously as the Water Street ship and the Ronson ship (after the developer whose proposed building construction was delayed by its discovery), this ship was old when abandoned sometime before 1750, for it was a crib hulk, a condemned vessel filled with rubble to act as cribbage for a wharf or expansion of the waterfront. Its location must then have been on the bank of the East River, but over the years the city has expanded eastward so that the vessel now lay two blocks from the river.

Warehouses had been built over it, and these were being removed for the erection of the proposed structure. Archaeologists under the direction of Warren Reiss and Sheli Smith recorded the entire hull and excavated as much of it as possible.

The hull had been filled with debris. Little of it related to the ship, which had been stripped of its rigging, gear and decorations before abandonment. The hull had the familiar apple-cheeked bow and elaborate head knee of the period. Timbers and planking were made of oak, while the deck was of pine. They were fastened with treenails of hickory and juniper, in combination with nails and bolts of iron. Seams were caulked in the manner of the Brown's Ferry vessel, although there was an additional layer of animal hair and pitch held in place with thin furring, a common sight on such early vessels.

Frame timbers were twice the size of those on the Brown's Ferry vessel, and they were doubled and closely spaced throughout most of the hull. In the bow, framing formed almost a solid wall of oak, each timber being about 15 in (38 cm) square. The heaviest planking, called wales,

A Ship beneath the City

When property developer Howard Ronson bought some New York City land in 1981, he little knew that beneath the ground lay the remains of an eighteenth-century ship.

34 (*left*) Near the spot where the Ronson ship was excavated, a similar merchantman rides at anchor in this 1712 engraving of New York Harbor.

35–37 The excavations: the Brooklyn Bridge in the background (*below left*) shows how far the Manhattan waterfront has been pushed back since the Ronson ship (*right*, bow to camera, *below*, the hold) was sunk to support a wharf.

was 4 in (10 cm) thick, twice that of the rest of the skin. There were three masts, and their locations suggest a standard ship rig. Although much of the construction seems to follow contemporary European documentation, researchers have yet to determine its registry and origin.

Tons of bow timbers have been excavated and are presently being preserved in solutions of polyethylene glycol. Like the Brown's Ferry vessel, these timbers will be reassembled and put on permanent display, in this case at the Mariners' Museum in Newport News, Virginia.

Jay Rosloff, a nautical archaeologist specializing in ship construction, made a preliminary reconstruction of the bow timbers. He found that the construction follows patterns which were well established by the eighteenth century. Instead of revealing previously unknown techniques or design features, the value of this vessel was one of confirming archival information and revealing the methods by which shipwrights applied practical expertise to known design and construction features.

The role of the Ronson ship as a crib hulk was by no means a rarity. Many a worn-out hull was filled with rubble and used to reinforce wharves and shoreline extensions where available machinery or economics did not permit more sophisticated construction. Although unfit for sea duty, they still maintained sufficient strength to serve as containers for the fill needed to stabilize shorelines and wharves.

When hulks were not available or wharf dimensions made them impractical, cribs were specifically built for the purpose. Colonial wharf cribs were variations of the cribbing used in Roman and medieval times. In their most basic form, wharf cribs were built somewhat like the sides of log cabins; logs or hewn timbers were stacked in overlapping right angles, their joints notched and fastened to provide a close-fitting box. The structure was then floated into position and sunk with rocks or other solid fill. In some cases the logs were simply overlapped without notching, leaving large gaps between the timbers. Such assemblies, called cobbs, had to be filled with rocks large enough to remain within the gaps.

Wharf cribbing was not limited to single structures, however. Two or more cribs could be assembled to make wharves of various shapes and dimensions. Most were capped with stone or smooth fill to provide roadways, some even supporting warehouses. Archaeologist Harding Polk, a specialist in colonial wharves, likens them to hour glasses – constricted avenues connecting port towns and plantations with the outside world, down which all merchandise, supplies and passengers must pass.

One of the few surviving crib wharves is the Follet site wharf, part of Strawberry Banke Museum in Portsmouth, New Hampshire. Strawberry Banke, the original name for Portsmouth, was settled in 1630 and flourished for more than a century afterward. Made of a small crib of rough timbers resting atop a larger foundation cribwork, the wharf is 60 to 80 ft (18.3 to 24.4 m) long and 40 ft (12.2 m) wide. Some of the fill material in the upper crib consists of flint nodules, which probably served first as ballast in a European ship. Known in the nineteenth century as Puddle Dock, the wharf may have been built as early as the late seventeenth century and has been repaired numerous times. It is an especially interesting site, since it exists among buildings and artifacts which represent the cultural changes of a port area whose history spans three-and-a-half centuries.

The Final Years

The last quarter-century of colonialism has so far provided no well-preserved shipwrecks along North American shores. Historical records indicate growth in all areas. By 1775 the population is said to have reached 2,500,000. Of the five largest cities, Philadelphia had 40,000 residents, New York City 25,000, Boston 16,000, Charleston 12,000, and Newport was thriving with 11,000 souls. All were major seaports, and all had expanding shipbuilding industries.

Although maritime records are more complete in this later period, and ship drawings and descriptions more elaborate, confusion and gaps remain in our understanding of late colonial seafaring activities. There were now many iron furnaces and foundries, sawmills and other supportive industries. Reputable shipwrights and ship masters worked in all areas of the coast. But how many ships were being built, how many were owned by colonial entrepreneurs, and how many tons were being shipped? Accurate answers to these questions are difficult, if not impossible, to assemble. These were years of dissension and rebellion; illegal trading and ambiguous recordkeeping were common enough to make many records suspect. But perhaps the beginnings of the American revolution bear sufficient testimony regarding the magnitude of maritime activities in the colonies during this period. In spite of the restrictions posed by divided loyalties, the British Navy was able to maintain a sizeable fleet far from home ports, while rebel American forces still somehow mustered the builders, suppliers and crews to send their own ships to sea.

CHAPTER SEVEN

Struggle for a Continent: Naval Battles of the French and Indian Wars

Kevin J. Crisman

Separated by nearly impassable wilderness, the French and English colonies established along the eastern shores of the North American continent in the early seventeenth century maintained for several decades a rival but essentially peaceful relationship. Peace was shattered in the latter part of the century by competition for New World resources and the eruption of wars in Europe. There followed four long wars, interspersed with brief periods of uncertain peace. Three of these conflicts, King William's War (1689–1697), Queen Anne's War (1702–1713), and King George's War (1744–1748), were initiated by the outbreak of fighting in Europe, but the final, climactic confrontation – the French and Indian War (1755–1763) – began in the colonies and spread to the other side of the Atlantic.

The outcome of the French and English wars in North America was especially dependent on naval mastery, both on the Atlantic Ocean and on the inland lakes and rivers. The absence of roads across the interior of the continent meant that an army and its supplies could move only by water. Building, equipping and maintaining small boats on the inland waterways presented severe logistical problems, but by trial and error the English eventually became masters at it; this was an important ingredient to their ultimate success.

Thousands of vessels, large and small, were employed during the colonial wars, but we know surprisingly little about how they were built and what they looked like; this is particularly true of the craft that navigated the rivers and lakes. Historical records of the seventeenth and early eighteenth centuries generally say little about naval construction, while contemporary depictions of vessels are often vague or inaccurate. Nautical archaeology provides the opportunity to fill gaps in our knowledge, although few wrecks from the French and British conflicts have yet been excavated and analyzed.

The European Colonization of North America
Despite their basic similarities as European outposts on the edges of an undeveloped continent, the French and English colonies did differ substantially.

The first major French settlement in North America, Quebec, was established on the banks of the St Lawrence River in 1608 by explorer Samuel de Champlain. In the decades that followed new towns and farms appeared along the river, including Montreal in 1642, but the rate of migration to 'New France' was low and the population grew rather slowly. With the exception of a few sparsely inhabited villages in Acadia (present-day Nova Scotia), the greater part of the colony remained concentrated in the St Lawrence Valley.

Fishing, farming and lumbering were common in Canada, but the most important occupation by far in terms of income for the colony was the fur trade with Indian tribes living in the interior. Felt hats made with beaver fur were at the height of fashion in Europe, and exports of this commodity proved highly lucrative for merchants and government officials who acted as middlemen between the natives and the markets in France. The colony was ideally situated for this business, for the St Lawrence provided direct access to the Great Lakes and the very heart of the continent.

New France may have been in an excellent position to exploit the fur resources of North America, but its location did have some drawbacks. From its inception the colony was heavily dependent on supplies, particularly foodstuffs and trade goods, from the mother country, yet the St Lawrence River froze solid for several months every winter, interrupting all shipments. This lifeline became even more tenuous in wartime, when the English concentrated their naval forces in the Gulf of St Lawrence to intercept transports and warships attempting to ascend the river.

The British colonies on the eastern shore of North America differed in size and purpose from their French neighbors to the north. Geography played a large part in this development: while the French were expanding the fur trade into the interior via the St Lawrence, the westward progress of English settlers and merchants was hampered by the Appalachian Mountains that ran parallel to the coast from Georgia to New England.

Some English colonists engaged in trade with the

1 *A Southwest Prospect of New York in 1756* provides an excellent view of several different types of oceangoing ships of the period.

Indians, but the majority were more interested in clearing land and building farms and towns. From small agricultural plantations in Virginia and Massachusetts the colonies rapidly expanded in both numbers and area through the seventeenth century, and these holdings were further increased in the 1660s by the acquisition of Dutch colonies on the Hudson and Delaware Rivers.

Britain's American colonies lacked the inland water routes enjoyed by the French, but their navigation of the Atlantic Ocean was never unduly restricted by season. New England fishing boats frequented North Atlantic fishing grounds in large numbers, merchant vessels carried on a brisk trade in fish, rum and other foodstuffs with the West Indies, and a steady flow of maritime commerce passed back and forth to Europe.

Contact between the French and English colonies was limited by a nearly impenetrable wilderness of mountains and forests that was traversed by only two navigable water routes. The most direct, and therefore the most important, was the Champlain waterway, consisting of Lakes Champlain and George. At their southern ends both lakes are only a few miles from the upper Hudson River, while Lake Champlain at its northern terminus empties down the Richelieu River into the St Lawrence. Conveyance of boats and equipment around rapids, or 'portage', was necessary at only a few points: between the Hudson River and Lakes George and Champlain, at the outlet of Lake George into Lake Champlain, and at the rapids of the Richelieu River. These portages could occasion much work and inconvenience, but traveling by water was infinitely easier and faster than overland travel.

The strategic value of the Champlain waterway was enormous, since it constituted both a location for defensive positions and a staging ground for attacks on enemy settlements. The two lakes became a focus of activity during each of the four colonial wars.

The second inland water route between French and British territories was more circuitous, stretching between the upper Hudson River and Lake Ontario via the Mohawk and Oswego Rivers. The passage was lengthy and involved several arduous portages, but for the British it proved to be the only way of entering the Great Lakes and challenging French domination of the interior.

Bateaux: Sturdy Transports on Rivers and Lakes

Travel on the lakes and rivers of North America entailed a rigorous procession of shallows, rapids, open water and overland portages of boats and supplies. Such conditions called for lightweight, shallow-draft vessels capable of enduring constant ill-treatment without falling to pieces. The bark canoes of the Indians partly fit this description, but they were somewhat unstable in rough water and generally not very durable.

The need for a sturdy, plank-on-frame inland boat was quickly recognized and met in the mid-seventeenth century with the invention of the bateau (spelled 'batteau' in much of North America). Peter Kalm, a Swedish naturalist traveling between the French and English colonies in 1749, has provided one of the finest contemporary descriptions of these vessels:

Battoe . . . are much in use in Albany: they are made of boards of white pine; the bottom is flat, that they may row the better in shallow water; they are sharp at both ends, and somewhat higher towards the end than in the middle. They have seats in them, and are rowed as common boats. They are long, yet not all alike, commonly three, and sometimes four fathoms long [18 to 24 ft, or 5.5 to 7.3 m]. The height from the bottom to the top of the board (for the sides stand almost

Replicas on Trial

Several full-size replicas of lightweight craft known as bateaux have been built by archaeologists and volunteers in recent years. Actual trials help assess handling qualities and provide a genuine experience of early American adventure on inland waterways.

2 (*right*) The replica of an eighteenth-century Lake George bateau gets underway from the shore at Basin Harbor, Lake Champlain in 1987. Compare ills. 5, 10–13.

3 (*below*) A replica based on the eighteenth-century bateaux found in Richmond, Virginia (ills. 14, 15), is poled through Seneca Bypass, a remnant of the Patowmack Canal.

perpendicular) is from twenty inches [51 cm] to two feet [61 cm], and the breadth in the middle about a yard and six inches [107 cm]. They are chiefly made use of for carrying goods, by means of rivers, to the Indians.

Kalm noted that French bateaux

are always made very large . . . and employed for large cargoes. The bottom is made of red, but more commonly of the white oak, which resists better, when it runs against a stone, than other wood. The sides are made of white fir, because oak would make the batteau too heavy.

Bateaux appear to have been entirely a New World invention, for Kalm observed that to his knowledge there was no similar boat type in Europe.

The earliest known mention of bateaux dates to 1671, when a special flat-bottomed boat was built at Montreal to navigate the rapids of the St Lawrence; once introduced, bateaux appear to have caught on quickly, and by the beginning of the eighteenth century historical documents contain accounts of carpenters assembling hundreds at a time for military use.

Journals and letters of military campaigns in the eighteenth century contain numerous references concerning the employment of bateaux, but it is clear that most soldiers and boatmen regarded them as commonplace and uninteresting, for practically nothing is said about their design or construction. Fortunately, it is possible to infer from the documents some idea of the capacity of these boats. The bateaux built by the English in 1759 were suitable for transporting twenty-three men with one

month's provisions; used as provision boats alone each could hold 30 barrels of flour or 16 barrels of pork, cargoes of slightly over 2 tons. French bateaux on Lake Champlain during the same period were reportedly able to freight up to 3 tons of supplies.

Bateaux were generally equipped with four to six oars and steered by an additional oar lashed to the stern. Long poles were sometimes carried to aid movement through shallow water and around rocks in rapids. Often rigged with a crude mast and sail when navigating on lakes, the flat-bottomed, shallow hulls were limited to sailing with the wind.

The bateaux beneath the museum. While thousands of bateaux were constructed in North America for military and commercial purposes, few have been found. This is perhaps not too surprising, since they were cheap, lightly built craft that most probably disintegrated soon after abandonment; some may have been broken up for firewood. The paucity of contemporary information about bateau construction and the lack of hull remains have combined to lend particular significance to archaeologically recorded examples of these craft.

During fall and winter of 1984–85 a veritable graveyard of bateaux was discovered during the construction of the Quebec Museum of Civilization in Quebec City's 'lower town'. The excavation of this remarkable find was directed by archaeologist Daniel LaRoche and sponsored by the Société Immobilière du Québec under a permit granted by the Ministry of Cultural Affairs.

In February 1985 I had the good fortune to visit the site and observe the uncovering and recording of two

4 Two of the eighteenth-century bateaux discovered during excavations in Quebec City's lower town. The endposts, frames and planking have been cleaned of mud and labeled prior to their being measured and photographed *in situ.* The eroded appearance of the timbers and the absence of boat-related artifacts suggests that these bateaux had been abandoned before their burial under the quay.

bateaux. Conditions at the site were extreme, combining frigid weather, frozen soil and an influx of ground water that was held in check only by the constant effort of three pumps. Despite tight construction deadlines, LaRoche and his crew successfully documented three bateaux *in situ* and recovered parts of five for preservation and further study.

The five nearly complete hulls were located in close proximity to one another, the first beneath the foundation of a house built in 1752, and the other four under a nearby quay believed to have been built in 1751. The hull timbers appeared to have suffered considerable deterioration prior to their interment, suggesting that the vessels were built, used and later abandoned on the edge of the St Lawrence River several years before the construction of the quay. The absence of any artifacts within the hulls further indicated abandonment rather than accidental sinking.

The boats averaged 33 ft (10 m) in length, the three measured examples being 30 ft 10 in (9.4 m), 31 ft 10 in (9.7 m), and 33 ft 7½ in (10.25 m) in overall length. Although similar in length, the construction techniques and timber dimensions differed slightly, suggesting that the hulls were the products of different shipwrights. The oak and pine timbers were fastened exclusively with iron nails, and the frames and endposts (only three endposts had survived) were carefully fashioned from naturally curved pieces of timber.

The Lake George bateaux. In the summer of 1960 a small fleet of partially buried bateau hulls was discovered by sport divers under the southern end of Lake George. Many of the fragile wrecks were torn to bits by

thoughtless souvenir-hunters, but fortunately a few examples were saved for archaeological study. The remains of two bateaux and part of a third were raised from the lake by a diving team directed by Dr Robert Inverarity of the Adirondack Museum, under a permit granted by New York State authorities.

The Adirondack Museum's effort proved to be one of the earliest successful underwater archaeology projects in the United States. The boats were cleared of mud and artifacts (one contained a cargo of 13-in [33-cm] mortar bombs), and raised to the surface; their iron fastenings had for the most part disintegrated, and at least one of the bateaux was recovered in pieces. The divers also collected loose timbers from nearby wrecks, including several stemposts. The wood pieces underwent lengthy treatments in polyethylene glycol to keep them from disintegrating upon drying out. One of the boats was partly reconstructed and is on display in the Adirondack Museum; the other two are in the possession of the New York State Museum.

In August 1985 Arthur Cohn, Scott Cooper and I visited the Adirondack Museum to record with measurements and photographs the construction of the bateau in the museum's collection. The existing hull consisted of the bottom planks, battens, the stempost and sternpost with their associated knees, the lower portions of the frames, and the lowest strakes of side planking, the garboards. Timber pieces that had been buried under Lake George's mud were in excellent condition, exhibiting original tool marks and tar stains, but endposts, frame tops and other pieces not protected by mud were considerably eroded. The bateau was 31 ft 10 in (9.7 m)

5 British bateaux and a sloop on Lake George during the French and Indian War. These vessels were built to transport British troops and artillery down the lake to attack fortifications on Lake Champlain. Expeditions against the French positions were initiated in 1755, 1756 and 1758, but the first two efforts came to nothing and the third ended in disaster. The bateaux in the print exhibit the narrow hulls and sharp ends typical of these craft.

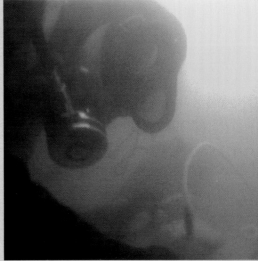

British Sloop, French Frigate

The French and Indian War (1755–1763) proved the climax of the struggle between Britain and France for control of the North American continent. Vessels like the British sloop *Boscawen* (ills. 6–8) and French frigate *Machault* (ill. 9) took part in minor naval engagements which helped decide the outcome of the war.

6 (*above left*) A main-deck beam of oak is brought ashore from the wreck of the Lake Champlain sloop *Boscawen* for measurement and examination. Such detached pieces were re-buried on the wrecksite after being examined.

7 (*above*) A diver records hull timber measurements on the wreck of the *Boscawen*. The site was in very shallow water, but dense weed growth and suspended silt combined to reduce visibility to a few inches.

8 (*below left*) Excavation project directors Arthur Cohn and Kevin Crisman examine a musket stock being cleaned by conservator Peggy Zak. The stock, recovered from inside the hull of the *Boscawen*, was originally part of a British Long Land-pattern musket.

9 (*right*) The wide variety of personal belongings retrieved from the wreck of the *Machault* provides a vivid picture of life aboard the flagship of a small French fleet defeated by the British in 1760.

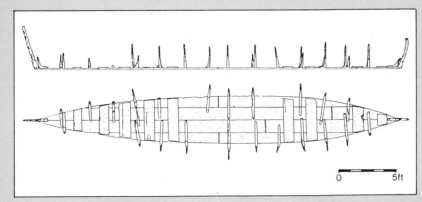

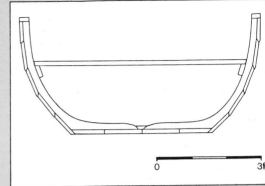

Building a Lake George Bateau

In 1987 the Basin Harbor Maritime Museum, Vermont, constructed a full-scale replica of a Lake George bateau. Boatbuilder Dexter Cooper assembled the hull from white pine planks and white oak endposts and ribs. Although quite narrow in proportion to its length, the bateau proved remarkably stable, but the shallow, flat-bottomed hull made it a poor sailing vessel.

10, 11   Profile and plan (*above left*) and reconstructed section (*above*) of the original bateau.

12, 13   The replica under construction: Robert Beach (*left*) of the Basin Harbor Maritime Museum fits a seat; view (*below*) from the stem aft. Compare ill. 2.

long on the bottom, 33 ft 2 in (10.1 m) in overall length, and 4 ft (1.2 m) wide on the bottom.

The bottom of the Lake George bateau was composed of four strakes of white pine planks, 1 to 1½ in (3.8 cm) in thickness and 12¾ in (32.3 cm) in maximum width. The outside edges of the bottom planks were beveled to fit the overlapping garboards. Plank battens, 1 in (2.54 cm) thick and 11 in (27.9 cm) wide, were nailed to the top of the bottom planking every 2 feet. The wrought iron nails used to fasten the battens to the strakes were quite small, but the carpenters used large numbers of them, about twenty nails per batten.

The stempost of the bateau was a curved piece of hardwood, probably oak, triangular in section, expanding from the front to the back. The bottom of the post was notched to fit over the forward ends of the bottom planks, to protect the weaker pine boards from splintering when the boat was beached. The after corners of the stempost were grooved to fit the side planking. The stem was reinforced by a small knee, nailed to the after face of the post and the bottom planking.

The sternpost consisted of a straight piece of oak or similar hardwood, also triangular in section. The post was spiked to the bottom planking and reinforced by a small knee. The after ends of the side planking overlapped the sides of the sternpost and were held in place with a few nails.

The frames consisted of naturally curved pieces of oak, tapered on each arm and thickest at the corner of the bottom and side; they were quite narrow, averaging only 2 in (5 cm) wide. Each frame was attached to the bottom planking with three or four nails. Five of the lowest side planks, the garboards, escaped the decay that destroyed the upper sides. The 1-in-thick (2.54-cm) pine planks were beveled on their upper edges to overlap the beveled lower edge of the next row of planks. This feature increased the

surface area of the seams, thereby making the relatively thin sides stronger and more watertight. Seams were sealed by a coating of tar.

The bateau in the Adirondack Museum was undoubtedly built in the British colonies, probably along the upper Hudson River in New York. A French expedition to the southern end of Lake George took place in 1757, but there is no indication that any of its boats were left behind. On the other hand, British records reveal that during the winter of 1758 hundreds of bateaux were sunk for preservation in this vicinity. The hulls recovered by the Adirondack Museum had holes drilled through their bottoms or sides, and were found lying in rows on the bottom, laden with rocks or mortar shells, evidence of intentional rather than accidental sinking.

The Lake George and Quebec City bateaux were quite similar in their design and assembly: they averaged about 33 ft (10 m) in length and consisted of a simple arrangement of planks and hardwood knees held together with iron nails.

James River bateaux. Although not very sophisticated in appearance or construction, the bateaux just described and thousands of others like them provided an inexpensive, practical means of transportation in the interior of North America during the colonial period. For the same reasons, they continued in use long after the period described in this chapter, as we are reminded by recent discoveries of late eighteenth- or early nineteenth-century examples in Virginia.

In 1983 William E. Trout III, President of the American Canal Society, and Richmond historian and canal buff Jimmy Moore followed with interest the excavation for a new building complex in downtown Richmond. They knew that the construction was situated just where the Great Basin of the James River and

Bateaux in Virginia

14 (*right*) Dig archaeologist Lyle E. Browning walks the length of boat 28, the only one of over sixty bateaux discovered in downtown Richmond, Virginia, to be excavated in its entirety. Note the walking boards running longitudinally. The pilings through the boat were driven down into the silt in the 1880s to support a rail yard by the C&O Railroad, which bought the old canal that once existed here.

15 Excavated bow section of one of the Virginia bateaux. Note the stern piece, the half-ribs at an angle, strengthening the bow planking, and the cross-piece here being measured, which supported the planking. A replica of one of the Virginia bateaux is shown in ill. 3.

Kanawha Canal had served as a terminus for river and canal boats between 1800 and 1880. Moore's persistence was rewarded when he was shown the remains of boats, including bateaux, 23 ft (7 m) below the modern street level.

While Faison Associates, developers of the land, delayed construction for more than a month, and even provided equipment and funds for the project, archaeologist Lyle Browning directed the recovery of the boats for the Archaeological Society of Virginia and the Virginia Canals and Navigations Society.

Subsequent building excavations in the vicinity uncovered the remains of over sixty additional bateaux, which were recorded by Trout and another canal buff, George Rawls; the Virginia Department of Transportation in cooperation with the Virginia Division of Historic Landmarks provided photogrammetric recording of five vessels. The press of construction and inadvertent damage by backhoes made it possible to excavate the entire length of only one bateau. It was 57 ft 6 in (17.5 m) long by 7 ft 6 in (2.3 m) broad, a bit broader than the James River bateaux measured by engineer Benjamin Henry Latrobe in the late eighteenth century at 60 to 70 ft (18 to 21 m) by 5 to 6 ft (1.5 to 1.8 m). If it had not been for a Patent Office fire, we would have actual plans of the original James River Bateau invented in 1771.

All of the bateaux in the Great Basin were similar, except that those used for hauling coal were more heavily constructed than the lighter 'Tobacco Boats' which were designed for white water. All were pointed at either end and had almost no sheer, and their nearly flat bottoms had no keels. Ends, frames and bottoms were made of hardwood, probably white oak, whereas sides were of lighter pine or poplar. Frames, composed in each case of five pieces scarfed together, were spaced from 22 to 27 in (56 to 69 cm) apart and fastened with iron nails driven from outside and often clenched over inside, although the

earliest hull found was also fastened with wooden pegs. A row of planks, nailed to the frames, ran lengthwise down either side of the interior; these were for walking upon while poling.

Protective canopies are known only from contemporary descriptions and woodcuts, but were identified on the bateaux by the characteristic holes in the gunwales. Cooking hearths of clay or earth were found between the third and fourth frames of most boats at both ends, enabling bi-directional travel by moving from one end to the other as in railroad locomotives.

Generally these bateaux were poled rather than rowed; iron posts at their ends supported steering oars.

More than a dozen replicas of the James River bateaux have been built, based on composite plans derived from the archaeological remains. Joe Ayers, especially, has been responsible for starting what Trout calls a Second Bateau Era in America, proving that 'a small group of volunteers can build an authentic replica in which to experience a genuine early American river adventure'.

King William's War

For several decades after their founding, the colonies of France and Britain had little contact with one another, the inhabitants being chiefly concerned with eking out a living in the unfamiliar landscape. Conflicts with local Indian populations further occupied the attention of the European settlers and hindered their expansion. The colonies were still recovering from recent altercations with Indian enemies when news arrived in 1689 of war in Europe. The French began the new war with a plan for the conquest of New York, formulated by ministers in Paris who had no appreciation of the difficulties of logistics and warfare in the wilderness. Briefly stated, the scheme involved an advance by 1,600 troops and militia down Lake Champlain and the Hudson River to New York City; once there, they would be met by two French warships that would assist in the siege and capture of the town. This impractical plan was quickly shelved by the governor of New France, who instituted in its place surprise attacks by French troops and Indians on isolated outposts, villages and farms on the frontiers of the English colonies.

New York, Massachusetts, and the other northern colonies reacted to these incursions by raising militia levies and impressing ships for invasions of New France via Lake Champlain and the St Lawrence River. Both enterprises met with failure. The troops ordered to proceed through the interior reached the southern end of Lake Champlain, but their further progress was arrested by a major oversight: they neglected to bring boats for the passage up the lake.

The attack by sea was commanded by Sir William Phips, a native of Massachusetts. With thirty-four vessels large and small, and 2,200 colonial militiamen, he sailed from Boston for Quebec City in August 1689, and after a lengthy voyage anchored below the town in October. Phips' request for an immediate surrender was declined, whereupon he ordered a landing and a bombardment of the city. These attempts did nothing to cow the French defenders, and Phips had no choice but to give up and return to Boston in late November.

This was the last major offensive of King William's War, but sporadic raiding of frontier settlements continued for seven more years. The Peace of Ryswick in 1697 brought a much-needed if only temporary peace.

Queen Anne's War

In 1702 England and France resumed their struggle in the Old World with the War of the Spanish Succession, and initiated a new series of attacks and reprisals in North America that have been called 'Queen Anne's War'. Strategists in France again advocated invasion of the British colonies and the destruction of Boston and New York City, but leaders of New France once more found themselves without the means to put these ideas into effect. They instead resorted to the tried-and-true method of sending raiding groups of soldiers and Indians through the wilderness to destroy the scattered, unprotected towns of the English.

The British colonies retaliated against these incursions by using their naval superiority to plunder French towns and shipping in Acadia. Invasions of New France via Lake Champlain and the St Lawrence River were attempted in 1709 and 1711, but each was frustrated by poor planning, bad leadership, or epidemics of smallpox and similar diseases. The attack on Quebec by sea in 1711 involved over seventy ships and 12,000 men, but through faulty navigation ten ships were wrecked with great loss of life in the Gulf of St Lawrence, so disheartening the leaders of the expedition that they turned back to Boston without attempting to ascend the St Lawrence River.

The British could claim one success in the midst of their sundry failures: in 1710 a powerful fleet descended upon Port Royal, Acadia, and after a short siege induced the French garrison to surrender. Possession of the fort (renamed Annapolis Royal by its captors) meant nominal control of this important Atlantic province of New France. When Queen Anne's War ended with the Peace of Utrecht in 1713, the British retained ownership of Acadia, giving them a foothold near the Gulf of St Lawrence and the ocean portals of the French colony.

For the next thirty years France and England were officially at peace, but in North America an intermittent war of raids continued. The French took measures during this time to fortify the approaches to their colony. The interior defenses originally consisted of Fort Chambly on the Richelieu River and Fort Frontenac at the outlet of Lake Ontario. These works were reinforced by the establishment of Fort Niagara at the head of Lake Ontario in 1726, and the building of Fort St Frédéric (called Crown Point by the English) near the southern end of Lake Champlain in 1734. The new positions protected the interior trade routes and the St Lawrence River heartland, while St Frédéric proved to be an ideal staging area for raids into New York and New England.

The loss of Acadia threatened the sea communications of New France. To rectify this situation a massive fortification was begun in 1720 along the shores of a large natural harbor on Cape Breton Island. The combination port and citadel, called Louisbourg, provided a haven for shipping in time of war and a base from which the French navy and privateers could harass English merchant and fishing vessels.

King George's War

Britain and France resumed their struggle in 1744, with the outbreak of 'The War of the Austrian Succession', which was echoed in North America as 'King George's War'. The inhabitants of New England quickly recognized the dangers that Louisbourg posed to their maritime trade and on their own initiative resolved to take the fortress. Over 4,000 militiamen signed on for the venture, and dozens of small merchant and fishing vessels were commandeered for transports.

The makeshift expedition departed from Boston in March 1745 and at the end of April landed several miles from the French fort. For the next six weeks the ill-disciplined but enthusiastic colonial troops used their siege guns to batter down the French walls. The land forces appear to have been about evenly matched, but the New Englanders had one crucial advantage: their supply vessels arrived on a regular basis, while those of the French rarely escaped the Royal Navy squadron that hovered off the shores of Louisbourg. The bombardment and blockade combined to bring about the surrender of the great fortress on 15 June.

Two French naval expeditions were sent to recover Louisbourg; the first, in 1746, was defeated by storms and disease, and the second, in 1747, was captured by the Royal Navy off the coast of France. Although the French

The Battle for Louisbourg

In 1720 the French began building Louisbourg, a massive fortress on Cape Breton Island, to act as a haven for their Atlantic shipping and a base from which to harass English vessels. It proved a sufficient threat during both King George's War and the French and Indian War for large contingents of men to be sent by sea to take it.

16, 17 Contemporary map (*above left*) and scene of colonial troops landing (*center left*) during the first siege of Louisbourg, 1745. At the outset of King George's War, New Englanders recognized the danger the French stronghold posed and mounted their own expedition to capture it. After a six-week struggle they succeeded, but three years later the battered fortress was returned to the French by the terms of the treaty of Aix la Chapelle.

18 (*below*) British boarding parties burn the *Prudent* and tow off the *Bienfaisant* at Louisbourg in 1758. These French ships-of-the-line were originally part of a twelve-ship force sent to aid the town. The destruction of the squadron during the siege gave the Royal Navy undisputed mastery of the Gulf of St Lawrence in the final years of the French and Indian War.

lost control of the sea, they maintained their ascendancy on the inland lakes and rivers, and parties of French and Indians used Fort St Frédéric as a base to carry out the customary attacks on New York and New England settlements. The treaty of Aix la Chapelle ended King George's War in 1748, and as part of its terms the fortress of Louisbourg was returned to its original owners.

The French and Indian War

The peace of 1748 temporarily ended the fighting in North America, but the continued expansion of Europeans into the interior of the continent made renewed disputes over territory inevitable. Open conflict began again in 1753 when the French built a series of forts on the upper reaches of the Ohio River (in what is now western Pennsylvania) to strengthen their claim to the region. In 1754 the English sent Virginia militia Major George Washington and a detachment of troops to drive out the French, but they were surrounded and defeated after a day-long skirmish.

War did not immediately break out, but during the next year each side sent troops and warships to North America while publicly declaring hopes for peace. The open rupture finally occurred on 8 June 1755 when a British naval squadron under Admiral Edward Boscawen encountered the French troopships *Alcide* and *Lis* off Cape Race, Newfoundland, and captured them after a brief fight. This may be considered the official beginning of the 'French and Indian War' in North America, but it was not until 1756 that England and France formally declared a state of hostilities that was known as 'The Seven Years War'.

The first three years of the French and Indian War proved disastrous for Britain and her colonies, whose forces suffered one setback after another on land and sea. In 1755 they began three campaigns to seize French positions on the Ohio River, Lake Champlain and Lake Ontario; all failed miserably, a result of either unskilled leadership or poor logistical planning.

The year 1756 was equally unfavorable for the British. During the previous year the French began a second fortification on Lake Champlain, near the outlet of Lake George; called Carillon by its builders and Ticonderoga by the English, the new work greatly improved French control of the Champlain waterway. A British expedition was organized to take the fort, and construction of bateaux and three small sloops was begun at Fort William Henry on the southern end of Lake George. The proposed attack was cancelled, however, after a French army under the command of Louis Joseph, the Marquis de Montcalm, descended upon Oswego, the under-manned and decaying British post on Lake Ontario, and captured it, along with the little flotilla of warships and bateaux that had been assembled there. The loss of Oswego deprived the English of their only outpost on Lake Ontario and kept them from challenging French control of the interior.

In 1757 the English resolved to recapture the fortress at Louisbourg, which the French had partially rebuilt and strengthened since its return at the end of King George's War. Troops were shipped from England and most of the defenses on the northern frontier of the colonies were stripped to provide men for the enterprise, but the warships and transports had to turn back while en route to Louisbourg when it was learned that three naval squadrons, comprising nineteen ships-of-the-line, had been sent from France and were waiting in the harbor.

While the British were occupied with their fruitless attempt on Louisbourg, General Montcalm assembled 4,000 men and 247 bateaux at Ticonderoga, rowed up the length of Lake George, and captured the undermanned garrison of Fort William Henry. The French employed a number of specialized bateaux during this attack; thirty-one pontoon boats for artillery were made by fastening pairs of bateaux side by side and building a platform above them. Another bateau was modified to serve as a gunboat capable of mounting an 11-pounder cannon and two small swivel guns.

The fortunes of war had reached their low point for England and her American colonies in 1757, but by 1758 naval power began to turn the tables on the French. On the high seas the Royal Navy recovered from earlier setbacks and began to choke off the vital shipments of supplies to New France. In the interior of North America, the British gained proficiency in the complicated business of building and maintaining a fleet of bateaux, and keeping the armies in the field well supplied. The operation of the bateaux was made substantially easier by the formation in 1756 of the 'Batoe Service', a special corps of 2,000 sailors and ship carpenters recruited from the seaboard.

In 1758 British strategy called for simultaneous attacks upon the outer defenses of New France. The capture of Louisbourg was deemed to be of the utmost importance, and a combined force of 11,500 men under General Jeffrey Amherst and 157 warships and transports under Admiral Boscawen was assembled for the undertaking. This siege proceeded much like that carried out by the New Englanders in 1745: Amherst landed his men in early July, ringed the citadel with batteries, and proceeded to demolish the stone ramparts. At the same time a squadron of French naval vessels, consisting of five ships-of-the-line and seven frigates, was trapped in the harbor by Boscawen's fleet and slowly destroyed. Six of the warships were scuttled by their crews to block the harbor entrance, two frigates attempted to escape (one successfully), and three ships were set afire by mortar bombs and burned to the waterline. On the night of 25 July, 600 British sailors in small boats boarded the two remaining vessels, the ships-of-the-line *Bienfaisant* and *Prudent*; the latter ran aground and was burned by her captors, but *Bienfaisant* was towed out of the harbor. The destruction of the ships at Louisbourg effectively ended French sea power in North America. Two days later the fortress surrendered for the second and final time. The British flattened the walls to ensure they would never be used again.

The most significant British success in the interior of the continent was the capture of Fort Frontenac at the outlet of Lake Ontario, a remarkable feat accomplished by a small, bateaux-borne army under Lieutenant-Colonel John Bradstreet, the experienced commander of the 'Batoe Service'. Bradstreet led his force over the Mohawk River route to Oswego, and thence around Lake Ontario to Frontenac. The French possessed five warships that easily could have blasted the tiny English flotilla to pieces, but they lay idle near Frontenac and were captured by the raiders. The fort itself, the keystone of the French western defenses, capitulated shortly thereafter and was destroyed by Bradstreet.

An earlier British expedition to capture Fort Ticonderoga on Lake Champlain ended disastrously when a 12,000-man army under the command of an incompetent general was repulsed by a force scarcely one-quarter its size. The French realized that despite this victory their ability to defend Lake Champlain was increasingly uncertain, and they began the construction of a naval flotilla of four small sloops and a schooner to augment the fortifications on land.

1759 – The decisive year. By 1759 the English forces were poised to deliver the coup de grace to New France. Royal Navy warships and privateers effectively prevented the arrival of most supplies or reinforcements, and large armies were prepared to invade the St Lawrence River Valley from the east and south.

The most important objective was Quebec, the capital and chief port of New France. In late June, twenty-two warships and 119 transport vessels under Admiral Charles Saunders sailed up the St Lawrence, anchored below the town, and unloaded an army commanded by General James Wolfe. The British bombarded the city for the next ten weeks, while the French in turn attempted to incinerate Saunder's fleet by floating burning ships and rafts downriver. The contest remained at a standoff until the night of 13 September, when the Royal Navy landed Wolfe and his troops above the city; the English and French armies met on the Plains of Abraham in the morning, where the British charged to victory and Generals Wolfe and Montcalm fell mortally wounded. The subsequent surrender of Quebec all but sealed the fate of the French.

At the same time two important interior defenses fell into British hands. Fort Niagara at the head of Lake Ontario surrendered after a brief siege, while an army under General Amherst forced the French to blow up and abandon Forts Ticonderoga and St Frédéric on Lake Champlain. Amherst intended to pursue his offensive down the lake and into Canada, but progress was checked by the small flotilla built by the French the previous year.

Amherst had foreseen the need for a navy of his own, and brought with him rigging, guns and shipwrights. He also brought Royal Navy Captain Joshua Loring to oversee the building and outfitting of vessels. During August and September, Loring and his small band of carpenters at Ticonderoga assembled and launched in short order an 18-gun brig of 155 tons, *Duke of Cumberland*, and a 16-gun sloop of 115 tons, *Boscawen*. These vessels were reinforced by a floating gun battery, or 'radeau', mounting six 24-pounder cannon, and several bateau-like gunboats mounting one cannon apiece.

In early October Loring sailed *Duke of Cumberland* and *Boscawen* to the northern end of Lake Champlain to locate and engage the rival flotilla. The two English vessels cornered three of the smaller French sloops in a bay, where the French crews elected to scuttle their vessels rather than face action. The sloops were raised and pressed into service in Loring's little navy, but it was too late in the year for Amherst to make much use of his mastery of the lake. The onset of winter weather forced the British to delay their conquest of New France for one more year.

The Sloop *Boscawen*

At the conclusion of the French and Indian War the naval squadron on Lake Champlain was stripped of guns, spars and other equipment, and laid up at the King's Dockyard below Fort Ticonderoga. The green-timbered warships quickly succumbed to dry rot and neglect, and sank one by one at their moorings, although the water was so shallow that their decks and upperworks remained partially awash. The exposed portions of the hulls were destroyed by winter ice and further decay, but their lower portions were preserved by a thick covering of mud. After two centuries under water little could be seen of the wrecks but a few eroded frame tops protruding above the lake floor.

In 1983 Arthur Cohn and I directed an underwater survey of Lake Champlain in the vicinity of Fort Ticonderoga, under the joint sponsorship of the Fort Ticonderoga Association, the Champlain Maritime Society and the Vermont Division for Historic Preservation. The water in this part of the lake is shallow and filled with masses of aquatic weeds, and thus is not particularly suited to survey with electronic instruments such as side-scanning sonar and magnetometers. Instead, the bottom was systematically examined by a team of divers swimming in a tight search pattern. Three nearly buried hulls were located and buoyed, and their positions plotted on the survey map. Subsequent test excavations produced artifacts dating to the French and Indian War period, and these, along with the dimensions and construction techniques of the hulls, permitted us tentatively to identify the three wrecks as part of Loring's naval squadron of 1759.

The first hull discovered was approximately 65 ft (19.9 m) in length, and was believed to be one of the French sloops built in 1758 and captured by the British in the following year. The second hull, 70 ft (21.3 m) in length and 25 ft (7.6 m) in beam, was identified as the British sloop *Boscawen*. Precise dimensions of the third hull could not be obtained, but it was flat-bottomed and resembled a large bateau or gunboat; its individual timbers were fastened with an unusual type of bolt also seen on the French sloop, and thus this wreck was judged to be French in origin.

Prior to the Fort Ticonderoga finds almost nothing was known about the design, construction, outfitting and appearance of the vessels in service on Lake Champlain during the French and Indian War. As the wrecks promised to yield much information about the living conditions of the sailors and soldiers who manned these small, fresh-water warships, we initiated a multi-year program of excavation and documentation; the Fort Ticonderoga Museum provided funding, the Champlain Maritime Society contributed technical expertise, and the State of New York, the legal owner of the wrecks, granted permits for archaeological excavation.

The English sloop *Boscawen* was studied first. We spent a total of ten weeks during the summers of 1984 and 1985 excavating the interior of the hull and documenting both its contents and its construction. Two 25-ft (7.6-m) square grids, subdivided into 5-ft (1.5-m) square excavation units, were suspended over the wreck to assist excavators in plotting the position of each find. Divers carefully stripped away the mud within their excavation units with the aid of water-powered dredges; fine-meshed net bags were attached to the dredge exhausts and examined after every 4-in (10-cm) level was dug to ensure that small items were not lost. After each unit was cleared of mud to the interior of the wreck, individual hull timbers and their iron and wooden fastenings were measured, sketched and drafted onto a master wreck plan. The waters of southern Lake Champlain are extremely murky, and visibility on the *Boscawen* seldom exceeded 1 or 2 ft (30 to 61 cm); the cloudy water conditions only slightly hindered the excavators, however, and a wide-angle video camera in an underwater housing allowed documentation of the work in progress.

The excavation of the *Boscawen* produced many surprises, not the least of which was the quantity and quality of artifacts contained within the hull. Prior to excavation we assumed that the sloop had been thoroughly stripped of equipment before abandonment, and that finds would consist of buttons, glass and ceramic sherds, musket shot and other minor debris. Small items of this nature were indeed found in abundance, but quantities of rigging components, tools, ordnance stores, small arms parts and personal possessions were also recovered. The unexpected variety of artifacts gave a vivid picture of living and working conditions aboard the *Boscawen*. The thick, airtight layer of mud which covered these materials for over two centuries kept most of them – even fragile rope, leather, cloth and straw – in an excellent state of preservation.

The array of rigging equipment scattered around the sloop's bilges included deadeyes, blocks, rope, iron hooks and thimbles, parral beads, fairleads, chain and a complete mast cap. Of particular interest were the ten single-sheave blocks recovered from the amidships and stern areas of the wreck. They differed considerably from one another in appearance and condition: three showed traces of red

19 (*left*) Several iron fasteners of this unusual design were found in the rib timbers of the two French vessels sunk at Fort Ticonderoga. After the bolt had been driven through two or more timbers, the protruding flange at the forward end was hammered over sideways, locking it in place. The bolt is 25 cm (9⅞ in) in length.

20 (*below*) Plan of the *Boscawen*'s excavated hull. Timbers beneath the mud were well preserved, including lower deck beams, pump wells and the single mast step. Protruding timbers were considerably worn by erosion and decay.

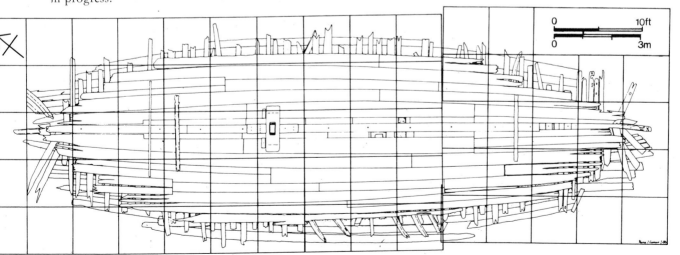

paint, while another was roughly carved and asymmetrical, suggesting that it was made on the lake to meet a deficiency in blocks. Yet another of the blocks was riddled with termite holes, indicating that it sat in storage for a time and may have suffered from old age when purchased by Joshua Loring for use on Lake Champlain.

The mast cap, used to attach the topmast to the upper end of the main mast, consisted of a rectangular block of white oak, $27\frac{1}{4}$ in (69 cm) in length, $12\frac{7}{8}$ in (30.7 cm) in width, and $7\frac{1}{2}$ in (19 cm) in height. One end contained a square notch that fitted the top of the main mast, while a round hole through the other end held the topmast. Three eyebolts were fastened to the underside of the cap to hold topping lifts, the blocks that raised and lowered the main yard and gaff. The mast cap is seemingly the only one yet discovered in a colonial-period shipwreck in North America.

Foraging tools – including a pickax and brush knife complete with wooden handles, two iron shovel blades and fragments of a wooden shovel blade, and an ax handle – were recovered from the amidships and stern portions of the hull. A hatchet head and fascine knife were also found, each stamped with the broad arrow mark that signified property of the British government. The three shovel blades were worn and broken, but the other implements appeared to be in good condition, and were plainly lost through carelessness rather than having been intentionally discarded. Other tools consisted of a hammer head, a mason's trowel and a small awl or gimlet; like the foraging tools, all seemed to have been in usable condition when they were left in the sloop's bilges.

Small arms repair must have been a frequent occupation of the *Boscawen*'s crew, to judge by the quantity of musket parts found. Divers recovered fragments of

walnut musket stocks, including two British Long Land-pattern musket butts complete with brass butt plates and pieces of the trigger guards. A Long Land-pattern gun lock, musket barrels, wooden ramrods, brass ramrod pipes, flint gunspalls, two bayonets and a small brass powderflask rounded out the inventory of gun parts from the wreck. The iron spear point from a boarding pike indicated that Joshua Loring outfitted the sloop with the same sorts of edged weapons that were carried on oceangoing warships of the time.

The personal possessions of the crew – the remains of their clothing, their diet and their diversions – best tell the story of life aboard the small, cramped *Boscawen*. With the exception of fragmentary remains of fabric encountered near the stern, nothing remained of the crew's clothing but metal fastenings such as buttons and buckles, half-a-dozen leather shoes and many shoe fragments. Buttons turned up in nearly every part of the wreck, and in very high quantities, suggesting that conditions aboard the sloop were not conducive to keeping uniforms intact. There was a wide range in the materials and styles of buttons: certain examples in brass were decorated with floral or geometric patterns, many were solid-cast from pewter and still others consisted of wooden disks. Brass cufflinks, buckles of various sizes, pins and a bell were also found on the inner planking and between the frames.

We learned something new about the crew's dietary habits. It was apparent from the bones, seeds, nut shells and other food remains found in the *Boscawen* that the crew supplemented their monotonous army diet with local wild foods. Several deer and waterfowl bones provided evidence that sailors or officers occasionally hunted to obtain fresh meat. Some type of squash, probably pumpkin, was consumed, along with shagbark hickory nuts, wild plums, wild grapes, butternuts and hazelnuts. Eating utensils consisted for the most part of simple, utilitarian items, like a pewter spoon with the owner's initials – 'HE' or 'HI' – scratched on the back, a pewter plate, an undecorated white delftware pot, and a crudely carved wooden ladle. Fragments from a delicate porcelain cup and pieces of a stemmed wineglass, however, indicate that there was at least one aesthete among the crew who was prepared to indulge in refined dining while

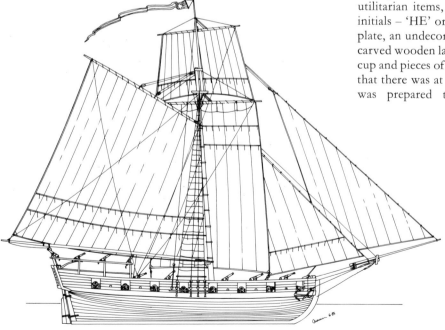

21 (*left*) Conjectural view of the *Boscawen* as she would have appeared on Lake Champlain in 1759. This drawing is based on the hull remains and contemporary information about the vessel. The sloop was about 23 m (75 ft) long on deck, and must have been incredibly crowded when her full complement of 180 sailors and soldiers were aboard.

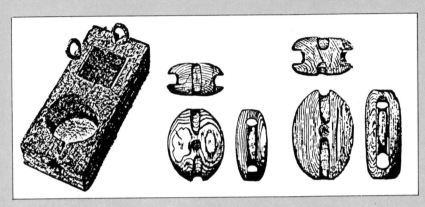

0   3ft

Aboard the 'Boscawen'

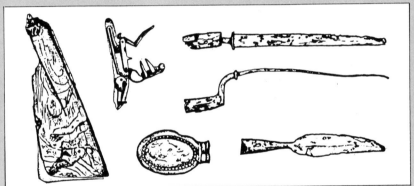

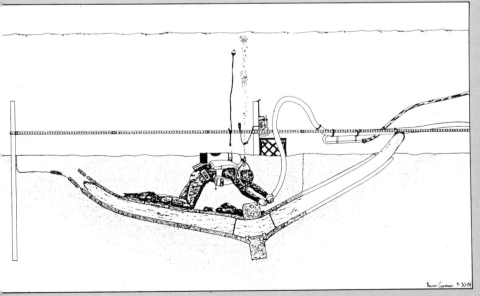

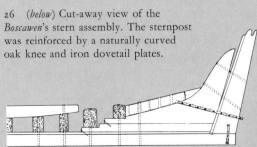

22 (*above*) The distribution of rigging-related materials in two excavation units. This concentration of rigging artifacts included deadeyes, single-sheave blocks, spare sheaves, iron hooks, parral beads and fairleads. Many pieces of cordage were also recovered from this vicinity. The loss or abandonment of this equipment suggests an attitude of carelessness among the *Boscawen*'s officers and crew.

23 (*upper left*) The mast cap (far left), viewed here from below, fastened the sloop's topmast to the upper end of the main mast. The single-sheave block in the center appears to have had little or no use. The right-hand block has termite holes, indicating that not all of the sloop's rigging equipment was good quality.

24 (*center left*) Small arms hardware found in the bilges of the *Boscawen*. Finds included (clockwise from far left) the broken stock from a British Long Land-pattern musket (see ill. 8), the lock mechanism from a musket, a bayonet, a pikehead and a powder flask.

25 (*below left*) A section across the *Boscawen*'s hull. The interior was filled with about 1m (3ft) of mud. When beginning the excavation of a new unit, divers often suspended themselves from the grid that overlay the wreck; as the trenches became deeper, however, most found it easier to work inside the hull.

26 (*below*) Cut-away view of the *Boscawen*'s stern assembly. The sternpost was reinforced by a naturally curved oak knee and iron dovetail plates.

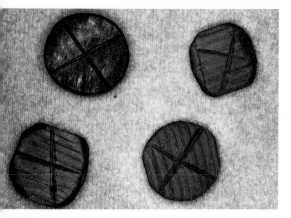

Amusement and Adornment

27 (*far left*) The purpose of round and square wooden counters found within the wreck of the *Boscawen* has yet to be determined, but it is possible that they were used as gaming pieces.

28 (*left*) French 2-sou piece. This was one of two coins found in the *Boscawen* with a hole drilled through the edge, possibly for carrying on a string.

campaigning with the naval squadron on Lake Champlain.

When not employed in operating or maintaining their warship, the men on board amused themselves in a variety of ways. Twenty round and square wooden counters for a game were discovered, each with an incised 'X' on one side. At least one member of the crew entertained himself (and possibly his shipmates) by playing an iron jew's harp. Smoking was evidently prohibited or strictly controlled below decks; only two broken kaolin pipe bowls and a few pipe stems were found. Drinking seems to have been a popular diversion, on the other hand, since a liquor bottle and dozens of fragments of others littered the inside of the hull.

Money either was in short supply for men living on the vessel or they were extraordinarily careful not to lose it. The excavation produced only four-and-a-half coins: two-and-a-half French 2-sou pieces dated 1738 and 1753, a British copper farthing dated 1718, and an unusual copper 1-heller coin from the German state of Bayreuth, dated 1752. The heller and one of the 2-sou pieces had holes drilled through their edges, perhaps for carrying on a string around the neck.

The *Boscawen*'s hull, of which about 40 percent remained, was the largest and most impressive artifact excavated. Hundreds of measurements and sketches made in 1984 and 1985 will ultimately allow a reconstruction of the hull on paper.

The keel, stempost and sternpost were all fashioned from durable white oak, and were fastened with iron bolts 1 in (2.5 cm) in diameter. The sternpost was secured to the keel by a pair of iron dovetail plates and reinforced by a large, naturally curved knee timber.

The *Boscawen*'s hull contained a total of twenty-six oak frames (ribs); each consisted of a floor timber fastened across the keel and a series of overlapping futtocks on each side of the floor. Each frame timber was fashioned from white oak, and averaged about 8 in (20.3 cm) square. Two water courses (also called limber holes) were cut into the bottom of every floor timber to permit bilge water to pass under the frames to the pump well, whence it was pumped from the hull. The individual frame timbers were

not fastened together in any manner, but were attached only to the 2-in-thick (5-cm) oak outer planking with iron spikes and oak treenails, indicating that the vessel was framed and planked simultaneously to save time; initially, three or four fully assembled 'guide' frames had been raised along the length of the keel to ensure that the port and starboard sides of the *Boscawen* remained symmetrical during framing and planking.

The interior of the hull included a mast step and several lower-deck beams. The step was shaped from a block of white oak 4 ft 3 in (1.3 m) long, slotted in the middle to hold the heel of the sloop's single mast. The block was fastened perpendicular to the centerline of the hull, slightly over one-third of the vessel's length aft of the stem. The beams for the lower deck consisted of white pine logs; the builders did not bother to de-bark the logs, but merely adzed their upper surfaces flat to form a platform for the lower-deck planking.

Study of the *Boscawen*'s hull remnants revealed some evidence of hasty construction, but in general the sloop was a very sturdy craft. The majority of the timbers that comprised the hull were fashioned from the preferred white oak, were of substantial dimensions and were fastened with adequate numbers of spikes, bolts and treenails. The *Boscawen* may in fact have been slightly over-built for the protected sailing conditions on Lake Champlain, but this is not surprising since most of Loring's carpenters were probably more familiar with oceangoing vessels.

Although the sloop was strongly built, its subsequent maintenance was poor. The carpenters took the time to cut limber holes in the bottom of every frame, but they failed to clear out treenail ends, bark, wood chips and other waste materials from between the frames. As a result, the water passageways were completely choked with debris from the time of launching, and the sloop would have sailed the lake with a foot or more of stagnant water in its bilges. The officers commanding the *Boscawen* also neglected to have the space below the lower deck cleaned out on a regular basis, and the area became filled with untidy heaps of wooden sticks and fragments, broken glass, scrap metal, food remains, charcoal, ballast stones and straw. Tools, rigging equipment, ordnance stores and many other useful items were lost in the debris-strewn bilges and never recovered; in one case excavators discovered a cache of rigging supplies carelessly buried under a pile of ballast stones. Clearly, once the *Boscawen* had performed its part in driving the French flotilla off Lake Champlain, it was of little worth to the British army, and was allowed to decay swiftly at its mooring below Fort Ticonderoga.

The *Machault*

By 1760 the French government was preoccupied with military operations on the European continent and had few resources to spare for its outnumbered army in Canada. That spring, however, a small naval squadron laden with military equipment and foodstuffs did sail from Bordeaux. This relief expedition was pathetically inadequate for the task of running the Royal Navy blockade and reinforcing the colony, as it consisted of only six vessels, the largest being the *Machault*, a frigate of 28 to 32 guns.

Two of the six ships were lost to the British Navy during the Atlantic crossing, one foundered in a storm and the remaining *Machault*, *Bienfaisant* (not to be confused with the ship-of-the-line of the same name mentioned earlier) and *Marquis de Malauze* found their route up the St Lawrence obstructed by enemy warships. The three vessels sought temporary shelter in the

1760: *Year of the British*

29 (*right*) The upper end of the *Machault*'s stempost and cutwater rise from the murky waters of the Restigouche River. This French frigate was scuttled by her crew on 8 July 1760 together with two sister ships, to prevent capture by a superior British force. Canadian archaeologists began excavations on the wreck in 1969 and four years later raised the stem and stern sections. Compare ill. 9.

30 (*below*) Contemporary drawing of a British gunboat used on the St Lawrence River in 1760.

31 (*below right*) Battle in the St Lawrence River between the French brig *Outaouaise* and British gunboats, 1760. After a lengthy contest the brig struck her colors, giving the British general, Jeffrey Amherst, undisputed command of Lake Ontario and the Upper St Lawrence River.

Restigouche River at the head of Chaleur Bay. In mid-June the English learned of the ships and sent a fleet to wipe them out. The French crews built gun batteries on the shores of the river and kept the Royal Navy at a distance for several days, but on 8 July they were forced to scuttle the vessels to prevent their capture. The English were unable to recover either the wrecked ships or their cargoes, and the shattered remnants of the last relief expedition to New France settled into the bottom of the Restigouche River.

In 1967, slightly more than two centuries after the fall of New France, the National Historic Parks and Sites Branch of Parks Canada began a long-term program to locate and investigate the wrecks. Searching with divers and magnetometers, archaeologists were able to find the flattened hulls of the *Bienfaisant* and the *Machault*. In 1969 a full-scale excavation of the frigate *Machault* was initiated under the direction of Parks Canada archaeologist Walter Zacharchuk. The work was undertaken to provide artifact dating and attribution information, and to answer questions about marine architecture, shipboard life and trade in the final years of the French colony.

Conditions for excavation in the Restigouche River were less than ideal, combining contaminated water, poor to non-existent visibility, tidal currents and considerable river-bottom debris. Nevertheless, excavators spent over 5,000 hours under water in the course of four field seasons. During the first three years the site was carefully excavated, with the divers using a grid divided into 5-ft (1.5-m) square units, to maintain archaeological control. The work was assisted by a wide array of specialized equipment, including a large dive barge (fitted with generators, compressors and a deck crane), airlifts for removing sand and silt overburden, and an underwater communication system that permitted contact between divers and surface personnel. In 1972, the fourth and final year of the *Machault* study, parts of the frigate's hull were detached with the aid of submersible chain saws and raised to the surface for detailed recording, preservation and eventual display. Recovered pieces included the stem and stern assemblies, and a midsection of the hull. The hull timbers were remarkably well preserved; both the stem and stern post still exhibited the incised roman numerals and lines that indicated the depth of the frigate's hull in the water.

The distribution of artifacts within the wreck provided some idea of stowage on board the *Machault*. Shot, boatswain's stores, cables and ropes, and sailmaker's tools were recovered in the forward end of the hull, while the amidships and after holds appear to have contained foodstuffs, water, spirits and ammunition. The cargo intended for the hard-pressed army in Canada proved to contain some unusual and seemingly impractical items. The hundreds of shoes and clay pipes recovered from the wreck might conceivably have aided the colony's defenses, but one wonders if the two or more barrels of Chinese export porcelain and the cache of tin-glazed earthenware bowls were necessary commodities for a supply expedition. Archaeologists analyzing the finds have theorized that the dishware was part of a small but potentially lucrative private trading venture by one of the *Machault*'s officers. Certain categories of artifacts, such as religious objects, surgical equipment, small arms and navigational instruments, were found in only small quantities or were entirely absent from the site, probably having been removed by the frigate's crew for use on shore sometime prior to the scuttling of their ship.

The Fall of New France

By 1760 the area of Canada still controlled by the French army was reduced to the vicinity of Montreal and the upper St Lawrence River, and the Royal Navy's command of the lower St Lawrence interrupted both supply and communication between France and its forces in North America. While the outlook for New France was grim, its leaders refused to surrender, hoping that a military miracle or peace might yet save the colony.

General Jeffrey Amherst's strategy for the defeat of New France in 1760 called for simultaneous advances on Montreal from three directions. One contingent of the British army was to sail up the St Lawrence from Quebec City, and a second was to proceed down Lake Champlain in the flotilla assembled by Joshua Loring during the previous year. The third and largest army group was to advance under the command of Amherst down the St Lawrence from Lake Ontario, and thereby prevent the French from retreating into the interior of the continent.

Amherst spent the months of June and July massing bateaux and troops at Oswego, while Joshua Loring prepared two brigs for service on Lake Ontario. This force entered the upper St Lawrence in early August, where the main body of Amherst's army was menaced by a French 10-gun brig, *Ottawa*. Loring's brigs were not present to deal with this adversary, but several small English gunboats managed to take the vessel after a four-hour action. After pausing to besiege and capture a small fort, Amherst sent his troops down the river's rapids in small boats and rafts; forty-six boats were destroyed and eighty-four men drowned in the turbulent waters, but the greater part of the army safely completed the passage.

On 7 September Amherst rendezvoused outside Montreal with the British armies invading from the east and south. The combined strength of the English at this time amounted to 17,000 men, whereas the French could muster a force of only 2,400. Montreal was incapable of resisting a prolonged siege by such a powerful and well-supplied enemy, nor was there any prospect of relief or re-supply by French warships. On 8 September the governor of New France surrendered, ceding the entire colony to its conquerors. The loss became official three years later, when the Seven Years War ended with the signing of the Treaty of Paris; by the terms of this agreement Canada became the property of England and its inhabitants subjects of the British crown.

CHAPTER EIGHT

Gunboats and Warships of the American Revolution

John O. Sands

The American Revolution was a war fought on the land. The names of the battles ring in our memories with unforgettable clarity: Bunker Hill, Saratoga, Brandywine, Yorktown. It was fought on the land, yet it was won on the seas. Control of the seas, and the access to supplies and trade that they represented, were the decisive factors in the entire war. Without control of the seas, American forces were fighting no more than a holding action; any hope of final victory was forlorn. With it, victory became a certainty. This was the first war of the modern era, the first war in which the vital relationship between disparate military forces became evident. The coordination of naval vessels, supply vessels and land forces was a complex experiment, an experiment vital to British victory, and an experiment that failed when the final test came.

The British were accustomed to fighting a war in the classic continental form, army against army in large carefully planned battles. The concept of an entire countryside at war eluded them for some time, to the detriment of their overall effort. British strategists imagined that the revolution was centered in the New England colonies, and their efforts to stamp out the rebellion were focused there. The belief that the American rebellion was a small family squabble that could be easily quelled gave way in the face of mounting evidence to the contrary. The entire conduct of the war was affected. With the slow realization that the rebellion was more widespread, strategy had to be restructured and broadened to include the whole of the colonies. The British found themselves in hostile country, thousands of miles from home and totally dependent upon supplies and resources from England for their support. That this was warfare unlike any they had previously encountered was evident to Richard Oswald, a British merchant of considerable influence who wrote in a strategy paper of 1779:

This American Land War is like no other War that ever was read, or heard of before. It prescribes action & conquest, but carries no coercive powers along with it over the Inhabitants of the Country. It courts

Allegiance, but cannot enforce any, either by Contribution of Property, or Penalty of Person . . . We call upon the Inhabitants then, to give us assurance of their Amity & Submission, by oath or affirmation. They decline it . . . We must leave them as we found them, and so must go in search of new adventures. We have a great deal to do. But must not go too far off, as we must eat. We would gladly Save our English Supplies as they come from a great way, & yet not being certain that the Country will kindly help us, & that it would displease them to be forced, we must not cash ourselves upon uncertainty & so must keep within a proper distance.

Without supplies from the countryside, no army could afford to venture far from the ships that carried their food and ammunition. The rebels had only to keep a force in the field to wear down the enemy, depending on the great expense of supporting an army abroad to sap the British will.

The expense of the war, and its poor progress, led the British ministers to look to the sea for a new approach. If it was impossible to subdue the Americans on their own ground, perhaps it would be possible to starve them out. Cut off from world trade, their supplies of weapons, ammunition and manufactured goods must eventually dwindle to the point that they would beg for peace. Thus, when Lord George Germaine, the British secretary of state for the Americas, appointed Sir Henry Clinton the new North American commander-in-chief, he instructed him to:

Embark such a Body of troops as can be spared from the Defence of the Posts you may think necessary to maintain, on board of Transports under the conduct of a proper number of the King's ships, with orders to attack the Posts on the Coast, from New York to Nova Scotia, and to seize or destroy every Ship or Vessel in the different Creeks or Harbours, wherever it is found practicable to penetrate, as also to destroy all Wharfs and Stores, and Materials for Ship building, so as to incapacitate them from raising a Marine, or continuing their Depredations upon the Trade of this Kingdom, which has been already so much annoyed by their Ships of War & Privateers.

While Clinton was supposed to be destroying the naval and maritime capabilities of the New England area, he was also instructed to look to the Southern colonies. For it was in the South that the principal export crops were produced, crops that in large measure were financing the war. Germaine explained that:

> The seizing or destroying their Shipping would also be attended with the important Consequence of preventing the Congress from availing themselves, as they have done, of their Staple Commodity, Tobacco, on which, and the Rice and Indigo of Carolina & Georgia, they entirely depend for making Remittances to Europe.

The strategy outlined by Lord Germaine coincided exactly with the thinking of Richard Oswald, who had also recognized the impossibility of achieving a final victory on land. He had concluded that an entirely new approach was called for, as 'there has been a great mistake in people's conceptions of the nature of this American business from the beginning'. The British fixation on their army was the result of a misunderstanding of the scope of both the rebellion and the continent. In view of the disparity between the 'capacity of resistance' on the part of the populace and the 'powers of enforcement' on the part of the British government, it was folly to have thought that a victory could ever have been achieved on land. Instead, the war should have been viewed as a problem of coastal blockade, a technique that centuries of warfare against continental powers had perfected. An embargo of the country's trade could have been effected with only a few strongholds along the coast to allow for the protection and resupply of the blockading ships. This would have permitted the total control of the trade of the rebellious colonies with virtually no commitment on the part of the army. It was unfortunate for the British that they realized their situation only after they had fought the rebellion for three years. That wasted time not only cost men and money, it allowed a shift in the balance of power. In 1778 the French signed a treaty of alliance with the rebellious colonies, significantly augmenting American capabilities. An internal rebellion had suddenly become a global war. Where the Americans had been virtually powerless on the seas during the early years of the rebellion, they now looked to the French navy for support. At the very time that the British recognized the importance of sea power, they had lost their monopoly on it. While they might ordinarily have been able to contain the French fleet with a continental blockade, the ships of the British navy were already engaged in America. Overextended as they were, any hope of maintaining control of the waters of the Atlantic was lost. This loss, more than any other, finally cost Britain the war.

In Search of Relics

HMS 'Augusta'. As with so many events, there was considerable interest in the American Revolution on the part of the surviving participants. Their interest in the documentation and memorialization of the events passed with them, however, and later generations of Americans were willing to let slip into obscurity both the memories and the physical remains of the war. There were a few who sought to preserve relics and tales from the days of the rebellion, but for most of the country the business of settling a continent was pressing enough. Occasionally, however, interest in the Revolution was inspired by the accidental discovery of a piece of the past. Such was the case with the wreck of HMS *Augusta*, in the Delaware River.

The *Augusta* was lost during the British attempt to seize Philadelphia, an attempt led by the brothers Richard and William Howe in the latter part of 1777. Theirs was a campaign aimed at the heart of the American colonies, a combined effort of the army and the navy. The British army sailed from New York for the Delaware River, but dallied for some months before attacking the rather meager fortifications there. During the delay the Americans had time to strengthen their positions, including the placement of obstacles in the river. These chevaux-de-frise on the river's bottom were intended to pose a hazard to any ship sailing up the river. They did their job well, if only for a limited time. In trying to avoid them while moving upriver, the 64-gun *Augusta*, accompanied by the 18-gun *Merlin*, was forced aground. This left her open to fire from shore batteries, and after several hours of shelling during unsuccessful attempts to refloat the vessel, she exploded suddenly. There was considerable loss of life, and the vessel was destroyed. There the story might have ended, had it not been for the fact that the ship lay in the middle of the channel, a hazard to navigation.

In 1869 the hazard was cleared, the vessel raised from the bottom and towed to the New Jersey side of the river. A contemporary newspaper reported that 'An intense excitement was created along the river and among the Jersey folks, who were anxious to see the vessel they had read of and heard so much about.' The salvors wasted no time in capitalizing on this interest; they threw up a canvas curtain around the hulk and charged 25 cents a look, with considerable success. Among the finds they displayed was a piece of metal 4 in (10 cm) long and 1 in (2.5 cm) wide, dated 1774, with the Lord's Prayer engraved on it. With great interest the visitors noted the fine state of preservation of the timbers, as well as the fact that only treenails were used for fastenings. This came as quite a surprise in the middle of the nineteenth century, when metal bolts had become commonplace in naval construction. The artifacts were finally distributed or sold, the hull began to deteriorate and the novelty wore off. The entire episode might have been forgotten had it not been for the Daughters of the American Revolution.

Relic of the Revolution

The wreckage of a British man-o'-war, HMS *Augusta*, lost during an attempt on Philadelphia in 1777, inspired new interest in the Revolutionary War when it was raised from the Delaware River nearly a century later.

1 (*above*) HMS *Augusta* burns in the Delaware River, downstream from Philadelphia, on 15 November 1777. After a drawing done on the spot.

2 (*right*) Timbers recovered from the wreck of the *Augusta* by the Daughters of the American Revolution provided the material to build the New Jersey room in their Continental Hall, Washington. The extraordinary craftsmanship evident in the room's construction, in combination with its historical associations, combine to make a strong patriotic statement.

Founded in 1890, the DAR sought to preserve the memory of the past. When they built Continental Hall as a national headquarters in Washington, each of the state chapters contributed a room to the building. The ladies of the New Jersey chapter still remembered the *Augusta*, although the hulk had been beached and was virtually covered with sand. Timbers were pulled from the wreck by men and horses, were allowed to dry for over a year and then were milled into lumber. The New Jersey room was paneled with this ancient oak, its plan copied from a Jacobean room in London. Thus the *Augusta* is preserved in a sense, both by artifacts to be found in several museums and by the spirit and enthusiasm embodied in the New Jersey room.

The Continental gunboat 'Philadelphia'. It was a ragtag group of rebels who twitched the tail of the British lion. They fought with little in the way of the war materials that we might take for granted today. Yet they managed to mount a war that eventually succeeded in freeing a country. It was a war filled with paradoxes, not the least of which was the fact that one of the most important American campaigns was led by a man who would later come to symbolize treachery, Benedict Arnold. Late in 1775, Arnold led an attack on Quebec, intending to neutralize that British possession to the northward. After a long winter's siege, the Americans were forced to withdraw in the spring of 1776. They moved south via the water route offered by Lake Champlain. The British were sufficiently impressed by the threat Arnold had offered that they followed him into the lake region. The Canadian governor Carleton saw an opportunity to open an offensive that would divide the New England colonies from the rest of the country. Lake Champlain thus became the unlikely site of a major naval engagement, hundreds of miles from the ocean.

Neither the British nor the Americans had any ships on the lake, nor did they have any way of getting them there. Each recognized the importance of the area, however, especially following the critical battles that had been fought there during the French and Indian Wars. So it was that both sides set to building vessels, the British to press southward and the Americans to stop them. By the fall of 1776, the British were able to muster some twenty-five vessels, ranging in size from a ship down to about twenty gondolas or gunboats. In return, Arnold could offer a few schooners and an assortment of gunboats, totaling seventeen vessels. Both sides had to use hastily built craft and incomplete equipment, but the Americans were outgunned and outmanned two to one. Nonetheless, they made a heroic showing.

General Arnold chose Valcour Island, near Plattsburg, New York, to take his stand. He arrayed his vessels across an arm of the lake on 11 October 1776, to fall in behind the English as they sailed south. Perceiving the trap, the British turned back upwind, engaged the Americans, and fought a hot action until darkness fell six hours later.

Arnold lost two vessels, the schooner *Royal Savage* and the gondola *Philadelphia*. The schooner was severely damaged and beached by her captain to allow the crew to escape; the British burned the hulk. The *Philadelphia* took a large number of shots at or below the waterline, and finally sank in about 60 ft (18.3 m) of water. With most of his ammunition spent, Arnold deemed it the better part of valor to slip away during the night. Although Carleton subsequently caught up with and destroyed the bulk of the American fleet, the delay forced him to abandon his campaign in the face of the approaching winter. The ragtag force had accomplished its goal, not through victory but through staying in the field.

The action was largely forgotten until 1932, when the wreck of the *Royal Savage* was discovered. Two years later, her remains were raised to the surface by Lorenzo F. Hagglund, a salvage engineer with the well-known firm of Merritt, Chapman and Scott. Since the vessel had burned, little remained save her bottom planks. The excitement generated by her recovery was sufficient to lead to a full-scale search for the *Philadelphia*, however. A large yacht was borrowed as the base of operations, and a chain sweep was dragged across the bottom of the lake. As might have been expected, a wide variety of debris was discovered during the two weeks of the search. On 1 August 1935, however, a major obstacle was encountered in 57 ft (17.4 m) of water. Investigation revealed the *Philadelphia*, her hull standing upright on the bottom of Lake Champlain, her mast still stepped. The cannons were removed to reduce the weight of the vessel, and she was raised by a floating derrick using lifting straps under the hull. The vessel was in surprisingly good condition. A tarpaulin passed under her bottom plugged the holes that caused her loss 150 years before, and the vessel was pumped dry. Following her recovery, the *Philadelphia* was displayed aboard a barge that traveled around the waterways of New York state. She was eventually brought ashore, and after Colonel Hagglund's death was given to the Smithsonian Institution. Arriving in Washington in 1961, she became a key element in the exhibits of the Museum of American History, and is to this day the only intact American warship from the American Revolution available on display.

Though not recovered with the archaeological precision that we have come to expect today, the *Philadelphia* still stands as a document of great importance. The hull is only 53 ft (16.1 m) in length, yet it played a vital role in the war. Such small vessels were critical to the American effort, as they could be quickly constructed yet could carry upwards of forty-five men and several large guns. They enabled access to the water by an otherwise landlocked army, and were utilized not only in the lake campaign, but also on Long Island Sound and in the Chesapeake Bay. As is typical with such hastily built vessels, there is virtually no documentation surviving. Without the *Philadelphia*, we would have scant concept of the meaning of the terms barge, gunboat and gondola.

The Battle of Valcour Island

3   A contemporary sketch of the 1776 battle on Lake Champlain shows American forces led by General Arnold concealed behind the island. The British forces in the foreground had to turn back upwind to engage the Americans, to their considerable disadvantage. The *Philadelphia* (ills. 4–6), one of Arnold's squadron, was one of only two American losses. The engagement delayed the British sufficiently long that eventually they had to abandon their campaign to isolate the New England colonies.

The gondola's flat-bottomed hull could be poled, rowed or sailed, depending on conditions. Though relatively small, it was sturdily built to withstand the strains imposed by carrying and firing artillery. That artillery consisted of three guns, the largest of which was the slide-carriage-mounted 12-pounder on the small deck in the bow. Her broadside consisted of two 9-pounders and a rail-mounted swivel, all on the midships deck. Her single mast carried not only a square mainsail, but a topsail on a separate topmast. With her flat bottom and lack of keel, she could not have been very weatherly, but the crew could always have rowed to windward.

For her size, the gondola carried a large number of men by our standards. Crowded into her short length these men had to live, sail and fight independent of any shore support. The artifacts recovered from the wreck give some insight into their lives. In addition to the cannon balls and ax heads associated with fighting afloat and ashore, there were buttons, spoons, pots and pans. Even the brick hearth on the midships deck that constituted the open galley was still in place. Life in this open boat must have been no more than rudimentary, yet the vessel and crew played a critical part in this campaign. A weapon need be no more than sufficient to its assigned task.

Far from being a static exhibit piece of no value to scholars, the *Philadelphia* continues to serve as a source of information. The Smithsonian Institution's Division of Naval History has completed an exhaustive study of the vessel and many related artifacts. This information is available in the form of a large set of plans detailing armament, rigging, hull design and living accommodations for this extraordinary survival.

Gunboat of 1776

She sank during the naval battle with the British on Lake Champlain in October 1776; 159 years later the American gunboat *Philadelphia* was discovered and raised, to become a prize exhibit of the National Museum of American History, Smithsonian Institution, in Washington, D.C.

4 (*right*) A scale model reconstruction of the *Philadelphia*, by Howard Hoffman, reveals constructional details. Only 53 ft (16 m) in length, this flat-bottomed gondola could be poled, rowed or sailed, depending on conditions.

5 (*below*) The remarkably well-preserved hull of the *Philadelphia*, now on display in Washington. Her main armament of a forward-mounted 12-pounder and a 9-pounder to port and starboard were recovered when the vessel was raised.

6 (*below right*) *Philadelphia* was photographed as she broke the surface of Lake Champlain on 9 August 1935. Note that her mast was still in place.

Penobscot Privateer

The 'Defence'. The British navy at the beginning of the American Revolution was among the most powerful fighting forces in the world. Arrayed against it was a miscellany of vessels assembled by the rebels. Not all were as simple as the *Philadelphia*, but certainly none approached the size or power of even the smallest British ship-of-the-line. Each of the former colonies was held responsible for constructing, buying or chartering its own naval force. These state ships, added to a meager group assembled by the Continental Congress, comprised the official navy of the United States. In addition, however, there was a fairly large number of private vessels authorized by Congress to take enemy shipping for private profit. These privateers carried letters of marque, and thus became legal representatives of the government. A well manned and sailed privateer could prove very profitable for her owners, and not a few investors entered this new field of endeavor. Frequently a ship that was already afloat was converted for use as a privateer, but the fastest and best ships were those built specifically for the task. Among the latter was the *Defence*, thought to have been built in Beverly, Massachusetts, in 1779.

Less than a year old, the *Defence* set out 19 July 1779 from Boston on 'her first voyage. She joined a fleet of forty-three vessels, nineteen of them armed. Included were ships of both the Continental and Massachusetts state navies, a number of privateers, and transport vessels for the army. This naval expeditionary force was the largest ever assembled by the Americans; its target was the new British outpost on Penobscot Bay, in what is today Maine. At the time Maine was a largely unsettled territory of Massachusetts, and the British had sent a force to establish what they hoped would be a colony loyal to the crown. The Americans set sail to counter this threat with overwhelming numerical superiority on their side. Yet only a month later, virtually the entire American fleet had been destroyed or captured, leaving the bottom of Penobscot Bay and River strewn with the wreckage of burned and abandoned ships. Among them lay the *Defence*.

The American effort was the victim of poor leadership, and of the inability of the army and the navy to cooperate. This important concept of joint command of both land and sea forces was new in the eighteenth century. The failure to cooperate proved disastrous to the American Penobscot expedition, and was to plague the British in later campaigns. Command of the American naval forces fell to Dudley Saltonstall, of the land forces to Solomon Lovell, with field artillery under none other than Paul Revere. On 25 July the fleet approached the British fortification called Fort George and opened fire. The fort's batteries promptly responded, but within three days the American troops were ashore, ready to storm the earthworks. Instead of storming, however, they dug in for a prolonged siege. The fleet under Saltonstall provided some supporting fire but failed to engage the three British warships anchored in front of the fort. Army and navy each waited for the other to take the initiative, unaware that British reinforcements were on their way from New York. On 13 August, when the stalemate finally ended and the army was about to attack, the additional British forces under Sir George Collier arrived. Although numerically superior, Saltonstall's fleet was outgunned and unsophisticated in comparison to the seasoned British veterans. He ordered a full retreat up the bay, and the attacker became the attacked. The trapped crews ran their ships into shallow water and scuttled them. The night sky was said to have been lit by the flames of burning ships, the evening quiet punctuated by the sound of exploding powder magazines. The crews that were able to escape took to the woods and walked back to Boston. The three officers in command of the expedition were court-martialed. Lovell was cleared of any wrongdoing, Revere was censured for his part but finally exonerated, while Saltonstall took the blame for the failure of the enterprise. His naval career was over.

Though the memory of this worst of all American naval defeats lived on, the location of the individual wrecks was forgotten. Not until 1972 did a summer class jointly sponsored by the Maine Maritime Academy and the Massachusetts Institute of Technology undertake a search for the *Defence*, while studying the construction and use of sonar equipment. Her location was reasonably well documented, and in only three days of surveying, the team was able to locate what appeared to be her remains. The wreck was marked by two cannon and a brick cookstove that projected above the bottom. The recovery of selected artifacts and the review of further historical records led to the conclusion that the wreck of the *Defence* had been discovered. By 1975, a cooperative agreement had been forged between Maine Maritime Academy, the Maine State Museum and the Institute of Nautical Archaeology to undertake the full excavation of this extraordinarily well-preserved wreck. The project was directed by David Switzer, with David Wyman as assistant director. Excavations in the cold Maine waters went on every summer through 1981, until the hull had been completely uncovered. The first ship of the American Revolution to have been fully excavated under scientific controls, the *Defence* revealed much about herself and the lives of those who sailed her.

The ship had been forced into a small harbor, where her crew scuttled the vessel rather than allow her capture. They set charges and hastily abandoned ship before an explosion ripped off the stern; the hull soon settled to the bottom. As a result of this precipitate departure, most of the supplies and ship fittings were left behind. Further, she sank without significant burning, so that the hull is better preserved than many others from the same fleet.

Archaeologists discovered that much could be learned from the placement of artifacts in the wreck as revealed by careful excavation records. Most of the foodstuffs were

Dissecting the 'Defence'

A Revolutionary War ship built privately and authorized to attack British vessels for profit, the *Defence* was scuttled by her crew after an abortive assault on Fort George, Penobscot Bay, in 1779. Almost two centuries later she was excavated by archaeologists led by David Switzer.

7, 8 The *Defence*'s main armament consisted of sixteen 6-pound guns. Cannon balls for the guns were held in so-called shot garlands, one of which is seen here (*above*) *in situ* before being raised (*left*) by the wreck excavators.

Digging a Yorktown Brig

Of the ships scuttled along the York River in 1781 by the besieged British commander, General Cornwallis, nine have now been located by underwater archaeologists. One, a merchant brig designated YO 88, has been the subject of a full-scale excavation under the direction of John Broadwater.

9 (*right, top left*) A cofferdam was built around YO 88 to provide controlled diving conditions. Bubbles escaping from the exposed timbers of the ship, here trapped under a layer of skim ice, outline the wreck below.

10 (*right, top right*) Archaeologists trace details onto clear plastic in the port bow.

11 (*right*) View facing port of a team of archaeological divers excavating casks in the bow of the wreck.

stowed forward in the vessel, beneath the forecastle. Approximately fifteen casks were found there, some still containing bone fragments and bearing stamps indicating their contents as salt pork. Amidships a wide variety of personal items, including many shoes and clothing buttons, showed where the crew must have slept and eaten. Aft of this section was the base of the bilge pump, surrounded by a box that separated it from the adjacent shot locker. It was in the shot locker that cannon balls were stowed, near the magazine holding the gunpowder supply, in the after end of the ship. When the ship was scuttled, an explosion in the area of this magazine left the after portion of the wreck rather badly damaged. A study of the distribution pattern of the artifacts in this section made it possible to determine the point of origin for the blast that sank the ship. Unfortunately the blast was centered below the officers' cabins, and little remains of them.

What was found of the ship itself is quite revealing. The hull is very sharp in design, with a V-shaped entrance forward. This is in marked contrast to the rather bluff-bowed entrance that the few surviving drawings from the colonial period might lead us to expect. The explanation seems to lie in the fact that the *Defence* was built specifically for use as a privateer and speed was essential. This may also explain the hasty construction indicated by certain features of the ship. While the keelson was carefully shaped and finished, the shot locker was roughly built and may have been a last-minute addition. As other American built vessels of the eighteenth century are excavated, it should be possible to form a better conception of typical design and construction techniques.

Among the most interesting features of the *Defence* was her galley. The brick galley stove was prominently visible above the bottom when the wreck was found, and continued to dominate the scene throughout the excavation. The stove, 5 ft (1.5 m) on a side, was built brick by brick around a large copper caldron. Holding 68 gallons, the caldron was of heavy riveted construction, divided down the center into two chambers. Fired from below, the two sections could hold salt meat and beans or vegetables. A surprising variety of mess equipment was found in the vicinity of the stove itself. The crew of 100 divided into mess sections of five men each. At mealtime each mess was issued a chunk of salt meat that was then boiled. The meat was identified by a small wooden tag tied to it, a tag marked with the mess's symbol. Each mess also had its own kid, a wooden tub about 1 ft (30 cm) deep and with a similar diameter. Food for the entire group was obtained at the galley stove and carried back to the men in this kid. Examples of both tags and mess kids were found. The largest number of eating utensils found, however, belonged to the men themselves. Apparently each man kept his own bowl and spoon, marked with the scratched initials of the individual owner. The various marks give some hope of connecting the artifacts to their original owners of 200 years ago.

From this survivor of an ill-fated expedition, we can begin to form some opinion of life aboard an American privateer during the Revolution. The *Defence* was clearly cramped and crowded. Of the 100 men aboard, the bulk lived and slept in the midships section, measuring only about 20 by 25 ft (6.1 by 7.6 m). With scarcely 6 ft (1.8 m) of headroom, they slung their hammocks, stowed their gear and ate their meals. In an overall length of less than 100 ft (30.5 m), room also had to be found for sixteen 6-pound guns, sails and equipment for a two-masted sailing ship, supplies for the officers and crew, and the small weapons and ammunition required by a successful privateer. She was a remarkably complex machine, though unfortunately for her owners, the *Defence* was never able to put all of this into profitable action.

12 (*left*) When British ships under Sir George Collier entered Penobscot Bay in August 1779, they trapped the largest naval expeditionary force that the newly formed United States had ever assembled. In short order the entire American fleet was destroyed, including the privateer *Defence*.

Archaeology of a Privateer

13, 14 (*right*) The excavated *Defence* with galleystove (*inset*) at the foremast and pump box and shot locker at the mainmast. The huge caldron in the galleystove provided cooked food for the whole crew of 100 men.

15 (*below*) The rich artifact deposit in a cross-section near the galleystove. Many of the loose boards came from casks.

16 (*bottom left*) Conservator Betty Seifert holds a successfully treated stand of grapeshot. Anti-personnel weapons, these iron balls wrapped in canvas on a wooden base were difficult to conserve because of dissimilar materials.

17 (*bottom right*) Graffiti were found on mess items, apparently individual property, like the pewter spoon.

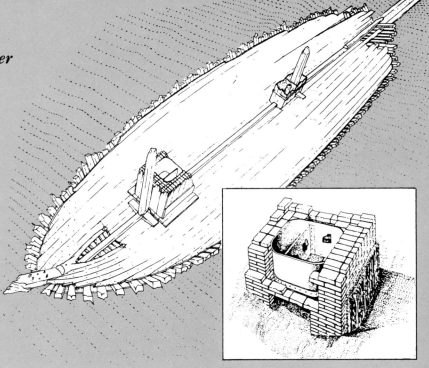

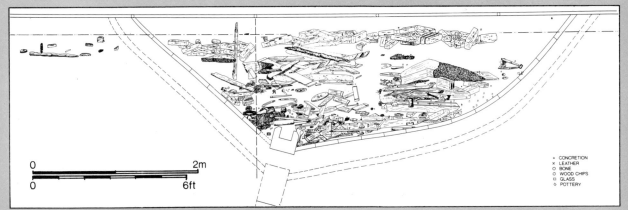

0   2m

0   6ft

+ CONCRETION
× LEATHER
○ BONE
□ WOOD CHIPS
□ GLASS
◇ POTTERY

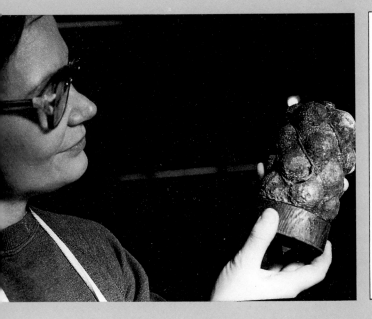

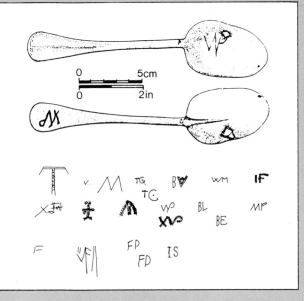

0   5cm

0   2in

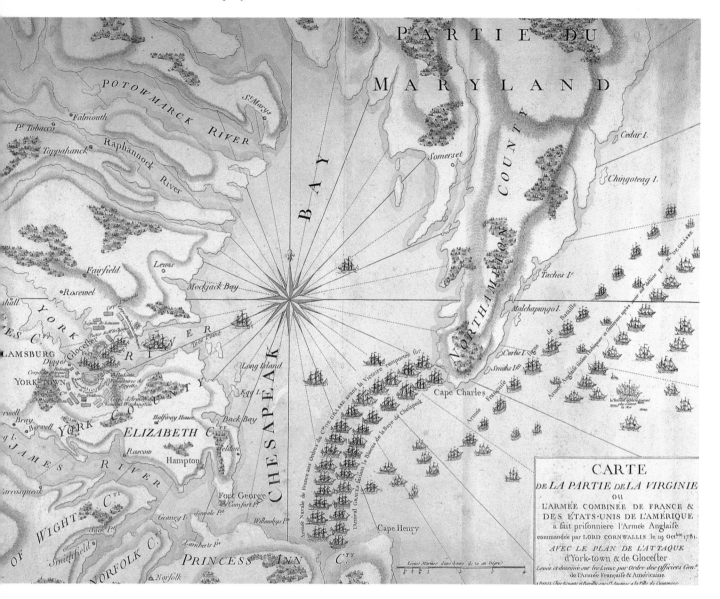

Yorktown: A British Defeat on Land and Sea

Sea power triumphant. By the summer of 1781, the British in North America faced fairly dismal prospects. Efforts to contain the insurrection in New England had failed, and a new strategy had been adopted. An army had been sent to the South, in the hope that the planters would prove more hospitable than their northern brethren. With good naval support, this British southern campaign had opened in Charleston, South Carolina, in January 1780. Responsibility eventually fell to General Earl Cornwallis, second-in-command for North America. He was able to capture and hold the major seaports in North and South Carolina, but he was totally unable to control the inland counties. By the summer of 1781 he had moved to the Chesapeake Bay, where the lucrative tobacco trade was centered. Having gained control there, he had essentially accomplished the purposes of the southern campaign from the strategic perspective. There was scant enthusiasm on the part of the population for a return to loyalist rule, however, and Cornwallis was able to maintain control only so long as he had naval vessels to hold the harbors. It was for this reason that he sought a harbor in the Chesapeake that he might permanently fortify and hold, thus providing ongoing control of the entire Bay. He ultimately chose Yorktown, in Virginia.

If the prospects of the British were dim, those of the Americans seemed even worse. Their army was under-equipped and exhausted after a war lasting six years. Finances, which always had been tight, were totally disrupted by the depredations in the South. There had as yet been few positive results from the alliance that was forged with the French in 1778. The most promising

The Battle for Yorktown

Naval power played a key part in the outcome of the battle in 1781.

18 (*facing page*) In this French map published soon after the battle, the strategic importance of the fleet under de Grasse is evident. It is shown both bottling up the mouth of the Chesapeake Bay and sallying forth to engage the British fleet coming to relieve Cornwallis.

19 (*above*) Washington (third from left) and his principal officers depicted by the artist Charles Willson Peale in front of recently captured Yorktown. Along the shore may be seen the sunken remnants of the surrendered British fleet, and the horses killed to prevent capture by the Americans. Downriver are two French ships-of-the-line, sailing into the harbor to assert naval command.

20 (*right*) General Earl Cornwallis, the British commander at Yorktown, in a portrait by Thomas Gainsborough painted in 1783, two years after his defeat.

21 Once it had Cornwallis trapped, the French fleet moved in to close the mouth of the York River, to ensure that no escape was possible for the British fleet.

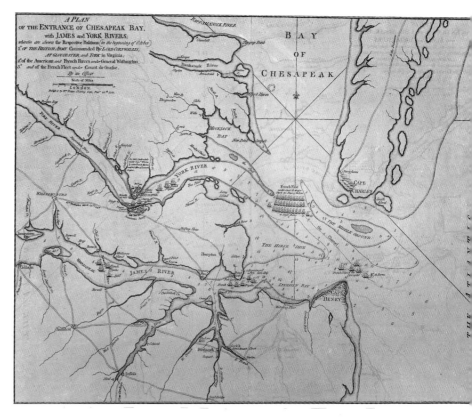

development had been the arrival of a fleet under Admiral Ternay, carrying the army of the Comte de Rochambeau. That fleet had never been able to coordinate properly with American land forces, however, and had been idle in Rhode Island for nearly a year. How delicate was the balance between Americans and British, and how dependent on the control of the seas, would soon become evident.

In the summer of 1781, the French finally responded to ongoing American entreaties to commit a major fleet to the fray in North America. A fleet of twenty ships-of-the-line sailed from Brest under the command of Admiral de Grasse, arriving off the entrance to the Chesapeake Bay on 29 August. When that fleet entered the Bay, the entire balance of power in North America shifted. Suddenly aggressor became defender, as the British army in the South was cut off from assistance from the main army in New York. Where Cornwallis had been bottling up the trade of the Chesapeake, he was himself now bottled up. The presence of an army of 10,000 men was cold comfort when all supplies and relief had to come by water. Washington lost no time in beginning to move his own forces to Virginia, to capitalize on the advantage that had been handed him.

That Cornwallis was in an untenable position was immediately apparent to the British command in New York, and the main British North American fleet was dispatched to attempt his relief. That fleet arrived off the Capes of the Chesapeake on 5 September and engaged de

Grasse, who sailed out to meet it. The battle was hotly fought but inconclusive. For the next five days the fleets sailed within sight of each other, each unwilling to reopen the fighting. Finally, Admiral de Grasse slipped away at night and returned to reestablish his blockade of the Chesapeake. He had come to the realization that his principal mission had nothing to do with the British navy, but rather with their army. Until that time navy had fought navy, army had fought army, and any cooperative effort was coincidental. With the recognition of the strategic role his fleet played, de Grasse took the step that broke the back of British control in North America.

On 28 September, Washington's land forces encircled Yorktown, while de Grasse held control of the Chesapeake. Having come to Yorktown by water, Cornwallis had not only his army in the town to protect, but a fleet of some sixty ships in the harbor to consider as well. There were five naval vessels, the largest being the *Charon* of 44 guns. The remainder were primarily transports that carried men, supplies, horses and artillery. Though they would have been vital to the survival of the army had it been able to reach the open ocean, they were a liability once trapped. Cornwallis therefore unloaded his supplies, stripped the naval vessels of their large guns for use ashore, and integrated the empty ships into his defenses. Drawn into shallow water along the beach at Yorktown, they were scuttled in a line. He thus created an obstacle to hinder an amphibious landing by the French, allowing him to concentrate his attention on his landward defenses. The force of numbers proved overwhelming, however. With no prospect of relief from New York getting through the French blockade, and outnumbered by Washington two to one, Cornwallis finally called for terms of surrender on 17 October 1781.

With the defeat of the second largest British military force in North America, the tide of the war turned. British public opinion swung against continuation of the war, whose costs both in men and money had become so great. Although it would take two more years to finalize the terms of the peace, the die was cast at Yorktown and the determining factor was a navy, not an army.

The Battle of Yorktown left behind not only a legacy of freedom, but also a legacy of shipwrecks. Beginning in 1972, I did extensive historical research to determine the extent and location of these wrecks. This archival research was paralleled by a series of remote sensing and underwater surveys undertaken with the assistance of a number of cooperating agencies. In the final analysis, nine shipwrecks of the Revolution were identified. This makes the site the largest assemblage of Revolutionary or colonial period wrecks presently known to exist, certainly warranting the continuing study they are now receiving. The extent of the wreckage should not be surprising in view of the scene the American observer St George Tucker described on 18 October 1781:

On the Beach of York directly under the Eye hundreds of busy people might be seen moving to and fro – At a small distance from the Shore were seen ships sunk down to the Waters Edge – further out in the Channel the Masts, Yards & even the top gallant Masts of some might be seen, without any vestige of the hulls. . . . A painter need not to have wish'd for a more compleat subject to imploy his pencil without any experience of Genius.

The Yorktown Warships

With the acquisition of approximately sixty ships at Yorktown, both the French and the Americans sought to capitalize on their captured spoils. Unfortunately for them, the bulk of the ships were under water, either as a result of artillery fire or scuttling. With no salvage equipment and few capable salvors, Washington opted to turn over the entire fleet, above and below the water, to the French. They succeeded in raising a number of ships, but when they abandoned the effort the following summer, many remained. There were desultory attempts at salvage, for both economic and historical reasons, over the next 150 years. It was not until 1934, however, that any systematic effort was made to recover artifacts from the river. This project was inspired by a growing historical awareness resulting from the sesquicentennial celebrations of 1931, and by the regular recovery of artifacts from the river bottom by watermen working in the area. A cooperative agreement was forged between two nascent organizations, Colonial National Historical Park and The

Mariners' Museum. The two parties agreed to undertake salvage work on the surviving shipwrecks and split the displayable artifacts.

The best-known naval event of the battle itself was the destruction of the 44-gun *Charon*, the largest British warship present at Yorktown. Only a year old, she was the pride of the naval contingent. When the town was encircled, her large guns were removed for use in the defensive works and she was moored to help defend one of the posts ashore. She did her job so well that when hostilities opened on the evening of 10 October, the *Charon* was the first target of the allies. A French battery fired heated shot at the ship, with memorable results. The American doctor Thacher reported:

A red-hot shot from the French battery set fire to the Charon, a British 44-gun ship, and two or three smaller vessels at anchor in the river, which were consumed in the night. From the bank of the river, I had a fine view of this splendid conflagration. The ships were enwrapped in a torrent of fire, which spreading with vivid brightness among the combustible rigging, and running with amazing rapidity to the tops of the several masts, while all around was thunder and lightning from our numerous cannons and mortars, and in the darkness of night, presented one of the most sublime and magnificent spectacles which can be imagined.

With such a description in hand, it is not surprising that the salvors of 1934 jumped to the conclusion that the wreck they first located was that of the *Charon*. Although a warship, evidence now suggests that it was not the spanking new *Charon*, but the ancient *Fowey*, of 24 guns.

The wreck was located off the beach at Yorktown, in about 40 ft (12.2 m) of water, a location that coincides with the last reported position of the *Fowey*. Over thirty years old, she was listed in the naval reports of 1781 as irreparable; on 16 October she had been pulled into shallow water and had holes drilled in her bottom. Among the artifacts recovered during the excavations were 6-pounder cannons, bar shot and similar armaments. Domestic artifacts included ceramics, pewter and glass, principally a collection of nearly 200 rum bottles. Though these suggested a state of continual inebriation on the part of the defenders, they represented a very small proportion of the total spirit ration normally provided for the crew. They do form, however, one of the largest assemblages of bottles of this period yet recovered. Artifacts related to the ship included parts of the chain bilge pump, anchors, sounding leads and parts of the ship's framing. Unfortunately, no attempt was made to differentiate the artifacts recovered from this first wreck and those subsequently discovered. Salvage conditions were admittedly difficult, with a professional helmet diver blowing mud aside with a water jet, resulting in zero visibility. Working entirely by feel and hearing, there was no chance for the diver to recover anything small. Although early plans called for the careful recording of locations for each

artifact, the pace of the recoveries soon overwhelmed the record-keeping system. Eventually everything was lumped under the generic categorization of having come from the *Charon*.

In the next year, the project moved across the York River to a wreck off Gloucester Point, Virginia. This vessel was clearly the victim of a fire, and a number of burned and melted artifacts were recovered. Before any detailed examination could be made, however, the work was stopped by a dispute over the destruction of oyster beds beneath the wreck. Fortunately for the long-term preservation of the wrecks, the excavations ceased.

Interest in the York River wrecks continued to be fired by displays at The Mariners' Museum and the Yorktown Battlefield, but it was not until I began research that any continuing official interest was taken. This coincided with the nomination of the site to the National Register of Historic Places, thus providing some measure of federal recognition and protection. Protective legislation was

22 (*left*) When salvage efforts were undertaken on the Yorktown shipwrecks in 1934, among the most numerous artifacts were rum bottles.

23 (*below*) Model of HMS *Charon* built by Major Raban Williams in the 1930s.

passed by the state legislature to add further protection. We were eventually able to undertake surveys of the area aimed at identifying new wrecksites and relocating those investigated earlier. Among those relocated was the wreck on the Gloucester side of the river, a wreck that seemed to merit closer investigation.

The Virginia Division of Historic Landmarks had assumed responsibility for the preservation and study of the wrecks at Yorktown, and they had invited the participation of the Institute of Nautical Archaeology at Texas A&M University. INA made a preliminary investigation of one of the wrecks on the Yorktown shore in 1976, to determine its condition and importance. A second field school, directed by J. Richard Steffy in 1980, sought to establish a firm identity for the wreck on the Gloucester side. The fact that the ship had burned and that its location coincided with a reasonable position for the *Charon* was suggestive. Fortunately, British naval vessels of this period are reasonably well documented, often with surviving plans and specifications. Because such information was available for the *Charon*, it was possible to use it as a guide to selective excavation. Measurements of the scantlings, of the length of the keel and the placement of features such as scarf joints in the keel, all coincided with expectations for the *Charon*. The wreck was copper-sheathed on the bottom, as an anti-fouling measure and for protection against *Teredo* worms. This was a relatively new concept at the time of the American Revolution, and was used only on warships. Finally, the location and design of the ship's pumps coincided exactly with those specified in plans for the *Charon*. By the end of the summer, it was possible to report conclusively that the wreck of the most famous ship at Yorktown had been located and identified. Because of the large amount of surviving documentation, and the deteriorated condition of the wreck, however, this ship would not have been the most informative to excavate fully, and attention was focused elsewhere.

HMS 'Charon'

The wreck of the 44-gun warship *Charon*, pride of the British fleet at Yorktown, was conclusively identified on the Gloucester side of the York River in 1980.

24 (*right*) When HMS *Charon* caught fire on the night of 11 October 1781, she drifted across the York River in a blazing inferno, setting several other ships alight in the process. In this inset from a French map made after the battle, Yorktown may be seen in the background.

25 (*below*) Construction plans of the *Charon* made it possible for archaeologists to identify her wreck by selective excavation. Among important clues were the placement of her pump box and the scarfs in her keel.

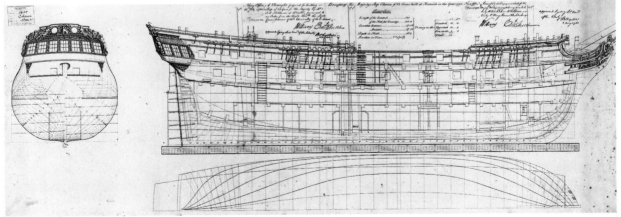

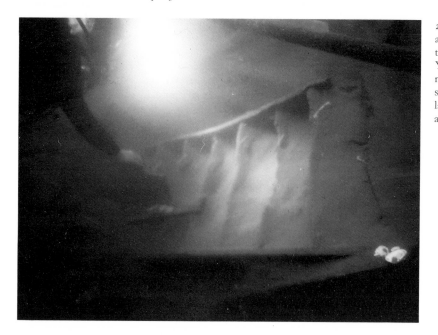

26 (*left*) An archaeologist cleans silt away from the accommodation ladder in the cabin area of the wreck known as YO 88, the remains of a British merchant vessel sunk on the Yorktown side of the York River in 1781. The ladder is also shown in the cross-section and plan, ills. 27 and 28.

The Yorktown Merchant Ships

Archaeology can be most informative when other sources are least informative. Properly done, it can augment the surviving historical record and provide us with information taken for granted and therefore not recorded in an earlier time. This is happily the case at Yorktown with respect to the merchant ships. That there should have been supply vessels attached to Cornwallis' army was such a commonplace matter that only the merest mention of them is made in the records. That Cornwallis used many of them to form his defensive line along the beach was also poorly documented. Yet the wrecks are there, lined up along the beach today as they were 200 years ago. This sheds an interesting sidelight on the tactics of the battle, but it has more important ramifications. While naval vessels of the eighteenth century were well documented by government records, commercial vessels rarely left behind a paper trail. They were built to traditional designs by traditional builders, often without any plans whatsoever. They lived out their lives in quiet trade, and were abandoned or scrapped to be replaced by new vessels with equally sketchy backgrounds. It is only when these anonymous ships have been caught up in the web of world events that we have an opportunity to see them more closely. Such was the case with the transports at Yorktown. The bulk of these ships were small British merchant vessels, typical of thousands of others, chartered by the military to carry supplies. A few others were captured prize vessels of various nationalities, just as poorly documented. The survival of the shipwrecks at Yorktown provides an opportunity to examine a variety of these ships.

The 1978 underwater survey of the river by John Broadwater and the Virginia Division of Historic Landmarks revealed six surviving wrecks along the Yorktown shore, bringing the total of known wrecks to nine. Of these six, one is presumed to have been the *Fowey*, while the remainder appear to have been merchant vessels. Each of the vessels was sampled with a test excavation, to determine the state of its preservation. On the basis of these preliminary tests, one wreck, known as YO 88, was selected for full-scale excavation. It offered the maximum amount of surviving hull, and had suffered little damage over the years from oystering and clamming. After a number of years of work in the York River, Broadwater was aware that he needed to improve the hostile diving conditions. It was nearly impossible to accomplish precision work with zero visibility, strong currents and persistent stinging nettles. After exploring many options, he finally decided that a cofferdam built completely around the site offered the most protection. The water within the cofferdam would be filtered to improve visibility, while the wreck itself would remain submerged.

The construction of the cofferdam involved major technological problems, not the least of which was the fact that the wreck sat on a deep bed of loose silt. The pilings to support the structure had therefore to be driven to great depths in order to provide adequate strength to withstand storm wave surge. In addition to the sheet steel that surrounded the wreck itself, a work platform had to be constructed. Finally, a pier of 500 ft (152 m) was built to provide shore access. The cofferdam was completed during the summer of 1982, and efforts at water clarification began at once. With approximately half a million gallons of water contained, filtration has been a significant problem. Round-the-clock pumping of the water through banks of sand filters has resulted in visibility as high as 25 ft (7.6 m), far better than the 2 ft

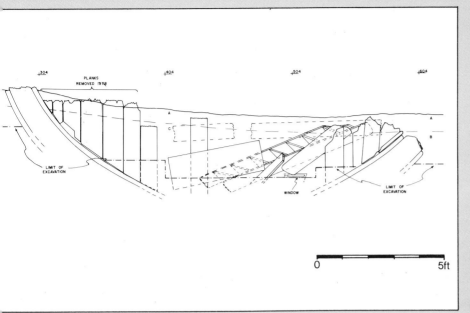

PLANKS
REMOVED 1978

LIMIT OF
EXCAVATION

WINDOW

LIMIT OF
EXCAVATION

0   5ft

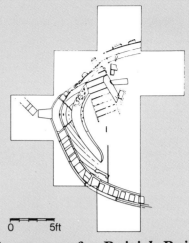

0   5ft

Anatomy of a British Brig

27, 28   Excavation in the stern of the
170-ton brig called by archaeologists
YO 88 (cross-section *above left*, plan
view *above*) has revealed much about the
life of the officers aboard. Beneath the
collapsed ladder was a finely worked
casement window, while next to it were
shelves from a carrying cabinet for a tea
service.

29   (*center left*) The site plan drawn in
1978 has provided the framework for
continuing excavation of YO 88.
Evidence of hull preservation provided
by this preliminary test excavation
ultimately justified the construction of
the cofferdam.

30   (*below*) The wrecks located along
the Yorktown beach by the Virginia
Historic Landmarks Commission survey
represent some of the ships intentionally
scuttled by the British to help defend
the shore area. The cofferdam built
around YO 88 is to the right.

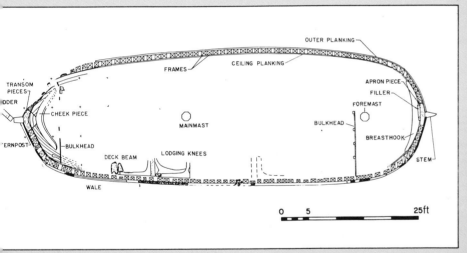

OUTER PLANKING

FRAMES

CEILING PLANKING

TRANSOM
PIECES

APRON PIECE

FILLER

RUDDER

FOREMAST

CHEEK PIECE

MAINMAST

BULKHEAD

BREASTHOOK

STERNPOST

BULKHEAD

DECK BEAM   LODGING KNEES

STEM

WALE

0   5   25ft

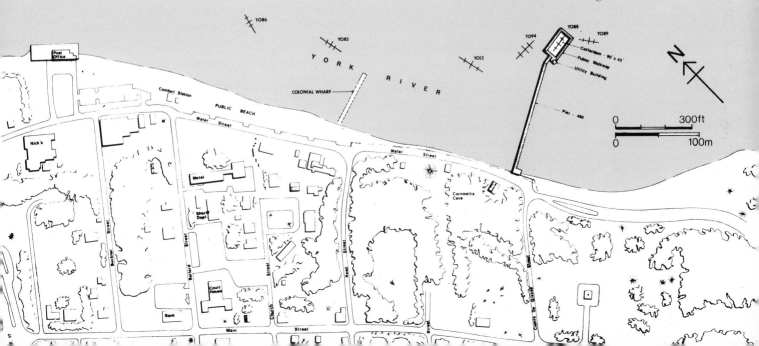

YO86

YO85

Post
Office

YO94

YO88   YO89

Cofferdam - 80' x 45'

YO12

Public Walkway

Utility Building

Comfort Station

Y O R K   R I V E R

PUBLIC BEACH

COLONIAL WHARF

Water Street

Pier - 490

Nick's

Water   Street

0   300ft

0   100m

Motel

Cornwallis
Cave

Sheriff
Dept.

Court
House

Bank

Main   Street

(61 cm) that is standard in the river. With vastly improved working conditions, teams of archaeologists have excavated in the bow and stern areas of the wreck to date. Already, a number of conclusions may be drawn.

The vessel was a brig of approximately 170 tons, with a preserved length of 74 ft 8 in (22.8 m). The stumps of her two masts still standing in the mud of the bottom bear testimony to her rigging plan and construction. Each mast is octagonal in cross-section, to permit wedges to be driven against mast partners. As her structure has been revealed, it is apparent that the ship was built much more heavily than might normally have been expected during the period. Her framing at the bow and stern is quite elaborate, and unlike any that has previously been found, suggesting extra heavy reinforcement. In addition to the traditional white oak frames, she is planked inside and out with white oak, adding further to her strength. The hull itself is quite bluff-bowed and beamy throughout, a design intended to carry maximum cargo. Her hull stands in sharp contrast to the deep-V of the *Defence*, built with speed in mind. One hypothesis that has been advanced is that the ship may have been a British collier, taken into the naval transport service at the beginning of the war. These extra stout vessels had long had a good reputation among British mariners, and many of them were chartered by the government.

Because the ship was almost certainly scuttled intentionally, it is not surprising that there are few artifacts aboard. Most of the items recovered have been directly associated with the operations of the ship itself, or her use as a defensive barrier. The few artifacts that relate to the lifestyle of her crew have come from the after cabin, again providing a contrast to the simple effects owned by the seamen of the *Defence*. Suggestive of the difference is the series of fitted shelves that formed a portable cabinet to carry a tea service, presumably once owned by an officer. That, with the fragments of raised wall paneling that survive, suggests an entirely different level of finish in this vessel built originally for commercial purposes. The large collection of barrels and casks already recovered represents a broad range of cooperage used to contain both wet and dry provisions. Many techniques of barrel construction, only hypothesized until now, have been confirmed. Particularly surprising is the extent to which the barrels were repaired and reused, with new heads fitted and even caulking between the staves to slow leaks. As the excavation continues in the midships section of the vessel, it will be interesting to compare the finds with those from the *Defence*.

The Future of the Past

The surface has barely been skimmed when it comes to studies of shipwrecks from the American Revolution. At all the sites discussed above, there are other wrecks that could and perhaps should be excavated. There are also many wrecksites that have been briefly examined but left largely alone for lack of resources to complete full excavation. HMS *Cerberus*, *Lark* and *Orpheus* are among the ships known to lie beneath the waters of Narragansett Bay. HMS *Culloden* went ashore on the tip of Long Island in 1781, and only selective recovery has been completed on her wreck. In the Mullica River of New Jersey, several American privateers were lost. Their wrecks, though located, have not been fully examined. In Virginia the state naval shipyard on the Chickahominy River has been located, along with the remains of two vessels of the period. Undoubtedly, there will be many more such discoveries in years to come.

The shipwrecks of the American Revolution offer us an extraordinary opportunity to look into our past, to discover how we came to be what we are today. It is an important period for more than the political, military and economic changes that occurred, however. It was a time when man stood poised on the threshold of a new era, the machine age. It was a time when handcraft technologies that had been the norm for thousands of years were soon to be abandoned. The physical remains of that period give us insight into our forefather's lives as the written remains of the period give us insight into their minds. It was a time rich with change.

CHAPTER NINE

The War of 1812: Battle for the Great Lakes

Kenneth A. Cassavoy and Kevin J. Crisman

The War of 1812 was a war that never should have been, a war which neither Great Britain nor the United States really won and which neither really lost. Some in the United States may have viewed it as 'America's second War of Independence'. And some Canadians saw it as part of the continuing struggle against American 'continentalism'. But there is little evidence to suggest that future relations between the two countries would have been different if the sides had more prudently sought a diplomatic resolution to their differences.

The war began primarily over issues of maritime rights on the high seas, yet there was no decisive battle on any ocean. Most of the fighting took place in the interior of the North American continent – on water as well as on land – as much as 1,000 miles from any coastline.

Neither side was in a state of readiness when war was declared. The American military consisted of a small, poorly equipped army, and a handful of frigates. Britain, embroiled with Napoleon in Europe, approached the conflict as if it were something of a backwoods skirmish, confident of controlling the seas. As she was soon to discover, however, defending her Canadian provinces from invasion from the south was a different matter. The small British regular army force had to defend a border with the United States which stretched over 1,000 miles, and the few ships of the Canadian Provincial Marine on the Great Lakes, used for hauling people and produce, had never been manned or maintained properly.

This was a war fought with one eye on the calendar. Five or six months of frantic activity during good weather was followed by six or seven of planning, preparation, and general 'hunkering down' around the fire while the lakes and countryside were gripped by the northern winter.

The least decisive events of the war probably occurred on Lake Ontario. Here, the American and British squadrons spent most of the war maneuvering around each other seeking the 'perfect' opportunity to engage, or taking turns in the building of a bigger ship to temporarily frighten the other off the lake. Many of the largest ships constructed on the lakes during the war never fired a shot in anger and ended up rotting at their wharves.

After two-and-a-half years, the conflict concluded on 24 December 1814, not by military might, but through diplomatic negotiations. The peace treaty specified a return to pre-war borders with no major concessions from either combatant, allowing both to claim victory.

In spite of the strange nature of the war, the conflict did involve significant events in terms of ships and shipbuilding. Because the belligerents were separated by the width of the Atlantic Ocean, a large part of the war revolved around naval actions. On the oceans the Royal Navy, hoping to strangle the United States into submission, used its superior forces to blockade American ports. The small U.S. Navy fought back, avoiding British naval squadrons whenever possible and attacking only merchant vessels or single warships. In a number of early one-on-one engagements on the high seas, the relatively young and inexperienced U.S. Navy was able to 'bloody the nose' of the seapower which dominated the oceans, but these victories were of limited strategic value.

Unlike the ocean engagements, major battles fought on the inland lakes were decisive, directly affecting future actions of the combatants on land as well as on the lakes. It is arguable that to some degree the entire course of the war was shaped by two or three critical lake engagements, which, in turn, depended on unprecedented feats of shipbuilding. Although the pace of shipbuilding and outfitting during the war left little time for record keeping, nautical archaeology is filling gaps in our knowledge of naval design and construction during the period.

U.S. and British Naval Policies up to 1812

United States. When the American colonies secured their independence in 1783, one of the first acts of the Continental Congress was to disband the small Continental Navy. During the next decade, however, the country's maritime commerce grew, and merchant vessels flying the stars and stripes were seen in ports around the globe. But because they sailed without the benefit of a navy, these vessels were subject to seizure by corsairs, particularly those of the piratical states of Algiers, Tunis and Tripoli on the North African coast.

By the early 1790s the need for a force capable of protecting merchant shipping was apparent, and the new national government moved towards the construction of a navy. In March of 1794 Congress ordered the building and outfitting of six frigates, but during the following year a peace treaty was established with Algiers, the most troublesome of the Barbary states. Construction continued on only three of the frigates, launched in 1797. One of them, the 44-gun *Constitution*, remains in commission to this day, although much rebuilt.

Trouble broke out again in 1798, when the warships and privateers of revolutionary France, paying little heed to neutrality, began depredations on American shipping. The result was an undeclared war, the 'Quasi-war', and a rapid increase in the U.S. naval establishment.

The election of President Thomas Jefferson in 1800 and the ratification of a peace treaty with France in 1801 combined to reduce the size of the U.S. Navy once more. Even a new war with Tripoli in 1802 did little to strengthen the fleet beyond the construction of several small cruising vessels and the purchase or building of gunboats for Mediterranean service. When the war ended in 1805, large warships not in use were allowed to fall into disrepair. The Jefferson administration, anxious to avoid the expense of maintaining a seagoing force, instead embarked upon the construction of small harbor and coastal gunboats, each capable of mounting one or two guns. This saved the government some money, but did little to protect American vessels on the high seas.

Great Britain. In the century and more before the American Revolution the British Navy had attained tremendous strength. From a position of struggling with powerful Dutch, French and Spanish forces it had moved to almost total dominance of the seas.

Following the humiliation of the war of 1776–1783, Britain quickly resumed a leading role in colonial and commercial activities. The Royal Navy was continually strengthened to protect merchant shipping and to discourage other countries from contemplating military action against England.

The year 1792 began over two decades of almost continuous war with France and her allies. At this time the British Navy reached a peak in size and power, winning an unbroken series of major naval engagements against French, Spanish, Dutch and combined fleets during a ten-year period. By 1805, following the decisive victory at Trafalgar, the British Navy was in absolute command of the seas and the number of her first- through third-rate ships was more than twice that of the combined fleets of France, Spain and the Netherlands.

This large navy required a roster which by 1812 had grown to over 5,000 officers and 145,000 men. Maintenance of such a navy demanded uninterrupted British commerce and financial stability. A strong and active merchant marine was needed, as was a strong navy to protect it. In the period just before the War of 1812,

during the long struggle with France and her allies, this British national imperative led to abuses of international maritime rights.

Just as President Jefferson was reducing the American Navy, the British increasingly interfered with neutral trade with France, much of it carried in U.S. bottoms. The Royal Navy also took to impressing sailors off American vessels to fill out the complements of its crews. Some were deserters from British ships or were of questionable American citizenship, but a great many simply were illegally pressed into service on His Majesty's ships.

As relations between the two countries soured, two naval incidents helped propel the United States and Britain into a state of war. On 21 July 1807, the Royal Navy 50-gun ship *Leopard* stopped the U.S. frigate *Chesapeake* off Norfolk, Virginia, and demanded permission to board and search for three men who had deserted from the British frigate *Melampus*. When the request was denied and *Chesapeake* appeared to be readying to engage, *Leopard* opened fire, killing three and wounding eighteen U.S. sailors and forcing the American ship to strike her flag. Although the British government disavowed the action and recalled the admiral involved, President Jefferson and Congress reacted angrily with two ultimately weak actions – an unpopular embargo on all foreign trade, and the building of 188 more of the ineffectual gunboats.

The U.S. Navy had a measure of revenge on 16 May 1811. During a confused night engagement off the coast of Virginia, the 44-gun frigate *President* battered the Royal Navy 18-gun sloop *Little Belt*, killing nine of her crew and wounding twenty-five. Although both sides claimed the other fired first, the true circumstances were never determined. The incident served mainly to embitter both countries still further and hinder efforts to settle differences through diplomacy.

Exasperated by the perceived high-handedness of Britain and her navy, Congress declared and President James Madison authorized a state of war on 18 June 1812. The British maritime imperative, in a high-seas collision with American national pride, had brought on the 'War of 1812'.

1812: An Indecisive Year

Shortly after war was declared, the few American warships in commission put to sea. While not numerous, the U.S. frigates were powerful vessels with sturdy hulls, large numbers of guns for their class, and superbly trained officers and seamen.

Britain maintained a fleet of close to 1,000 warships, including 236 ships-of-the-line, on patrol in the English Channel, the North Atlantic, the Mediterranean, the West Indies and the Indian Ocean. The difficulties of keeping a fleet of this size manned and repaired, however, meant that the quality of individual ships suffered. Despite its earned command of the seas, the British fleet found its resources stretched to the limit. Also, in the years after Trafalgar, without a serious challenger for control of the oceans, the British seaman had lost some of his sharpness.

When the frigates from the two navies met in single-ship actions in 1812, a nearly unbroken string of American victories resulted. In August, the *Constitution* defeated the *Guerriere*, in October the *United States* captured the *Macedonian*, and December saw the *Constitution* victorious over the *Java*. Such early successes did not materially harm the Royal Navy, but were a blow to its prestige.

On the interior lakes, naval activity was limited in 1812. Shortly after the declaration of war, the U.S. Navy Department ordered Lieutenant Thomas Macdonough to Lake Champlain to assume command of its forces – two decrepit gunboats built in 1808 to enforce Jefferson's embargo. Macdonough augmented this miserable flotilla

by commandeering and arming three small merchant sloops owned by the army. The resulting fleet was larger than anything the Royal Navy could assemble, and Macdonough sailed the lake unchallenged through the remainder of 1812.

On Lake Erie, the Canadian Provincial Marine mustered a patchwork squadron of four small schooners, one brig and the ship *Queen Charlotte* carrying 16 carronades. In opposition to this, the Americans had only the *Adams*, a small 6-gun brig. After being captured and recaptured within a short time after the war began, the unfortunate *Adams* was ultimately burned by her U.S crew to keep her from falling again into British hands. The Royal Navy's virtually unopposed presence on the lake stymied any American western offensive; ambitious American plans for the invasion of Upper Canada, halted

'Old Ironsides'

1, 2 USS *Constitution* earned her 'Old Ironsides' nickname during her defeat of HMS *Guerriere* in August 1812 (*right*) when a sailor observed enemy cannon shot bouncing off her stout oak hull. *Constitution* survives as the oldest commissioned warship afloat in the world, accessible to visitors (*below right*) in the Charleston Navy Yard in Boston, Massachusetts, near the site of her October 1797 launch.

by General Isaac Brock's early and unexpected capture of Detroit, would have to wait until the U.S. Navy could somehow gain ascendancy on Lake Erie.

On Lake Ontario there was at least minor action in 1812. The Provincial Marine commanded by Captain Hugh Earle included the ship *Royal George* of 22 guns and four or five smaller vessels. The United States had only the 16-gun brig *Oneida*, commanded by Lieutenant Melancthon T. Woolsey. In July, Earle proceeded with his squadron from his naval base at Kingston to Sackets Harbor, New York, the major U.S. naval facility on the lake. Under his inexperienced command, a planned preemptive strike against the base ended as something of a farce. After inflicting only minor damage, Earle hurried back to Kingston. In November, Captain Isaac Chauncey, the new U.S. commander on the lake, returned the Canadian visit. With the *Oneida* and a group of schooners, he chased the *Royal George* into Kingston harbor. He exchanged fire with the harbor batteries but, in the end, accomplished no more than Earle had with his hesitant attack on Sackets Harbor. These two non-engagements set the pattern for most ensuing confrontations on Lake Ontario – plenty of maneuvering, considerable skirmishing, little action.

In November 1812, the launching at Sackets Harbor of the U.S. ship *Madison*, rated at 20 guns, started the real battle of Lake Ontario – the battle of the shipwrights.

1813: Year of the Shipwrights

The U.S. squadron under the command of Lieutenant Thomas Macdonough maintained control of Lake Champlain through the fall of 1812, but in early June of the following year Macdonough's 'flagship' – a large sloop – ran aground and needed repairs. Meanwhile, the two remaining sloops blundered into the British-controlled Richelieu River at the northern end of the lake and were captured after a four-hour battle. Macdonough commandeered more sloops, but before these could be armed, a British raiding party entered the lake with the two sloops, three gunboats, and forty-seven bateaux carrying approximately 1,000 troops. U.S. army barracks in Plattsburgh, New York, were burned, the town of Burlington, Vermont, was bombarded, and eight privately owned lake vessels were captured or sunk. Macdonough regained control of the lake by early autumn, but his reputation as naval commander was severely injured.

Early in 1813 the U.S. Navy Department chose Lieutenant Oliver Hazard Perry to command an American force on Lake Erie and hired two New York City shipwrights, the brothers Adam and Noah Brown, to assemble the necessary warships. How Noah Brown built a squadron for Lieutenant Perry, despite setbacks and shortages, is one of the legends of the War of 1812.

When Brown and his small band of carpenters arrived in late February 1813 at Presque Isle (now Erie), Pennsylvania, they found almost nothing to work with besides standing timber. Tools, iron for spikes and bolts, caulking, and other essential shipbuilding materials were in short supply or impossible to obtain. Brown laid the keels for two 20-gun brigs and labored through the spring to complete them, despite strikes by his half-starved carpenters, and the constant threat of a British raid. While completing the brigs *Lawrence* and *Niagara*, he also built a small schooner, two gunboats, a blockhouse, a guard house, barracks buildings, fourteen small boats for the squadron, and all necessary woodwork, from gun carriages to masts and spars.

Outfitting of the vessels was delayed by shortages of cannon and men, but the U.S. naval squadron was completed in late summer and Perry was ready to take on the British fleet on Lake Erie.

Meanwhile, Captain Robert Heriot Barclay took command of the British squadron. Already at the far end of a disastrously long supply line, his Lake Erie fleet was dealt a fatal blow when the American capture of York (present-day Toronto) carried off or destroyed most of the equipment destined for Lake Erie. Barclay's new 19-gun flagship *Detroit* never received its guns and went into action armed with a patchwork of cannon taken from the bulwarks of Fort Malden at Amherstburg. Because the cannon were without the standard gunlocks of ocean-going warships, it was necessary to use the powder flash from a pistol fired over their touch-holes to set them off!

On 10 September, Perry and Barclay met at the western end of Lake Erie. Although the British were able to force Perry to strike his flag and leave the *Lawrence*, they were unable to follow up their advantage and the Americans ultimately captured all of Barclay's warships, clearing the way for a U.S. advance into Canada. The Americans had won because they were able to build and equip, in record time, a stronger squadron than that of the British. Much of the credit for the turnaround in the U.S. fortunes of war on the western frontier, then, was due to Noah Brown.

After the war the American warships on Lake Erie were laid up in Misery Bay and later intentionally sunk to preserve their hulls. One of the brigs, the *Lawrence*, was raised in the 1870s and cut into thousands of souvenir pieces. The second Brown-built brig, *Niagara*, was raised in 1913 and restored as part of the centennial celebration of Perry's victory. Original plans of the Lake Erie vessels could not be found, and thus the reconstruction of the *Niagara*, still on display in Erie, Pennsylvania, was based on existing hull remains and conjecture.

Lake Ontario saw the greatest naval activity on the U.S.-Canadian border in 1813, but, although both sides considered the lake of the utmost strategic importance, the real contest again was one of shipbuilding.

The 1813 navigation season began with new commanders. Captain Isaac Chauncey, as noted, took command of the U.S. squadron. Provincial Marine Captain Earle was replaced by Royal Navy Captain James Lucas Yeo, and all British forces on the lake came under his direction.

Naval Heroes

3   Under the command of Lieutenant
Thomas Macdonough (*near right*) a U.S.
squadron sailed Lake Champlain
unchallenged in 1812. British raids
during the summer of 1813, however,
severely tested that supremacy, and it
was some time before Macdonough
could regain control.

4, 5   On Lake Erie, Lieutenant Oliver
Hazard Perry (*far right*) fought a
successful campaign against the British
in 1813 – thanks in no small measure to
the brilliance of his chief shipwright,
the legendary Noah Brown. Brown and
his small band of carpenters labored
throughout the spring and summer of
that year to build two 20-gun brigs, a
small schooner and fourteen other small
boats for the U.S. squadron. By the
time of the battle of Lake Erie, on 10
September (*right*), the American force
was strong enough to take on and
defeat British opponents.

When Chauncey arrived at the U.S. Navy's base in
Sackets Harbor in the fall of 1812, he brought with him a
remarkable shipwright, Henry Eckford of New York
City. Eckford's yard in New York was adjacent to that of
the Brown brothers, and he shared with them the ability to
design and build sturdy warships on extremely short
order.

Chauncey's confidence in Eckford was not misplaced.
In the fall of 1812 the shipwright launched the sloop of
war, *Madison*, and the following year he constructed a fast
dispatch schooner, *Lady of the Lake*; the ship *General Pike*,
rated at 24 guns; and the schooner *Sylph*, rated at 16 guns.
The two latter vessels were completed in the summer and
did not participate in the early actions on the lake. These
vessels augmented Chauncey's existing squadron of the
brig *Oneida* and a varying number of armed merchant
schooners.

On the Canadian side of the lake, Yeo worked to
reinforce his squadron of six vessels by beginning the
construction of two 24-gun ships, one at his base in
Kingston, and the other at York. The British fleet was half
the size of its American counterpart but overall was more

efficient. With one exception – *General Simcoe* – it consisted
of vessels designed as warships, most built at Point
Frederick naval facility in Kingston and finished up to
ocean standards under the supervision of master-builder
John Dennis. In contrast, the unequal sailing qualities of
Chauncey's large warships and armed schooners made for
a very clumsy squadron under sail.

The rival navies had several encounters in August and
September 1813, but they involved primarily elaborate
maneuvers and exchanges of cannon shot at long range. In
truth, both Yeo and Chauncey were reluctant to risk a full-
scale battle unless victory was absolutely assured, which it
never was. During this summer skirmishing Chauncey
learned that hastily armed merchant schooners made poor
substitutes for true warships. The over-gunned and top-
heavy schooners often were more of a menace to their
crews than they were to the enemy.

The *Hamilton* and *Scourge*

From the time the ice went out in 1813, the armed
schooners *Hamilton* and *Scourge* had been part of the dozen
or so vessels of the American squadron cruising Lake

Ontario. *Hamilton* was the former U.S. merchant schooner *Diana*, built in Oswego, New York, in 1809. She was constructed under the supervision of shipwright Henry Eagle, and purchased by the U.S. Navy at the outset of the war. She had a length on deck of approximately 73 ft (22 m) and a beam of close to 22 ft (6.7 m). The *Scourge* was the former Canadian merchant schooner *Lord Nelson*, built at Niagara (now Niagara-on-the-Lake) in 1810–11. Somewhat smaller than the *Hamilton*, with a deck length of perhaps 57 ft (18 m) and a beam of around 20 ft (6 m), the *Scourge* was built by shipwright Asa Stanard for James and William Crooks. On 5 June 1812, thirteen days before the war began, *Scourge* was seized by the U.S. Navy brig *Oneida* on questionable charges. Offered at public auction in Sackets Harbor soon after, the vessel was snapped up by the U.S. Navy (the beneficiaries of the Crooks family finally received compensation for the loss of the vessel 118 years later!).

Both *Hamilton* and *Scourge*, topsail schooners, were refitted and pressed into service; like many vessels of the time, they could be propelled by long oars (sweeps) if becalmed. *Hamilton* was equipped originally with 9 or 10 guns and the *Scourge* with 8, adding considerable firepower to the U.S. squadron. The weight of these guns, however, made the merchant schooners top-heavy and unstable; one crew member of the *Scourge* referred to his armed merchant ship as a 'floating coffin'.

The U.S. and British fleets avoided direct contact during early summer in 1813. On 7 August the fleets finally met off Niagara. After a day of maneuvering, they settled down for the night, out of range but within sight of each other on the calm lake waters. In the dark, early morning hours of 8 August, a sudden, deadly squall sprang up. Both the *Hamilton* and *Scourge* were blown over and foundered within minutes.

The *Hamilton* and *Scourge* lay undisturbed until they were discovered over a century-and-a-half later, in 1973, during a search spearheaded by Dr Daniel Nelson, a dentist of St Catharines, Ontario, and initiated in 1971 under the auspices of the Royal Ontario Museum. The discovery was confirmed in 1975 when sonar images of an earlier magnetometer contact provided vivid silhouettes of two vessels, a quarter-of-a-mile apart, sitting upright at a depth of 300 ft (91 m), and subsequent video pictures from an unmanned submersible showed a vessel of the right period with cannon shot lying nearby; the shot could only be from the *Hamilton* or *Scourge* since all ordnance had been banned from lake vessels after the Rush-Bagot treaty of 1817. Films taken in 1980 from a manned submersible showed the *Hamilton* to be in excellent condition. In the same year, title to the vessels was transferred to the City of Hamilton, Ontario, by the United States Navy through the United States Congress via the Royal Ontario Museum.

In May 1982 the Hamilton-Scourge Foundation (aided by a financial contribution by the Ontario Heritage Foundation, Ministry of Citizenship and Culture,

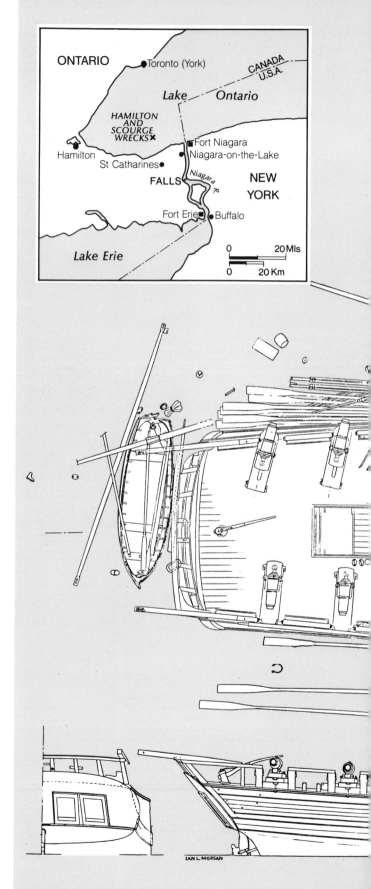

'Hamilton' and 'Scourge'

Merchant schooners pressed into service by the U.S. Navy on Lake Ontario, the *Hamilton* and *Scourge* were top-heavy with extra guns when they encountered a British squadron off Niagara on 7 August 1813. That night a sudden, deadly squall sprang up, sending both vessels to the bottom. More than a century-and-a-half later, in 1973, a team led by Daniel Nelson located the ghostly outlines of the ships resting upright at a depth of 300 ft (91 m).

6 (*far left*) The location of the wrecks.

7 (*left*) A dramatic side-scan sonar image of the *Hamilton* made in 1975 reveals the ship in black, casting a white acoustic shadow that outlines her masts.

8, 9 The *Hamilton* as found on the lake bed (*center left*) and in profile (*below left*) as she once appeared. These 1986 Hamilton-Scourge Project drawings, by marine heritage artist Ian Morgan,

working with research assistant John Ames, are derived from mainframe database indexing of approximately 28 hours of videotape and 2,800 35-mm slides taken in 1982 during a Hamilton-

Scourge Foundation/National Geographic Society survey. Referencing for the index was provided by preliminary archaeological drawings made in 1982 by Kevin Crisman. The second-stage drawings confirm the accuracy of primary historical documents such as naval purchase orders and inventories. Courtesy of Hamilton-Scourge Project.

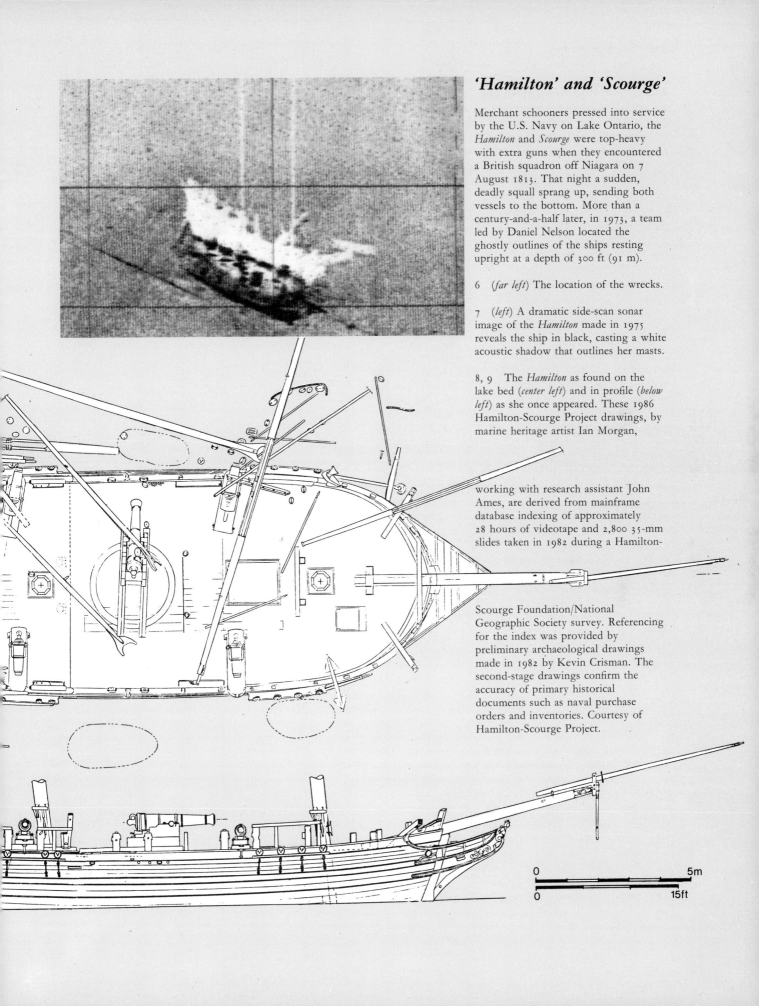

| 0 | | | | | 5m |
| 0 | | | | | 15ft |

Province of Ontario) and the National Geographic Society sponsored a full-scale photographic survey of the two shipwrecks. A Remotely Piloted Vehicle (RPV) carrying both still and videotape cameras was maneuvered carefully around the wrecks by a pilot operating from a barge on the surface. Project Archaeologist Ken Cassavoy interpreted the resultant photographs and videotape footage. With the help of Kevin Crisman, a colleague at the Institute of Nautical Archaeology and Texas A&M University, he developed preliminary plans of the ships.

The ships rest upright on the lake bottom, listing perhaps 16 to 18 degrees to port, with masts reaching upward 50 ft (15 m) and more. Except that ropes holding spars, blocks, deadeyes, anchors and fittings have virtually all rotted away, allowing such material to drop to the decks or to the lake bottom, the ships probably look much as they did when they sank. Scattered around the vessels are skeletal remains of some of the fifty-three men who went down with them.

It seems likely that when the *Hamilton* foundered, her carronades slid to port and helped tilt the vessel in that direction as she sank, then struck and stabilized on the bottom. A similar scenario fits the *Scourge*, whose port guns probably tilted directly downward when she was blown over on her side and stayed in that position as the ship sank, while the starboard guns remained relatively upright in their ports. The distribution pattern of artifacts around the ships clearly results from their port lists. On the *Hamilton*, with her open bulwarks, some material undoubtedly went over the side on impact with the bottom. In the case of the *Scourge*, closed bulwarks suggest that a considerable amount of loose material, now invisible under silt, has lodged along the inside edge of the port bulwark.

The initial survey of the *Hamilton* shows sweeps, large and small spars, blocks and deadeyes littering the wreck area. Ordnance includes 8 carronades, 18-pounders, and one long pivot gun, probably a 12-pounder. Powder ladles, grape-shot pedestals and cannisters have also been identified. The ship carried two wooden stock type anchors at her bow. A number of cutlasses are visible. At the stern of the *Hamilton* rests a ship's boat, which was undoubtedly pulled down still fastened on its davits when the ship sank.

The inventory of material on the *Scourge* site is similar; on the deck are ten long guns of smaller caliber, probably a combination of 4- and 6-pounders. The ship carries two iron sliding-stock anchors. Crossed pairs of cutlasses are fastened above the gun ports on the bulwarks, and a number of boarding axes are stowed inside the starboard stern quarters. Contrary to most descriptions of armed lake schooners, the *Scourge* has true bulwarks with gunports cut into them; the *Hamilton*, on the other hand, has no bulwarks, but only rails with openings cut for carronade and long-gun clearance. There is some evidence that sweeps were stored along the rails of the *Hamilton*, possibly to provide some protection for gun crews.

Probably the single most striking element of each ship is its figurehead. That of the *Hamilton* is thought to represent the goddess Diana, celebrating the vessel's original name. This bust-type figure is of a style common in the nineteenth century, the highly decorative garland at its base being unusual but not unique on ships of the period. The *Scourge* figurehead initially was thought to honor the admiral who inspired the vessel's original name, *Lord Nelson*. Since other known figureheads of Lord Nelson clearly depict him with one arm and even his blind eye, this suggestion is now discounted. The full-figure, walking style of the figurehead is common on ships of the nineteenth century.

The depth (with a resultant constant temperature of 3 to 4 degrees celsius), the absence of destructive marine organisms, the absence of light, and the fresh, virtually currentless waters have combined to protect the two ships. There is no evidence of structural damage to the outside of the hulls either from the initial impact or later deterioration, although some surface softness is evident. The strakes seem to be in good condition with caulking still in place and seams tight. The decks do not appear to have weakened; the heavy guns show no signs of falling through. Cannons and carronades exhibit severe surface oxidation, but this has probably not affected their overall strength. Smaller metal objects such as shot cannisters are considerably corroded.

Below open hatches silt covers the storehouse of material which unquestionably lies beneath the decks of each vessel. Clothing, tools, personal effects, even food should have survived as it was on the night of 7 August 1813, much of it excellently preserved in the relatively oxygen-free environment.

The ships allow us to compare historical accounts with archaeological evidence. Interesting, if minor, points already indicate disagreements between these sources. At least one historical document refers to the *Scourge* as carrying '12 guns', but other sources, perhaps partly confusing it with the *Hamilton*, say the *Scourge* carried 'one long 32 and 8 short twelves'. Photographs show that, at least at the time of her sinking, the *Scourge* carried 10 guns.

James Fenimore Cooper based a book on the tale of Ned Myers, one of the crewmen who survived the sinking of the *Scourge*. Photographic evidence now presents minor contradictions to the eye-witness account Myers gave the novelist, including a description of cannons leaving their ports and one gun 'capsized . . . directly over the forward hatch. . . .' From photographs of the *Scourge* we can see that none of the guns has capsized back on the deck and certainly none has moved over the forward hatch. All the guns are still in their respective ports and it is likely that at least the starboard cannons never left the positions we see them in now. Perhaps based on the Myers-Cooper story, many accounts of the sinking of *Hamilton* and *Scourge* refer to 'the guns breaking loose' on deck.

Hamilton and *Scourge* were quite ordinary ships of the period, built as simple Canadian and American merchant

A Tale of Three Wrecks

10 (*near right*) Archaeologist Brian Robinson traces construction features on a frame timber recovered from the hull of the U.S. Navy brig *Eagle*, excavated recently in Lake Champlain.

11 (*far right*) A portion of the *Tecumseth*, salvaged from the harbor at Penetanguishene, Ontario, in 1953, is all that may be seen today of the British armed schooner, preserved at the Penetanguishene Historical Naval and Military Establishments.

12 (*below*) The decayed hull of the U.S. Navy 17-gun schooner *Ticonderoga*, facing aft from the stem. The remains of this vessel were raised from Lake Champlain in 1958 and placed on display behind the Skenesborough Museum in Whitehall, New York. The surviving lower portions of the frames suggest she was narrow and nearly flat-bottomed, indications of the *Ticonderoga*'s commercial steamboat origins.

schooners. They were the transport trucks of their time, and as such are extraordinarily important as representatives of traditional shipbuilding techniques of the early nineteenth century. They also are representative of their period in a symbolic way, one built in Canada, the other in the United States. Paralleling the experience of the citizens of their warring countries, these average, hardworking merchant ships found themselves drafted into military service and pressed onto the field of battle.

The corporation of the City of Hamilton, Ontario, Canada, holds title to *Hamilton* and *Scourge*. If the ships are eventually raised, they will be housed in a museum in that city. In the meantime, the Hamilton-Scourge Project operates an Interpretive Center during July and August.

1814: The War Ends

Britain, roused by attacks on its naval and merchant vessels, concentrated its naval might on the east coast of the U.S. The blockade established in 1813 had by 1814 slowed commercial maritime traffic along the coast to a trickle. The abdication of Napoleon at this time freed additional British vessels and thousands of troops for duty in North America, and the Royal Navy began raiding coastal towns, particularly in the Chesapeake Bay area. Although victorious in several single-ship actions at sea in 1814, the U.S. Navy was incapable of defending its shores.

On Lake Ontario, adversaries Chauncey and Yeo, each disappointed by results of the previous summer, resolved to outbuild one another. At the Sackets Harbor and Kingston shipyards, hundreds of carpenters shaped green timbers into new warships. The British got a headstart in the autumn of 1813 by laying the keels for two very large ships, the 60-gun *Prince Regent* and the 44-gun *Princess Charlotte*. While lumber was still relatively close at hand, virtually all other materials for the ships had to follow a long, difficult route to Kingston. This was problem enough in terms of nails, pulleys, paint, rope, lead, sails

and dozens of other items, but became a nightmare when ordnance was involved. In one instance, 200 teams of oxen secretly hired in Vermont and New Hampshire pulled 46 cannons, only a portion of those needed, from Montreal to Kingston. Crews for the new ships followed an even more difficult trail, entailing for some a 1,000-mile midwinter trek by snowshoe and sleigh.

Chauncey was slower to act. It was not until 11 January 1814 that Henry Eckford joined him at Sackets Harbor to begin the new American shipbuilding marathon. He quickly laid the keels for two 20-gun brigs and a 44-gun frigate, the latter lengthened on the stocks to carry 58 guns to counter the British frigates building at Kingston. Despite frigid weather and sickness among the carpenters, Eckford managed to launch the brigs *Jones* and *Jefferson* in April, and the 58-gun *Superior* in early May. He immediately began work on a second frigate, the 42-gun *Mohawk*. The outfitting of the new vessels was delayed by the late arrival of guns and stores, largely shipped via ice-choked rivers or rutted roads from New York City.

Yeo was the first to enter Lake Ontario in 1814, his squadron strengthened by the addition of the *Prince Regent* and the *Princess Charlotte*, both launched on 15 April. The Royal Navy first attacked and destroyed the depot at Oswego, New York, where some supplies intended for the U.S. squadron were captured, and then began a blockade of Sackets Harbor. Yeo raised the blockade in early June, but it was not until the end of July that Chauncey completed outfitting his vessels and sailed into the lake. He immediately began a blockade of Kingston that continued until October when the British finished the 112-gun ship-of-the-line *St Lawrence*, and the U.S. Navy was, in turn, forced to seek the shelter of its base.

This state of affairs on Lake Ontario, with Chauncey and Yeo launching larger and larger ships but assiduously avoiding a showdown, gave every indication of continuing into the next summer. Each side had

enormous ships-of-the-line on the stocks when news of peace arrived in February of 1815, putting an end to the most expensive and also the least decisive shipbuilding race of the war.

The brig 'Jefferson'. After the war the U.S. Navy's Lake Ontario squadron was laid up at Sackets Harbor with guns, masts and spars removed and the decks housed. The warships were kept afloat for several years, but their timbers eventually rotted and, one by one, they settled to the bottom. The half-submerged wrecks were sold to a salvager in 1825 on condition that he remove the hazards from the harbor.

At least one vessel, believed to be the 20-gun brig *Jefferson*, was undisturbed. New York diver Richard Van Gemert examined the wreck in the 1960s and found the bottom of the hull and most of the port side intact. The forward end of the hull suffered considerable damage a few years later when a marina was built over it, but reports that the hull was entirely destroyed were unfounded. In fact, the volume of boat traffic generated by the marina has protected the *Jefferson*'s fragile timbers from relic-hunting divers.

In 1985 the New York State Bureau of Historic Sites sponsored a week-long archaeological survey of the wreck. The fieldwork, directed by Kevin Crisman and Arthur Cohn, involved photographic and video recording of exposed timbers, and documentation of the assembly and curvature of a typical frame located near the midship frame (the widest rib on a hull, indicated by the symbol ⋈).

The *Jefferson* was found to be about 50 percent intact, including the after one-half of the keel and keelson, the sternpost and its associated deadwood timbers, and most of the port side, including nine gunports. The vessel had listed to port and was filled with mud nearly to the top; only gunports, keelson and odd bits of wreckage were

exposed. The damage to the forward end of the hull made it impossible to locate the midship frame precisely and thus we had to select a frame for study that was slightly aft of midships.

Crisman and Cohn excavated a trench 5 ft (1.5 m) wide across the inside of the hull at the frame, removed the interior (ceiling) planking and recorded the construction of the frame. Individual timbers were fashioned from white oak and hard maple, and were substantial in dimensions. Although wartime conditions greatly accelerated the construction of the *Jefferson*, the carpenters nevertheless had taken extraordinary care in shaping and assembling the frames; the timbers were perfectly squared off and each had been smoothly finished with an adze. Surprisingly, the bottoms of the frames had no limber holes, the small drains that allow bilge water to flow underneath frames and collect in the pump wells. The bilges of the brig must have been perpetually filled with a foot or more of stagnant water.

Measurements made possible the reconstruction of a section view of the frame examined. Although this was not the widest point on the hull, it was close enough to the midship to provide a good idea of Eckford's design for the brig. The reconstruction indicated that the *Jefferson*'s frames had very sharp deadrise, giving the warship a distinctive V-shaped bottom. The hull was also relatively shallow compared with contemporary oceangoing warships of the same class. The sharp deadrise and shallow hull probably combined to make the *Jefferson* a very fast vessel under most sailing conditions, but they also made her highly unstable when she carried a deckload of heavy guns. In September 1814 the brig was caught out on the lake in a gale and twice blown over on her side. The crew were forced to throw ten guns overboard to save the vessel. Historical documents suggest that several of Eckford's Lake Ontario creations suffered from Chauncey's tendency to over-gun them, and carried extra

13 (*left*) The British fleet attacks Fort Oswego, Lake Ontario, on 6 May 1814. The naval vessels on this lake resembled oceangoing warships in many respects, but their hulls were generally shallower in draft and considerably sharper, since they were not required to carry large quantities of provisions or fresh water.

14 (*right*) A modern artist's copy of a contemporary depiction of the U.S. Navy brig *Jones*, sister ship of the *Jefferson*. Although this rendition contains some inaccuracies – the masts are too short and the overhang of the stern is exaggerated – it does provide an idea of the appearance of Chauncey's 20-gun brigs.

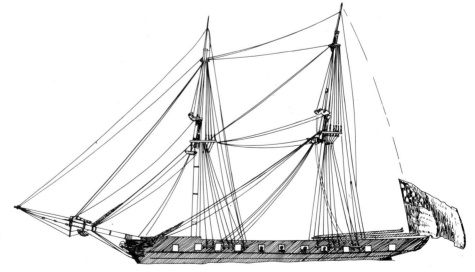

Ghostly Relics of the War of 1812

Images of the *Hamilton* and *Scourge* appear like apparitions from the deep on television monitors and in remarkable underwater photographs.

15 In order to analyze the sites and draw the original plans of the *Hamilton* and *Scourge* wrecks, Ken Cassavoy (*left*) and Kevin Crisman spent three months studying the slide and videotape images sent back by the Remotely Piloted Vehicle (RPV) from the depths of Lake Ontario. The wooden stock of the

Hamilton's starboard anchor can be seen on the upper screens, a fluke and the arms of the same anchor, hooked over the bulwark, appear on two of the lower screens.

18 (*right*) An 18-pound carronade has remained aimed through the *Hamilton*'s rail for over 175 years, as seen in this photograph taken with a Remotely Piloted Vehicle. A pair of deadeyes lie below the vehicle's claw.

16, 17 The figurehead of the *Scourge* (*below*, drawing *near right*) shows the excellent state of preservation of this schooner on the bed of Lake Ontario. The theory that the figurehead represents Lord Nelson, who inspired the vessel's original name, has been discounted since two arms are clearly depicted and other known figureheads of the admiral show him with one arm and even his blind eye.

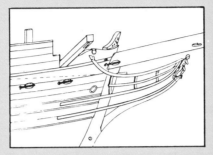

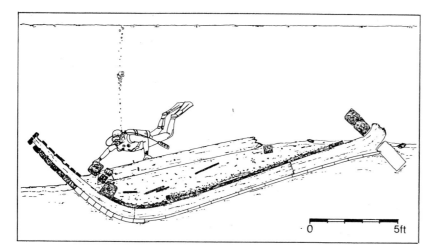

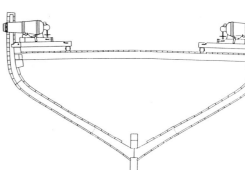

0   5ft

ballast to keep them from capsizing when under full sail.

The archaeological study of the *Jefferson*'s hull revealed shortcuts used by Eckford to hasten the brig's construction, perhaps the most obvious being the omission of knees, naturally curved pieces of wood, often cut from branches or roots, that strengthen wooden vessels by preventing important structural timbers from separating, as at the juncture of the deck beams and frames, or the sternpost and keel. Eckford simply increased the size of the longitudinal clamp and waterway timbers that locked the deck beams into the side of the hull, and he fitted wedges of wood between the keel and sternpost. These expedients no doubt saved a great deal of construction time, reduced weight in the upperworks, and only slightly lessened the overall strength of the brig's hull.

In all, the *Jefferson* proved to be a superbly built vessel, fashioned from white oak and white pine timbers that were generally larger in dimensions than those used in high-seas vessels of equivalent size. The unusual design, with a sharp yet shallow hull, was admirably suited to the sailing and fighting conditions on Lake Ontario.

The Kingston Fleet after 1814

By the end of 1814 the British fleet on Lake Ontario was stronger than ever, led by the 112-gun *St Lawrence* – a ship as large and powerful as Nelson's *Victory*. With the signing of the Treaty of Ghent in 1815, however, this proud fleet began the voyage to a perhaps more igno-minious end than the U.S. naval squadron across the lake.

At the close of hostilities the first-rate *St Lawrence*, the frigates *Prince Regent*, *Princess Charlotte*, and the newly launched *Psyche* all were at anchor in Kingston harbor. The ships *Montreal* (ex-*Wolfe*) and *Niagara*, brigs *Charwell*, *Star* and *Netley*, several schooners, and two powerful three-deck ships, *Wolfe* and *Canada*, ready for launching, were also all at Kingston. With the signing of the Rush-Bagot treaty in 1817, limiting naval armament on the Great Lakes, the guns and gear were removed from the now idle fleet and the ships were housed over for

protection. Despite costly efforts to keep them in good repair, the ships gradually deteriorated. Eventually, the navy ordered the six largest vessels, including the never-launched *Wolfe* and *Canada*, to be sold at public auction. The mighty *St Lawrence* was sold for £25. There were no bids on the others. The *St Lawrence*, towed to a nearby pier to serve as a storehouse for steamship wood, eventually sank at her mooring to become a source of souvenirs for swimmers. The rest of the fleet rotted in the mud along the shore or was broken up and hauled away to be sunk in a less congested area. Some of the hulks may have suffered further from demolition charges set off by units from the adjacent Royal Military College. Sizeable sections of at least three are apparently still at the bottom of nearby Deadman Bay. A 1951 underwater survey concluded that one may be the frigate *Kingston*, another the sloop *Montreal*. Plans for all the vessels exist, reducing their archaeological importance, but a detailed evaluation of the remains seems appropriate for the future.

Lake Champlain – The *Ticonderoga* and the *Eagle*

In 1812 and 1813 Lake Champlain had played only a minor role in the conflict, but in September 1814 it was the scene of what historians have termed 'the most decisive naval battle of the War of 1812'.

When cold weather and ice ended the 1813 navigation season, U.S. squadron commander Macdonough, still smarting from losses that summer, led his small squadron 7 miles up the winding Otter Creek to Vergennes, Vermont, a town boasting saw mills and an iron foundry, and surrounded by forests of oak and pine. Here, protected from British raids over the frozen lake, he began preparations for the construction of several warships. The Navy Department engaged Adam and Noah Brown, the builders of Perry's squadron, to direct the construction of the new Lake Champlain vessels.

Noah Brown arrived at Vergennes in late February. Macdonough had originally intended to build only gunboats, but when he learned of a large British sailing

19, 20 Cross-section approximately amidships of the *Jefferson* on the bed of Lake Ontario (*far left*) and in a reconstructed view (*left*). This U.S. Navy brig was abandoned after the War of 1812 and eventually sank, listing over to port. The diver hovers over a broken main-deck beam. The brig's shallow, sharp V-bottom resulted in a fast ship, but one that was topheavy when weighted with heavy cannon.

21 (*right*) In this 1828 engraving several ships of the now idle British fleet at Kingston are shown housed over for protection.

vessel in frame on Isle aux Noix in the Richelieu River, he decided to construct a similar warship. Brown built and launched Macdonough's new flagship, the 26-gun *Saratoga*, in only forty days, and at the same time completed six 75-ft-long (22.9-m) 2-gun gunboats.

Brown was not the only shipwright working in Vergennes that spring. Near the U.S. Navy's temporary shipyard a steamboat was under construction, the inaugural vessel of the newly formed Lake Champlain Steamboat Company. The Company's choice of time and place to begin their new enterprise was unfortunate, for in late April Macdonough commandeered the unfinished hull and Brown began converting it into a warship. They considered completing the hull as originally intended, which would have made it the first steam-powered warship in the world, but Macdonough reported to the Secretary of the Navy:

> It cannot be done within two months owing to the machinery not being complete and none of it here; this delay, and the extreme liability of the machinery (composed of so many parts) getting out of order, and no spare parts to replace, have induced me to abandon the idea of fitting this vessel to be propelled by steam but to have her directly fitted for twenty guns in the rig of a schooner.

The steamboat-turned-schooner was launched on 12 May, armed with 17 guns of varying size, and christened *Ticonderoga*. The new American squadron emerged from Otter Creek in late May and immediately began a blockade of the Richelieu River.

During the winter of 1813–14 British shipwrights on Lake Champlain had also been busy, assembling a squadron made up of a 16-gun brig, the *Linnet*, the sloops *Chubb* and *Finch*, and a flotilla of gunboats. The appearance of the decidedly superior American squadron in May forced the Royal Navy to build a massive frigate, *Confiance*, the largest warship ever to sail the lake. *Confiance* was to carry twenty-seven 24-pounder long guns, and four 32-pound and six 24-pound carronades.

When news of the frigate under construction reached Macdonough, he petitioned the Navy Department for permission to reinforce his command with a 20-gun brig. In early July Noah Brown's brother Adam received orders to proceed immediately to Vergennes and run up the vessel. Assisted by 200 New York City shipwrights, Brown laid the keel on 23 July and launched the 117-ft-long (35.7-m) hull only 19 days later on 11 August. The brig, named *Eagle*, was hastily rigged and armed with eight long 18-pounder cannon and twelve 32-pounder carronades. An acute shortage of sailors on Lake Champlain at this time forced the *Eagle* to fill out its 150-man complement with musicians from a military band and 40 convicts from a chain gang.

On 1 September a British army of over 10,000 veteran troops crossed the U.S.-Canadian border and began an invasion of the western shore of Lake Champlain. The force advanced into Plattsburgh, New York, and halted across the Saranac River from a U.S. Army fortification to await the arrival of the Royal Navy. Macdonough prepared to meet the British squadron by positioning his ships in a 'line ahead' formation across the opening of Plattsburgh Bay and laying a series of anchors and spring lines around each vessel, enabling them to shift their broadsides to meet an attack from any direction.

With the army ready to move forward, British Commander-in-chief General George Prevost urged – some say hounded – the new British squadron commander, Captain George Downie, to bring his fleet into action against Macdonough. With carpenters still at work on the decks of the just-launched *Confiance*, Downie, against his better judgment, proceeded down Lake Champlain with his fleet.

At 9 o'clock on the morning of 11 September 1814, the Royal Navy squadron sailed into Plattsburgh Bay. A point-blank fight ensued. Fifteen minutes after the battle began Captain Downie was killed. By 11 o'clock the *Saratoga* and *Confiance* had pounded each other into wrecks, with most of the guns on their engaged broadsides unusable. Macdonough resorted to his pre-

Closing Years of the War

22 (*left*) A replica of the transport schooner *Bee* – seen here under main, fore, jib, flying jib and gaff topsail in Penetanguishene Bay – was launched in 1984 as a reminder of the 'Durham boats' once used at the naval station established there in the latter part of the war.

23 (*below*) The battle of Plattsburgh Bay, Lake Champlain, 11 September 1814 – the most decisive naval engagement of the war. In support of a British invasion force of 10,000 men, the Royal Navy attacked a U.S. squadron under Macdonough. A gruelling point-blank fight ensued, but American forces won the day thanks to pre-arranged anchor-lines which enabled them to turn their ships to present fresh broadsides. Macdonough's victory helped bring about the end of the war.

arranged spring lines and anchors to turn the *Saratoga* so as to present a fresh row of guns. The *Confiance*, unable to complete a similar maneuver, soon struck her flag, followed by the *Linnet*. Meanwhile, most of the British land force had crossed the Saranac and driven the American defenders into a nearby wood. But with the defeat of Downie's squadron, the ever-cautious Prevost, who had watched from shore, recalled the troops and ordered them back to Canada. British naval support for the British land offensive was finished. Macdonough's victory helped convince many British leaders that invading the United States would be a difficult proposition and undoubtedly hastened peace negotiations.

The onset of winter induced Macdonough to lay up all the warships at the southern end of the lake near Whitehall, New York. When news of peace arrived in February 1815 the vessels were stripped of armament and stores, and their decks were housed over. The Navy half-heartedly maintained them, but by 1825 the green-timbered hulls had rotted and sunk. The Lake Champlain squadron was sold to local scrap merchants, who extracted iron fittings exposed above the water.

The schooner 'Ticonderoga'. The hull of the schooner *Ticonderoga* was raised from the bottom of Lake Champlain in 1958, and displayed behind the Skenesborough Museum in Whitehall, New York. In 1981 the vessel was surveyed under the direction of Kevin Crisman, to permit preparation of construction plans, and to determine how Brown had converted it from a steamboat into an armed schooner. Hull remains included the keel, the sternposts and deadwood, the frames to the turn of the bilge, and portions of the keelson. Although a significant amount of the hull was damaged or missing, it was possible to identify at least one of Brown's modifications, and to make some general observations about the *Ticonderoga*'s qualities as a sailing warship.

The 113-ft 9-in (34.7-m) keel was composed of seven pieces of white oak; the two uppermost keel timbers extended the full length of the hull, and probably constituted the original keel. The five lower timbers added 14 extra inches (36 cm) to the depth of the *Ticonderoga*, and were no doubt added by Brown to strengthen the schooner's hull and improve its stability under sail.

The remnants of the schooner's frames consisted for the most part of the floor timbers and first futtocks. They had a very slight deadrise, giving the *Ticonderoga* a nearly flat bottom and a sharp turn of the bilge. The boxy shape of the frames was ideal for the hull of a commercial steamship, as it provided a maximum of passenger and cargo space. At its widest point the vessel was originally about 26 ft (7.9 m) in beam, making it very narrow in proportion to its overall length of 120 ft (36.6 m). The narrow beam permitted faster and more efficient travel, while the weight of the engine and boilers in the hold would have stabilized the steamship by giving it a very low center of gravity.

The long, narrow lake-steamer hull was probably not well suited to conversion into a sailing warship, and when Noah Brown completed the vessel in May 1814, he undoubtedly made some changes. The keel, as noted earlier, appears to have been enlarged to strengthen the hull and give it a deeper 'bite' into the water. Brown presumably strengthened the deck and its supporting structure to bear the strain of heavy guns. The weight of guns and masts high in the narrow hull would also have adversely affected stability, and an unusually large amount of ballast may have been required to lower the center of gravity. Even with Brown's modifications, it seems likely that the *Ticonderoga* was an awkward sailing vessel, although certainly adequate for Lake Champlain's protected waters. Her 17 guns proved crucial to the American squadron at the Battle of Plattsburgh Bay.

The brig 'Eagle'. After the completion of the *Ticonderoga* study in 1981, a search of the lake around Whitehall was organized by Kevin Crisman and Arthur Cohn to locate the remains of other vessels from Macdonough's 1814 fleet. By systematically groping in the mud at the murky southern end of Lake Champlain, divers discovered the remains of three warships: a 75-ft (22.9-m) U.S. gunboat, possibly the *Allen*; a 56-ft (17-m) midship section from the Royal Navy brig *Linnet*; and the 117-ft (35.7-m) U.S. brig *Eagle*. The *Eagle* was particularly well preserved, with the keel, stem, stern and portside all more or less intact. The remnants of ten gunports were still evident on top of the port side.

In 1982 a two-year project was initiated to study the three wrecks, under the direction of Crisman and Cohn, sponsored by the Champlain Maritime Society and the Vermont Division for Historic Preservation. We decided to concentrate our efforts on the *Eagle*, since the hull was in good condition and historical sources contained little information about the brig's design and appearance. Ten divers recorded the construction of the *Eagle* by measuring and sketching the individual timbers and recording the curvatures of the stempost and five frames. As the wreck contained few artifacts and was almost free of overburden, the task was completed in as little as five weeks.

Despite the *Eagle*'s construction in less than three weeks, the hull proved to be surprisingly substantial and well-fastened. The 106-ft 5-in (32.4-m) keel was composed of three timbers flat-scarfed end-to-end, the first two being of hard maple and the aftermost of white oak. The stempost, gripe, apron, sternpost and stern deadwood were fashioned from tough, long-lasting white oak, and all were heavily fastened to the keel with iron drift bolts.

The frame timbers were of large dimensions and were securely bolted together; the frames themselves were closely spaced along the top of the keel. A wide assortment of woods found their way into the frames,

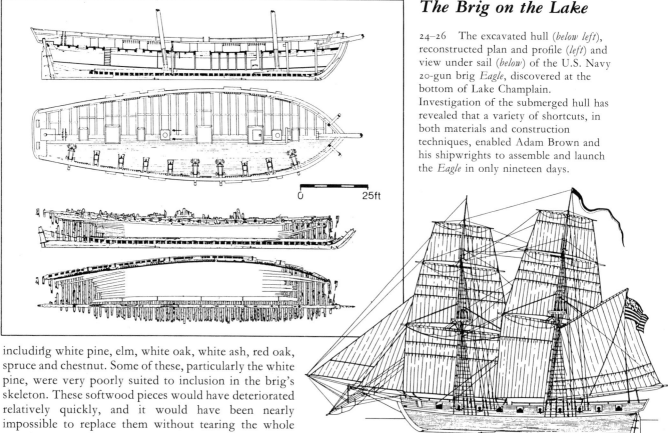

The Brig on the Lake

24–26 The excavated hull (*below left*), reconstructed plan and profile (*left*) and view under sail (*below*) of the U.S. Navy 20-gun brig *Eagle*, discovered at the bottom of Lake Champlain. Investigation of the submerged hull has revealed that a variety of shortcuts, in both materials and construction techniques, enabled Adam Brown and his shipwrights to assemble and launch the *Eagle* in only nineteen days.

including white pine, elm, white oak, white ash, red oak, spruce and chestnut. Some of these, particularly the white pine, were very poorly suited to inclusion in the brig's skeleton. These softwood pieces would have deteriorated relatively quickly, and it would have been nearly impossible to replace them without tearing the whole vessel apart. The *Eagle*'s builders obviously considered long-term preservation of little importance, and used almost any tree growing in the vicinity of the shipyard. Further evidence of haste in the assembly of the frames was exhibited by some of the timbers' original rounded log surfaces, complete with bark.

Adam Brown and his shipwrights also resorted to the expedient practiced by Henry Eckford on the brig *Jefferson*: they did not install reinforcing knee timbers in the *Eagle*'s hull. The stern deadwood contained two wedges of wood in lieu of a stern knee, and the ends of the main deck beams were not braced by either lodging or hanging knees. In the case of the deck beams, Brown greatly enlarged the supporting clamp and waterway timbers to lock the beam ends to the inside of the hull. Omitting knees from an oceangoing vessel would have seriously weakened its hull, but on the generally calmer lakes it was an acceptable shortcut, saving the Navy's carpenters days, if not weeks, of precious construction time.

Seven of ten gunports we measured on the *Eagle* retained their bottom sills, five of them equipped with flat iron plates, each pierced in its center; these pivoting points for carronade carriages indicated the positions of the *Eagle*'s 32-pounder carronades. The waterway (a longitudinal timber situated at the junction of the deck and bulwarks) was hollowed on its top surface between

the gunports to hold round shot in convenient proximity to the guns.

The reconstructed lines of the *Eagle* show the design limitation imposed on sailing ships by the shoal water conditions of Lake Champlain. The hull was 117 ft 3 in (35.7 m) in length between perpendiculars, and 34 ft 9 in (10.6 m) in molded beam, giving it a length-to-beam ratio of 3.37:1. The brig had an extremely shallow depth of hold of only 7 ft 3 in (2.2 m) at the midship frame, and unlike the sharper, deeper *Jefferson*, the *Eagle* had a rounded, almost tubby, hull section. The Lake Champlain brig probably drew less than 9 ft (2.7 m) of water, and could have navigated most of the lake; at the same time it appears to have been a stable vessel, capable of sailing quite fast under certain conditions. Despite severe time limitation, Adam Brown and his men had produced a warship that was both well designed and strongly built.

Lake Huron

Lake Huron saw relatively little naval action during the war. For most of the conflict, U.S. forces could not be spared to control the waters of this large lake or to eliminate the remaining British stronghold at Michilimackinac.

After the Americans gained control of Lake Erie, the Canadians were forced to rely solely on an inland

27 (*left*) Remains of the British schooner *Nancy* – destroyed by her crew in 1814 to prevent capture – were excavated in 1923.

28 (*below*) The Penetanguishene naval slipway used in the repair of the British Upper Lakes fleet.

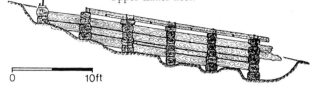

0   10ft

waterway and portage route to carry supplies from York up to the shores of Georgian Bay, then across the bay and up Lake Huron to Michilimackinac. This fort and trading post controlled access to Lake Michigan, and thus the Upper Mississippi and the old Northwest. Captured from U.S. forces during the first month of the war, it was held through assaults and blockades to the end.

The 'Nancy'. A sturdy merchant schooner, *Nancy*, built of oak and red cedar in Detroit in 1789, was pressed into government service in 1812 to supply the isolated post at Michilimackinac, transporting goods from the end of the York-to-Georgian Bay portage route to the north end of Lake Huron. For a good part of the war, the *Nancy* was the entire British fleet on the lake. In 1814 the U.S. Army sent a large assault force into Lake Huron aboard six vessels of the Navy's Lake Erie fleet. An attempt to recapture Michilimackinac was unsuccessful, but part of the squadron – the brig *Niagara* and schooners *Scorpion* and *Tigress* – trapped the *Nancy* on the Nottawasaga River where she was destroyed by her crew to prevent her capture. The same crew, using small boats, shortly boarded and captured the *Tigress* and later took the *Scorpion*. This bold action broke the blockade of Michilimackinac and returned control of Lake Huron to the Canadian forces. The two captured vessels, renamed *Confiance* and *Surprise*, became the core of the British fleet on the lake. The remains of the *Nancy* lay in the

Nottawasaga River near present-day Wasaga Beach, Ontario, for a century or more but eventually were relocated and raised. In contrast to so many other fleet ships after 1814 – including *Confiance* and *Surprise* which rotted and sank at their moorings at the mouth of the Grand River in Ontario – the remains of the *Nancy* have been well treated. They now form the centerpiece for the Nancy Island Historic Site Museum in Wasaga Beach.

Penetanguishene. For a short time the captured *Confiance* and *Surprise* were regular visitors at a newly created naval establishment at Penetanguishene on Georgian Bay, where the British, late in 1814, began to build a dockyard for an Upper Lakes fleet. Two armed schooners, *Tecumseth* and *Newash*, built near Niagara Falls just after the war ended, were sent up to Penetanguishene. Each was 70 ft (21.3 m) on deck with a beam of over 24 ft (7.3 m), and each was designed to carry two 24-pounder long guns on circle pivots, one toward the bow, the other amidships, and two 32-pound carronades, one on each quarter. After the Rush-Bagot treaty, like their counterparts in the Lake Ontario fleet, the two schooners and other small vessels at Penetanguishene were allowed to rot at their moorings or were towed out of the way and sunk. In 1953 a large portion of the *Tecumseth* was pulled from the harbor bottom by a crude dredging method. The badly broken pieces, including the keelson, parts of the stem and sternpost, frames and planks, are now displayed at the

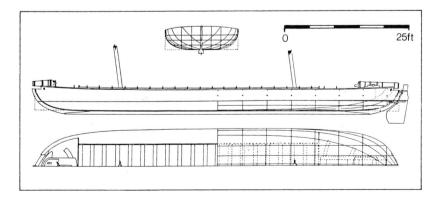

29 A U.S. Navy row galley. This particular design, prepared by naval constructor William Doughty, specified a hull 75 ft (23 m) in length with seats for forty oarsmen. A number of boats were built according to these lines for use on Lake Champlain and in the Chesapeake Bay Flotilla.

0   25ft

Historic Naval and Military Establishments at Penetan-guishene, Ontario. The remains of the *Newash* still lie in shallow water in the harbor, a source of souvenirs for local swimmers.

In 1974 and 1975, as part of an archaeological and historic investigation of the Penetanguishene facility, the naval slipway used in the repair and maintenance of the Upper Lakes fleet was studied by a Government of Ontario underwater excavation directed by Ken Cassa-voy. Little was known about the method of constructing slipways in this period, in spite of their important role in any shipyard. The project revealed a structure 30 ft (9.1 m) by 16 ft (4.9 m), its principal feature a pair of long rails, similar to railroad tracks, on which a ship could be hauled out of the water on a cradle. The sturdy oak rails were secured 11 ft apart, fastened to large oak beams, and supported on a series of columns made up of massive pine 'sleepers'. The simple structure most probably was built near the water's edge, then carefully – it lacks any major structural pieces to stop the beams and 'sleepers' from shifting – pulled into the water, positioned and slowly sunk by filling its extensive cribwork with rock ballast. It appears likely that detailed soundings were made of its proposed location, then the height of each supporting column matched to the soundings to give the rails the proper slope.

During the excavation of the slipway, an underwater survey around nearby Magazine Island located the possible remains of a transport schooner, sometimes called a 'Durham boat', used extensively at this naval station. A full-scale replica of such a vessel, based on and named after the *Bee*, which served at Penetanguishene, was built and launched in 1984. It now serves the museum as a working, sailing example of vessels of the period.

Gunboats. The flotillas of gunboats or 'row galleys' stationed along the coast of the United States in the early nineteenth century proved to be nearly useless in wartime. Mounting only one or two guns, they were markedly inferior in armament to most other types of warships, and their small unsteady hulls made it difficult to aim the guns with any accuracy. A large number of sailors were required to man their oars. Gunboats also swamped easily in rough weather, limiting their range to protected harbors or bays, where they offered little resistance to blockading warships. The boats did, however, enjoy some popularity in the lake service for patrolling shallow areas. Three gunboats played an important role in the British capture of two U.S. Navy sloops in the Richelieu River's restricted waters in 1813. The opposing navies at the Battle of Plattsburgh Bay also each contained a flotilla of gunboats, but the exposed crews showed little enthusiasm for actively engaging regular warships, and their contribution to the outcome of the battle was minimal.

Most of the U.S. Navy's gunboats sat out the war, Commodore Joshua Barney's Flotilla of the Chesapeake being an important exception. This force was first conceived in 1813 when the Royal Navy's blockade of the Chesapeake Bay included raids on farms and towns in the tidewater region. Barney perceived that the British whaleboats and launches carrying the raiding parties were vulnerable when separated from the main fleet, and he advocated the construction of row galleys capable of operating in shallow water, where they could wreak havoc among enemy transports yet avoid action with the larger cruisers. The Navy Department authorized Barney to outfit a flotilla at Baltimore.

During the winter of 1813–14 Barney purchased and rebuilt a number of existing boats and constructed thirteen row galleys from two designs specially prepared by naval constructor William Doughty. The plans called for double-ended vessels, the first to be 50 ft (15.2 m) in length and 12 ft (3.7 m) in beam, and the second 75 ft (22.9 m) in length and 15 ft (4.6 m) in beam; both sizes were to mount a cannon at the stem and stern, and carry either one or two lateen-rigged masts.

Barney's flotilla of eighteen vessels confronted the British on 1 June 1814, and was promptly forced to seek refuge inside the mouth of Maryland's Patuxent River. Over the next few weeks they fought a series of pitched battles against the British fleet, on one occasion driving off two frigates, but they were unable to escape their cul-de-sac. The flotilla retreated further up the river, where, threatened with capture, the gunboats were blown up by their crews on 22 August. Three days later government buildings in Washington, D.C., were burned by British troops in probably the most successful raid of the war.

During a magnetometer survey directed by Donald Shomette and Ralph Eshelman, sponsored by the Calvert Marine Museum and Nautical Archaeology Associates, Inc., and funded through the Maryland Historical Trust, the deeply buried hulls of several of Barney's gunboats were discovered under the Patuxent River in 1979. The following year Shomette and Eshelman investigated the construction and contents of one of the hulls with a team of divers who dug a trench 10 ft (3 m) by 20 ft (6.1 m) inside a plywood cofferdam installed over its forward end.

Despite poor visibility, the excavators exposed deck beams, planking and a large open hatch. Inside the wreck they found a surgeon's kit comprising a tooth extractor, forceps, scissors, scalpels, pharmaceutical bottles, apothecary mixing bowls and a pestle for grinding medicinal compounds. Other artifacts in the hold included ordnance-related items, carpenters' tools, lanterns, barrel staves and a sandstone 'camboose' or deck stove.

The wreck was in good condition, although timbers near the bow were twisted and splayed by the blast which scuttled the vessel. The overall dimensions of the hull, determined by probing in the mud, were 48 ft 7 in (14.8 m) by slightly over 16 ft (4.9 m). Although the exact identity of the boat was not determined, the excavation of what surely was part of Barney's fleet gave another glimpse of naval construction and naval life during the War of 1812.

CHAPTER TEN

Steamboats on Inland Waterways: Prime Movers of Manifest Destiny

Joe J. Simmons III

The invention of the commercially viable steamboat was not the work of a single person. As with most important technological innovations, it was the successful combination of a number of previously developed elements: a dependable power plant of sufficient strength and acceptable size; a method of communicating the work of the engine to efficient propulsive devices (e.g., paddle wheels and screw propellers); and a hull able to withstand the punishment inflicted by massive, constantly working machinery.

Although steam's expansive properties were apparently appreciated by ancient Greeks and Romans, its elasticity, or ability to expand when hot and contract when cool, and how this could be applied to move pistons inside cylinders, was not well understood until the end of the seventeenth century.

Denys Papin, a French engineer of the late 1600s, produced the first steam engine with a piston, and the first piston engine in which condensation was utilized to create a vacuum. Papin suggested that multiple engines, insuring continuous motion, might propel vessels by turning paddle wheels.

Another Frenchman, the Marquis Jouffroy d'Abbons, is commonly credited with first propelling a boat with steam power, but his engine was of a type already proven incompatible with watercraft. In 1705 the Englishman Thomas Newcomen had patented an engine capable of pumping water from mine shafts and powering mills, but trials from about 1735 showed that it was too massive for watercraft, and that it required prohibitive amounts of fuel. Nevertheless, the marquis used the Newcomen engine again in 1776 and 1783. The 1776 trial failed when the vessel's duck's-feet propulsion unit proved ill-conceived. The second vessel moved successfully against current, but the two-cylinder Newcomen engine shook its hull so badly that it was beached in a sinking condition and abandoned after its first and only run.

Important modifications made on the Newcomen engine by Scottish engineer James Watt in the last half of the eighteenth century were primarily responsible for the efficient application of steam power to watercraft. The development of the low-pressure, double-acting condensing steam engine, in which the steam acted on each side of the piston alternately, increased power output considerably, allowing a corresponding reduction in the size of the power plant. Additionally, by insulating the boiler and steam carrier pipes against heat loss, Watt greatly improved fuel consumption. As a result, a number of attempts to propel vessels with Watt or Watt-inspired engines were made during the last twenty years of the eighteenth century in Europe and North America.

The Birth of the Steamboat as a Commercial Venture

John Fitch. The first commercial steamboat venture in the Western Hemisphere appears to have been that of John Fitch and his simply named *Steamboat*, or *Steam-Boat*, of 1790. Although he had experimented with stern- and side-mounted paddle wheels, paddle chains, and even the screw propeller, Fitch utilized a peculiar configuration of vertically suspended paddles at the stern of the *Steamboat*. She ran on a regular schedule on the Delaware River from May to September 1790, at 6 to 8 miles per hour, covering better than 2,000 miles during her single season of operation. But relatively high rates for passengers and freight could not compete with those of stage lines operating along the river's easily traveled banks, and public anxiety over the safety of this 'floating sawmill' and her boilers inhibited its acceptance.

Other Americans in the race to demonstrate steam-propelled vessels successfully included James Rumsey, John Stevens and Robert Livingston. A list of their partners reads like a *Who's Who* of the early United States, including Thomas Jefferson, Ben Franklin and George Washington. Even though each inventor touted his vessel as the 'first true steamboat', none ever received official recognition. Rival claims for recognition from the newly formed federal government, in fact, led to the formation, in 1790, of the first Board of Patent Commissioners, chaired by Thomas Jefferson.

Fitch, Rumsey and Stevens all filed immediately for patents. In a baffling decision by the Board, all three petitioners were granted patents with the same wording and the same date of issuance. This decision only forced the claimants to seek steam navigation monopolies from individual states, added litigations to the docket, and generally clouded the issue. In effect, the Patent Commissioners' decision delayed the advent of practical steam navigation for another sixteen years, until 1807, when Robert Fulton entered the picture.

Robert Fulton. During the nearly twenty years he spent in England and France, the American Robert Fulton observed many steamboat attempts, and at the same time was familiar with the pioneering work of Fitch, Rumsey, Stevens and others in North America. In 1803, three years before he returned to the United States, he even made marginally successful trial runs with a vessel of his own design on the Seine. Fulton's talents of observation and deduction, his knowledge of engineering and hydro-dynamics, his familiarity with the work of other inventors, and his ability to discard unworkable elements and combine successful ones into new power-train and propulsion configurations were the keys to his success. Where others suffered repeated failures with virtually unaltered equipment, Fulton made changes where appropriate, and eventually developed the first steamboat design which had widespread commercial potential. His considerable talents at public relations, his organizational ability, and his knack for befriending powerful persons also contributed to Fulton's success. One of his few shortcomings was a lack of business sense. For this he relied on his backers, and on one man in particular: Robert R. Livingston, delegate from New York to the First and Second Continental Congresses, Chancellor of New York State, the man who administered the oath of office to George Washington, U.S. Minister to France who was largely responsible for negotiating the Louisiana Purchase, and inventor of various steamboat designs himself. Livingston was to be Fulton's partner from their meeting in France in 1802 until the Chancellor's death in 1813.

In August 1807, Fulton piloted the *North River Steamboat of Clermont* on her maiden voyage up the Hudson River. The vessel made the 150 miles between New York and Albany in 32 hours, for a speed close to 5 miles per hour. This rate was more than enough to meet the 4-miles-per-hour minimum which had been stipulated in the requirements of New York State's sixteen-year steam navigation monopoly, to be awarded to the operators of the first vessel to attain certain pre-set conditions.

The *North River Steamboat of Clermont*, named for the Lower Hudson, or North, River and Livingston's estate on the Hudson (Clermont), was built by Charles Brown of Manhattan Island under Fulton's supervision – an arrangement continued for most of Fulton's subsequent vessels. She was around 140 ft (43 m) long, 16 ft (4.9 m) in beam, and had a depth of hold of 7 ft (2.1 m) and a draft of 28 in (71 cm). She measured about 100 tons and her hull was flat-bottomed, with a hard chine; the sharp angularity at bow and the squared-off stern belied canalboat origins. A pair of uncovered side paddle wheels 15 ft (4.6 m) in diameter and 4 ft (1.2 m) wide were positioned approximately one third of her length back from the bow and forward of the Boulton & Watt bell-crank motion engine and a 20-ft long (6.1-m) low-pressure boiler. All the machinery was placed well down in the hull, the boiler resting on a masonry foundation. The *North River*, her proper abbreviation, was equipped with two auxiliary masts for the added use of sails when wind and intended direction of travel coincided.

Faced with increasing competition on eastern rivers and the seaboard, Fulton and Livingston strengthened their commercial position while Fulton continued experimentation. After studying the first Boulton & Watt engine he had purchased, he made all but one of the subsequent engines used in his vessels, constantly improving their efficiency. He rebuilt the *North River* in 1808, increasing her size and covering her paddle wheels. The *Car of Neptune*, a side-wheeler built in 1808–9, followed, as did the *Paragon* and the *New Orleans* of 1811, and at least two New York-to-Jersey ferries, the *Jersey*, a center-wheel catamaran, and the *York* of 1812.

The *Fulton*, built in 1813 by Fulton for Elihu S. Bunker, a former competitor, marked a departure from the typical flat-bottomed, wall-sided hulls. Designed for service on the open waters of Long Island Sound, the *Fulton*'s more seaworthy hull shape was a combination of lines taken from deep-water sailing vessels and flat-bottomed craft. Unable to serve as intended, owing to the British blockade

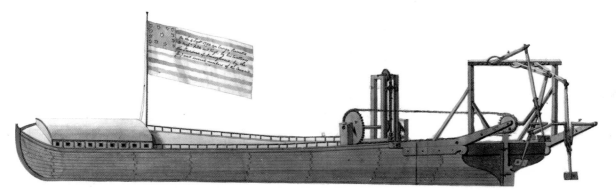

during the War of 1812, she plied the Hudson with her flat-hulled cousins. Her performance led Fulton to embody her lines, or slight variations thereof, in all of his subsequent steamboats. The last vessel he designed, the *Chancellor Livingston*, was launched in 1817, two years after his death.

Besides the change from flat- to round-bottomed hulls, other changes are discernible in the distinguished line of twenty-one steamboats which Fulton either built or designed: tonnage was increased (from 100 tons for the *North River* to more than 500 tons for the *Chancellor Livingston*) as the length-to-beam ratio was reduced (from the *North River*'s *c.* 10:1 to the *Chancellor*'s 4.7:1).

Even though a number of Fulton's vessels were lost, none has been found. However, the contemporaneous remains of the first two steamboats on Lake Champlain, the second body of water regularly traversed by these 'fire canoes', have yielded important information. The *Vermont*, a side-wheeler built in 1809, was the first steamer on the lake. She made scheduled runs until 1815, when a thrown connecting rod pierced her hull and caused her to sink in the Richelieu River. The vessel, recovered in 1953 by a private salvage firm, exhibited a flat bottom, hard chine, and exaggerated length, similar to those of Fulton's early boats; she had no keelson. The hull remnants were taken to the site of a planned museum, which failed to materialize. Sadly the vessel was removed and destroyed sometime in the 1970s.

The second steamboat on Lake Champlain, the *Phoenix*, built in 1814, caught fire and sank in 1819 with a loss of six souls. Historically blamed on an unattended candle in the galley, the conflagration may have been the work of competing, sail-powered lake interests. A side-wheeler (146 by 27 ft [45 by 8.2 m], 325 tons) known to have been built in the style of Fulton's later vessels, with a comparatively round bottom, reduced length-to-beam ratio, keelson, and auxiliary mast forward, she has been examined *in situ* by Arthur Cohn and members of the Lake Champlain Maritime Society. The *Phoenix* sits upright in 60 to 110 ft (18 to 34 m) of water just off Colchester Point where she was grounded and heavily salvaged before sinking. As was often the custom, her machinery was

Fitch and Fulton: Steamboat Pioneers

1 (*facing page*) The peculiar stern-paddle steamboat designed, built and run by American John Fitch in 1790 – the earliest commercial steamboat venture. The paddles at the back pushed down into the water and propelled the vessel with duck-like kicks. This is an 1811 copy of one of two drawings included in Fitch's 1791 patent; an original still exists in the French Patent Office.

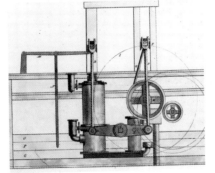

2–4 Robert Fulton (portrait in 1806, *above, far right*) developed many new steamboats. His *North River Steamboat of Clermont* (Fulton's own 1809 patent drawings: *center* on trial, and *above, near right*, machinery) was the first commercially successful steamboat operation in the world. Note the enclosed paddle wheels.

5 (*below*) Side elevation of Fulton's *Chancellor Livingston*, built in 1815–16 by the New York North River Steamboat Company.

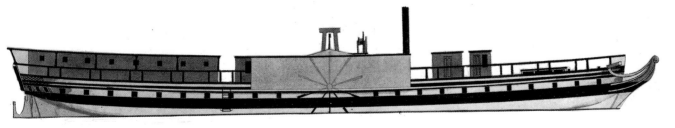

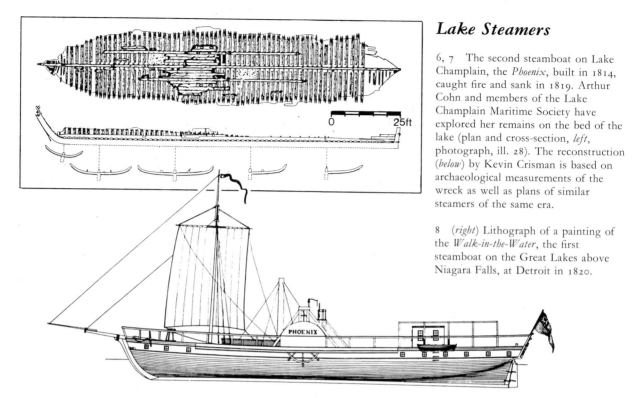

Lake Steamers

6, 7 The second steamboat on Lake Champlain, the *Phoenix*, built in 1814, caught fire and sank in 1819. Arthur Cohn and members of the Lake Champlain Maritime Society have explored her remains on the bed of the lake (plan and cross-section, *left*, photograph, ill. 28). The reconstruction (*below*) by Kevin Crisman is based on archaeological measurements of the wreck as well as plans of similar steamers of the same era.

8 (*right*) Lithograph of a painting of the *Walk-in-the-Water*, the first steamboat on the Great Lakes above Niagara Falls, at Detroit in 1820.

transferred to another vessel; in this case, the *Phoenix II*. Today she serves as a piece of living history, both for continuing research and for visits by experienced sport divers, in one of the lake's Underwater Historic Preserves managed by the State of Vermont.

The remains of what would have been the second steamboat on the lake, the *Ticonderoga* of 1814, were recovered by local sport divers in 1958 from East Bay, Whitehall, New York, and displayed at the Skenesborough Museum in Whitehall (see Chapter 9). Her round bottom, similar to that of the *Phoenix*, would have made her the first steamer with that hull shape on the lake had she not been purchased by the U.S. Navy while under construction and converted to a schooner rig. Similar framing patterns in both the *Ticonderoga* and the *Phoenix* were designed to strengthen their hulls about one third of the way aft of their bows. It was there that the hulls supposedly suffered the greatest strains from prolonged mechanical vibrations.

No physical remains of later eastern-style inland steamboats have been examined archaeologically in North America, but the magnificently preserved wreck of the *Eric Nordewald*, a side-wheeler sunk in a fresh-water lake in Sweden, gives a partial idea of what they and their equipment were like because they share several features, such as high length-to-beam ratios, general types of engines and boilers and their placement within the hulls, and deck-structure configurations. This recently discovered vessel, dating to around 1832, is a specialized type of canal-steamboat whose paddle wheels were slightly recessed into its hull. The resultant shape resembled that of a violin, giving the type the name 'fiddle boat'.

Steamboats on the Great Lakes

Even before the *Phoenix* was lost in Lake Champlain, steamboats which closely resembled the later eastern-style vessels had made their debut on the Great Lakes. The first steamer to operate on the vast lake system was the 231-ton side-wheeler *Ontario*, built in 1817 at Sackets Harbor, New York, for service on Lake Ontario; the *Frontenac* had been launched earlier in Canada, but did not enter service until later. The premier steamboat on the lakes above Niagara was the *Walk-in-the-Water*, a 338-ton side-wheeler built in 1818 and based in Buffalo, New York. Three years later she was stranded on the shore of Lake Erie and abandoned near her home port.

Steamboats were relatively late to gain acceptance and widespread use on the Great Lakes largely because of the comparative ease and better economics of sailing from port to port using the area's ample winds. The introduction of the screw propeller and its use by steamers on the Great Lakes as early as 1842 was the key reason for the decline of wind-driven commercial craft on their waters. Even after the paddle wheel had been largely replaced by the screw, the relatively deep, wave-tossed lakes and their sluggish currents led to a prolonged dependence on the ship-like hull of the eastern-style steamboat configuration. A single-piston engine from the wreck of the *Indiana*, a propeller-driven steamer built in 1848, was recovered for display in the Smithsonian Institution – the earliest

example of a power plant from a commercially successful screw vessel.

No archaeological examples of early Great Lakes steamboats are known. However, a number of excellently preserved wrecks from the late nineteenth century are protected in the waters of the Isle Royale National Park in Lake Superior.

Western Steamboats

Considering the Missouri [River] its main branch, [the Mississippi] is the longest river in the world – four thousand three hundred miles. It seems safe to say that it is also the crookedest river in the world, since in one part of its journey it uses up one thousand three hundred miles to cover the same ground that the crow would fly over in six hundred and seventy-five. It discharges three times as much water as the St Lawrence, twenty-five times as much as the Rhine, and three hundred and thirty-eight times as much as the Thames. No other river has so vast a drainage basin: it draws its water supply from twenty-eight States and Territories; from Delaware, on the Atlantic seaboard, and from all the country between that and Idaho on the Pacific slope – a spread of forty-five degrees of longitude. The Mississippi receives and carries to the Gulf water from fifty-four subordinate rivers that are navigable by steamboats, and from some hundreds that are navigable by flats and keels. The area of its drainage basin is as great as the combined areas of England,

Wales, Scotland, Ireland, France, Spain, Portugal, Germany, Austria, Italy, and Turkey. . . .
Mark Twain, *Life on the Mississippi*, 1883

In 1810, most of the length of the Mississippi was virtually uninhabited by those of European stock. The settled portions of the Mississippi watershed consisted primarily of the valleys of the Ohio River and its tributaries and the area around New Orleans; the Spanish and French authorities, who until 1803 controlled the mouth and a great deal of the surrounding territory of the Mississippi River, did not encourage the northern movement of settlers out of New Orleans.

As pioneering families moved west the wilderness was tamed, agriculture took root, and a market-oriented economy borne principally by watercraft developed. Preferred routes of travel were established along which the tide of settlement and commerce flowed.

Three natural gateways linked this new land and its extensive waterways with eastern North America and, from there, with the rest of the world: the Northern, the Northeastern and the Southern. The eastern terminus of the Northern Gateway was New York City. From there it stretched along the Mohawk River, or up the Hudson and the St Lawrence, and then westward across the Great Lakes. The Erie Canal, completed in 1825, followed by the completion of the Welland Canal which skirted Niagara Falls, and improvements in the St Lawrence River were the major developments of the Northern Gateway.

9 An 1858 wood engraving of several different aspects of transportation on the Mississippi River. Confronting one another are a canoe, flatboat (broadhorn), two steamboats and the railroad.

The Northeastern Gateway, originally a largely overland route, linked Pittsburgh and Wheeling on the Ohio River to Baltimore and Philadelphia on the Atlantic Coast. Inland navigation along this gateway, primarily by canal boat, intensified when the Pennsylvania canal system between Pittsburgh and Philadelphia opened in 1834.

New Orleans was the entrance of the Southern Gateway. The major development in this area was the post-1812 establishment of steamboat services throughout the vast expanse of the Mississippi and Missouri valleys. New Orleans, in turn, was linked to the East as early as the 1820s by regularly scheduled packet services to and from New York City.

Keelboats, flatboats, broadhorns, barges, bateaux, canoes and other types of craft had conducted commerce, transported pioneers and otherwise supported the frontier on western rivers for some time before the first steamboat shattered the calm of the Ohio and Mississippi Rivers. Fulton's *New Orleans*, built in 1811 under Nicholas J. Roosevelt's direction in Pittsburgh, holds that honor.

Roosevelt had been appointed supervisor of the western interests of Fulton and Livingston after they had obtained a navigation monopoly from the Territory of Louisiana earlier in the same year. Both Livingston and Fulton had had their eyes on the Ohio and Mississippi Rivers and their tributaries for a considerable period, certainly as early as the formation of their steamboat partnership in 1802, when Livingston was negotiating the Louisiana Purchase.

The *New Orleans* was built generally in the style of other early Fulton boats with a flat bottom, deep draft and a moderately high length-to-beam ratio; she measured 371 tons, and had most of her machinery, including a low-pressure engine with a 34-in (86-cm) diameter cylinder, placed low down in the hull. She was intended to be a stern-wheeler, but difficulties during construction necessitated a change to side paddle wheels. Auxiliary masts were placed fore and aft.

Over the winter of 1811–12, during their 2,000-mile voyage of more than a hundred days from Pittsburgh to the city for which this vessel was named, passengers on the *New Orleans* experienced fire on board, delays due to low water, the birth of a new Roosevelt and the devastating New Madrid Earthquake. The deep draft proved repeatedly troublesome in the shoal waters of the Ohio and Mississippi, a fact which was to greatly influence subsequent and divergent developments in western steamboats.

The *New Orleans* was not designed with sufficient power to run for any distance against the Father of Waters; she was assigned to a Natchez-to-New Orleans route following her glorious arrival at the mouth of the Mississippi. After carrying General Coffee and his troops to assist in Jackson's defense of New Orleans during the War of 1812, the first steamboat on the western rivers was caught by a fall of the river while tied up near Baton Rouge in July 1814. Receding water left her impaled on a stump and subsequent attempts by the crew to free her only enlarged the hole. The *New Orleans* slid swiftly beneath the murky waters of the Mississippi; the exact location of her remains is unknown.

Henry M. Shreve and the western steamboat. Several subsequent steamboats proved too weak to steam upriver. Not until 1815 did David French's *Enterprise* (80 by 29 ft [24.4 by 8.8 m]), commanded by Henry M. Shreve, an experienced keelboat captain, steam from New Orleans to Louisville, but this was against a swollen, sluggish

Mississippi and Ohio. Apparently, she too had a relatively deep draft like other early steamboats of the west, but had no trouble with shallows on this voyage because of the high water.

Only two years later Shreve was behind the wheel of a unique vessel, the *Washington*, constructed according to his explicit design. Under normal conditions the *Washington* steamed the 1,440 miles on her second trip in 1817 from New Orleans to Louisville in twenty-five days, less than a quarter of the time normally required for the arduous up-river voyage in keelboats.

According to traditional knowledge, this was the first steamboat built in the 'western', or flat-bottomed, shallow-draft fashion, the type of vessel which opened western North America to vast settlement. There is evidence, however, that the vessel may not have been the shallow-draft prototype she is commonly thought to have been: her hull might have been as deep as 12.5 ft (3.8 m) – one of the deepest drafts of all the early steamboats on western rivers. Other fundamental features of the *Washington* are hotly debated. In short, the inability of scholars to agree on the appearance of Shreve's *Washington* raises serious doubts as to the vessel's uniqueness and traditionally assigned starring role in the development of the classic western steamboat. Clearly, the evolution of this specific type of steamboat was not the work of a single man, just as the invention of the steamboat was not due solely to Fulton. The flat-bottomed, shallow-draft hull of western steamboats developed gradually over a period of about three decades, from the early 1820s to the 1850s.

Generally, the shallow waters of the west demanded a powerful yet lightweight engine designed so that its mass could be distributed over a large area of shallow hull. This and virtually unlimited supplies of wood fuel led to the development of the high-pressure steam engine which operated at pressures of 50–125 pounds per square inch (3.5–8.75 kg per square cm) or greater. One innovation of the *Washington* unquestionably attributed to Shreve was the horizontal, high-pressure, noncondensing, direct-acting engine which powered her. It was exactly this type of engine that was used throughout the remainder of the steamboat era.

In the *Washington* the engine was probably placed in the hull, while the four boilers were paired on either side of the main deck. In the fully developed western steamboat, however, the high-pressure engine, a battery of boilers, and other major machinery were all placed on the main deck.

The resulting loss of space to machinery on the main deck was compensated in later steamboats by the erection of another level, or boiler deck (thus named, even though the boilers were below), over the main deck. In the first multi-decked steamboats small partitioned areas arranged around a central salon on the boiler deck were forerunners of generally more comfortable and even opulent accommodations in later steamers; arranged with the men's section forward and ladies' aft, each of the crude

early cabins was named for a state in the Union, thus introducing the term 'stateroom'. On the roof of the second deck a pilothouse was erected well forward, and usually forward of this two tall smokestacks topped with ornamental crowns rose from the furnaces under the boilers. On larger, fully developed western steamboats, a third and fourth deck, the hurricane and texas, respectively, appeared.

Another question regarding the *Washington* is whether she was equipped with side-mounted paddle wheels or a single stern wheel. A stern wheel is favored by most scholars because Shreve's horizontal, direct-acting engine was probably designed so that the power of the engine could be more easily communicated to the stern than that from an engine whose cylinders moved vertically, as in earlier high- and low-pressure engines. Stern-mounted paddle wheels, used extensively on post-bellum steamboats, were particularly good on the narrow and shallow upper reaches of many western rivers because the boats using them were characteristically narrower and of less draft than side-wheelers. In some cases, the stern wheel could be raised as needed. A heavily laden western-style steamboat 200 ft (61 m) in length, with a 30-ft (9.1-m) beam, could float easily in only 2.5 ft (74 cm) of water. One smaller steamer which ran some 10 tons of goods on only 8 in (20 cm) of water had a watering can proudly hung at the bow by her owners – as if she could float on its contents alone!

Scholars do not even agree on how Shreve's most famous vessel met her end, although all affirm that she suffered the fate to which many subsequent high-pressure steamboats were to succumb. Some say there was a boiler explosion on the *Washington*'s maiden voyage in 1816, although they do not mention her subsequent loss; others state that she was sunk after a boiler explosion in 1819; the Lytle-Holdcamper List gives her date of abandonment as 1823. Regardless of its exact date and nature, the explosion caused the first major steamboat catastrophe and, as such, served as a cautionary signal for the public.

Widespread apprehension over the tendency of early high-pressure boilers to explode led to a brief spate of safety barges. Towed behind steamboats, these opulently outfitted barges removed passengers from harm's way by the length of their tow cables. Lessening public concern during a relatively explosion-free two-year period, however, led to the safety barges' decline around 1830, although the problem of confining high-pressure steam had not been solved. In fact, 1838 and 1850 witnessed more explosions than any other years of the steamboat era. Charles Dickens, who steamed on the Ohio, wrote in 1840 that traveling on high-pressure steamboats 'conveyed that kind of feeling to me which I should be likely to experience, I think, if I had lodgings on the first floor of a [gun] powder mill'.

Explosion was not the major cause of steamboat losses, although it caused the greatest mortality. Mark Twain mentions an average of a wreck every mile in the 200 miles between St Louis and Cairo, Illinois. Tabulations of records between 1819 and 1925 show that snags – wholly or partially submerged tree trunks – were twenty times more likely to cause loss or damage to steam traffic on the Missouri River, and even ice, fire and collisions with bridges resulted in more sinkings.

In addition to his development of the standard high-pressure engine used on western steamboats, Captain Shreve contributed to inland navigational safety as U.S. Superintendent of Western River Improvements during the administrations of Presidents Adams, Jackson and Van Buren. Perhaps his most important contribution here was as inventor of the snag boat; the catamaran snag boat *Heliopolis*, built in 1829, received U.S. Patent number 913 in September 1838. Shreve insured his fame by clearing some 300 miles of the Mississippi, south from Cairo, Illinois, of thousands of snags with the first of 'Uncle Sam's toothpullers', as snag boats became known, and by breaking up the Great Log Raft of the Red River, thus opening up 150 miles of previously unnavigable water in northwestern Louisiana. Shreveport was named for him.

Yet another honor for Captain Shreve was won through litigation. Until his death, Fulton, his associates and, afterwards, their heirs were repeatedly taken to court over disputes about navigation on nearly every river from the Mississippi to the Hudson. In 1819, Shreve and his backers defeated the monopolistic claims which the Fulton/Livingston partnership had on the Mississippi River system. Rival factions continued battling in various state and federal courtrooms until 1824, when a Supreme Court decision (*Gibbons vs. Ogden*) effectively negated the claims of Fulton's heirs and others to sole navigation rights and royalties due them from contested state monopolies. This reinforced the decision made in favor of Shreve and placed the conveyance of people and goods by steamboat into the realm of a national free-market system unhindered by state or territorial boundaries. In other words, it signaled the beginning of a golden era of the steamboat – a period which lasted until several years before the Civil War started.

Now free to be utilized for a variety of purposes on practically every body of water in the continent,

steamboats evolved to fill many different niches. Hull configurations, power plants, propulsive systems, and superstructures were split generally into two traditions based on hydrographical factors: those designed for use on deep, often wave-tossed waters with rather sluggish currents vs. those intended for use on shallow, or periodically shallow, waters with relatively swift currents. The former had deep, seaworthy hull shapes, were usually powered by economical low-pressure engines, and were used primarily on the eastern seaboard and in the deeper rivers of east, northeast, and northwest North America and in the Great Lakes. The latter, or western-style steamboats, had flat, shallow-draft hulls with a length-to-beam ratio of from around 5:1 to 8:1, were usually powered by comparatively uneconomical high-pressure engines, and ran predominantly on midwestern and western rivers or on bodies of water in other parts of the continent with similar conditions.

As the frontier areas of North America moved steadily westward, so the western-style steamboat followed. On frontier rivers from the Republic of Texas to the Territories of Arizona, California, Utah and Montana, steam-powered vessels of shallow draft ranged widely. After the discovery of gold in California in 1848, marine and inland steamboats of both traditions quickly arrived in considerable numbers off the coast and in the major river valleys of western North America. Some inland vessels made the hazardous passage around the Horn; others were shipped overland in pieces to be reassembled in the west. By the end of 1850, there were some 700 steamboats plying the western rivers.

Builders of steamboats, engines, boilers and related equipment soon appeared. In 1853 the first steamboat built on the West Coast, the *Shasta* (110 by 23 ft [33.5 by 7 m] by 3.5 ft [1.1 m] depth of hold, 18 in [46 cm] draft, and 120 tons burden) was launched from the Rincon Point yard of Littleton & Company. Others quickly followed.

Steamboats found their way to northwest and far northwest North America as swiftly as did miners, merchants and settlers. Fairly well-preserved remains of several vessels were seen along the shore of the Yukon River as late as 1975.

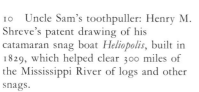

10 Uncle Sam's toothpuller: Henry M. Shreve's patent drawing of his catamaran snag boat *Heliopolis*, built in 1829, which helped clear 300 miles of the Mississippi River of logs and other snags.

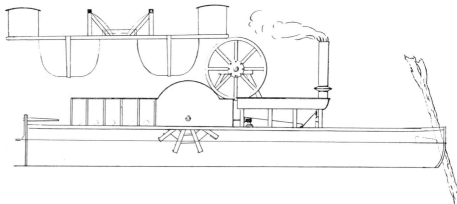

Relics of a Bygone Age

11 (*right*) The rotting hulks of ancient steamboats are still to be seen. Here the Canadian stern-wheeler *Schwatka* lies abandoned at an old shipyard across the Yukon River from Dawson, Yukon, in this photograph taken in the early 1980s.

12 (*below*) The ghostly remains of a snagged and abandoned side-wheeler, from *Harper's Weekly*, 1888.

Diversification of the Western Steamboat

Although the greater variety of physical situations and transportation demands on western rivers, as compared with those in the eastern part of the continent, led to the evolution of equally varied steam-powered craft, these western craft all shared an extremely shallow draft, lightly built superstructures and powerful engines.

Packet boats. By far the most numerous steamboats on the western rivers were packet boats, general-service vessels which carried both freight and passengers. The decks of side-wheel packets were characteristically lozenge-shaped, tapering toward their bows from the widest portions of their hulls at the paddle wheels. The decks,

usually two (main and boiler), were wider than the beam dimensions owing to the guards – prominent overhangs of the decks on either side; thus, the main deck was protected by the boiler-deck guard which served as a promenade deck. Stern-wheel packets were ordinarily built with narrower guards and, in plan, the sides of these vessels were nearly parallel.

Because of the increased strain on hulls which supported aft-projected paddle wheels, wooden hogging frames, or iron-rod hogging chains, usually were prominent on stern-wheelers. Hogging chains prevented a hull from hogging, or sagging, by supporting areas strained by the weight of machinery, while simultaneously keeping the hull supple enough to be able to slip over sandbars and shoals. Nevertheless, the heavy wear

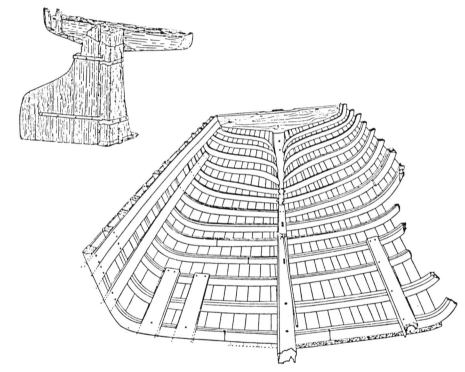

13–15   The side-wheel cotton-packet *Black Cloud*, built in 1864 and abandoned nine years later in the Trinity River, Texas, is one of the few western steamboats studied by archaeologists. Her bronze bell (*above*) was presented to a local church in Liberty, Texas, soon after her abandonment. Texas A&M University archaeology students recorded the *Black Cloud*'s rudder assembly (*above center*) and hull remains (*above right*) on the river bed. See also ill. 27.

16   (*right*) The remnants of the *Cremona*, a stern-wheel packet of 1852, were located by archaeologists in Mobile Bay, at the mouth of the Alabama River. Her unusual joinery at the angular turn of the bilge, between futtocks and first side strakes, is shown here. The bases of the futtocks are set in mortises cut into the lowermost side strakes of the box-like hull.

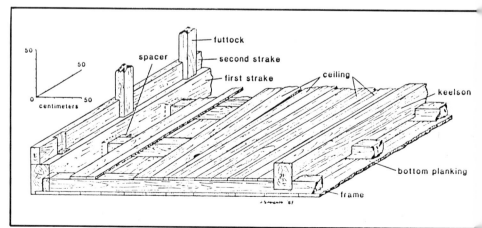

inflicted on the wooden hulls accounted for an average steamboat lifespan of only five years.

Some type of cross-chain system of support was similarly necessary on side-wheelers, particularly on the extra-wide main decks of the specialized side- and stern-wheel cotton packets which hauled staggering quantities of highly flammable cargo; cotton bales were often stacked so high that the only light which entered salons and cabins came through the overhead skylights.

The *Black Cloud*, a side-wheel cotton packet built in Orange, Texas, in 1864 and abandoned in the Trinity River at Old Green's Ferry Crossing on the Atascosita Road in Liberty County, Texas, is one of the few western steamboats examined to any degree by archaeologists. The location of the *Black Cloud* apparently has always been known to at least local historians and the property owners in the immediate vicinity. At periods of extreme low water, portions of the vessel's hull and paddle wheels were exposed to view. In fact, the ship's bell was at the time of the *Black Cloud*'s abandonment in 1873 a gift by one of the owners to a church in Liberty, where it still resides.

While laying a gas pipeline across the river in 1965, equipment operators encountered the *Black Cloud* and recovered pieces of a paddle wheel, hogging chain and fragments of wood. A contemplated second pipeline led to a magnetometer survey by the Texas Antiquities Committee and the Natural Gas Pipeline Company. As a result, the second pipeline was laid without disturbing the wreck.

The wreck offered an excellent training opportunity for nautical archaeology students at nearby Texas A&M University, who hoped to add to local history and to the rather sparse physical evidence of commercial river steamers. No large-scale excavations resulted, but during the course of three weekend's work, we uncovered, mapped and drew the stern transom and rudder assembly, the bed of fire bricks under the forward-mounted furnaces, main-deck hatch coamings and details of framing and deck beams forward and amidships. Additionally, some forty-five artifacts representing primarily structural components of the hull and the drive train were recovered, conserved and recorded.

A number of other side-wheel packets are now being sought. Among them is the *Mittie Stephens*, tragically burned in 1869 on Lake Caddo between Texas and Louisiana, and now the object of a search directed by S. Ruby Lang of the Mittie Stephens Foundation.

The *Cremona*, a stern-wheel packet built in 1852 at New Albany, Indiana, for service on the Alabama River, was located in Mobile Bay in 1983 by archaeologists contracted by the U.S. Army Corps of Engineers. One of several vessels sunk as part of a defensive harbor obstruction during the mid-years of the Civil War, the *Cremona* is the earliest stern-wheeler located to date. Significant portions of the hull survived their long immersion in the fine silts on the floor of Mobile Bay, enabling researchers to observe the spoon-bill bow,

square stern, flat bottom and rather unusual construction at the angular turn of the bilge, where the futtock frames were mortised into the first side strake.

'*Mountain boats*'. Special stern-wheelers of exceptionally shallow draft were used on the upper sections of the Missouri, Niobrara, Yellowstone, Colorado and other rivers, often shallow, muddy paths winding through tortuously narrow canyons. The normal head of navigation on the Missouri, at Fort Benton, Montana, was almost 3,600 river-miles from the Gulf of Mexico and 3,300 ft (1,000 m) above sea level.

Fully developed by the late 1860s, chiefly as supply boats for western military installations and gold-mining operations, mountain boats had characteristically bowl-like spoon-bill bows, no guards, a minimum number of decks with shortened cabin structures and, usually, 'grasshopper' rigs. These were pairs of large spars carried at the bow with which steamboats could pull themselves over sandbars and shoals. This was accomplished by sinking the spars into the riverbed, jacking the bow of the vessel up with the help of derricks, spar straps and steam-powered winches, then running the boat forward under a full head of steam until she fell off the spars. Thus repeated until the bar was crossed, the action resembled that of a large, slow-motion grasshopper.

The best archaeological example of either the eastern or western type of inland steamboat is that of the *Bertrand*, a western steamer lost on the Missouri River less than a year after her construction in Wheeling, West Virginia. Although possibly a specially constructed mountain boat, the *Bertrand* more probably was a modified stern-wheel packet of the Upper-Ohio class, as she did not have the characteristic spoon-bill bow and carried both guards and a 'grasshopper' rig. She was 161 ft (49 m) in length, 32 ft 9 in (10 m) in beam, had a depth of hold of 5 ft 2 in (1.6 m), measured 251 tons, and was said to draw only 18 in (46 cm) when unloaded, or 'light'. While en route from St Louis to Fort Benton in the Montana Territory, she sank in less than five minutes on 1 April 1865, surprisingly with no loss of life, after hitting a snag at Portage La Force below De Soto Bend, some 25 miles north of Omaha, Nebraska.

The remains of the *Bertrand* were located on U.S. Government property (De Soto National Wildlife Refuge) by two salvors searching for treasure trove – mainly the gold, whiskey and mercury reputed to have been aboard the locally legendary vessel. The searchers were aided by newspaper accounts and other documents relating to the sinking and contemporaneous salvage attempts. Maps from the period prepared by the U.S. Army Corps of Engineers and more recent aerial photographs helped reduce the search area. Finally, magnetic anomalies detected by a magnetometer in the prime search location were sampled with a truck-mounted auger 6 in (15 cm) in diameter. Extensive wooden remains, glass, brick, leather boot fragments, brandied

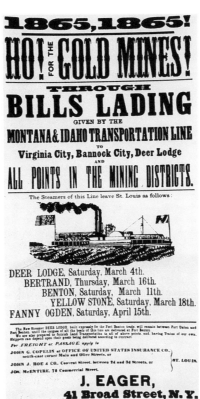

The Romance of Steamboating

17, 18 The *Deer Lodge* (photograph, *far left*) was a mountain boat exhibiting all the characteristics of this type of vessel: spoon-bill bow, no guards and grasshopper spars. Her shallow draft allowed her to navigate the upper reaches of rivers such as the Missouri. The *Deer Lodge* was built by the owners of the *Bertrand*, both of which are advertised in the 1865 handbill (*left*) announcing their departure dates from St Louis.

19 (*right*) This gouache and collage on paper of the *Saloon or Main Cabin of the Steamboat Princess* is the earliest known painting of the interior of a Mississippi River steamboat. The figures are mostly hand-colored cutouts from newspapers or magazines. French-born artist Adrien Persac did the painting in 1861 in memory of his wedding trip from Baton Rouge to New Orleans on the *Princess* a decade earlier.

cherries and other items were encountered in late February 1968 under an average of 26 ft (8 m) of sediments, well below the water table in an old ox bow of the river. Bolstered by this evidence, the finders submitted a plan of excavation to the Chief of the Midwest Archaeological Center, National Park Service, and this resulted in a contract which specified that excavation of the site could be conducted only under the direct supervision of National Park Service archaeologists. The discoverers were to receive 60 percent of the trove, specified as mercury, whiskey and gold. The United States Government was to retain 40 percent and ownership of 'any artifacts (to include all man-made objects or parts thereof) or other valuable historical items'. As in most ventures of this type, the finders' dreams were not fully realized; only nine containers of mercury and two cases of 'mixed' spirits were located in the hold. The absence of most of the *Bertrand*'s machinery and few traces of her superstructure and deck freight suggest that the vessel was heavily salvaged shortly after sinking.

The *Bertrand* was excavated during the latter part of 1968 and throughout most of 1969. About 15 ft (4.6 m) of overlying sediments were readily removed by dragline and bulldozer to a level 5 ft (1.5 m) below the water table. A small floating dredge, placed in the water-filled excavation, removed large volumes of the overburden which was screened to capture dislodged artifactual material. Once the level of the boat was reached, excavation proceeded with shovels, trowels and high- and low-pressure water jets to loosen the formidable Missouri River mud. An extensive well-point system operated constantly to keep the water table low enough for work to continue.

In addition to the entire lower portion of the hull up to the main, or first, deck, close to 2,000,000 individual artifacts were located and removed. The enormously varied cargo recovered had a total volume of around 10,000 cubic feet (283 cu. m), consisting generally of foodstuffs, clothing, agricultural and mining supplies including liquor, patent medicines and quicksilver, and numerous and varied objects of leather, wood, glass, porcelain and other ceramics. Fabrications of iron (wrought, cast and drawn), hard rubber, shell, textiles (wool, cotton and silk), bone, ivory, copper, brass, tin and lead, as well as ammunition for the Army's 12-pound mountain howitzers in the Territorial forts, were included among the *Bertrand*'s cargo. About 300,000 of the artifacts were determined 'to warrant stabilization and/or restoration for purposes of future study and museum exhibition'.

The wreck was identified by the words 'Bertrand Stores' inked on some of the wooden crates taken from the hold, by comparison of consignees' initials and marks on some of the cargo crates, and by correlation between labeled personal effects and known passengers. Perhaps the most touching example of the latter was the classroom chalkboard of Fannie Campbell found in the hold among other lost family possessions.

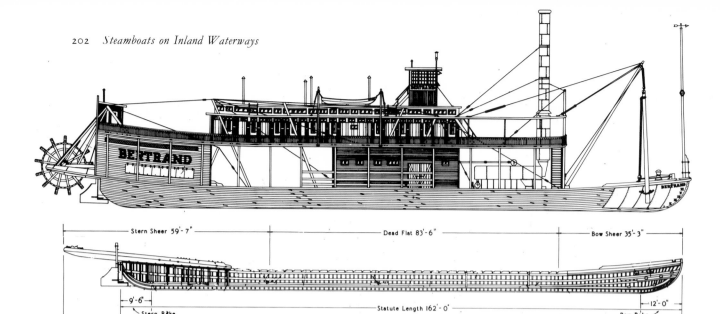

Stern Sheer 59'-7"   Dead Flat 83'-6"   Bow Sheer 35'-3"

9'-6"
Stern Rake   Statute Length 162'-0"   12'-0"
Bow Rake

Actual Length 178'-4"

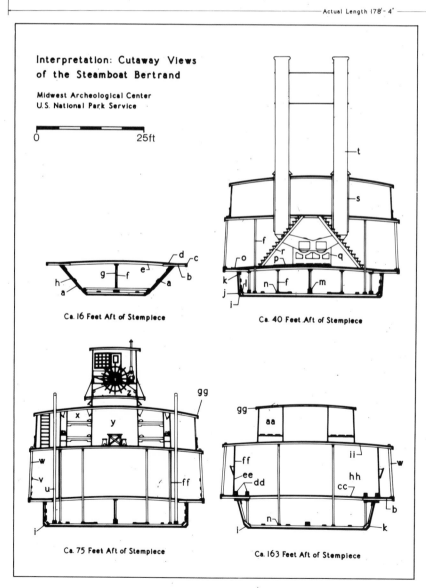

Interpretation: Cutaway Views of the Steamboat Bertrand

Midwest Archeological Center
U.S. National Park Service

0   25ft

Ca. 16 Feet Aft of Stempiece

Ca. 40 Feet Aft of Stempiece

Ca. 75 Feet Aft of Stempiece

Ca. 163 Feet Aft of Stempiece

On Board the 'Bertrand'

20, 21   (*above*) Cross-section as found and reconstruction of the western steamer *Bertrand*, which sank on hitting a snag in the Missouri River in 1865.

22   (*left*) Cutaway views: *a* ice shield, *b* outriggers, *c* guard, *d* main deck, *e* deck beams, *f* stanchions, *g* bulkheads, *h* side planking, *i* knuckle, *j* cocked hat (futtock), *k* top wale strake (clamp), *l* bilge keelson, *m* main (central) keelson, *n* floor strake, *o* ash trap door, *p* ash trough and fire brick, *q* firebox and boilers, *r* stairway to boiler deck, *s* head jacket, *t* stacks, *u* hog chain brace, *v* rails, *w* stationaries, *x* berths, *y* dining area and kitchen, *z* pilot house, *aa* toilets, *bb* boiler deck, *cc* main deck, *dd* cylinder timbers, *ee* engine room ventilators, *ff* bulkheads, *gg* cabin roof, *hh* engine room, *ii* carlines.

Facing page:
23   (*top left*) The side of a soap case.

24   (*right*) The *Bertrand* yielded hundreds of glass and ceramic bottles, in at least thirty different shapes. Perishable contents included wine, champagne, domestic and imported ale, 'Dr J. Hostetter's Celebrated Stomach Bitters' (191 cases), 'Bourbon Whiskey Cocktail from A. Richard' (packed 24 quarts to the case), catsup, essence of ginger and Worcestershire sauce.

25   (*above left*) Cargo included ironstone china packed in barrels along with water glasses.

After documentation of the hull and its contents, and the removal of the cargo and other artifacts, the vessel was filled again with silt and covered by a layer of polyethylene and then a layer of steel aircraft landing-strip, with a layer of silt between. Then the well-point system was shut off and removed, allowing the water table to rise to its natural level. The well-protected site now appears as a small, oval pond between two piles of earth.

This remains the only large-scale excavation of a steamboat of any kind, and as such is of great importance to the first-hand study of the vessels which were the key to North America's westward expansion. Data obtained during the *Bertrand*'s excavation has added particularly to our knowledge of the construction of specialized western steamboats in use on the Upper Missouri River. New insights into everything from the stowage of cargo to the nature of life aboard western steamboats have also resulted from the work on the wreck.

Frontier historians have also benefited because the size and diversity of the *Bertrand*'s cargo impart a sense of what life amid the bustle of the Montana gold rush must have been like, and vividly represent the 'mining technology and frontier economy of mid-19th-century [North] America'. The impact of the *Bertrand*'s loss to frontier enterprises is better appreciated by noting that her cargo represented some 13 percent of the entire tonnage shipped to Ft Benton in 1865. Coupled with the loss that year of another steamboat engaged in the same trade, economic repercussions were serious.

Towboats. Towboats, vessels which in fact pushed freight barges, were usually constructed without guards and with only protective, squared-off nosings at the bows of their narrow hulls. They were almost exclusively stern-wheelers, but even the finest floating palaces, side- and stern-wheeled alike, towed a barge or two when necessary. Pool towboats, which operated on lakes (pools) behind dams where bridge clearances were drastically reduced, had specialized forms, including shortened smokestacks. At least one side-wheel towboat, the *John Fraser* – sunk during the 1890s in Lake Nipissing off Georgian Bay, Ontario – has been examined archaeologically.

Ferryboats. Side-wheel, stern-wheel and center-wheel ferryboats all possessed broad, unobstructed main deck areas, leading to many strange arrangements of smokestacks and pilothouses. Usually loaded from floats, vehicles entered from one side and exited from the other. Transfers, or railroad ferries, were equipped with tracks which ran lengthwise down the centers of their main decks; their massive cargoes necessitated elaborate bracing with stout hogging frames and chains; and their pilothouses were supported over the tracks on bridges.

The Golden Age of Steamboats

The five or six decades from the building of the *Phoenix* in 1814 to the sinking of the *Bertrand* in 1865 and the *Black Cloud* in 1873 were the golden years of steamboating.

26 (*right*) The steamboat *Bertrand* being uncovered beneath 26 ft (8 m) of sediment which had accumulated since she hit a snag and sank in 1865. After hundreds of thousands of artifacts were removed for conservation and study, the hull was covered again for long-term preservation.

27 (*below*) At extreme low water, traces of the side-wheel cotton-packet *Black Cloud* have remained visible in the Trinity River, Texas, since she was abandoned over a century ago. So far only limited excavations have been carried out on the wreck (ills. 13–15).

28 (*bottom*) In 1985, the first Vermont State Underwater Historic Preserve was established over the remains of the *Phoenix*, which burned and sank in Lake Champlain in 1819. Here two divers examine the bow structure.

29 *Robinson's Floating Palaces* – a typical showboat. The steamer at the far end provided the propulsion and actually pushed the 'show-barges'.

Showboats. Contrary to their Hollywood images, show-boats were not steamboats at all. They were simply theaters installed on unpowered barges, usually towed (i.e., pushed) by dilapidated stern-wheelers. The unwieldy duo was controlled remotely from the pilothouse of the showboat, the tiller lines and engine-room bells having been connected from showboat aft to steamboat by cables. The extent of entertainment on an ordinary steamboat was apt to have been a simple, well-stocked bar and a twenty-four-hour poker table.

Channel maintenance vessels. Among the various vessels designed for maintenance of channels, ports and navigational hazard approaches were snag boats, steam-powered dredges and light tenders.

The Decline of Steamboating

Of the thousands of variously designed steamboats that plied the inland waters of North America, only six nineteenth-century craft – two paddle-wheelers (the *Moyie* 1898 and the *Eureka* 1890) and four screw boats – are left. The economic depression following the boom years of the Civil War negatively affected river-borne commerce, particularly in the Midwest. Coupled with the growing importance of railroads, originally designed as feeder systems for steamboat traffic, and an increasing reliance on towboat and barge fleets, it sounded the death knell of the steamboat. A history of nineteenth-century commercial transportation, in this case for the Mississippi Valley specifically, can hardly be given more succinctly than by Mark Twain:

> Mississippi steamboating was born about 1812; at the end of thirty years, it had grown to mighty proportions; and in less than thirty more, it was dead! A strangely short life for so majestic a creature. Of course it is not

absolutely dead; neither is a crippled octogenarian who could once jump twenty-two feet on level ground; but as contrasted with what it was in its prime vigor, Mississippi steamboating may be called dead.

> It killed the old-fashioned keelboating by reducing the freight trip to New Orleans to less than a week. The railroads have killed the steamboat traffic by doing in two or three days what the steamboats consumed a week in doing; and the towing fleets have killed the through-freight traffic by dragging six or seven steamerloads of stuff down the river at a time, at an expense so trivial that steamboat competition was out of the question. . . .

Life on the Mississippi, 1883

Eventually, late-blooming steamboat traffic in west, northwest and far northwest North America was affected by and finally succumbed to similar, unavoidable economic determinants.

And yet, steamboating remains one of the most invitingly romantic subjects of nineteenth-century North America and westward expansion. The keen interest of a large number of steamboat *aficionados* and the brisk business captured by diesel-powered steamboat replicas are indicators of its widespread appeal.

The archaeological community is awakening to the potential of steamboat excavations and the copious information they can add to our knowledge of these important vessels. Literally thousands of steamboats of all kinds lie concealed in river sediments throughout the continent; virtually every navigable waterway holds promise for steamboat archaeology. To study one of Fulton's early vessels or to answer the myriad questions about the true nature of Shreve's *Washington* are but two of the almost unlimited goals available to steamboat archaeologists.

CHAPTER ELEVEN

The Civil War at Sea: Dawn of an Age of Iron and Engineering

Gordon P. Watts, Jr

When the thunder of heavy artillery awakened residents of Charleston, South Carolina, at 4:30 am on 12 April 1861, few expressed surprise. Months of negotiations with the Union Army garrison occupying Charleston's Fort Sumter had failed to produce a peaceful surrender of that strategic harbor fortification. In response to a final rejection of Confederate demands, batteries under the command of General P. G. T. Beauregard had initiated what most Charlestonians believed inevitable – a reduction of Fort Sumter by force. Throughout the newly formed Confederate States of America, Beauregard's attack confirmed that the United States could not be dissolved peacefully. For all Americans, news of the hostilities made it clear that complex sectional, political, economic and social differences between the North and South could only be resolved by war.

Determined to preserve the nation, newly elected President Abraham Lincoln responded to the Confederate attack on Fort Sumter by calling on those states remaining loyal to the United States to provide 75,000 militia for immediate service, and by formulating an offensive strategy that included a blockade of the Confederate coastline, to isolate the South from sources of foreign support; a Union army attack on Richmond, Virginia, to destroy the army defending the Confederate capital; and a second offensive operation to divide the southern states by regaining control of the Mississippi River. With the entire run of the Mississippi again under Union control, Chattanooga could be captured and developed as a base for an invasion of the deep south that would destroy the Confederacy.

The Confederate Congress reacted by enacting legislation to provide for an enlistment of 100,000 men. While the Union adopted an offensive strategy, President Jefferson Davis and other southern leaders were determined to achieve success through defense of the South and diplomatic recognition in Europe. Strategic priorities of the Confederacy included a successful defense of Richmond, repelling Union advances into southern territory, securing diplomatic recognition abroad and demonstrating the ineffectiveness of the blockade.

The American Civil War has been traditionally characterized by massive army operations, but naval and maritime activities were instrumental in the strategic objectives of both sides. For the United States, naval support was essential in reestablishing control of the Mississippi and other western rivers, launching offensives against the Confederate capital, supporting invasions of the deep south and southern coastal plain, and maintaining a blockade of Confederate ports. While the most celebrated of Confederate maritime activities are associated with commercial and military efforts to run and raise the blockade, the Confederacy also assembled and maintained a variety of small defensive fleets, authorized privateering and sponsored successful commerce raiders that disrupted Union merchant shipping and whaling.

Both the Union and the Confederacy took advantage of dramatic technological innovations spawned by the scientific and industrial revolution. The development of steam propulsion, iron ship construction, shell guns, naval armor and other products of nascent engineering disciplines were undermining the traditional character of both maritime commerce and naval power. The destructive power of ironclads confirmed the passing of the great age of wooden sail-powered fighting ships. Steam provided commerce raiders with an unprecedented mobility, making helpless victims of traditional sailing vessels. Efforts to run and enforce the Union blockade of Confederate ports also generated new technological demands: in spite of the initial success of wooden sailing vessels like the schooner yacht *America*, steam-powered iron- and ultimately steel-hulled ships like the blockade runner *Phantom* displaced even the fastest sail. And semi-submersible and submersible vessels for the first time demonstrated the ability to sink enemy ships. Still, industrial production could not completely satisfy the needs of either the North or South, and makeshift gunboats were also employed by both sides.

The First Ironclads

A staccato of drums brought the crew of the USS *Cumberland* scrambling to quarters on the morning of 8

Discovering the 'Monitor'

It took 111 years for the wreck of the most famous Civil War vessel, the Union ironclad *Monitor*, to be located off Cape Hatteras.

1, 2   Finally discovered in 1973 at a depth of 230 ft (70 m), the *Monitor* underwent detailed survey later in the decade. The manned submersible *Johnson-Sea-Link I* (*above right*, being launched) dived more than fifty times on the wreck in 1979. Archaeologists breathing a mixture of helium and oxygen (*center right*, Gordon Watts using a special television camera) were able to spend up to one hour at a time on the wreck working from the submersible.

3   (*below*) The world's first battle between steam-powered, ironclad warships: the *Monitor* and Confederate *Virginia* confront each other in the Hampton Roads, Virginia, 9 March 1862. The result was inconclusive but the psychological impact of the battle gave impetus to the construction of numerous similar ironclad warships.

4 (*right*) Tracking an ironclad: the *Monitor* was known to have sunk under tow in December 1862, and a hunt through the towship's log narrowed the search to a rectangular area south of Cape Hatteras. Using a magnetometer, side-scan sonar and cable-slung cameras, a team of scientists on board the research vessel *Eastward* finally located the wreck on 18 August 1973.

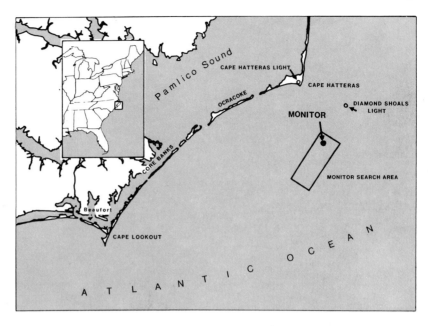

March 1862. To the southeast of the powerful frigate's anchorage off Newport News, Virginia, a pall of black smoke confirmed that the Confederate ironclad ram CSS *Virginia* was underway. Within minutes *Cumberland*'s decks were cleared for action. and her ordnance run out for battle. Lieutenant-Commander Thomas O. Selfridge, Jr, later recalled 'her crew standing at their guns for the last time, cool, grim, silent and determined Yankee seamen, the embodiment of power, grit, and confidence'.

Within the armored casemate of the recently completed CSS *Virginia*, that same resolution was recorded by Captain William H. Parker as the ironclad steamed down the Elizabeth River, ' . . . no voice broke the silence of the scene; all hearts were too full for utterance, an attempt at cheering would have ended in tears, for all realized the fact that there was to be tried the great experiment of the ram and iron-clad in naval warfare'.

Within hours the *Virginia* had forever altered the conduct of naval warfare. With virtual impunity the casemated ironclad, constructed from the remains of the scuttled steam frigate USS *Merrimack*, had destroyed the frigates USS *Congress* and USS *Cumberland* and damaged the stranded frigate USS *Minnesota*.

As the *Virginia* created havoc among the wooden warships in Hampton Roads, the steam tug *Seth Low* labored through the Atlantic off Cape Charles, Virginia. Astern, awash in storm-driven swells, rode a second ironclad, the USS *Monitor*. The *Monitor*'s executive officer, Lieutenant Samuel Dana Greene, wrote of the vessel's arrival at Hampton Roads:

An atmosphere of gloom pervaded the fleet, and the pygmy aspect of the newcomer did not inspire confidence among those who had witnessed the day before. . . . Reaching the *Minnesota*, hard and fast

aground, near midnight we anchored. . . . Between 1 and 2 AM the *Congress* blew up – not instantaneously but successively. . . . Near us, too, at the bottom of the river, lay the *Cumberland*, within her silent crew of brave men, who died while fighting their guns to the water's edge, and whose colors were still flying at the peak.

The following day, 9 March, the *Virginia* returned to Hampton Roads to confront this new adversary, and at 6:00 am, steamed directly for the stranded frigate *Minnesota*. The *Monitor*, ordered to protect the *Minnesota*, steamed for the *Virginia*. For four hours the two ironclads engaged each other, but in spite of close, frequently point-blank ranges, neither vessel was seriously damaged. Less than conclusive, the celebrated battle was the first between steam-powered, ironclad warships.

Each vessel represented a different approach to the demands of 'modern' warfare and the availability of resources and industry. The *Virginia*'s design had been developed by Confederate Lieutenant John M. Brooke to utilize the remains of the USS *Merrimack*, which had fallen into Confederate hands when the State of Virginia withdrew from the Union. By mid-July 1861 the *Merrimack* had been raised, and engineers and carpenters were converting the frigate hull into an ironclad ram.

The hull of the *Merrimack* was cut down to the berth deck and an inclined casemate, constructed over all but the bow and stern, was armored with 4 in (10 cm) of iron plate. Within the protective casemate was a formidable battery of six 9-in Dahlgren cannon, two 7-in, and two 6.4-in Brook rifled guns. A 1,500-pound iron ram installed on the bow made the vessel an even more potent threat to the wooden fleet of the United States Navy. On 17 February 1862, the converted USS *Merrimack* was commissioned into the Confederate States Navy as the CSS *Virginia*.

While the construction of Union ironclads was not initiated solely as a response to the threat posed by the *Virginia*, news of her construction contributed to the atmosphere of urgency under which the program was adopted. In August 1861, Congress authorized appointment of an 'Ironclad Board' to evaluate proposals for armored warships and to recommend allocation of $1.5 million appropriated to finance construction of vessels meeting their approval. The Board approved three designs.

Two of these were for conventional armored ships similar to ironclads already in service in England and France. The third design was submitted by Swedish-American engineer John Ericsson of New York. Ericsson proposed such a radical departure from traditional warship design that considerable effort was required to convince the Ironclad Board to approve the concept even conditionally. The design called for a low-freeboard, armored raft supported by an iron displacement hull that contained both machinery and quarters. The unique 'Ericsson Battery' was a revolving armored turret that carried the vessel's ordnance.

Ericsson, backed by several influential industrialists, began construction in October 1861, and launched the *Monitor* on 30 January 1862. The assistant secretary of the navy telegraphed: 'Hurry her to sea as the *Merrimack* is nearly ready at Norfolk.'

The combatant careers of the *Virginia* and *Monitor* were brief. For two months the ironclads challenged each other from safe distances, each captain aware that the loss of his ship would risk far more than a tactical victory could achieve. Then, drawing too much water to escape up the James toward Richmond following a Union invasion of the peninsula between the York and James Rivers, the *Virginia* was abandoned. At midnight on 10 May, the ironclad was fired. After burning furiously for four hours, she exploded and disappeared beneath the Elizabeth River.

The *Monitor* was freed of duty by the arrival of other Union ironclads in October. On 29 December 1862, after having assisted in engagements elsewhere, she was being towed toward Beaufort, North Carolina, by the steamer USS *Rhode Island* when favorable weather south of Cape Hatteras deteriorated to squalls and heavy seas. The *Monitor* rapidly took on water around the turret, through the anchor well, and down engine-room air intakes. She was largely abandoned when, at approximately 1:30 am on 31 December, she disappeared. Sixteen men were lost, washed away by the storm or carried down inside the ironclad.

Search for the *Monitor*

While most of the remains of the *Virginia* were salvaged after the war, the *Monitor*'s site remained unknown for 111 years. Location and identification of the 'Cheesebox-on-a-Raft' depended on sophisticated electronic technology that did not exist until after World War II.

In August 1973, with support from the National Science Foundation and the National Geographic Society, oceanographer John G. Newton of Duke University, physicist and electrical engineer Harold E. Edgerton of the Massachusetts Institute of Technology, geologist Robert Sheridan of the University of Delaware, and I formed a multidisciplinary team on Duke University's research vessel *Eastward* to search for the *Monitor* in an area identified by historical research.

On 18 August, during examination of the second of twenty-two magnetic and acoustic targets, our closed-circuit television camera revealed a semi-circular object partially obscured by a massive beam. Using a scale attached to the camera frame, we confirmed that the objects corresponded in size to the *Monitor*'s turret and armor belt. Although the remains could not be conclusively identified aboard ship, photographs and videotapes provided a wealth of data for analysis throughout the fall and winter. By January 1974, additional historical research had matched sufficient features of the wreck with design and construction details of the *Monitor* to satisfy us that our survey had been a success.

Our evidence did not convince a cadre of skeptics until May 1974, when we returned to the site aboard the research vessel *Alcoa Seaprobe*. Using the *Seaprobe*'s sophisticated computer-controlled positioning system, we photographed the entire ironclad, leaving little doubt of its identification.

Protection of the site was now urgently needed. On 30 January 1975, with the approval of President Nixon, the *Monitor* was designated as the first National Marine Sanctuary by the National Oceanic and Atmospheric

5 (*left*) One of a half-dozen stereoscopic photographs of the *Monitor* taken after the 'victory' over the *Virginia*. This view on the starboard quarter shows the turret and armored pilot house near the bow.

6 (*right*) This *Harper's Weekly* illustration captures the scene on the night of 31 December 1862. In the words of the *Monitor*'s paymaster, he and the crew 'gathered on top of the turret, stood with a mass of sinking iron beneath us, gazing through the dim light, over the raging waters with an anxiety amounting almost to agony for some evidence of succor from the only source to which we could look for relief.' In the background the towship *Rhode Island* stands by as small boats attempt a dangerous but successful rescue of all but sixteen of the crew. Designed for operations in the shallow southern rivers and sounds, the *Monitor* proved no match for the Atlantic.

Administration (NOAA), thereby providing both protection and an administrative vehicle for regulated, systematic research.

Two years later NOAA, the North Carolina Division of Archives and History, and Harbor Branch Foundation joined forces to continue investigation of the *Monitor*. Although the site had been documented by remotely controlled videotape and oceanographic cameras, the research vessels and manned submersibles of the Florida-based Harbor Branch Foundation now permitted first-hand, on-site operations.

Diving on the 'Monitor'. The first dive created tremendous excitement. Marshall Flake and I, in the forward sphere of the *Johnson-Sea-Link* I, reached the sandy bottom at a depth of 230 ft (70 m) and saw on the submersible's sonar that the wreck lay less than 200 ft (61 m) away. Some 40 ft (12 m) from the wreck we found the first evidence of Ericsson's ship: a brass marine navigation lantern partially exposed on the sand. On a subsequent dive, when Richard Roesche was locked out of the submersible to recover the lantern, we found that it contained a red Fresnel lens, suggesting an ironic possibility: the first evidence of the *Monitor* on the seabed appeared to be the last evidence of the sinking ship observed by rescuers from the USS *Rhode Island* in 1862 – a red distress signal displayed above the turret.

Observations and photographs made on more than fifty dives to the site, as well as a sample of the ironclad's hull plate, provided new information for use in developing a program for the *Monitor*. After two years of analysis and planning, the same three organizations combined in a second, more complex investigation in which archae-ologists conducted mixed-gas excavations of the site.

Excavation inside the *Monitor* called for us to operate alone for a maximum of two one-hour periods each day while totally dependent on the submersible's power. Following comprehensive physical examinations and rigorous training, John Broadwater, Richard Lawrence and I joined the Research Vessel *Johnson* off Cape Hatteras and for the next thirty days we dived once a day for two days in the submersible and worked aboard the *Johnson* every third day. The schedule permitted decompressions of four-and-a-half hours for each hour of work on the site.

Our excavation was monitored by closed-circuit television, and our notes and observations were mostly recorded acoustically. An aluminum frame supporting a 35mm camera system permitted stereoscopic photo-mapping of excavated areas, and elevations within the excavation were controlled by a specially designed level. We removed overburden with a hydraulic dredge powered by a centrifugal pump operated by one of the submersible's thruster motors.

As the small dredge removed successive levels of sediment, the disposition of artifacts within the excavation confirmed that the ironclad had rolled over and gone down by the stern. The archaeological record also confirmed that the hull had survived intact for a considerable period prior to catastrophic collapse, lending some support to the theory that the shipwreck, mistaken for an enemy submarine, had been depth-charged during World War II.

With television and 35mm cameras, we recorded the condition of the interior of the historic ship. Forward of an amidships bulkhead the lower hull had collapsed and exposed the quarters of the officers and crew. Here structural damage was extensive, but a variety of artifacts were found intact. Amid shoes, crockery and weapons that surrounded one of two ruptures in the *Monitor*'s deck, I recovered a jar of relish, preserved by a patented rubber seal. In a storeroom inboard of the port armor belt and immediately forward of the amidships bulkhead we recovered a number of glass vessels containing pepper and mustard.

Aft of the amidships bulkhead the engineering space had been protected by the remains of the lower hull. Details of the galley and engine room proved readily identifiable. In the galley, *Monitor*'s cast-iron stove had collapsed after falling to the deck as the ship rolled over on sinking. Close by, near the port armor belt, lay the remains of a large centrifugal pump, perhaps the high-capacity Adams pump installed to keep the bilges clear of water. The Martin boilers, although separated from their beds, rested on deckbeams near their original locations. About 10 ft (3 m) aft of the boilers we found the complex and imposing engine designed by Ericsson. Starboard and port of the unique engine were the blowers that provided forced draft ventilation for the boilers. Close examination

Ironclad on the Ocean Floor

7–9   The *Monitor* lies bottom up (*right*), her displaced turret now supporting the nearly intact after section containing galley, coal bunkers and steam machinery. Towards the bow at top right the lower hull has collapsed, exposing crew quarters and storage areas. The turret detail (*below right*) shows an archaeologist working from the submersible. The photomosaic (*bottom*) is made up of some 2,000 exposures put together by the U.S. Navy.

of the port blower confirmed historical records which indicated that heavy leather belts used to drive the blowers had become soaked and slipped off their pulleys. With the exception of a sample of coal recovered from a port bunker we disturbed nothing in the engineering space.

Because the hull of the ship had come to rest on the turret, our examination of potential avenues of access to the interior of the turret required work under the hull. Some of the large armor plates covering the vessel's wooden deck were loose, so this work was kept to a minimum. Once the gunports had been examined, found

closed, and photographed, we attempted to locate access hatches in the bottom of the structure. Probing the wooden base of the turret with a high-pressure gas probe confirmed that the wood was intact but that its cellular structure had deteriorated. No access was identified; examination of the turret's interior would have to wait for a future investigation.

Unlike wrecks buried in bottom sediments, the *Monitor* is deteriorating in a high-energy environment. Unless the stress created by the position of the turret is relieved, intact portions of the ship will doubtless collapse. In 1983

Finds from the 'Monitor'

10 (*right*) Conservator Curtiss Peterson prepares the *Monitor*'s unusual four-fluked anchor and a section of stud-link chain for electrolytic conservation. Carried out in a makeshift conservation laboratory at East Carolina University, the process took more than two years to complete. All artifacts recovered from the *Monitor* have been consigned to the Mariners' Museum in Newport News, Virginia, for display and permanent curation.

11 (*below*) Glass vessels from the *Monitor* included a champagne bottle and several small octagonal containers for mustard and pepper embossed to identify their contents on one side and 'U.S. Navy' on another. An embossed storage jar found amid shoes, crockery and weapons around one of two ruptures in the *Monitor*'s deck contained relish preserved by a well-designed and patented rubber seal.

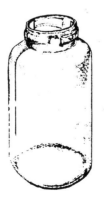

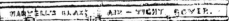

NOAA, East Carolina University and Harbor Branch Foundation conducted a short investigation to collect additional archaeological and engineering data to identify options for stabilizing or recovering all or portions of the structure. During these operations, the *Monitor*'s large iron anchor was located and recovered, providing insight into the problems associated with preserving additional material from the wreck.

Today NOAA works in conjunction with the National Trust for Historic Preservation to develop plans for preserving the *Monitor*. At all costs, NOAA must be committed to a management policy that will not result in the sort of inadvertent destruction characteristic of other Civil War ironclad recovery projects.

Ironclads Triumphant

The initial success of the *Virginia* had demonstrated to the South that the disparity in available vessels could be minimized by investing in heavily armed armored steam warships. The performance of the Confederate ironclad *Arkansas*, one of five ironclads laid down prior to the Hampton Roads engagement, increased support for casemated vessels. Constructed in spite of myriad technological and industrial deficiencies that plagued southern warship construction, the *Arkansas* was ready for action only four months after the *Virginia* fought the *Monitor*. She descended the Yazoo River for Vicksburg, Mississippi, and, near the mouth of the Yazoo, successfully engaged three Union vessels from Admiral David Farragut's Mississippi River squadron. Although the *Arkansas* was destroyed by her crew when her engines seized during a subsequent attack on Baton Rouge, the ironclad had demonstrated its destructive potential and survived each punishing engagement.

The success of Confederate ironclad warships generated support for the construction of approximately fifty similar vessels, almost half completed and placed in service before the end of the war. Although generally fitted with less than effective steam machinery, the vessels were well armed and reasonably armored. For river and harbor defense, they served the South effectively.

In the North, the *Monitor*'s timely 'victory' over the *Virginia* and the threat of additional Confederate ironclads garnered considerable support for the construction of armored vessels. Now riding the crest of a wave of tremendous popularity, engineer Ericsson designed and built new and more powerful classes of 'Monitors'; before the end of the war twenty-seven had been launched by various contractors. While the losses of the *Weehawken*, *Keokuk* and *Patapsco* off Charleston, South Carolina, and the *Tecumseh* in Mobile Bay led to further criticisms of the design, most of the vessels served well throughout the war.

There were still other classes of ironclads on both sides of the conflict. In fact, Union ironclads were already under construction at Carondelet and Mound City, Missouri, where John Ericsson signed a contract to build the

Monitor. The Missouri ironclads had been proposed by retired civil engineer James B. Eads in the weeks that followed General Beauregard's attack on Fort Sumter. Eads contracted to construct seven flat-bottomed vessels, each with three keels and each powered by an internal paddle wheel. The vessels would be fitted with iron casemates similar to that on the CSS *Virginia*.

The 'Cairo'. The first of Eads' vessels was commissioned before the end of December 1861, and the rest followed on 15 January 1862. One of the latter, *Cairo*, would have remained little known had she not been assigned the task of clearing torpedoes from the Yazoo River. In December 1862, near Drumgould's Bluff, the *Cairo* was rocked by two explosions and, according to the First Class Boy, 'the water rushed in like the roar of Niagara'. Despite efforts to beach the vessel, the *Cairo* slipped into deep water and disappeared within twelve minutes. No lives were lost, but her commanding officer received considerable criticism, one Union officer writing: 'On December 12 Lieutenant-Commander Selfridge of the *Cairo* found two torpedoes and removed them by placing his vessel over them.' For the first time in history a powerful ironclad warship had been destroyed by an electrically detonated torpedo, in this case made from a five-gallon glass demijohn.

A modern search for the *Cairo* by National Park Service historian Edwin C. Bearss, Don Jacks of the Park Service, and geologist Warren Grabau located the ironclad on 12 November 1956. Armed with information from historical records, they used a simple magnetic compass to detect the mass of iron they knew would be associated with the ironclad. Reconnaissance dives confirmed the vessel to be virtually intact, and in 1959 divers raised artifacts including a soap dish, wash-bowl, mirror, can of shoe polish and bottles of medicine from the pilot house. An anvil, vice, hammers and other tools in the vessel's blacksmith shop were found in good condition.

The *Cairo* was salvaged in stages. Operation *Cairo*, Inc., a non-profit organization, recovered the vessel's distinctive pilot house in 1960. Divers also removed tons of sediment as well as potentially dangerous explosive ordnance from the hull in preparation for full recovery. An attempt to lift the vessel in 1963 failed, but Operation *Cairo* secured funding for a second attempt the following year. Faced with pressing deadlines, this attempt began without additional assessment of the ship's condition or the removal of tons of sediment still inside. Results were disastrous. Lifting cables sliced deeply into the hull. As portions of the ironclad appeared above the water, the increased weight caused one of the cables to cut the *Cairo* in half. Attempts to recover the bow section caused additional damage as portions of the starboard casemate collapsed. The condition of the wreck forced salvors to cut the hull again. After the bow section was floated onto a submerged barge, the midship section of the hull was raised. As it was lowered onto a second barge, the

Union Gunboat

12 (*right*) The USS *Cairo* was one of seven vessels built for operations on western rivers. Flat bottomed with three keels and powered by an internal paddle wheel, she sank in Mississippi's Yazoo River on 12 December 1862 after Confederate mines exploded against the hull.

13, 14 (*below*) In their haste to abandon ship the *Cairo*'s crew left behind many treasured possessions, such as this daguerreotype of an unidentified woman and child, as well as items like this mess plate and cup, spoon, comb, knife, razor and pocket watch.

15, 16 (*center right* and *below right*) Although the *Cairo* was largely destroyed during efforts to raise and preserve her, the National Park Service has developed an impressive exhibit at the Vicksburg National Military Park, conveying an accurate sense of the original vessel.

structure collapsed and a section of the starboard casemate fell back into the Yazoo with many associated artifacts. The stern section was lifted onto a barge, but slid back into the water when the barge listed; several days later it was raised to the river bank, but damage was extensive. When the barges at last reached Vicksburg, the 'once-proud ship', according to the Natchez *Democrat* of 24 December 1964, 'lay in ruins atop two barges'.

Although artifacts including arms, mess gear, clothing, photographs and personal items such as razors and combs received some care, no plans had been made for conservation of the vessel's structure. The remains were transported to a Pascagoula shipyard for restoration, but funds ran out and the *Cairo* was abandoned for thirteen years. When the National Park Service finally acquired title to *Cairo*'s remains in 1973, more than half of the recovered wood had disintegrated beyond recognition.

In spite of the condition of the ironclad, the National Park Service elected in 1977 to truck its pieces to Vicksburg National Military Park, where surviving sections are reassembled and exhibited, with missing portions stylistically reconstructed, next to a museum which displays artifacts from the vessel.

Blockade Runners

When President Lincoln proclaimed a blockade of the Confederacy on 19 April 1861, the United States Navy consisted of only 90 vessels. Less than half were in commission and only 8 were in U.S. waters. Secretary of the Navy Gideon Welles responded to this critical shortage by authorizing the purchase of 136 ships, the construction of 52, and the repair and recommission of another 76 in only nine months. Within a year more than 14,000 enlisted men and 1,000 officers had been added to Navy enrollments.

For the blockade, the southern coastline was divided into four theaters – the North Atlantic, South Atlantic, East Gulf and West Gulf – with separate squadrons for each. Plans called for the capture of several small, defensible harbors as convenient bases of operation. By midsummer 1862 the blockade that most southerners had dismissed began to take effect. Of more than 250 sailing vessels documented to have run the blockade of Carolina ports in 1861, only 145 were still operating the following year. In 1863 that number had diminished to 55, and in 1864 only 14 sailing vessels were engaged in blockade running. In addition to eliminating sailing vessels, the increase in Union warships began to make even the operation of steam-powered blockade runners increasingly risky.

The steamer 'Modern Greece'. Pearson and Company of Hull, one of the first English firms to engage in blockade running, dispatched seven vessels to Confederate ports between May and August 1862. Six were captured, and the 753-ton steamer *Modern Greece* forced aground immediately north of Fort Fisher, North Carolina. To prevent explosive projectiles fired from pursuing Union ships from setting the steamer afire and igniting a cargo of powder, the garrison at Fort Fisher fired solid shot through the abandoned ship to flood her hull. The Confederate strategy worked well and salvage vessels recovered at least four valuable Whitworth breech-loading rifled cannon, hundreds of Enfield rifled muskets, powder, shot, lead, side knives, surgeons kits and a revealing assortment of non-military material listed for

auction in the 1 July *Wilmington Journal*: dry goods, hardware, boots and shoes, blankets, ready-made clothing, felt hats, pepper, pimento, bicarbonate of soda, soda ash, mustard, drugs and medicine, gunny bags, salt, cognac, champagne, red and white wine, scotch whiskey, claret, sparkling burgundy and 'various other articles'. Despite Union efforts to disrupt salvage, Confederate engineers and divers also succeeded in recovering the steam machinery from the *Modern Greece*.

The location of the *Modern Greece* remained known, but the wreck was protected by sand and sediment until Good Friday 1962, when a storm exposed the site. Navy divers shortly thereafter discovered much of the hull and cargo intact and were authorized to remain in the state to assist in a systematic salvage of the vessel.

The divers recovered an impressive collection of weapons, tools, supplies and other materials. Enfield rifled muskets, bayonets and bullet molds were still packed in shipping cases. Enfield rifle bullets, crated projectiles for Whitworth rifled artillery, and pigs of lead for casting additional bullets were packed among coils of wire, pigs of tin and sheets of tinned steel for use in the construction of canteens, cartridge boxes and the like. A variety of casks contained pocket and side knives, military and household utensils, hardware and tools. In addition to hoes and picks the cargo of the *Modern Greece* contained boxes and kegs of drills, bits, saws, files, taps and dies, hammers, gouges, chisels and axes. A number of surgeon's medical kits contained tongue depressors, knives, bone saws, scalpels, tourniquet presses and a scarifier for relieving high blood pressure.

Although this material was removed without regard for archaeological context, the salvors recovered a valuable study collection of material brought through the blockade. More than 11,000 artifacts were raised in 1962 and 1963.

Custom-built blockade runners. Unlike the *Modern Greece*, many other wrecks in the vicinity of Cape Fear are of vessels specifically designed to run the blockade. As the strength of Union fleets increased, British and Confederate firms engaged in shipping material through the blockade could no longer rely on large, deep-draft steamers to evade the United States Navy. Although large transoceanic steamers continued to carry supplies out of Europe, most delivered their cargoes to ports in Bermuda, Nassau or Havana for transfer to smaller, faster, shallow-draft steamers.

In search of suitable blockade runners, British and Confederate firms purchased fast steamers designed for river and channel mail and passenger service, but as these ships were captured or destroyed, British shipyards began to produce vessels especially designed for the purpose.

Perhaps the first of these was the 214-ft (65-m) side-wheel steamer *Banshee*, built on the Mersey. Although the light gauge of her steel plates made her dangerously fragile, the *Banshee* became the first steel vessel to cross the Atlantic. Following two weeks of repairs in Nassau, she made sixteen successful trips through the blockade.

Side-wheel steamers proved successful, but many blockade-running captains preferred twin-screw propelled ships. The first of these was the 161-ft (49-m) *Flora*, built of iron in London. Both her short masts and telescoping smoke funnel could be lowered to reduce the ship's profile. She registered 14.12 knots during speed trials, and easily outdistanced the cruiser USS *Tuscarora*

17, 18 *Blockade Runner Ashore (far left)*, painted in 1863, depicts a stranded steamer being unloaded through the surf. Her size and configuration suggest this is the British steamer *Modern Greece*, forced aground near Fort Fisher, North Carolina. The fort garrison salvaged part of a valuable cargo. Sheffield side knives from the *Modern Greece (left)* reflect styles popular in America over a decade before the Civil War and lend weight to theories that English merchants shipped unsaleable goods to a captive market in the South.

19 *(right)* Possibly the first British vessel specially designed for blockade running, the *Banshee* became the earliest steel vessel to cross the Atlantic and completed sixteen successful trips through the blockade. This painting captures the sleek design of the *Banshee* or a later and slightly larger *Banshee II* launched in Liverpool in 1864.

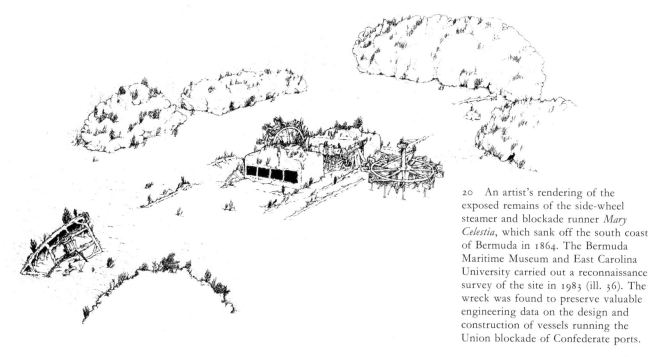

20 An artist's rendering of the exposed remains of the side-wheel steamer and blockade runner *Mary Celestia*, which sank off the south coast of Bermuda in 1864. The Bermuda Maritime Museum and East Carolina University carried out a reconnaissance survey of the site in 1983 (ill. 36). The wreck was found to preserve valuable engineering data on the design and construction of vessels running the Union blockade of Confederate ports.

while operating on only one screw. In eleven trips through the blockade it was said that she 'laughed at her adversaries'. Eventually she was sold to the Confederate Government and operated on the Cape Fear River until being scuttled following the fall of Fort Fisher.

In spite of the risks, blockade running provided strong financial incentives for both British and Confederate firms. In December 1864, the United States Consul at Liverpool reported that virtually every class of English society was speculating in the trade:

> Members of Parliament, mayors, magistrates, aldermen, merchants, and gentlemen are all violating the law of nations. Nine-tenths of all vessels now engaged in the business were built and fitted out in England by Englishmen with English capital, and are now owned by Englishmen.

Firms like the Anglo-Confederate Trading Company were formed solely for the purpose of blockade running.

Profits were also great for large transoceanic vessels which delivered cargoes to neutral British ports in Bermuda, the Bahamas, Nova Scotia and the Spanish port of Havana, Cuba. As Savannah and Charleston became more difficult to enter, Havana became more important for vessels operating in the Gulf of Mexico, and Bermuda more important for vessels operating through Wilmington, North Carolina. By 1864, Wilmington, almost impossible to blockade effectively because of geography and a complex system of coastal fortifications, had become the major Confederate port facility. This made Bermuda the preferred neutral port, in spite of dangerous coral reefs and the treacherous channels that provided access to harbors at St Georges and Hamilton. Reconnaissance

conducted in 1983 and 1986 by East Carolina University and the Bermuda Maritime Museum confirmed that two victims of these hazards – the side-wheel steamers *Nola*, sunk in 1863, and *Mary Celestia*, sunk in 1864 – offer excellent opportunities to study the design and construction of blockade runners.

Within the Confederacy, the opportunity to realize high returns on capital investments stimulated the formation of organizations like those in Britain and Bermuda. The *Kate*, owned by John Fraser and Company, operated so consistently that the term 'packet' was used to describe her activities. Before hitting a snag and sinking in the Cape Fear River, she brought invaluable commercial and military cargoes into the Confederacy and generated staggering revenues from cotton carried on each outward voyage. Her captain reportedly received $2,000 in gold for each successful trip. The high wages paid to the crew of the *Venus* confirm that the trade was not without recognized risk:

Rank	Wage
Captain	$5,000
First Officer	1,200
Second Officer	750
Third Officer	750
Chief Engineer	2,500
Crew	250
Pilot	3,500

On 21 October 1863, risk turned into disaster. The *Venus* was run aground and set on fire north of Fort Fisher. Today her remains lie just south of Carolina Beach inlet in the vicinity of the wreck of the *Hebe*, a sistership of the twin-screw *Flora*.

In an effort to circumvent skyrocketing commercial freight rates, the Confederate Ordnance Department began to purchase and operate its own blockade runners in 1862. Some of the Confederate states also resorted to operating their own vessels or purchasing percentage interests in ships owned by commercial firms. It was not enough. In August 1863, Confederate commanders in Wilmington, North Carolina; Charleston, South Carolina; and Mobile, Alabama, were told that all private blockade runners had to turn over half their outward cargo space to the Confederacy in return for a 'liberal freight rate'.

For the North's part, in an effort to increase the effectiveness of the blockade, Union crews were offered shares of revenues generated by the sale of prize vessels.

Blockade running increased dramatically when there was little moonlight or poor weather. One Union officer, after sleeping all night for the first time in two weeks, noted that 'as the moon was bright I done so with a clear conscience', and another, on the Wilmington Station, wrote on 9 May 1863 to the *Scientific American*: 'I am sorry to say that two more steamers ran in last night and had the impudence to blow their whistles – I suppose to give us warning to keep out of the way or else be run down.'

In spite of such frustrations, the blockade produced measurable results. Nearly 1,400 vessels – 300 of them steamers – were captured by Union warships. Modern surveys of the shallow inshore waters in the vicinity of Wilmington, Charleston, Mobile and Galveston have identified the remains of vessels that were run ashore. In the vicinity of Cape Fear, near channel entrances to the Port of Wilmington, at least thirty blockade-running steamers were lost. Although the blockade failed to deny foreign commerce to the South, the Confederacy acutely felt the steady decline in trade.

The Commerce Raiders

Taken aback by her appearance, few of the British garrison could believe that the strangely proportioned Confederate steamer anchored in the Bay of Gibraltar on 18 January 1862 was the commerce raider CSS *Sumter*. But the converted mail steamer had captured or destroyed eighteen American merchant ships during a cruise that carried her from New Orleans, through the Caribbean, along the coast of Brazil, and then across the Atlantic to Gibraltar.

The *Sumter*'s cruise proved that Confederate commerce raiders could successfully attack the United States merchant marine, not only disrupting commerce but also occupying the attentions of warships that would otherwise be engaged in more destructive activities. Captured cargoes and the sale of captured merchant vessels were additional benefits.

Early in the war Confederate President Davis issued letters of marque to privateers, a practice already discredited in Europe. Although President Lincoln proclaimed that captured crews of privateers would be treated as pirates – in a proclamation that was virtually ignored – the Union's blockade of the South, closing ports where captured vessels could be sold, did more to curtail private raiding. The operation of Confederate cruisers, however, continued to justify their destructive activities.

The 'Florida'. Two months after the *Sumter* reached Gibraltar, a second cruiser, the 185-ft (56-m) wooden gunboat *Oreto*, cleared Liverpool, where she had been built under false pretenses to prevent her confiscation. Armed, supplied and renamed the *Florida* in Nassau, the

21–23 The highly successful Confederate commerce raider *Florida* (model *below*) sank mysteriously in the Hampton Roads in 1864, probably at Union hands. In the 1980s archaeologists recovered from the wreck such items as a pewter pitcher (*far right*) and (*right*) champagne and brandy bottles, and a ceramic jar with a name and address from the French port of Brest, where the *Florida* made repairs.

warship was coaled in Barbados before beginning a five-month cruise that resulted in the capture and destruction of fourteen prizes. The brig *Clarence*, armed and manned with a crew from the *Florida* after being taken off the coast of Brazil, took five additional prizes. The schooner *Tacony*, last of the five, was armed with ordnance from the *Clarence* and was able to capture an additional ten vessels. After making repairs at the French port of Brest, the *Florida* recrossed the Atlantic, destroying an additional twenty-two ships before being controversially captured by the sloop-of-war USS *Wachusett* in Brazilian territorial waters and brought to Hampton Roads, where she sank mysteriously after an 'unforeseen accident' with a U.S. army vessel. The *Florida*, seized in violation of Brazilian neutrality, was now effectively beyond Confederate recourse through international law.

After an unsuccessful magnetometer survey for the *Florida* in 1980, archaeologists working for popular author Clive Cussler used information from both historical research and local watermen to narrow their search to a small area off the Horne Brothers Shipyard pier, where anomalies were detected with a depth recorder. Working in low visibility and strong currents, divers found a large, nearly intact section of exposed deck leading to an iron cylinder more than 4 ft (1.2 m) in diameter, possibly a support for the ship's mizzenmast. Near two large iron cylinders thought to be boilers, they established that the copper-sheathed hull's beam was in excess of 23 ft (7 m), and measured the vessel's 6½ by 7 in (17 by 18 cm) frames. Artifacts, including a wooden shot box containing over 400 .557-caliber bullets for British Enfield rifled muskets, a pistol handle and a small cannon fuse, were in keeping with a Confederate commerce raider. Perhaps the most exciting recovery was a small white ceramic pharmaceutical jar bearing the seal of the Paris School of Pharmacy and the name and address of a Brest druggist. The rich collection of brass, leather, glass and other materials in an excellent state of preservation suggests the potential for additional research.

The 'Alabama' and 'Nashville'. Little more than four months after the *Florida* put to sea from Liverpool, a second Confederate cruiser sailed from the same city, despite diplomatic protests from the United States Consul and efforts to have the vessel seized for violations of the Foreign Enlistment Act. In the Azores the recently christened *Enrica* received her crew, officers, ordnance, ammunition, supplies and coal, and was renamed the *Alabama* before departing for the North Atlantic.

Within two months the *Alabama* had captured and burned twenty prizes. Later she sank the Union steamer *Hatteras* off Galveston, Texas, and then, after depositing the crew of the *Hatteras* at Port Royal, Jamaica, headed south and destroyed several additional vessels before sinking ten more off the coast of Brazil. Next she rounded the Cape of Good Hope for a six-month cruise to the East Indies, on which she destroyed seven vessels before

returning to the Cape and a return passage to Europe. Before finally being sunk by the USS *Kearsarge* off the coast of France near Cherbourg, the *Alabama* had captured or destroyed a total of seventy-six vessels, a record never equaled.

Unlike British-built commerce raiders, the CSS *Nashville* had been built in New York prior to the Civil War. Confiscated in Charleston following the attack on Fort Sumter, the ship was operated as a Confederate cruiser and then as the blockade runner *Thomas L. Wragg*. After being chased into the Ogeechee River near Savannah, Georgia, the ship was armed, rechristened *Rattlesnake* and issued a letter of marque by Confederate Secretary of State J. P. Benjamin. Attempting to escape to sea, the *Rattlesnake* ran aground and was destroyed by the Union ironclad *Montauk*. Returning down river, the *Montauk* struck a Confederate mine. As her crew made repairs to keep afloat, one member observed fragments from the burning *Rattlesnake* floating downstream and wrote:

> As these silent witnesses of the havoc drifted past us, they seemed to show a determination that, if we could not allow the NASHVILLE to run the blockade as a whole, she was going to run the blockade in pieces.

Efforts were made to salvage the *Nashville* shortly after the Civil War, but no progress was made until 1959, just prior to the Civil War Centennial Celebration, when divers joined the Georgia Historical Society in recovering much of the *Nashville*'s machinery for display in a proposed museum at Fort McAllister. Few records survive to document this project.

A decade later a second group of divers, although unable to secure a permit from the State of Georgia, began excavation of the *Nashville*. Five field seasons were devoted to excavation, artifact recovery and historical research before the state ordered the operations to cease. Although the investigation ended in litigation, the publication of material salvaged from the *Nashville* has provided the opportunity to examine material from one of the more successful Confederate commerce raider/blockade runners.

The remains of the *Florida*, *Nashville* and the recently located *Alabama* are monuments to perhaps the most successful Confederate navy campaign. Commerce raiders destroyed a total of $46 million in United States merchant vessels. The effect on the New England whaling industry was little short of disastrous. While their activities may not have turned the tide of war, Confederate commerce raiders carried the war to New England as certainly as General William T. Sherman made it felt in Georgia.

The Gunboats

Although Confederate Secretary of the Navy Stephen R. Mallory favored the construction of ironclad warships, he recognized the lack of facilities for the construction of

24 Officers and crew of the USS *Hunchback* photographed on the James River in 1864–65. A New York ferry converted to serve as a gunboat, the *Hunchback* provides an excellent example of the numerous ersatz warships used by both the Union and the Confederacy. While these vessels were structurally vulnerable and offered limited protection for their crews, they served as highly effective platforms for transporting ordnance on protected rivers and sounds.

armored vessels. He also acknowledged the need for coastal defense vessels and intense political pressure to build wooden gunboats for river and harbor defense. Steam gunboats about 100 or 120 ft (30 or 37 m) long, carrying two guns apiece, could be constructed quickly, cheaply and locally. In December 1861 the Confederate Congress authorized construction of up to 100 gunboats and appropriated $2 million to support construction.

The 'Chattahoochee'. The Confederate States Navy Yard at Saffold, Georgia, was typical of some of the temporary yards established for the purpose of constructing gunboats. Located on the plantation of David S. Johnson, the Saffold site was selected in part because of an abundance of available oak and pine. On 19 October 1861 Johnson was awarded a $47,500 contract to build a 130-ft (40-m) gunboat equipped with two engines, boilers and propellers. Construction was beset by problems of logistics, design, labor and poor management. By the time the *Chattahoochee* was launched in 1863, nearly a year late, the contract with Johnson had been revoked. Modifications still underway forced the gunboat to be towed downriver on her maiden voyage to Chattahoochee, Florida. Within two hours the *Chattahoochee* had grounded, smashing the rudder and springing the sternpost. On arrival at her destination the vessel was, according to Lieutenant George Gift, '. . . in a splendid

condition for service, a strong leak and no engines. I wish the confounded vessel in Jerico'.

On 26 May 1863, about to return to Chattahoochee after an unsuccessful attempt to rescue a captured schooner, the *Chattahoochee*'s boilers exploded, killing seventeen men and sinking the gunboat. The Confederate Navy raised the hull in August and towed it back to the Saffold shipyard of David S. Johnson who, in spite of past performance, received a contract to repair the vessel. Ready for service again on 20 April 1864, the *Chattahoochee* suffered continued breakdowns and groundings until she was set afire by her own crew and sunk 15 miles south of Columbus, Georgia.

In the 1960s the United States Army Corps of Engineers identified the *Chattahoochee* as an obstruction to navigation on the Chattahoochee River. The Confederate Gunboat Association worked with the Corps to salvage the vessel, but during lifting operations the gunboat's keel snapped and much of the wreck settled back to the bottom. Only the stern section of the hull was actually recovered. This and the remains of the Confederate Ram *Muscogee* became the focal points of the James W. Woodruff Confederate Naval Museum in Columbus.

In summer 1983, the Confederate Naval Museum joined East Carolina University to relocate the *Chattahoochee*'s remains for a new study. Approximately 90 ft (27 m) of the lower hull survive, some badly charred.

Confederates on Display

Today the remains of the Confederate gunboat *Chattahoochee* and ram *Muscogee* (also known as the *Jackson*) are focal points of the James W. Woodruff Confederate Naval Museum in Columbus, Georgia.

25, 26 When the U.S. Army Corps of Engineers began a study of navigation on the Chattahoochee River in the 1960s, they identified the remains of the *Chattahoochee*. The Confederate Gunboat Association was formed to work with the Corps of Engineers to salvage the vessel. Unfortunately during the salvage the *Chattahoochee*'s keel snapped and only the stern was recovered (*below*; on display, *left*).

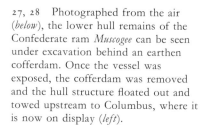

27, 28 Photographed from the air (*below*), the lower hull remains of the Confederate ram *Muscogee* can be seen under excavation behind an earthen cofferdam. Once the vessel was exposed, the cofferdam was removed and the hull structure floated out and towed upstream to Columbus, where it is now on display (*left*).

From the remains of the stem to a break in the keelson where the stern separated during salvage attempts, the hull is well preserved below the turn of the bilge. Even part of the starboard side survives intact to almost the level of the main or weather deck. Lines of the hull, design and construction details, and plans of the steam machinery were recorded to provide a more complete picture of the gunboat, a picture enhanced by artifacts recovered from the wreck.

The 'Iron Age' and 'John F. Winslow'. The remains of two Union gunboats in North Carolina provide opportunities to compare the problems encountered by the Confederacy with those of the United States. Unlike the Confederacy, the North was able to contract with established shipbuilders to produce and launch vessels in approximately ninety days; twenty-three 507-ton screw gunboats were under construction from Delaware to Maine. Even so, the Union's demand for gunboats quickly exceeded the supply, forcing her procurement officers to turn to ferries, tugs, coastal transports and river boats.

Nathaniel L. Thompson of Kennebunk, one of five Maine shipbuilders contracted to build 'ninety-day' gunboats, laid the keel for a 144-ft (44-m) iron-ore carrier with a beam of 25 ft (7.6 m) and a draft of 12 ft 6 in (3.8 m). The heavily framed 424-ton wood hull was suitable for gunboat service and on 28 April 1862 Thompson delivered the sail-rigged vessel to Boston, where she was fitted with steam machinery and, as the USS *Iron Age*,

transferred to the North Atlantic Blockading Squadron on 11 September 1862.

The *Iron Age* was stationed off the mouth of the Cape Fear River as part of the Union squadron blockading Wilmington, North Carolina. In assisting the USS *Montgomery* in trying to refloat the paddle-wheel blockade runner *Bendigo*, which had been fired and abandoned at the entrance to Lockwood's Folly Inlet west of the Cape Fear River, a hawser parted and the USS *Iron Age* was grounded near the *Bendigo*. At least two cannon were thrown overboard to lighten the vessel, but she could not be freed and, to prevent capture, was blown up on 11 January 1864.

While the forward section of the vessel is today covered by inlet sediments, the gunboat's exposed after hull and machinery pose a threat to navigation. Laboring in strong currents, archaeologists working for the U.S. Army Corps of Engineers have studied the *Iron Age*'s boiler and steam machinery inside her intact lower hull. Aft of the boiler the remains of a single-cylinder vertical operating steam engine lie on a bed of coal and debris. Steam pipes, ventilators and pumps were found amid anthracite coal spilled from bunkers located aft of the engineering space. The four-bladed iron propeller remains in position aft of

29, 30 When a hawser parted during an unsuccessful attempt to salvage the blockade-runner *Bendigo*, the USS *Iron Age* ran aground on a shoal and was destroyed by her crew on 11 January 1864. Evidence of explosions that destroyed the warship survives in the disarticulated remains near the mouth of the Cape Fear River. The machinery and stern (*right*) have been examined by underwater archaeologists working in conjunction with U.S. Army Corps of Engineers. Among the finds was this navigation lantern (*far right*).

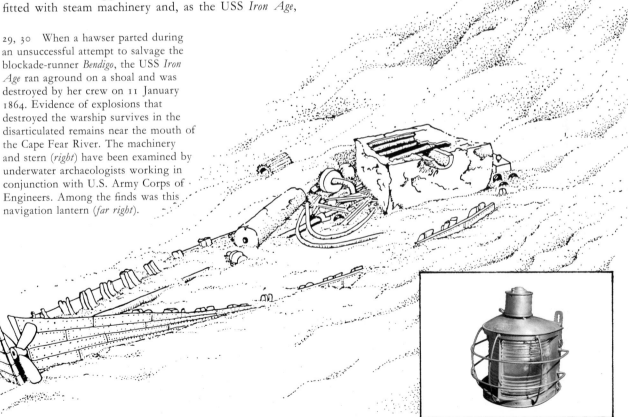

31 (*left*) An artist of the *Illustrated London News* recorded the gunboat USS *Picket* (at right) leading the vessels of Brigadier-General Ambrose E. Burnside's North Carolina expedition through Hatteras Inlet in 1862. Constructed around the iron hull of the *John F. Winslow*, a barge built in New York in 1845, the *Picket* inspired little confidence and was not considered one of the most attractive assignments under Burnside's command.

32 (*right*) Run aground on shoals in one of the many shallow inlets along the coast of North Carolina, the British-built paddle-steamer *Bendigo* is preserved and protected by sands that trapped the blockade runner. Like many Civil War vessels she is visible from the air and attracted the attention of pilots spotting schools of fish for commercial vessels.

the sternpost, partially concealed by the brass-sheathed wooden rudder. Along the turn of the bilge oak frames, oak exterior planking and bilge ceiling, possibly of pine, were measured. Planking was secured to the frames with both bronze spikes and treenails, and copper sheathing was attached to the hull with brass sheathing tacks. Finds included a brass navigation lantern, ironstone china and fragments of dark green bottle glass. Further work on the *Iron Age* is difficult to justify at this time since other, better-preserved Union gunboats are known which offer equally valuable archaeological data in a safer operational environment.

One of the more unusual products of the Union gunboat procurement program was the *John F. Winslow*, constructed as an iron barge in New York in 1845, but converted for military service during the war. In addition to the installation of steam machinery, boilers and a screw propeller, the *Winslow*'s iron hull was planked over with wood. A new wooden bow and stern, extending beyond the original hull, increased the vessel's length more than 30 ft (9 m) to 129 ft 7 in (40 m). Her interior was fitted with coal bunkers, quarters, storage and a magazine. A superstructure not unlike that designed for tugs was installed over the deck, and sponsons were added to the sides of the hull to increase both beam and stability.

On 20 December 1861 the *John F. Winslow* was commissioned USS *Picket* in Philadelphia. She was immediately dispatched to Hampton Roads, Virginia, to join a joint army/navy invasion of the North Carolina sounds. On 11 January 1862 approximately 100 vessels departed Hampton Roads. Perhaps to increase confidence in the curious assortment of ersatz gunboats making up the fleet, Brigadier-General A. E. Burnside selected the

'small propeller called the Picket . . . the smallest vessel in the fleet' for his flagship. Although rough weather off Cape Hatteras caused the loss of the *City of New York*, *Pocahontas* and *Zouave*, the *Picket* survived to support the amphibious landing that brought Roanoke Island under Union control.

On 6 September 1862, during an engagement at Washington, North Carolina, the *Picket* was lost. The *New York Times* of 15 September reported that the *Picket*, 'after firing one gun, blew up from the explosion of her magazine, killing nineteen of those on board', and suggested that the 'accident was occasioned by the carelessness of someone who entered the magazine, which happened to be left unlighted, with a burning candle'. To prevent Confederate salvage, the *Picket*'s ordnance and machinery were recovered and she was burned to the waterline.

The *Picket*'s remains received little attention until 1973, when local divers found much of her hull surviving on the river bed. With the assistance of the North Carolina Division of Archives and History, archaeologists mapped and sampled the site in 1976, to provide a frame of reference for additional examination. Local divers working through the Beaufort County Historical Society confirmed that the wooden hull of the *Picket* had been damaged by nineteenth-century salvage activity, but still survived in an excellent state of preservation. Excavation within the bow, stern and amidships section of the gunboat produced a more exciting discovery. Within the wooden hull of the USS *Picket*, the iron hull of the *John F. Winslow* remained intact. As such it represents one of the best-preserved early iron hulls produced in the United States.

Submarines

When Philadelphia Harbor Police discovered an iron 'submarine monster' in the Delaware River in May 1861, there appeared little question about the diabolical intent of the craft's operators. They were arrested and the submarine confiscated. Even though the mysterious vessel was towed back to the Noble Street wharf about 2 o'clock in the morning, an alert reporter from the Philadelphia *Evening Bulletin* had a chance to examine it. On 17 May he reported that the vessel:

> had the appearance of a section of boiler about twenty feet long, with tapered ends, and presenting the shape and appearance of an enormous cigar with a boiler iron wrapper. . . . The after end was furnished with a propeller, which had a contrivance for protecting it from coming in contact with external objects. The forward end was sharkish in appearance . . . as only the ridge of the back was above the water, while the tail and snout were submerged. Near the forward end was a hatchway or 'manhole', through which egress and ingress were obtained. This hole was covered with a heavy iron flap, which was made airtight, and which was secured in its place by numerous powerful screws and hooks. Two tiers of glass bulls' eyes along each side of the submarine monster completed its external features, afforded light to the inside. . . .

Permitted aboard by the harbor police, the reporter squeezed through the 'manhole' and found himself inside a vessel about 4 ft (1.2 m) in diameter with 'a crank for the purpose of operating the propeller . . . [and] steering rods, connected with the fins outside, which could be moved at pleasure, and which had something to do with steadying the sinking craft'.

The submarine's crew revealed that the vessel had been constructed by French engineer Brutus de Villeroi in Philadelphia two years earlier with the financial support of Stephen Girard. Although de Villeroi had successfully tested a submarine in France as early as 1832, the French government expressed no interest in the novelty, and he had come to Philadelphia in 1859 to promote his invention. After numerous successful trials of the Philadelphia submarine, operation of the craft was curtailed due to Girard's death. The outbreak of civil war provided the Frenchman the opportunity to garner new support for his invention.

De Villeroi's trouble with the Philadelphia police was temporary. After a rigorous inspection, a Navy Board on 7 June 1861 reported that both the engineer and his invention would be of the greatest value to the government. The Board found that the submarine could dive and resurface after remaining submerged for extended periods. It had excellent mobility. It could investigate the bottoms of rivers and harbors and assist in the location and salvage of shipwrecks. And the fact that divers could leave the vessel while it was submerged would provide ample opportunity to attach an 'engine of destruction' to a ship's hull while undetected from the surface.

The 'Alligator'. In spite of subsequent favorable recommendations, the Navy was slow to pursue this new development. The Chief of the Bureau of Yards and Docks recommended only that a second and larger vessel be built to destroy Confederate shipping at Norfolk, Virginia; in case of failure, de Villeroi and his supporters would receive no compensation for their efforts.

Accepting these terms on 1 November 1861, Martin Thomas of Philadelphia signed a contract with the Navy to build the vessel in forty days at a cost of $14,000. Thomas then contracted with de Villeroi to supervise construction in a Philadelphia shipyard, but the vessel was not completed within the specified time. The CSS *Virginia*'s attack on Union vessels in Hampton Roads made delays especially frustrating. On 26 March 1862, Louis Hennet, an engineer working on the submarine, wrote to the *Philadelphia Public Ledger* that had the submarine been in service, 'the MERRIMAC would have been destroyed, or at least rendered harmless'.

The submarine was finally launched on 30 April, with critical design changes. Instead of being powered by a hand-turned screw propeller, the vessel was provided with a series of sixteen oars. Each oar was designed to operate like the foot of a duck, closing like a book on forward motion and opening to catch the water when an operating crank inside forced the oar aft.

The *Alligator*, as de Villeroi's submarine was identified, was ordered to Hampton Roads to clear obstructions in the James River and perform other submarine work. Her first assignment was to destroy bridges in the vicinity of Richmond and on the Appomattox River near Peters-burg, but after only four days the navy ordered the *Alligator* back to Hampton Roads with a total lack of confidence in the vessel. Later experiments confirmed the vessel could not make sufficient speed or remain submerged due to lack of air. Discouraged, if not terrified, another skipper turned in a derogatory report and dismissed his crew. Finally, while under tow for Port Royal, South Carolina, the *Alligator* was cut adrift during a violent storm off Cape Hatteras.

Confederate submarines. Confederate engineers were meanwhile experimenting with similar designs but with dramatically different results. In New Orleans James R. McClintock and Baxter Watson designed a submarine strikingly similar to that of de Villeroi. With financial support from Horace L. Hunley and a few wealthy merchants, the Leeds Foundry began construction of the novel vessel during autumn 1861. Built of iron, the vessel measured approximately 20 ft (6 m) in length, 4 ft (1.2 m) in depth, and 6 ft (1.8 m) in width. There was a small hatch amidships, and a small hand-cranked propeller at the stern; two diving vanes were located at the stem.

Successful trials near New Orleans in Lake Ponchartrain included the submarine's diving beneath and sinking a barge by means of a towed 'magazine of powder' equipped with sensitive detonators. On the basis of this experimental torpedo attack, Hunley and his associates secured a letter of marque from the Confederacy classifying the newly christened *Pioneer* as a privateer. Before an attack could be made on Union vessels in the Gulf of Mexico, however, New Orleans was evacuated and the *Pioneer* was scuttled in the lake.

Undeterred, Hunley, McClintock and Watson moved their operation to Mobile, Alabama, to build a larger and more sophisticated submarine. Made of boiler iron, the new vessel was to be equipped with a battery-powered electro-magnetic engine. When the engine failed to develop sufficient power, the design was altered to accommodate human power, which produced only marginal results. While being towed toward Fort Morgan, the submarine was unfortunately swamped by rising seas.

Hunley, McClintock and Watson immediately started work on a third vessel! To save time, a 25-ft (7.6-m) ship's boiler was selected for the hull. The ends of the reinforced boiler were faired and fitted with watertight bulkheads and tapering bow and stern sections. Both the bow and stern held ballast tanks and pumps for submerging and surfacing; diving vanes at the bow helped control ascent and descent. The submarine was equipped with a crank-turned propeller and improved compass. Hatches near the bow and stern afforded access and observation. During open water tests in 1863, the new submarine successfully sank a barge in Mobile Bay with a towed torpedo, but in later experiments the towed torpedo was abandoned in favor of a more controlled spar torpedo mounted on the bow of the vessel.

Attracted by a high regard for General Beauregard and a $100,000 reward for the destruction of the Union warships USS *New Ironsides* or USS *Wabash*, offered by John Frazer & Company of Charleston, Hunley and his associates freighted their 'fish boat' to Charleston by rail. After a number of practice dives there by her volunteer crew, the vessel was readied for an attack on *New Ironsides*. Shortly after midnight she departed Fort Johnson on the south side of Charleston harbor, but, with her hatches open, she was swamped by the wake of a passing steamer. Only her commander, Lt John Payne, CSN, was able to abandon ship before the submarine settled to the bottom.

The disaster pointed out the need for experienced personnel and adequate training. General Beauregard brought Hunley to Charleston to supervise the submarine's operation. After the vessel was raised and repaired, Hunley and Lieutenant George Dixon, now in command, began training a new crew. Exercises in the Ashley and Cooper rivers became routine. With training almost over, however, the submarine dived too sharply and stuck in viscous bottom sediments. In spite of efforts to pump out the ballast chambers, drop keel ballast pigs and open the hatches, the submarine could not be freed, and the whole crew was asphyxiated.

Divers found the vessel in nine fathoms of water, her bow buried in the mud. For a second time the 'fish boat' was raised. Hunley was found in the forward hatchway, his face contorted in an expression of 'despair and agony'. His right hand was over his head, where it had been pressing against the hatch, and in his left was a candle. Thomas Park, in charge of the repair and service of the submarine, was found in the after hatch, his hand also pushing the cover. Below, the bodies of the crew were 'tightly grappled together'.

With a new volunteer crew, Dixon cleaned and repaired the submarine and began rigorous training exercises across the harbor from Charleston, with nocturnal cruises extended into the Atlantic when weather permitted. After the newly christened CSS *H. L. Hunley* had made a lengthy and successful dive, General Beauregard authorized Dixon to proceed with plans to attack 'any vessel of the enemy'.

On the night of 17 February 1864 the weather was ideal as the *Hunley* slipped into the Atlantic. Off Beach Inlet Lieutenant Dixon found the 1,800-ton corvette USS *Housatonic*. Although the *Housatonic* almost escaped after the officer of the deck observed something in the water off her starboard quarter, Dixon drove the torpedo into the

33 A rare photograph of a steam-powered semi-submersible David torpedo boat lying in Charleston harbor after the city was captured. Unlike the submarine *H. L. Hunley*, Davids could not submerge. However, their steam powerplant provided speed and maneuverability unavailable using manpower. Under the command of William T. Glassel a David severely damaged the powerful ironclad USS *New Ironsides*, putting the ship out of action for almost a year.

Blockade Runners off Bermuda

By 1864 Wilmington, North Carolina, had become the major port from which Confederate vessels could run the Union blockade, collecting vital supplies from the neutral British islands of Bermuda. But where Union gunboats failed, Bermuda's treacherous reefs occasionally succeeded in sending Confederate ships to their doom. The side-wheel steamers *Mary Celestia* and *Nola* suffered just such a fate – but their loss has been the archaeologist's gain.

34, 36 Recorded in watercolor by a Bermudian artist (*far left, above*) the *Mary Celestia* plunges to the bottom less than eight minutes after striking a coral head off the south coast of Bermuda in 1864. Archaeological investigation of the remains of the steamer and historical research confirm the painting's accuracy. The wreck lay south of the Gibbs Hill Light with the bow down to the southwest. In the photograph (*above left*) East Carolina University students record engineering details of the steam machinery on the *Mary Celestia*. Although much of the hull structure has collapsed, the boilers, engines and paddle wheels survive in excellent condition and offer exciting possibilities for investigation. The starboard paddle wheel at right is equipped with patented feathering boards to improve both speed and efficiency.

35 (*below left*) Unlike the majority of those blockade runners lost in low-visibility seas along the southeast coast of the United States, the remains of the British-built blockade runner *Nola* are highly visible and readily accessible. Wrecked in less than 30 ft (9 m) of water near Western Blue Cut Off Ireland Island, Bermuda, in December 1863, the *Nola* offers virtually unrestricted opportunity to study iron hull construction. A 1986 survey of the site revealed that almost 70 percent of the hull structure lies exposed.

corvette just forward of her mizzen mast. The explosion lifted the *Housatonic* by the stern before she heeled to port and sank. Dixon's attack was a success, but the CSS *Hunley* and her crew never returned.

Although more than one historical source indicates that the remains of the Confederate submarine were salvaged from the immediate vicinity of the USS *Housatonic*, other sources imply that the vessel may have made signal for range lights to be set off Breach's Inlet. For author Clive Cussler the possibility that the *Hunley* escaped was sufficient to sponsor a search during the summers of 1980 and 1981. Both investigations employed highly accurate radar ranging systems and magnetometers. The surveys located the unsalvaged remains of the *Housatonic* and several other Civil War shipwrecks, but no evidence of the *Hunley* was identified.

While the fate of the *Hunley* remains as intriguing as ever, Charleston Harbor could contain the remains of one or more Confederate 'Davids'. These were small warships of wood and iron about 50 ft (15 m) long, designed to operate *almost* submerged. A small steam engine provided power to a propeller in the stern of each. With ballast tanks flooded, only a David's armored deck and funnel were exposed, allowing the vessel to deliver a spar torpedo against an enemy hull without attracting much prior notice.

Although the impact of Confederate submarines was largely psychological, Union Rear Admiral John A. Dahlgren recognized their potential. In discussing 'Davids', he wrote:

> Among the many inventions with which I have been familiar, I have seen none which have acted so perfectly at first trial. The secrecy, rapidity of movement, control of direction, and precise explosion indicate, I think, the introduction of the torpedoe element as a means of certain warfare. It can be ignored no longer. If 60 pounds of powder, why not 600 pounds?

As a result of the hazards of wartime commerce and the frequent and often dramatic confrontations between Union and Confederate vessels, more than a thousand ships were lost or destroyed during the American Civil War. Today these wrecks preserve valuable evidence of vessels that reflected the vanishing shipbuilding traditions of the eighteenth century as well as those that contained the seeds of modern naval and marine architecture and shipbuilding. Civil War shipwrecks preserve exciting opportunities to explore one of the most catastrophic events in American history. Through systematic investigation Americans have the opportunity to investigate what is perhaps the largest surviving, and yet virtually untapped, source of Civil War information. Although few Civil War wrecks have been scientifically investigated, salvage and archaeological surveys have demonstrated their potential for research, education and recreational activities.

CHAPTER TWELVE

The End of the Age of Sail: Merchant Shipping in the Nineteenth Century

Paul Forsythe Johnston

The nineteenth century marked a revolution in the history of seafaring, a turning point whose impact upon worldwide cultural, economic and technological development is still being felt today. Nowhere was this impact greater than in the Americas, where the tenuous European toehold had evolved into a solid grip on the continent. Over the course of the century, tens of millions of Europeans voyaged from the Old World to the New, making it their new homeland. At first, these immigrants traveled aboard small wooden sailing vessels that took anywhere from four to twelve weeks to cross the Western Ocean. By the century's end, immense steel steamships were making regularly scheduled passages over the same route in as little as five days and had laid transatlantic telegraphic cables providing instantaneous intercontinental communications.

During the same period, American merchant ships sailed the world's seas and oceans in search of new products and profits. In the course of their voyages, merchants also often discovered new cultures and regions, filling gaps in contemporary world maps and adding to man's scientific and humanistic knowledge of our global environment. The New England whaling fleet alone is credited with the discovery and exploration of more than 400 islands in the Pacific Ocean. The cargoes that these mariners landed quite literally provided the basis for the United States government: until 1913 most federal revenues were derived from duties collected on foreign goods landed at custom houses throughout the nation.

Despite the critical role of the merchant marine in the growth of the United States into a world power in the nineteenth century, the ships of the era have received little attention from the archaeological community, with a few notable exceptions. Fortunately, however, these vessels are well documented in various other ways, and many representative examples still exist for scholarly study and public enjoyment.

Trade Expands: The Century Begins

By the opening of the nineteenth century, American mariners had raised their new nation's flag in every major port throughout the world from Archangel to Zanzibar. Yankee ingenuity, daring, skill and more than a little luck, combined with the hard-won freedom to trade anywhere, encouraged a search for exotic cargoes from the 'richest ports of the Far East' and the Pacific basin, including pepper, teas, silks, coffee, animal furs and skins, spices, ivory, porcelains, bêche-de-mer, furniture, sandalwood and many others. Taking advantage of their neutral status during the war between France and England and the resulting disruption of normal trading patterns, Americans stepped into the breech and also established regular commerce routes along the shores of continental Europe, India and Africa, exporting fish, lumber, textiles and leather goods in exchange for manufactured products, iron, gum copal, finished textiles, slaves and spices.

Highly developed coastal trade along the shores of North America also prospered in the early years of the nineteenth century, partly the result of population growth in communities all along the eastern seaboard. In the absence of decent roads, watercraft provided the quickest, most reliable and regular service between all sizes of settlements, supplying transportation for passengers, the mails and the transshipment of cargo to and from the major ports for distribution along the coast.

Initially, the ships used in the deepwater and coastal trades were little different from their colonial counterparts. Centered in New England in the early part of the century, the nation's shipbuilding industry gained such a fine reputation for providing seaworthy, well-founded ships that the vessels were often sold to European merchants along with their cargoes.

During the eighteenth century, sloops, ketches and small square-rigged vessels had dominated the coasting trade. By the start of the next century, however, the two-masted schooner had proved more efficient and was in widespread use throughout the Atlantic seaboard and the West Indies. Its fore-and-aft rig was more weatherly, allowing the vessel to head closer to the wind and permitting a close-hauled schooner to outsail a much larger square-rigged ship. Moreover, it enabled the running rigging to be handled from the deck rather than

Bound for Foreign Ports

Taking advantage of their new status after the War of Independence, Americans established themselves as major international sea traders by the late eighteenth century.

1 (left) The *Samuel* of Boston, entering Naples in 1797, portrays a typical topsail schooner of around the turn of the century. Although small, such vessels were used for both coastal and deepwater trading voyages.

3 (right) *Cap Cook Cast A Way on Cape Cod 1802.* The ship *Ulysses* was one of a fleet of three vessels that cleared Salem for foreign ports in 1802. All three wrecked at Cape Cod during a storm shortly after departure. At this time merchants preferred to ship cargo aboard small vessels to minimize potential losses and spread the risk.

Prosperous Merchants

2 (right) Crowninshield's Wharf at Salem in 1806. The Crowninshields were one of the wealthiest families in New England in the early nineteenth century, having made a fortune privateering during the American Revolution. At the inner (left) end a vessel is hove-down for repairs; three pump-makers, a sail loft and a ship smithy are also visible. Farther down is the yellow horsecart of George Crowninshield, Jr, future owner of America's first oceangoing luxury yacht, *Cleopatra's Barge*. Along the wharf are tied up *America*, *Fame*, *Prudent* and *Belisarius*, all Crowninshield-owned. The merchants' warehouses served not only as storage facilities, but also contained their business offices, called counting houses.

aloft, thereby requiring a smaller crew and lowering operating costs. The rig was also easier to bring about and maneuver in shallow or confined coastal waters, where a fast tack could make the difference between a profitable voyage and a vessel's total loss. As the volume of traffic increased, a third mast was added around 1800, and the two- and three-masted American schooner soon became a common sight in the harbors and fisheries of North and South America and along the coasts of Europe and Africa.

For the deepwater trade of the times, especially with China, the East Indies and the Mediterranean, the three-masted square-rigged ship and its two-masted variant, the brig, were the vessels of choice for Yankee mariners. Although they required far larger crews than the schooner, they were bigger and more heavily built than their fore-and-aft rigged cousins, averaging from 400 to 600 tons burden. These design requisites were necessary for long voyages that might include circumnavigation and passages through the world's most difficult waters at the Cape of Good Hope and Cape Horn in the Southern Hemisphere. Although the risks were great for these voyages, which could last well over a year, profits could be spectacular. Many vessels paid for themselves with a single trip to the Orient, and a 700 percent profit for a particularly successful cruise was not unknown.

Aside from an occasional costly skirmish with the Barbary Pirates, the loss of a vessel or crew to French privateers, British impressment, Fijian cannibals or shipwreck, there was no reason for the mariners of the nineteenth century's first decade to suspect that American seaborne commerce would not continue to expand and prosper. In 1807, however, at the time Robert Fulton's *North River Steamboat of Clermont* was demonstrating the commercial viability of steam (Chapter Ten), a series of international events began that disrupted the normal and carefully nurtured trade patterns. The first was the Jefferson Embargo Act of 1807, which unilaterally banned all American ships from participating in foreign trade. All legitimate international enterprises, along with their subsidiary support industries, were devastated; only smugglers and merchants creatively interpreting the law's wording profited. Subsequent nonintercourse and embargo acts passed by Congress continued to restrict international trade until the onset of the War of 1812, which further deepened the depression in the merchant marine. Crews and vessels from all facets of the maritime economy were pressed into naval service or lured into the lucrative privateering industry. Although limited foreign trade resumed during the war, it was on a much reduced scale, and the attrition rate was high. To the north, the ports of New England and New York suffered less than ports in the Delaware and Chesapeake Bays on account of the increased British presence in the southern regions.

Although commerce suffered, ship design advanced during the War of 1812. One of the chief developments was the refinement of the southern-built pilot schooner, the prototype of the swift Baltimore clipper schooner, which grew sharper and faster in order to evade British blockading squadrons patrolling the mid-Atlantic coastline. It has been estimated that these small vessels accounted for more than half the nation's wartime foreign trade, also finding widespread use in privateering, the coastal trade and the less honorable but highly profitable smuggling and slaving industries. As a type, these schooners were so successful that shipbuilders along the eastern seaboard adopted certain of their design characteristics relating to speed and handling, and the little two-masters soon became popular throughout the New World.

The Heyday

The period between the War of 1812 and the Civil War has appropriately been called the Golden Age of American maritime enterprise. The half-century of peace witnessed the commercial development of the steamship, the rise of the transatlantic sailing packet, the brief and dramatic genesis of the famous clipper ship and its even more rapid demise, the settlement of the Pacific Northwest, the successful and efficient pursuit of the whale and food fish, and the overall growth of the American continent into a worldwide maritime power.

Recovery from the War of 1812 was initially slow. First to rebound were the fisheries and coastal trade, aided by the 1817 'Act Concerning the Navigation of the United States'. Still in force today in even stronger form, this protective legislation prohibited trade between any ports in the nation in vessels wholly or even partly foreign-owned. Almost immediately a lively exchange resumed between the West Indies and the southern cotton ports of Mobile, Charleston, Savannah and New Orleans and the northeastern ports of Boston, New York, Albany, Philadelphia and Baltimore. Among the most important bulk products shipped north were cotton, tobacco, sugar and molasses, which were traded for lumber, fish, stone and lime. Northern ports also imported coal and flour from the mid-Atlantic region to fuel their industrial and manufacturing centers. As the volume of traffic increased, regularly scheduled service for freight, passengers and mail between the major eastern port cities developed aboard medium-sized square-riggers, called packets after their cargo of subsidized packets of mail. Smaller sloops and schooners distributed these cargoes between the hub cities and outlying settlements.

Around the same time, the new steamboat made its appearance along the shores of the Northeast. As the steam navigation monopolies that Fulton and his father-in-law Robert Livingston had been granted were being successfully challenged in the courts or were expiring following Fulton's death in 1815 (see Chapter Ten), other entrepreneurs appeared, attracted by the potential of smaller crews than on sailing vessels, more regular schedules independent of wind and weather, greater speed and maneuverability, and increasingly reliable engines and boilers. By the 1820s, small wooden-hulled side-wheel

4 The Black Ball Line packet ship *James Foster, Jr* was built at New York in 1854 by the famous shipbuilder William H. Webb. Starting in 1836 at the age of twenty, Webb constructed all the Black Ball liners as well as many famous clipper ships. One of the largest packets of her day at 171 ft 6 in (52 m) in length and 1,410 tons, *Foster* averaged thirty-six days on westbound passages from Liverpool to New York over her twenty-four-year career as a Black Baller.

paddle steamers operating along the East Coast and inland waterways were taking the most lucrative passenger, mail and freight service away from the sailing packets.

The deepwater trade of the period followed a different course from the coasting business. Oceangoing merchantmen were increasing in size, and more often than not larger vessels bearing foreign cargoes set their sails for the port of New York. Located midway along the East Coast, with easy access to both inland and coastal markets, New York in the late eighteenth century had surpassed Boston in the volume of foreign trade. In the process, it became the nation's largest seaport, and many merchants formerly centered in New England migrated there to take advantage of the growing market for their products.

Chief among the factors responsible for the renaissance of foreign trade and continued growth of New York was the inauguration of a transatlantic sailing packet service between that city and Liverpool in 1818 by the British textile merchant Jeremiah Thompson and his partners. British mail bags had regularly crossed the Atlantic from the mid-eighteenth century, and owners of individual ships had offered service between specific ports at various intervals during the same era, but now the Black Ball Line provided a fleet of ships willing to sail punctually on specific days of each month of the year, with or without full holds. Although a risky idea, the advantages of the new service were obvious, and within six years several competing lines offered similar service between New York and Liverpool, Le Havre and London. Boston, Baltimore and Philadelphia made sporadic efforts to compete with New York for the packet business, but the eastbound volume of cargo from these ports was too low to support regular services, and they were forced to ship their products to New York for transshipment. The most profitable westward cargo was 'fine freight', consisting of textiles, hardware, cutlery, books and luxury items, followed by cabin passengers, mail and specie. Less profitable emigrants and heavy freight (British iron,

French millstones and wine), or even bulk salt and coal, filled out the westbound manifests. At first, the merchants of New York had trouble finding cargo desirable to Europeans. The only regional products available in quantity were flour, wheat, furs, skins, salt meat and flaxseed, and the British Corn Laws prohibited importation of the first two. However, the problem was solved early on by the shipment to New York of cargo from ports as far south as the Gulf of Mexico. Chief among these southern cargoes was raw baled cotton from New Orleans, Charleston, Savannah and Mobile, along with smaller quantities of tobacco, rice and naval stores (tar, pitch and turpentine). To accommodate this coastal trade, small packet companies sprang up from Portland, Maine, to New Orleans, to serve as trunk or feeder lines for New York-bound export cargo and as distributors of the incoming products.

The ships built for the transatlantic packet service were among the strongest and most durable in the annals of merchant sail. Virtually all were full-rigged ships, growing from around 350 tons burden at the outset to more than 1,000 tons in the mid-1840s. Their length-to-beam ratio averaged a capacious 4:1, with 'frigate-built' full bows and two decks for passengers and cargo. In order to survive stormy winter crossings and hard-driving masters intent on keeping or bettering scheduled passages, many ocean packets had caulked inner or ceiling planking as additional protection. Around 90 percent of the American ocean packets were built at the East River in New York, and their strength was legendary: only three of the 150 or so vessels built for the trade foundered at sea, and to the astonishment of many Europeans, many others which grounded or went ashore were refloated and returned to service. Luxurious accommodations were provided for cabin passengers, and officer service aboard the vessels was highly desirable as a fast track to command of one's own ship. Conditions and pay for the common sailor, however, were poor by contemporary standards.

The Climax of the Clipper

The sleek oceangoing clippers of the mid-nineteenth century caught the popular imagination. During the California Gold Rush, almost any full-rigged ship in east coast ports was called a clipper, so anxious were shippers to fill westbound vessels. But the true clipper was a ship capable of making the voyage from New York to San Francisco in 110 days or less.

5 (*left, above*) This painting by John Stobart portrays the Gold Rush ship *Niantic* at left after she was beached and converted to a storeship in San Francisco harbor. Also shown in the center is the English-built *Vicar of Bray* drying her sails. Abandoned at Port Stanley in the Falkland Islands and hulked there in 1880, *Vicar*'s hull is still preserved, and she may one day be returned to the United States.

6 (*left, below*) Shipbuilder Donald McKay's *Great Republic* was the largest and most magnificent wooden sailing ship ever built. Some 334 ft (102 m) in length, the clipper displaced 4,555 tons and carried splendid mahogany furniture and stained glass windows on board. Sadly she never achieved her potential. In late 1853, just before her maiden voyage, she burned to the waterline in a New York City fire. Sold off, she was rebuilt with a reduced hull and rig. In this formal oil painting by James A. Butterworth, the original ship is shown under full sail. Usually commissioned by the owner or captain of a ship, formal ship portraits were required by their owners to be extremely accurate renditions.

7 (*right*) The bow of the extreme clipper *Snow Squall* at Port Stanley, in the Falkland Islands, shows how well the low temperatures near Cape Horn preserved the vessel before she suffered damage during the conflict between Britain and Argentina in 1982. Launched in South Portland, Maine, in 1851, the *Snow Squall* went through many adventures – including victory in a race from China to New York – before being forced into Port Stanley after suffering irreparable gale damage in 1864. Today her remains have been returned to her port of origin in Maine, where they are being put on display.

8 (*left*) The people of Boston were so pleased that their city was the Cunard Line's American terminal that they cut a 7-mile passage through the ice to help the line's flagship *Britannia* maintain her schedule.

The Rise of the Steamship

The Atlantic packet service continued to expand for around three decades, until the same factors that made it so successful in the early part of the century caused its demise in the middle years of the era. The chief cause of its obsolescence was the development of a regular transatlantic steamship service, which had competed with the slower square-riggers from 1840. Steamers required smaller crews than the two or three dozen men commonly manning a 1,000-ton sailing ship. Moreover, they were faster, and less reliant on weather in maintaining scheduled arrivals and departures. Once the screw propeller was developed and tested by the British in the 1830s to replace the side-wheel paddle, it was only a matter of time before the ocean steamship became practical.

The Cunard Line. Like the packets before them, transatlantic steamers were less of a new idea than an idea whose time had come. As early as 1819, the American side-wheeler *Savannah* had crossed from Georgia to Liverpool in less than a month, but public prejudice guaranteed her economic failure and she was sold by her owners shortly afterwards. Not until the 1830s were similar ventures undertaken, but these were intermittent and unprofitable. Developments in the reliability, mechanical efficiency, safety and economic viability of coastal steamers progressed, however, and in 1839 the British government accepted bids for a heavily subsidized steamship mail service between Liverpool and the New World. Nova Scotian merchant and shipowner Samuel Cunard won the contract and immediately began construction of four identical sisterships, each measuring 207 ft (63 m) in length and 1,156 gross tons. With the departure from Liverpool for Boston of the foursome's most famous member, *Britannia*, on 4 July 1840, the age of the ocean steamship began. The Age of Sail, which had ruled the world's waterways for thousands of years, was drawing to a close.

The Cunard Line to Boston, which shifted its base of operations to New York in 1848, was an immediate success, winning the most valuable transatlantic freight and passenger business away from slower sailing packets. When the attention of the American shipping industry was diverted to California in the late 1840s because of the Gold Rush, several rival British steamship companies sprang up to service the increasingly important North American market, funneling freight and emigrants from Western Europe to New York, Boston, Philadelphia and Baltimore.

Brunel: From the 'Great Western' to the 'Great Eastern'. The most significant of Cunard's early competitors on the Atlantic Ferry was Isambard Kingdom Brunel, the famous British civil engineer. Brunel's first steamship was the *Great Western* of 1838, specifically built to be the first steamer to cross the Atlantic using only steam power. Built of wood and measuring 236 ft (73 m) and 1,321 tons burden, *Great Western* lost the race for a place in history by only a few hours to the British steamer *Sirius*, which arrived at New York on 22 April 1838 under charter to the British and American Steam Navigation Company.

Undeterred, Brunel began construction of another transatlantic steamship, the *Great Britain*, measuring 274 ft (84 m) in length and 3,270 tons. Among her most radical features were an iron hull divided by vertical watertight bulkheads, a propeller drive, standing rigging of wire, six hinged and progressively raked masts, a balanced rudder and a clipper bow. Such innovations delayed *Great Britain*'s launch until 1843, and after a single voyage to New York in 1845 she went aground on the rocks at Dundrum Bay, Ireland. Nearly a year later she was refloated and subsequently served as a passenger ship in the England–Australia immigration and freight service.

Isambard Kingdom Brunel

This British engineer devoted twenty years of his life to building steamships for the Atlantic crossing.

9 (*above right*) Brunel's first steamship was the *Great Western*, built of wood and 236 ft (73 m) long, seen here arriving off New York in 1838.

10 (*center right*) The iron-hulled *Great Britain* in an 1844 view by a pioneer of photography, Fox Talbot.

11 (*below*) In 1969 the hulk of the *Great Britain*, towed on a pontoon, began the triumphant voyage back to her home port of Bristol, England, after over eighty years in the Falkland Islands, where she had been abandoned.

12 (*below right*) Brunel's colossal *Great Eastern* ready for launching in 1857. She remained the largest steamship in the world for almost fifty years.

The Grave of a Gold Rush Ship

A China packet converted to a whaler, the *Niantic* joined the rush of ships bound for San Francisco after news of the California gold discovery broke in 1849. Within a week of arrival she had been deserted by most of her crew and was later converted into a storeship (ill. 5). In May 1978 her remains were discovered during building work for a new office block and archaeologists quickly undertook a salvage excavation.

13 (*above right*) A San Francisco fire had reduced *Niantic* to a charred hulk and landfill had then buried the remains. The salvage excavations are viewed here from the stern.

14 (*center right*) A cross-section of the 4,000 artifacts from the wreck of the *Niantic* shows all phases of her restless career: a flensing spade from her whaling days, a tin of truffled sausages and champagne from France, a fragment of Chinese export porcelain, a hand scale for gold prospectors, and a leather-covered blank book for accounts and record keeping.

15 (*below*) A forest of masts in San Francisco harbor in 1853 gives some idea of the huge number of ships laid up there at the height of the Gold Rush.

16 (*right*) This contemporary lithograph depicts the sinking of the Collins liner *Arctic* on 27 September 1854. Collins' own family was aboard the *Arctic* and perished with 345 other souls following the collision with the French steamer *Vesta* in mid-Atlantic.

After nearly forty years, in 1886 *Great Britain* sustained severe damage during a storm off Cape Horn at the tip of South America. His crew threatening mutiny, her captain turned toward nearby Port Stanley in the Falkland Islands and intentionally beached the ship. There she was purchased for $2,000 by the Falkland Islands Company for use as a floating wool and coal storage hulk before abandonment nearly fifty years later. Interest in her was rekindled in the 1960s, and surveys indicated that her condition was sound enough to warrant preservation. Accordingly, in 1970, *Great Britain* was towed back to the dock where she had been built in Bristol, England. There she may be seen today, a testimony to the durability and strength of the British iron shipbuilding industry in the mid-nineteenth century.

Although Brunel's first two steamers were financial disasters, in 1854 the engineer began designing one more such vessel, the gargantuan *Great Eastern*. Nearly five times larger than any ship built previously and unsurpassed in size for nearly half a century, *Great Eastern* measured an astounding 680 ft (207 m) in length and 18,914 gross tons. She accommodated 4,000 passengers and carried enough coal in her bunkers (15,000 tons) for non-stop voyages from England to Australia and on to India. Brunel was uncertain as to the most efficient means of propulsion and incorporated sail, screw and side-wheel paddles. Also included were a cellular double bottom and a steering engine, both features common on today's large oceangoing vessels. *Great Eastern*'s size and technology were so far ahead of their time that construction delays bankrupted no fewer than three consecutive sets of owners before the ship was even launched. Moreover, Brunel died prior to her launch. Without his guidance, she too was unprofitable in the transatlantic trade. After enjoying limited success as a telegraphic cable-laying ship between 1866 and 1873, *Great Eastern* was laid up, ending

her days as a tourist attraction and floating billboard for a British department store.

The Collins Line. In the pioneering years of the Atlantic Ferry, Samuel Cunard had one other major rival aside from Brunel: Edward Knight Collins, the only American to successfully challenge the British steamship's domination of nineteenth-century transoceanic trade. A native of Cape Cod with many seafaring ancestors, Collins entered the shipping industry in 1827 with a packet line servicing New York and Veracruz, Mexico. In 1832 he sold his interest in that line to finance the acquisition of one of the lesser packet companies plying between New York and New Orleans. In a few years he was able to consolidate his profits and begin the famous New York–Liverpool packet service known as the Dramatic Line, naming his ships after well-known figures in historic drama. However, recognizing that the future lay with steamships, Collins petitioned the federal government as early as 1838 to subsidize an American transatlantic steamship mail service along the lines of the British system then being considered. Congress balked until 1847, its leaders finally capitulating in an effort to break the ever-stronger British monopoly of ocean steam navigation. The government contract called for an annual subsidy of $385,000 and the construction of five steamships of a certain size and speed, convertible to wartime duty should the necessity arise. As low bidder, Collins won the contract and sold off his two packet lines to finance his new venture, The New York and Liverpool United States Mail Steamship Company. He also ordered the construction of four identical steamships, and when the Collins Line, as it became known, inaugurated service in 1850, *Atlantic*, *Pacific*, *Arctic* and *Baltic* were the largest, fastest and most luxuriously outfitted steamers in the world. Measuring around 283 ft (86 m) in length and 2,783 gross tons, these side-wheel paddle steamers offered such amenities as stained-glass skylights, steam heat, steward service in the staterooms and 3,500-bottle wine cellars.

Passengers flocked to the new line, and Cunard was forced to lower his rates to stay competitive. Proud of the new flagships of the American merchant marine, Congress patriotically increased Collins' annual subsidy to $858,000 in 1853 to offset some 'trifling' losses; around the same time British competition was temporarily hampered as merchant steamships were requisitioned by Parliament for service in the Crimean War.

Collins and his steamers enjoyed record passages and profits until fall 1854, when *Arctic* collided with another steamship in fog off Newfoundland. *Arctic* had been driving under full steam in hazardous conditions to maintain the line's reputation for speed, and 348 persons, including Collins' wife and two children, were lost as a result. Subsequently, in early 1856, *Pacific* departed Liverpool for New York with around 150 passengers and was never heard from again. The public outcry against Collins for operating at unsafe speeds was tremendous, and the line could not maintain its regular schedule with only two vessels left. The Cunard Line, which had never lost a passenger, was quick to advertise that fact, and the public's allegiance to the Collins Line evaporated. Later the same year the government mail subsidy to the Collins Line was reduced to the original amount, and in spite of the construction of a new steamship, the line ceased operations in February 1858. Nevertheless, Collins had introduced to the public the concepts of speed and luxury at sea; together with safety, they were to prove the dominant factors in steamship design for the next century. By 1861, when the Cunard Line phased out side-wheel paddles in favor of the propeller, the engine-powered ship had eclipsed the sailing vessel on the world's most lucrative Western Ocean trading route, a position it would never relinquish.

Despite this, the windship remained the most efficient means of transport for certain types of coastal and deepwater trade in the Americas. Along the Pacific Coast the population was too low to warrant regular steamship service of any magnitude, and there were too few coaling stations in the Pacific and Indian Oceans to justify the steamship's presence in the Far Eastern trade.

The Gold Rush Ship *Niantic*

Following the discovery of gold at Sutter's Mill in Coloma, California, in December 1848, people from all over the world, and in particular the East Coast of North America, were desperate for passage to San Francisco, gateway to the gold fields. Once there, prospectors required food, clothing, shelter, outfitting and other basic services. Virtually anything afloat, from New York harbor tugboats to condemned whaling barks, was pressed into use to supply these needs. In 1847, the year before the discovery, an estimated 7,000 people were in California. Five years later, the population was 207,000.

In 1849 alone, more than 775 ships sailed for San Francisco from ports all over the world. One such vessel was *Niantic*, a small ship originally built in Connecticut in 1835 as a China packet and converted to a whaler in 1844. In late 1848 she cleared Rhode Island for the Pacific Northwest on her second whaling voyage. After rounding Cape Horn in January 1849, *Niantic* stopped at Paita, Peru, for provisions and repairs, and there her master learned of the California gold discovery. Seizing the opportunity, he immediately abandoned his plans for a lengthy whaling trip and set sail for the Isthmus of Panama, where hundreds of stranded prospectors were clamoring for passage to San Francisco. At the isthmus, *Niantic*'s blubber trypots were converted to cookpots and, refitted for passengers, she loaded 246 forty-niners at $250 for cabin-class accommodations and $150 for steerage. Within a week of her arrival at the Golden Gate in early July 1849, *Niantic*'s human cargo had dispersed along with nearly all of her 23-man crew, who had deserted to join the prospectors. She joined the large fleet of empty ships swinging at anchor in San Francisco harbor, idled for want of a crew.

Niantic's career was not yet over. She was sold to realtors who beached her and stripped her of masts and rigging, converting her into the community's first storeship. The novel idea caught on quickly under pressure from the local population explosion and consequent shortages in housing, building materials and labor. By 1851, 148 surplus ships had undergone similar conversions along San Francisco's waterfront, serving as warehouses, jails, saloons, office buildings, hotels and shops. In that year, however, a fire destroyed twenty-two city blocks along the waterfront, burning *Niantic* and several other storeships. Landfill soon covered the charred hulk and within four months a house was built overhead, succeeded by a hotel, a commercial building and an office building over the years. Rather than damaging *Niantic*, these later constructions effectively sealed her off from deterioration. In May 1978 she was uncovered during excavations for the foundation of a new commercial building, now twelve blocks from the modern waterfront.

With severe time and funding constraints, only limited salvage was possible for archaeologist Isabel Bullen of the National Maritime Museum of San Francisco. Nevertheless, a remarkable amount of material data was recorded and recovered, shedding new light on one of the nation's most famous phenomena: the California Gold Rush and the consequent growth of San Francisco into the West Coast's largest and most important urban center in the mid-nineteenth century.

Some 4,000 artifacts were removed from *Niantic*'s hold, representing the largest known Gold Rush deposit of commercial merchandise and displaying the wide range of imported goods available to local consumers from all over the world. Luxury items from France, such as champagne, sherry and truffled sausages, suggest a high level of disposable income and the tastes to indulge them, as might be expected in a town where gold was abundant. San Francisco's image as a hard-drinking community during this era was supported by the discovery that 97 percent of the hundreds of bottles recovered from *Niantic* were for alcoholic beverages, mainly imported spirits from France, England and Holland. Associated fragmentary casks and barrels for the storage of beer and whiskey fill out this aspect of social activity. American, British and German stationery and printing items, including leather-bound blank books, pencils, paper, pens, ink bottles, scissors, paper cutters, calendars and two complete copy presses bespeak a busy commercial community. English, European and American firearms and weapons, ranging from a sword to muskets, carbines, pistols, bullet molds and powder gauges, are indicative of the more violent side of frontier society. Among many other types of tools stockpiled aboard *Niantic*, a hand scale for weighing gold, fragmentary assay crucibles and shovels would have been used in the gold fields; large quantities of kitchenware, glassware and tableware might have seen use in either the field or the city. The picture is enhanced by textiles associated with carpets, clothing and bedding, along with a charred roll of wallpaper, ceramics (including Chinese and European export porcelain), clothing and footwear. A set of navigating dividers, a fragmentary telescope, a flensing spade for cutting blubber, and a rotary hand pump harken back to *Niantic*'s career as a whale hunter.

Clipper Ships

In 1844 a treaty opened several new Chinese ports to trade with the United States, giving it relative parity with Great Britain and other nations that had been trading regularly in the Orient. Tea and luxuries were the primary cargoes, and the first ships of the season to return laden to the mother country garnered the highest profits for their owners. Speed also protected the tea and expensive textiles from mold in the hot and humid latitudes and guaranteed a faster turnaround of merchants' capital. As a result, shipyards in Britain and America began building swifter ships, sacrificing some cargo capacity in exchange for longer, more streamlined and lighter hulls capable of carrying immense amounts of canvas on their spars. Fueled by pride, profits, the press and popular imagination, these vessels came to be known as clipper ships, one of the best-known yet shortest-lived phenomena in maritime history.

The origins of the clipper ship are as manifold as they are disputed. The term 'clipper' first appeared in the early nineteenth century in connection with the Baltimore schooner, which was designed to outsail British naval vessels or privateers and was later used by slavers, smugglers and opium runners as well. Derived most probably from speed-related slang such as 'at a fast clip' or 'clip along', the term was gradually applied to any fast, streamlined sailing vessel. Certainly the full-rigged tea ships and transatlantic packets also contributed design

17 The most detailed contemporary drawings of Baltimore clippers were published in 1824 by Frenchman M. Marestier, who had originally come to the United States to study American steamship technology. These illustrations from his publication depict two variants of the two-masted Baltimore clipper schooner.

elements, notably those relating to stability, weatherliness and the capacity for withstanding a hard-driving crew sailing through heavy winds and weather. The popular equation of speed with progress, and, most importantly, the California Gold Rush were also major factors in the meteoric rise of the clipper ship.

In order to fill westbound passenger and cargo manifests, shippers back east took to calling nearly any full-rigged ship loading at the wharf a clipper ship or at least 'clipper-built', and the press enthusiastically cooperated in exaggerating the claims. As a result, more than a century later it can be difficult to separate fact from fiction. Most authorities, however, are agreed on certain basic features and criteria in discussing the ship type. Generally, the term 'clipper' is restricted to those hundred or so wooden sailing ships capable of making the voyage from New York to San Francisco in 110 days or less, or an equally swift passage between other major ports such as Hong Kong or Shanghai and London. Other factors being equal, a clipper might sacrifice up to a third of the cargo capacity of an equally large vessel for the sake of streamlined, fine lines. The low hulls were characterized by sharp, even hollow entrances below the water, with a long, fine run. Above the water was a strongly raked stem, which came to be known as a clipper bow. The stern was also inclined, with an overhanging counter to reduce the wetted surface. Length-to-beam ratios averaged around 4.5:1, although for extreme clippers this could approach 6:1. Clippers normally carried heavier spars and far more canvas on their three square-rigged masts than other deepwater ship types, and they required crews of up to 100 officers and men to permit operation in all weathers and waters. Although they were lightly built for speed, rivalry between competing owners and builders required that they be well finished and outfitted for passengers.

18–20 The great ship designer Donald McKay (*below*, in 1855) built many famous clippers at his East Boston shipyard (*right*), including the *Flying Cloud* and *Great Republic* (ills. 6, 22), as well as packet ships like the *Star of Empire* and *Chariot of Fame* (original profile drawing, *below right*).

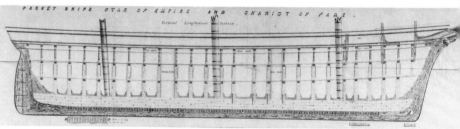

Although American clippers were built throughout the Northeast, most of the speed records fell to vessels built by Donald McKay at East Boston and William Webb at the East River in New York. Webb is remembered best for his fine designs, and McKay for the durability and speed of his ships. Certainly no commercial sailing vessel ever matched the two 89-day record passages between New York and San Francisco set by McKay's extreme clipper *Flying Cloud*, and none ever exceeded the top speed of 22 knots achieved by his *Sovereign of the Seas* in 1854.

Typically, a California clipper loaded passengers and cargo at New York. At the height of the Gold Rush in the early 1850s, the freight rates to San Francisco were astronomical – up to $60/ton – and a new ship could pay for her construction, fitting out and insurance in a single voyage. She sailed west via Cape Horn, making San Francisco in three to four months depending upon the weather at the Cape and the season of the year. Inevitably, some crewmen joined the Gold Rush, and more than one ship lay at anchor at the Golden Gate for weeks without a soul aboard. If a crew was available, the ship might clear port in ballast with a few chests of gold bound for New York, or she might set out across the Pacific for a load of Chinese export products. From the Far East she could depart for London or New York via the Cape of Good Hope, in the process casually circumnavigating the globe in a matter of months, only a few centuries after the epic three-year voyage of Magellan's *Vittoria* around the world.

The 'Snow Squall'. Despite the clippers' romantic image, preserved through the written word and pictures,

comparatively little is known of the vessels themselves. Recently, however, the rediscovery of the hulk of the only known example of the American extreme clipper, beneath a dock at Port Stanley in the Falklands, has promised to add significantly to our knowledge of these ships.

Built in 1851, *Snow Squall* was one of three clipper ships constructed by Alfred Butler at his shipyard in South Portland, Maine. Considered small for the type though finely built, she measured 163 ft (50 m) in length by 31 ft (9.5 m) in breadth and 742 registered tons. Over her peripatetic thirteen-year career, *Snow Squall* visited many ports in North and South America, Europe and the Far East. Among her adventures were a victory over Donald McKay's giant clipper *Romance of the Seas* during a race in 1854 from China to New York, and a narrow escape from capture by the Confederate raider *Tuscaloosa* in 1863. Although her early performance was disappointing, in 1856 *Snow Squall* set both the one-way and roundtrip records between New York and Rio de Janeiro (respectively 28 and 53 sailing days) on a coffee voyage.

Clearing New York on 2 January 1864 for San Francisco, *Snow Squall* encountered a fierce gale at the Straits of Le Maire off Cape Horn and was driven aground, sustaining severe damage. Her master, James Dillingham, elected to turn back for repairs at Port Stanley in the Falkland Islands, a common haven and provisioning spot for Cape Horners. The local facilities were unable to repair the damage, however, and Dillingham was forced to sell the vessel to the Falkland Islands Company. She was stripped and grounded, and then used as a storage hulk for wool, the Company's main export. The deteriorating hull was finally abandoned and a dock was built over that portion of it still above water.

In 1982, a team of archaeologists led by Dr Fred Yalouris of the Harvard Peabody Museum initiated a survey of *Snow Squall*'s nearly intact hull with the long-term objective of measuring, recording and recovering the most significant elements for exhibition at the Spring Point Museum in South Portland, Maine, near where she had been built. Since then, Yalouris has led three more expeditions to Port Stanley, resulting in nearly 50 tons of the bow and starboard hull being removed, cleaned, treated and transported back to Maine, where further research and conservation treatment are being conducted prior to reassembly and display. Over the next few years, *Snow Squall* is expected to provide the only detailed plans of an American extreme clipper ship.

The demise of the clipper ship. During the heyday of the clipper era, every new ship that slid down the ways seemed destined for glory. Stories abound of hard-driving captains pushing their crews and ships mercilessly over the world's deepest and most distant waters, crowding on every available foot of canvas short of actually driving their ships under the waves, shortening sail only when necessary and then only at the last moment. In truth, many records were set not so much by the ships as by their crews. Many of the vessels were so badly damaged by demanding captains that they had to undergo extensive repairs after each voyage, losing money for their owners and shortening their working lives. Nevertheless, hyperbole was heaped upon exaggeration and, then as now, the public loved it.

Few clippers were more deserving of sensationalism than Donald McKay's masterpiece, *Great Republic*. Everything about her, from her dimensions (334 ft [102 m] in length and 4,555 registered tons) to her amenities (velvet and mahogany furniture, oil paintings, stained glass windows) and crew size (100 men and 30 boys) was intended to slay the competition. She carried four decks and 15,653 yards of canvas spread over four masts. She was the largest and most magnificent wooden sailing vessel ever built.

Unfortunately, *Great Republic* never had an opportunity to achieve her potential. Towed to New York and loaded for her maiden voyage to Liverpool in late 1853, she burned to the waterline during a general fire in the city the day after Christmas. McKay wrote her off as a total loss and collected $455,000 from the underwriters, who sold her as she lay to A. A. Low & Brother. *Great Republic* was subsequently rebuilt, and sailed with a reduced hull and rig for several owners until abandoned after a gale off Bermuda in 1872.

At the time of *Great Republic*'s fire, there were a full dozen new clippers waiting for full holds at New York, along with several older vessels. Earlier that same year, many other clippers had been forced into the despised Pacific nitrate trade, and still others had been transferred to the cotton or lumber trade by their owners just to keep

21, 22 Among the earliest examples of mass marketing, these sailing (or clipper) cards announced the imminent departure of clipper ships. One bears the only known picture of *Snow Squall*; the other advertises McKay's famous clipper *Great Republic*.

them and their crews busy. One of the problems was that overbuilding from Maine to New York had glutted the shipping market and depressed freight rates. The economic depression of the mid-1850s, culminating in the panic of 1857, further drove rates downward to a low of $10/ton. The clippers, with their reduced cargo capacity, suffered accordingly. In addition, the lightly built and heavily sparred vessels incurred high operating costs on account of frequent maintenance and repairs, and the large crews they demanded. These and other factors made the ships uneconomical after only a decade or so of use; by the start of the Civil War most had been broken up or sold.

As early as 1856 some shipowners and builders recognized the writing on the wall and began ordering vessels with greater cargo capacity. An example of these, known as medium clippers, was *King Philip*, built in Maine in 1856 and grounded in 1878. Her remains have recently been identified in the sands of Ocean Beach, California, by archaeologist James P. Delgado of the United States Department of the Interior, who reports that 45 percent of the hull is intact.

Whaling and the Beginning of the End

The clippers were not alone in suffering a decline during this period. All American maritime-related enterprises were affected by the same circumstances to a greater or lesser degree, and with the onset of the Civil War, foreign deepwater trade in American bottoms practically disappeared. Many ships and crews were transferred to naval and army transport service, and fear of the Confederate raiders drove up insurance rates and caused Northern shipowners to sell off or transfer registry of

End of an Era

23 (*right*) The hull of the medium clipper *King Philip* awash in the intertidal zone at Ocean Beach, California, where she beached in 1878. In 1869 and again in 1874, *Philip* was set afire by mutinous crews. After grounding near the Golden Gate in 1878 during a gale, the ill-fated vessel was stripped and the hull was blown up.

24 (*below*) The *Charles W. Morgan*, built in 1841 and preserved at Mystic Seaport in Connecticut, is the only surviving American whaling ship. Between her construction and 1921 the *Morgan* made thirty-seven voyages.

some 1,300 vessels to foreign nations during the war. Many others that remained in deepwater trade were lost or captured, with the New England whaling fleet serving to illustrate the hardest-hit elements of the merchant marine.

Prior to the Civil War, the whaling industry had grown for over a century in size and profits. During that period, New Englanders had embarked upon voyages lasting up to four years in search of the world's largest animal, gradually expanding the hunt from the waters off New England to the Pacific and Arctic Oceans. Fine oil made from boiling whale blubber in tryworks aboard the ships was in great demand world-wide as lamp fuel, a lubricant and a softener for rope-making fibers. Spermaceti, a liquid wax from the brain cases of sperm whales, was used for candles, industrial detergents and fine machine oil. Whalebone found such diverse uses as ladies' corset stays, umbrella ribs and buggy whips, and the carved ivory teeth of the sperm whale were especially prized as gifts for sailors' sweethearts and families. Most valuable of all was ambergris, a substance found only in the stomachs of diseased whales. Used in Europe as a fixative for expensive perfumes, the rare material commanded a price of up to $400/pound.

The industry peaked in 1846 with 736 ships in the business, nearly all originating from ports in southern New England and Long Island Sound. The most prominent whaling port of all was New Bedford, Massachusetts, which as late as 1857 fielded 329 whalers. Although the introduction of coal gas for illumination and the 1859 discovery of petroleum in Pennsylvania threatened to superannuate the industry within a few decades, it was the Civil War which was most responsible for reducing the fleet size.

The first major incident involving the whaling fleet during the Civil War resulted from the Northern blockade of 3,000 miles of southern coastline from Virginia to the

25 (*right*) In 1861 the Union forces sent a fleet of twenty-five obsolete whaling vessels to the South to be deliberately scuttled to block the channels to major Confederate ports. The whaling industry never recovered from this and other losses to the Union cause.

Texas–Mexico border. In 1861 the Federal Navy decided to focus and tighten the blockade by purchasing old ships, loading them with rocks and sinking them at the mouths of Confederate harbors. Accordingly, forty-five ships, mostly laid-up whaling vessels from New Bedford and New London, were purchased and loaded between October and December of that year. The first fleet of twenty-five ships was dispatched to Savannah, Georgia, where a few were sunk; the remainder, which came to be known as the Stone Fleet (or the Rat-Hole Squadron), was diverted to Charleston, South Carolina, anchored and scuttled. Shortly afterward the other fleet was sunk nearby. Unfortunately for the North, the Stone Fleet's sinking deepened rather than blocked the channel to Charleston, prompting Herman Melville's rhyme 'A failure, and complete/Was your Old Stone Fleet'. Moreover, a fleet of considerable postwar potential had been lost.

Many other whalers were lost to Confederate raiders. One group of twelve was captured and burned in mid-1862 by the famous *Alabama* off the Azores, a popular hunting ground. Another fleet of eight New Bedford whalers was captured and burned in the Arctic, out of a total of thirty-eight ships caught by Captain James I. Waddell during a single cruise. Waddell had cleared England in October 1864 aboard *Shenandoah* with the express purpose of destroying the Arctic whaling fleet. Although he was aware that General Lee had surrendered at Appomattox twelve weeks earlier, on the basis of a report that Confederate forces were still active in North Carolina, Waddell burned the whalers and several other prizes on 28 June 1865. This event, the last hostile action of the war, caused Waddell to flee to England for fear that he might be tried as a pirate. Although the dollar value of the catch from the whaling industry remained steady or increased in the postwar years, the fleet never recovered.

Down-Easters: The Last American Square-Riggers

The rest of the American merchant marine was similarly affected. In 1860, just before the start of the war, American bottoms transported around two-thirds of the nation's foreign imports and exports, but by war's end this figure was less than one-third. The deepwater trade never regained its pre-eminence. Many hundreds of ships were lost, sold or transferred to flags of convenience, and national shipbuilding, naval and labor interests conspired to prevent the transferred vessels from re-adopting the American flag. Moreover, a shortage of skilled shipwrights drove up postwar shipbuilding costs by more than 50 percent, and during the war the British had filled the gaps in the disrupted American trading patterns. Also, led by the British, European shipyards were making the transition from wooden to iron ships at a time when there was a severe shortage in America of iron manufactories and stiff tariffs on essential imported shipbuilding supplies such as copper, iron, hemp and canvas. Finally, European shipyard wages were considerably lower than those in America.

In spite of these problems, there remained one area where American merchant ships competed successfully with foreign rivals on the high seas. This was the trade in grain from the rich farming valleys of California, which produced a hard wheat unaffected by long voyages and in great demand in Europe. A type of ship was developed in northern New England shortly after the Civil War to transport this and other overseas bulk cargoes. Known as 'Down-Easters', these vessels, a late form of the medium clipper, combined the best qualities of the packet and clipper ships, with the full bottoms of the former and the sharp bows of the latter. They averaged 200–300 ft (61–91 m) in length, and although they carried less sail than the Cape Horn clippers, they were nearly as fast and far

26   The hull of the huge Down-Easter *George R. Skolfield* is pounded by the surf shortly after stranding at Ludlum Beach, New Jersey, in 1920. By this time *Skolfield* was schooner-rigged by her owners for economy's sake.

more economical to operate. Insofar as their design was matched so closely to their intended use as bulk cargo carriers, many authorities consider the Down-Easter to be the highest development in the history of the wooden square-rigged sailing ship; it remained a practical and profitable alternative to the Clyde-built iron ship in the grain trade into the late 1880s. However, the march of progress was inevitable: the steamship and lighter iron- and steel-hulled sailing vessel combined to sweep the traditional wooden windship from the international deepwater trade by the turn of the century. The Down-Easter, the last and finest manifestation of that millennia-old tradition, lasted another decade or two into the twentieth century along the Pacific Coast, transporting lumber, coal and Hawaiian sugar and servicing the seasonal Alaska salmon industry.

The 'George R. Skolfield'. One of the last true Down-Easters was the *George R. Skolfield*, built in 1885 at the Skolfield Brothers yard in Brunswick, Maine, and named after her owner. Measuring 232 ft (71 m) in length and 1,645 registered tons, *Skolfield* was the last and largest vessel built by this family of shipowners and builders. The huge wooden square-rigger celebrated her maiden voyage by circumnavigating the globe eastward to China, San Francisco and Liverpool. For the next fifteen years she worked Pacific ports primarily in India and the Far East, acquiring the reputation of being a reliable, if somewhat slow, sailer.

In 1900 *Skolfield* was sold to the Seaboard Transportation Company of New York, which converted her to a schooner rig for economy's sake. She was used as a coastal barge for bulk cargoes until 5 February 1920, when she

27   This panoramic photograph of Casco Bay, Maine, taken around 1902, shows a remarkable cross-section of coastal sailing vessels, including two-, three-, four-, five- and six-masted schooners.

28 The only seven-masted schooner ever built was the *Thomas W. Lawson*, which sank in the Scilly Isles on her maiden transatlantic voyage in 1907.

grounded near the beach at Sea Isle, New Jersey. Although the crew was rescued, *Skolfield* could not be salvaged, and she broke up several years later during a storm.

In 1971, after more than half a century, another storm revealed wooden remains to local resident and amateur historian Susan Langston. Mr J. Richard Steffy, accompanying his associate George Bass, then of the University of Pennsylvania, confirmed the hulk's probable date and type; after several months of intensive research Langston was able to identify the remains as those of the *George R. Skolfield*. Her investigations also uncovered the vessel's figurehead at the Mariners' Museum in Newport News, Virginia, several photographs documenting the ship's career and loss, and the original builder's half-hull model and logbook in the possession of a Skolfield family member in Brunswick, Maine.

Langston's research resulted in the acquisition of the 10-ton section of hull by the Maine Maritime Museum in Bath in 1973. The remains have been integrated into an exhibition on Maine shipbuilding at the Percy and Small Shipyard, and the museum has also mounted an exhibit devoted to the Skolfields and their contribution to the local shipbuilding industry. Although comparatively little remains of *Skolfield*'s hull, her hand-hewn and wedged treenails and sawn frames graphically document the final days of American wooden square-riggers.

The End of the Century

In spite of the disappearance of the American deepwater sailing vessel in the latter half of the nineteenth century,

the nation's coastal shipping industry continued to thrive under governmental protection from foreign competition. Among sailing vessels, the economical wooden schooner remained the rig of choice, with the tern, or three-master, enjoying the most widespread use on both coasts. They were especially practical for tramping bulk cargoes of lumber, lime, coal, building brick and stone, grain, flour, sugar and oil from their sources to urban industrial centers along the coast. When the tern schooner reached its practical size limit of around 800 tons, shipbuilders responded by enlarging the hulls even further and adding extra masts; the first specially designed four-master appeared in 1880 and the first five-master in 1888. In the early 1880s, the use of steam donkey engines for operating the running rigging aboard these large vessels also became commonplace. Although this development was humane, labor-saving and economical, it also allowed shipowners to hire smaller and less experienced crews to man the schooners, which were growing larger and harder of handling. The first of a total of ten six-masted schooners slid down the ways in 1900, and two years later the world's only seven-master, *Thomas W. Lawson*, followed.

The dangers of these gigantic coasters is perhaps best illustrated by the fleet of fifteen multi-masters owned and managed by William F. Palmer around the turn of the century. Palmer, a mathematics teacher and high school principal, entered the shipping business in his early forties after teaching himself naval architecture. Beginning in 1900, he amassed the largest fleet in New England of successful and profitable colliers, thirteen of which he designed himself. However, over the fleet's lifetime, only one of his schooners, *Rebecca Palmer*, had a peaceful end. Six others sank or were abandoned at sea; four were wrecked along the coast; two collided with steamships; one burned at sea, and one was torpedoed during World War I.

Thomas W. Lawson fared no better. Built of steel and launched at Quincy, Massachusetts, in 1902, she measured 375.6 ft (114 m) in length and 5,218 gross tons, with a length-to-beam ratio of 7.5:1. On her maiden voyage she ran aground even though only partly loaded, establishing a pattern she was to follow. *Lawson* was so large, deep and crank that even her designer, B. B. Crowninshield, was forced to admit that 'tacking . . . was sometimes difficult and occasionally impossible'. Uneconomical as a collier, *Lawson* was converted to an oil tanker. On her maiden transatlantic voyage, heavily laden with oil, she carried a crew of only seventeen officers and men, in marked contrast with her mid-nineteenth-century predecessors. Near the Scilly Isles she encountered back-to-back gales and, unable to wear ship or tack, was wrecked on 13 December 1907 with the loss of all but two of her crew.

Combining economy with impracticality, the immense multi-masted schooners were the last widespread manifestation of American working sail. Relegated to a tramp's life, they transported only slow-moving and less valuable bulk cargoes along the coast, where local and regional steamship lines had long since taken the most valuable passenger and freight business away from the sailing ship.

But just as the steamboat eclipsed the sailing ship in the late nineteenth century, so too was it superseded for all but local or specialized applications by alternate means of transportation. Foremost among these was the railroad, which by 1869 had crossed the North American continent, not only offering competing rates for transporting passengers and cargo, but also consuming most of the limited output of the nation's engine, boiler, steel and iron manufacturers. During a period when the entire country was beginning to look inland rather than to the sea for economic prosperity, the overall effect was to increase the British advantage in the production of iron and steel steamships.

By the opening years of the twentieth century, large, efficient and heavily subsidized British firms were operating dozens of steamships capable of five-day passages over the Atlantic. The challenge of competition for the coveted Blue Riband of the Atlantic for the fastest voyage by a steamer was answered only by the Germans and French until midway into the present century.

In the present century, aside from brief increases during the world wars, the American merchant marine has been practically non-existent due to high labor and operating costs. Nearly all the world's deepwater bulk cargoes are transported by immense, highly efficient supertankers and containerized freighters registered under various flags of convenience for tax and insurance purposes. Many of these colossal ships, the largest moving objects ever created by mankind, are too large to enter even the deepest ports. Instead, they load and discharge cargo at distant offshore terminals, spending their entire working lives out of sight of land. Once the foreign products reach our shores, for the most part they are distributed by the trucking and railroad industries.

It is perhaps ironic to consider that, in this age of conservation of natural resources, there is a movement in the shipping industry toward the development of auxiliary sail for large engine-powered ships. Successful experiments indicate that multiple rigid-wing sails controlled by computers from a ship's bridge could save up to 30 percent of a vessel's operating costs under certain conditions, without increasing crew size. Should this development find practical application, it is possible that the Age of Sail may enjoy a renaissance, and once again we might see forests of masts crowding our waters.

Epilog

George F. Bass and W. F. Searle

What does the future hold for ship and boat archaeology in the Americas?

Allow two veteran divers – one with a background in nautical archaeology and the other in navy and commercial salvage and wreck clearance – to close this book by speculating on the answer.

There is no question that there are and will be many sites for future study. 'Statistics for the eighteenth and nineteenth centuries', states Willard Bascom in *Deep Water, Ancient Ships*, 'indicate that approximately 40 percent of all wooden sailing ships ended their careers by running onto reefs, rocks, or beaches made of rock, sand, or coral.' Another 10 to 20 percent, Bascom estimates, sank offshore in deeper water.

Lloyd's List demonstrates that losses at sea remain a daily occurrence. One can add to this the myriad small craft that sink in ponds, lakes and rivers across the continents on any given date.

Although most shipwrecks studied in the near future will be in relatively shallow water, deeper wrecks are in many instances better preserved. Largely as a by-product of military research and development, there already exist the means to locate and inspect even the deepest shipwrecks or, as in the case of the *Breadalbane*, those under Arctic ice.

Breadalbane

In 1846 a British expedition led by Sir John Franklin, looking for the elusive Northwest Passage between the Atlantic and Pacific Oceans, was trapped by Arctic ice while aboard the ships *Erebus* and *Terror*.

When no news had arrived from the explorers by 1847, a series of search teams were dispatched to find the lost men. One team sailed in 1853 aboard the ten-year-old British bark *Breadalbane*. But *Breadalbane* survived the cruel Arctic no better than the ships she sought. She was sunk by ice – fortunately without loss of life.

Breadalbane's crew did not know that they were already too late to rescue Franklin and his men. An 1859 rescue team would find on King William Island skeletons and a written account of the last days of the original, ill-fated

expedition: their ships crushed by the ice, and their leader and two dozen fellow crewmen already dead, the remaining men had abandoned the ships on 22 April 1848. The account stopped only three days later. An Eskimo witness described how the starving men had fallen and died as they walked. In 1984 archaeologists discovered some of the sailors in frozen, shallow graves.

More than a century after the *Breadalbane* went down, a team of modern explorers set out to locate her remains. The problems associated with finding a shipwreck under 6 ft (1.8 m) of ice and 340 ft (100 m) of water were great, but the search, directed by Canadian physician and underwater explorer Joe MacInnis, was successful. In 1980 a Klein Associates sonar, just as on the *Hamilton* in Lake Ontario several years earlier (see Chapter Nine), printed out the ghostly silhouette of a ship still upright on the seabed, her masts standing tall.

Sonar detects wrecks by emitting sound waves and measuring with extreme accuracy the length of time it takes these sound waves to bounce back from the sea or lake bed to the sonar unit. Thus if some obstacle rests on or protrudes from the sea or lake bottom, the sound waves return from it sooner than from the bottom beyond, and this time differential is recorded on a paper chart. Sometimes the obstructions are simply rock outcrops, but as sonar becomes increasingly refined these can be distinguished on the paper from the recognizable shadows of sunken ships – such as the *Breadalbane*.

Three years after *Breadalbane* was found, MacInnis directed a large team, supported by airplanes and a snow tractor, which cut through the Arctic ice on which they were camped and lowered diver Doug Osborne to explore the remarkably preserved ship. Osborne rode in a recent invention, the WASP, a kind of one-person, surface-powered submersible with arms. The team cut another hole, through which yet another invention, a Remotely Piloted Vehicle (RPV), was lowered to enable *National Geographic* photographer Emory Kristof to record both Osborne's work and the wreck. The results show how well isolated Arctic sea water, free of marine borers, can preserve a wooden ship for more than a century.

Frozen Tombs in the Arctic

1, 2   Petty Officer John Torrington, whose deep-frozen corpse (*below right*) lies buried in the permafrost of northern Canada's Beechey Island, was a member of the ill-fated British expedition trying to discover a Northwest Passage in 1846. The *Breadalbane*, sent in search of the lost explorers in 1853, herself was sunk by the ice. A team led by Joe MacInnis tracked down the wreck in 1980 and three years later sent diver Doug Osborne (*right*) to inspect the hull 340 ft (100 m) down in a kind of one-person submersible, the WASP.

But the technology used on *Breadalbane* would not have existed, or been so refined, had it not been for earlier work on more recent and equally tragic catastrophes – not on the sea, but under it and in the sky.

The Beginning of Deep Search and Recovery

Comet. On 10 January 1954 a British Comet jet liner, with twenty-nine passengers and a crew of six, broke apart and dropped from the sky near the Italian island of Elba. The steps taken to discover the cause of the crash were similar to those used today by marine archaeologists (and were used more recently, in 1986, to explain what went wrong with the space shuttle *Challenger* after it fell into the Atlantic Ocean). It was necessary to locate the wreck, raise the pieces, and study them.

Within days of the Comet's loss, British naval vessels were on the scene, searching in 400 ft (120 m) of water. Witnesses to the crash, and reports both from the aircraft which spotted floating wreckage and from Italian sailors who picked up the only recovered bodies, narrowed the search field to an area of about 100 square miles. As with the *Breadalbane*, the first contact with the wreck was by sonar, or, as it is called in Great Britain, ASDIC. In those days, however, underwater television or manned observation capsules used for identifying sonar contacts were simply lowered, or 'dunked', from surface vessels. The only means of moving them through any kind of search pattern was to alter the position of the surface vessel by shortening or lengthening the mooring cables, or otherwise moving her about. The method was inefficient – impossible in high seas – but in this case, it was successful. The underwater television showed the sonar contact to be the Comet.

Once located, the scattered pieces of the Comet were recovered, some by a grab directed from the sea floor by an observer in a watertight capsule, but many trawled up in nets. The urgency of the operation was heightened when, on 8 April of the same year, a second Comet disappeared over the Mediterranean under similar circumstances. In seven months about 70 percent of the first Comet had been recovered. Painstaking reconstruction pointed to the cause of the disaster – metal fatigue – and allowed successful changes in the Comet's design. No attempt was made to recover the second Comet, which sank in water more than half-a-mile deep.

'Thresher'. How far search and recovery techniques advanced in less than a decade was demonstrated by the search for the USS *Thresher*, a 278-ft (85-m) nuclear-propelled attack submarine, lost with her crew of 129 men on 10 April 1963. The submarine was making a test dive about 200 miles off the coast of New England when her surface escort, the Submarine Rescue Ship USS *Skylark*, heard over her underwater, sonar-like communications system sounds of what may have been an attempt to surface, a few garbled words and then silence. Although there was no chance of finding the submarine's crew alive in water $1\frac{1}{2}$ miles deep, a search was immediately initiated. A fleet that grew to three dozen ships, some employing sonar and underwater cameras, was ultimately successful.

This time, however, a new dimension was added. The search was not conducted exclusively from surface vessels. The Navy employed its famous research bathyscaphe *Trieste*, which three years earlier had dived to the deepest part of any sea, almost 7 miles down. In late June, at a depth of 8,400 ft (2,600 m), and with Lieutenant (now Rear Admiral) Brad Mooney at the controls, *Trieste II*'s crew spotted bits and pieces of what seemed to belong to the *Thresher*. In subsequent dives which continued through August, *Trieste II* not only photographed structural parts of the lost submarine, but, with an externally mounted mechanical arm, retrieved among other things several pieces of *Thresher*'s copper nickel piping. These dives led to confident conclusions as to the systems which failed and caused the submarine to be lost, and consequently led to corrective design and shipbuilding techniques.

H-bomb. On 17 January 1966 a mid-air collision between an American strategic bomber and its refuelling tanker caused four unarmed hydrogen bombs to be dropped near Palomares, Spain. Three of the bombs impacted on land and self-destructed in non-nuclear explosions. The only remaining bomb, with its parachute intact, fell well out to sea where it promptly sank in deep water. Even though great strides had recently been made in deep ocean search and recovery techniques, the problems presented by the missing H-bomb severely tested these new capabilities.

Many of the advances were the result of study by the post-*Thresher* Navy-sponsored Deep Submergence Systems Review Group. There were other catalysts, however, than the loss of the *Thresher*. Methods of retrieving tested weapons from the sea floor, as well as mine countermeasures technology after the Korean War, led to the development of underwater robotic equipment systems which could swim down, search out objects on the sea floor and, as necessary, work on them. By the mid-1960s the result of this was the Navy's CURV (Cable-controlled Underwater Research Vehicle), the first successful, work-oriented ROV (Remote Operated Vehicle). CURV was the key to the successful manipulation which led to the recovery of the H-bomb.

A pair of manned research submersibles, *Aluminaut* and *Alvin*, both launched after the *Thresher* tragedy and both capable of diving to greater than 6,000 ft (1,800 m), were instrumental in the search and identification phases, and were critically involved in the recovery phase. Once *Alvin* had located the bomb, *Aluminaut*, with her longer battery life, drew baby-sitting duty and kept the bomb in view while *Alvin* was readied on the surface for a recovery attempt. *Alvin*'s job was to attach lines to the bomb's parachute harness by means of grapnels. But this lifting attempt failed when the bomb, only a short distance off the bottom, broke free and tumbled farther down the submarine canyon in which it had been found. After several stressful days of renewed searching, the errant bomb was relocated at 2,850 ft (870 m). This was frighteningly near the maximum depth to which CURV was limited, but CURV was now given the assignment of rigging the lift lines to the bomb's parachute harness. CURV successfully attached two lift lines. Then, while maneuvering to attach a third line, its propulsion propellers became entangled in the parachute nylon,

presenting a dilemma to the controllers on the surface. In short order the decision was made to carefully lift the entire entanglement – CURV, parachute and bomb. The three were successfully raised to some 60 ft (18 m) below the deck of the lifting platform (Submarine Rescue Ship USS *Petrel*), at which point divers entered the water and attached a heavy lifting strap directly to the bomb, which was hoisted onto the ship's afterdeck. This successful operation had demonstrated for the first time the employment of both manned submersibles and unmanned vehicles in deep ocean recovery.

'Scorpion'. When another nuclear attack submarine, *Scorpion*, was reported missing in 1968, somewhere between the Azores and her destination in Norfolk, Virginia, the U.S. Navy was presented with a far greater challenge. The search area was enormous. The distance between the Azores and Norfolk is nearly 2,500 miles, the depth of water sometimes 4 miles. Both submarines and a fleet of surface vessels were brought into the task which lasted from May through October and involved thousands of men. Eventually the Navy's Oceanographic Research Ship USNS *Mizar*, which had photographed *Thresher* five years earlier, discovered the *Scorpion* nearly 2 miles deep and about 400 miles from the Azores.

The following year *Trieste II* dived with submarine designer/naval architect Captain Harry Jackson on board to inspect the *Scorpion* and evaluate, or at least postulate, the manner in which she was damaged and the reason for her loss. This basic lesson must not be lost on those who explore shipwrecks from submersibles. Just as physicians are called to observe patients for medical diagnoses, those observing historic shipwrecks from submersibles should include people trained to evaluate hull damage, state of preservation and other pertinent factors.

Titanic

The search and survey techniques developed by the Navy in the 1960s and afterward eventually made possible the discovery and inspection of the most famous shipwreck of modern times.

Everyone knows the story of the 'unsinkable' *Titanic*, the largest and most modern ship of her day: How she sank on her maiden voyage in April 1912 after striking an iceberg in calm seas. How radioed pleas for help were unheeded by other ships in the vicinity. How 1,522 lives were lost. As children we learned of cowardice and bravery, of insufficient lifeboats, of dying cries in the night.

Now everyone knows how a joint project from the United States and France, under Dr Robert Ballard of the Woods Hole Oceanographic Institution, and Jean-Louis Michel of the Institut Français de Recherches pour l'Exploitation des Mers, located the ship on 1 September 1985. A video cassette of the expedition became the largest selling television documentary in history, showing the interest the public has in historic shipwrecks.

Final Resting Place of the 'Titanic'

The largest and most modern ship of her day, the *Titanic* struck an iceberg and sank on her maiden voyage in April 1912, 350 miles southwest of Newfoundland. Now, through a triumph of present-day underwater technology, the liner has been located, mapped and explored 2½ miles deep on the ocean floor. But her discovery has created a controversy over salvage, brought to a head in July 1987 when a separate expedition raised more than 300 items from the shattered ship.

3 (*above left*) The U.S. research submersible *Alvin*, rebuilt with a strengthened hull to dive to 13,000 ft (4,000 m), being launched from the support ship *Atlantis II* in 1986, as part of the research expedition led by Robert Ballard of the Wood's Hole Oceanographic Institution.

4 (*center left*) This ghostly image – one of thousands of photographs taken of the wreck – records the edge of the *Titanic*'s bow on the starboard side, with two bollards and railing visible. A 3-ft (1-m) long fish swims over the deck.

5 (*below*) Profile of the *Titanic*. It now appears that when she sank on the night of Sunday 14 April, her hull broke in two, the stern section pivoting round in the opposite direction from the bow. The two halves today lie 1970 ft (600 m) apart on the floor of the Atlantic.

Although not in classical domestic American waters – she lies 350 miles southeast of Newfoundland – *Titanic* was nearing North America when she sank, and her discovery is included here as an example of the use of modern technology in finding an historic wreck so far at sea, 2½ miles down on a mountainous seabed, with conflicting contemporary reports of her last position!

The wreck was spotted by video cameras that are part of *Angus*, an unmanned search system that also carried sonar and other electronic equipment down to just above the ocean floor. The following year, during a second expedition, Ballard and his colleagues inspected and photographed the wreck, inside and out, by means of *Alvin*, now rebuilt with a strengthened hull to dive to 13,000 ft (4,000 m), and *Jason Jr*, a robot tethered to *Alvin* that swam down stairwells to photograph the interior of the rusting giant.

Although no ship designers or naval architects were involved in these submarine inspections of the *Titanic*, the explorers decided that the great vessel had not been sunk, as believed, by a long gash inflicted by the iceberg. It seemed to them, instead, that the ship's riveted plates had simply separated under the blow. More surprising to them was the extensive damage caused by pressure on the hull as it sank. The stern, torn away and turned completely around, lay 600 ft (180 m) from the rest of the ship. All wood had disappeared, although ceramic, glass and other artifacts appeared like new in expedition photographs.

Deep Cargo Salvage

When Searle was a midshipman at Annapolis in the 1940s, the 'deep ocean' commenced at the 100 fathom line, or 600 ft (180 m), leading to the phrase to 'deep six' materials such as code books, crypto wheels and the like, which meant jettisoning them deeper than 100 fathoms, where they were beyond the limits of location and retrieval. It was only after the successful search for and recovery of the H-bomb off Palomares that the jettisoning limits were redefined. But will this redefinition affect marine archaeology in the near future? Now that the deepest and most isolated wrecks can be located and visited – systems under development will soon allow the U.S. Navy to record 98 percent of the ocean bottom – what are the possibilities of actual excavation at depths inaccessible only a generation ago?

It is true that salvage operations have been conducted at appreciable depths for some time. Millions-of-dollars-worth of gold and silver was salvaged in 1932–35 from the wreck of the *Egypt*, sunk 400 ft (122 m) deep in the Bay of Biscay in 1922, and additional millions in gold bars were recovered in 1941 from the *Niagara*, sunk at a similar depth off New Zealand in 1940. In both cases an observer, dangling in a metal chamber over the wreck, directed by telephone the movements of a grab sent down from the surface. And in both cases the salvors simply blasted their way through the ships with explosives. Neither technique could be employed in careful archaeological excavation.

It was the development of self-contained underwater breathing apparatus (SCUBA) that revolutionized underwater archaeology around the world in the middle of the twentieth century, for it gave divers and archaeologists, for the first time, the mobility to do delicate work. Excavations conducted with SCUBA, however, are limited to depths seldom exceeding about 150 ft (46 m). There are two reasons for this. Firstly, nitrogen, which constitutes 80 percent of the air we breathe, becomes narcotic under pressure; at depths much greater than 150 ft, the diver can become confused and disoriented, incapable of careful excavation or even safe diving. Secondly, the deeper one dives and the longer one stays at depth, the greater the length of time it takes to return to the surface without risking the bends, the painful and sometimes fatal illness caused by the formation of bubbles in the bloodstream and body tissues; for the deeper one dives, the greater the pressure of the air one breathes to prevent being crushed by the increasing weight, or pressure, of the water surrounding the diver. The diver avoids the bends by rising slowly to the surface, usually in stages, pausing for certain lengths of time at various depths determined by how deep he or she has been and how long the dive. At each pause, or stage, the diver breathes off more of the pressurized nitrogen in his system. This is called decompression. A twenty-minute dive at 150 ft (46 m), for example, calls for more than eleven minutes of decompression. A one-hour dive at the same depth, however, calls for nearly two hours of decompression, which is totally impractical in any extended diving operation, especially since archaeological teams, for safety, usually decompress much more than is required, often using pure oxygen to hasten the removal of nitrogen from their bodies.

There are methods of overcoming both nitrogen narcosis and the impracticality of inordinately long decompression following each dive. If a diver breathes something other than air, most commonly heliox (a mixture of helium and oxygen rather than the normal nitrogen and oxygen of air), nitrogen narcosis is avoided. Avoiding intolerable decompression periods after extremely long, deep dives, however, is more complex and is dependent on a technique known as saturation diving.

As described above, the deeper one dives and the longer one stays at depth, the more pressurized gas (whether air or heliox) one absorbs into the system, thus necessitating decompression periods of ever-increasing lengths. At some point, however, the diver's body has absorbed all the pressurized gas it can hold. After this saturation point, the length of decompression is not increased, regardless of how much longer the diver stays at depth.

Saturation diving allows divers to live under pressure for days or weeks at a time. Normally they live in pressurized metal chambers aboard surface vessels, and are lowered to the seabed in pressurized capsules from which they can exit and work for several hours. At the end of their work period, they re-enter the capsule, seal its hatch, and are raised back to the surface where the capsule is mated with the deck chamber in which they live. After days or weeks or even months the amount of decompression will be great – several days – but once the diver has become saturated his decompression penalty will not increase.

This was the method used in 1981 to salvage £45 million in Soviet gold bullion from the HMS *Edinburgh*, sunk during World War II in 800 ft (250 m) of water 170 miles north of Murmansk.

Saturation divers may, alternatively, live on the seabed in an underwater habitat, but when they do surface they must still be raised in a pressurized capsule and locked into a deck chamber for the proper period of decompression.

Both approaches to saturation diving have been used on another famous shipwreck.

Andrea Doria

At 11:10 pm on 25 July 1956, 50 miles south of Nantucket Island, the 697-ft (212-m) *Andrea Doria*, pride of Italy's passenger fleet, collided with the Swedish liner *Stockholm* and settled on her starboard side in 240 ft (73 m) of water. Thirty-four people were killed by the collision, but the ship did not stop claiming victims. Because she can be reached by air diving, but only at great risk, she remains especially dangerous.

Immediately following the disaster, divers descended at least to the ship's uppermost structure, 165 ft (50 m) deep, to obtain 'front page' or 'cover' photographs, and these dives were followed by more-or-less 'official investigation dives', during the training for which one diver died while using an unfamiliar mixed-gas breathing system.

In the intervening years since the *Doria* went down there have been numerous diving expeditions to her, both surface-based air dives and at least three expeditions using saturation techniques. Dive-shop gossip has it that freelance divers have hacksawed away a statue of Admiral Doria – leaving the feet welded to the pedestal. (The statue is variously reported to be in a bar room in Norfolk, in a museum in Florida, or elsewhere.) Sport divers, additionally, visited the wreck both for the thrill and for souvenirs. At least two died, and Bass knows a third who was paralyzed by the bends from her 'ultimate dive'.

Clearly, saturation dives were necessary for any reasonably long visits to the ship. Alan Krasberg of Boston was the first when he used a two-man, towable, winch-itself-down underwater habitat in a 1968 'salvage' attempt.

'The habitat', Krasberg wrote to Searle in July 1987, 'was intended to be attached via a winch and wire rope to a locked toggle through a porthole near the promenade deck thru-way. Diver gas was carried on board.'

Luck was against Krasberg. Day after day high seas prevented his team from placing the toggle, and a diver/photographer for a news magazine almost died from what must have been an air embolism, requiring immediate treatment in the expedition's combination habitat-decompression chamber. 'The next day the sea was flat calm at last', Krasberg continued, 'but we were now on our way back to shore with the man in the chamber.'

'All I have to show for it', he added by telephone, 'is half of one porthole and a sign from the ship that says "Men's Room".'

Nearly two decades later, saturation diving of the type used in offshore oil work allowed a team led by the late Peter Gimbel and his wife Elga Anderson to actually explore the *Doria*'s interior. Gimbel had dived on the wreck the day after she went down, when he was only twenty-eight years old, not knowing that his curiosity about the tragedy would become an obsession to which he devoted much of the second half of his life. In 1985, with hundreds of tons of diving equipment mounted on an offshore supply vessel moored to four 3-ton anchors, Gimbel's divers remained under pressure for a month, lowered each day to the wreck in a 4-ton steel bell from which, attached to umbilicals bringing air and warmth, they cut a hole in the hulk and swam inside. Although not an archaeological project, Gimbel's curiosity was the same kind of curiosity that drives the archaeologist. Did this virtually 'unsinkable' ocean liner truly go down because a crucial watertight door had been left open? Gimbel's well-organized and fully manned expedition confirmed that the door was open, but a 65-ft (19-m) gash he found in the *Doria*'s hull made the question more or less academic, thus confirming the post-accident inquiries in the federal court in New York, as well as in the London insurance community.

Were rumors of fortunes stored in two of the *Doria*'s safes true? The safe Gimbel raised contained paper money and certificates, but not the rumored fortune. Bass cannot believe, however, that Gimbel thought he could recoup from those safes the costs of the expedition he mounted. He is convinced it was a mixture of curiosity and challenge that pushed Gimbel on.

Shipwrecks and Society

Shipwrecks in American waters can now, regardless of depth or temperature, be located and partly or completely recovered. This has led to intense interest in what happens to them, as shown by a sheaf of contemporary clippings sent by Searle to Bass:

'Divers Hope to Hoist Ship's Safe Tomorrow' (*Post-Intelligencer*, Seattle, Washington, 31 July 1987) and 'Ship Salvage Plan Draws Protest' (*The Daily News*, Longview, Washington, 27 July 1987), concerning objections by the Underwater Archaeological Society of British Columbia to a salvage team's plans to recover $10 million in valuables from the *Governor* which sank in U.S. waters in 1921 with loss of life. 'Treasure Hunters Ordered Not to Damage Coral Reef' (*The Houston Post*, 25 July 1987): 'A federal judge refused Friday to allow a group of treasure hunters to tunnel into an already damaged Gulf of Mexico

Last Moments of a Luxury Liner

6, 7 On 25 July 1956, eleven hours after colliding with another liner, the *Andrea Doria* sank (*right*) 50 miles south of Nantucket Island. Thirty-four people died, and the wreck continues to claim victims as divers chance their luck on the ship, whose uppermost structure lies at 165 ft (50 m). In 1985 a saturation-diving team explored the *Doria*'s interior and brought up the ship's safe (*below*) containing paper money but not the rumored fortune.

Death of a Battleship

8, 9 Over 1,000 sailors lost their lives in the sinking of the battleship USS *Arizona* (*far right*) at Pearl Harbor on 7 December 1941. The great ship now serves as a national memorial, and is protected on the harbor bottom (*below right*) as a National Park.

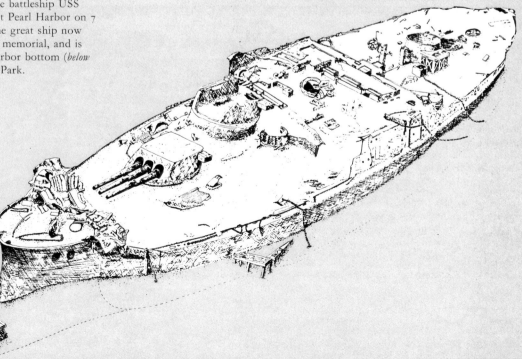

coral reef in search of a sunken Spanish galleon that purportedly carried $100 million in gold and other valuables.' 'Salvors Vie for Sunken Treasure off [*sic*] Central America' (*The Virginian-Pilot*, 9 July 1987), 'Treasure Hunters Claim $450 Million Shipwreck' (*Washington Post*, 18 July 1987), and 'Ship Defies Court Order, Hunts Sunken Treasure' (*The Virginian-Pilot and the Ledger-Star*, 18 July 1987), all concerning the 1857 wreck of the sidewheel steamer *Central America*, lost during a hurricane on a voyage from Havana to New York. 'Controversial Titanic Expedition Delayed by Bad Weather, Intention to Salvage Artifacts from Wreck Called "Grave-Robbing"' (*Washington Post*, 25 July 1987) and, later, 'Inquiry On Titanic Jewels: Descendant of Victim May Claim Satchel' (*Washington Post*, 3 September 1987), the last raising insurance and other questions that eventually must be decided by courts of law.

The *Titanic*, especially, has roused strong emotions over the question of 'to-touch' or 'not-to-touch'. A bill was even introduced into the United States Senate that would have prevented import into the United States of any of the artifacts being raised from the vessel. But this is not an archaeological matter. The *Titanic* is no more an archaeological site than is the *Andrea Doria*, yet there have been no outcries about disturbing the latter. It is said that the *Titanic* should not be disturbed because lives were lost during her sinking, but such reasoning would put both salvors and nautical archaeologists out of business around the world. Presumably, then, the rationale for leaving the *Titanic* undisturbed is the same as that which led to the raising of private funds to save and restore New York's famed Carnegie Hall when it was destined to be torn down: some structures are simply so venerable that a sufficient segment of society wants them left intact for posterity.

Such respect for certain noteworthy vessels is warranted, regardless of their archaeological value. An example is the USS *Arizona*, sunk during the Japanese attack on Pearl Harbor in Honolulu on 7 December 1941. Three battleships – *West Virginia*, *Oklahoma* and *Arizona* – were sunk by dive bombers, fighters and torpedo planes that day, but the single greatest disaster was the loss of the USS *Arizona* with 1,102 sailors on board. Now protected as a National Park, the USS *Arizona* National Memorial includes a concrete and steel structure which spans the ship's remains as they lie on the bottom of Pearl Harbor. The park attracts over a million visitors annually.

Certainly not all World War II wrecks should become national monuments. The debate over historic preservation on land – Are we saving too much? Are we saving the right things? – must include historic preservation under water. It would seem wrong to allocate large sums for the preservation of one ship simply because she lies on the ocean floor, when an identical sister ship, rotting at her moorings, might legitimately and ethically be cut up and sold for scrap. Yet some preservationists seem still not to recognize this double standard.

With tens or even hundreds of thousands of wrecks in the Americas, the public may believe that this debate over what to save may be postponed, but such is not the case. Although only a fraction of existing wrecks warrant archaeological excavation, it is exactly that fraction – wrecks of historical importance, or those rich in artifacts – that attract treasure-hunters who are not motivated by the desire to recover and restore the past of the Americas. As pointed out in Chapter Three, all the known wrecks of the Age of Exploration were damaged by modern looters before archaeologists reached them.

An example of a wreck that *does* warrant scientific examination is the British frigate *Hussar*. At 3 pm on 23 November 1780 she struck Pot Rock in the gauntlet of reefs called Hell Gate in New York's East River, and finally sank at 7 pm several miles upstream in the Bay of Brothers at a depth of 42 ft (12.8 m). Some $3 million in gold specie had supposedly been boxed and stored earlier beneath the ballast of the *Hussar* by a few trusted British tars; a new crew had then been recruited and only two officers notified of the existence of the gold. At Wallabout Bay in New York Harbor the *Hussar* was said to have taken on seventy American prisoners and an additional $1.8 million in gold from the backup ship *Mercury*, before sailing up the East River.

After over 200 years and a score of treasure-hunting expeditions the mysteries of the *Hussar* remain unsolved: Did she have gold aboard at all, or was it transferred to the *Mercury*? If she took four hours to sink, did she tie up and unload the gold? Why, in those four hours, did not the 107 men reported lost save themselves, and why in that time were the American prisoners not released? The answers to these questions will be found only when a proper archaeological expedition is mounted at the Bay of Brothers.

Society must decide, then, which wrecks should be protected from commercial exploitation, just as society protects certain structures on land while others of equal vintage are razed. In some cases this is easy. We would not allow an entrepreneur to dismantle either Mount Vernon or the Alamo for private gain. Why, then, should a diver be allowed to dismantle one of Columbus' or La Salle's ships to sell or own for personal benefit? Some historic wrecks should be preserved through excavation and conservation; others should be preserved under water for the pleasure of future generations of visiting divers.

Society must also decide the cost it will bear in order to learn about and preserve the past. In the near future, new knowledge will continue to come from relatively shallow or even underground wrecks. Will archaeology be able to take advantage of the new technologies to search and work deeper? Only the tiniest fraction of the millions spent on the H-bomb search would ever be available for seeking an archaeological site under similar conditions. The United States was willing to pay the necessary millions of dollars for the *Titanic* search primarily because it provided a test of equipment with potential military value. The cost of saturation diving on HMS *Edinburgh* was more than offset by the value of gold recovered.

Archaeologists will not come by such vast sums in their search for knowledge. Should deep wrecks then be left to entrepreneurs who might pay for their recovery through sales of artifacts? Or should they be saved for the future, when new techniques could lower costs of working at great depth?

Education must play a role in the study of whichever wrecks do warrant archaeological study. Although often commendable, some of the pioneering research described in this book was conducted by divers with only a smattering of historical knowledge, or by archaeologists with scant familiarity with ship design.

Nautical archaeology remains an infant branch of archaeology, however, and most projects described in the preceding chapters were conducted only within the past two decades. Meanwhile, the number of archaeologists capable of excavating and interpreting both land and underwater sites is growing, as evidenced by the authors of those chapters.

Over the years Bass' teams have learned, both in the Mediterranean and in the Caribbean, that for every month of diving, two years must be spent on the conservation of excavated artifacts, including entire hulls; on the cataloging, drawing and photographing of these finds; on library, archival and museum research; and on interpreting and publishing the discoveries. The nautical archaeologist need not be expert in every phase of this research, but must have sufficient training to choose and evaluate able assistants and colleagues in each area. And he or she must remember that the cost of conservation and restoration in true archaeological work usually exceeds the cost of diving, even on wrecks more than 150 ft (46 m) deep.

Humans being fallible, mistakes will be made in the attempt to draw distinctions between wrecks of social or historic significance and those of more commercial value. 'Significance' is in the eye of the beholder. Yet the public has agreed that looters should not be allowed to bulldoze any native American mounds for pottery to sell. The public should come to see historic monuments under water simply as historic monuments.

At the same time the public, and especially the news media, must recognize the difference between those who excavate historic ships for knowledge and those who recover them solely for monetary gain. The press too quickly bestows the title 'underwater archaeologist' on any diver who raises artifacts from the deep. There is a long and honorable tradition of salvage at sea, but it must not be confused with archaeology. Nor should legitimate salvors be confused with plunderers and pirates, as U.S. statute makes clear:

> Whoever plunders, steals, or destroys any money, goods, merchandise, or other effects from or belonging to any vessel in distress, or wrecked, lost, stranded, or cast away, upon the sea, or upon any reef, shoal, bank or rocks of the sea, or in any other place within the admiralty and maritime jurisdiction of the United States, shall be fined not more than $5,000 or imprisoned not more than ten years, or both. (18 U.S. Code 1658).

In the debate over historic shipwrecks, care must be given to truth. Bass has published a list of more than a dozen myths spread by treasure-hunters in order to justify their often destructive work: that they are 'saving' the wrecks from future storms; that they do not need to record or preserve the hulls they destroy while searching for treasure because detailed plans of galleons and other early ships exist in Spanish archives; that hulls in the New World are not as well preserved as those in the Mediterranean and thus deserve no special care; that the only way to pay for underwater survey and excavation is through the sale of artifacts; that duplicate artifacts have no archaeological value; that the only incentive for looking for and excavating early shipwrecks is monetary gain. Perhaps this book will put some of the myths to rest.

The quest for history is as exciting as any search for treasure. It is a quest that benefits us all. It is a quest that has begun in earnest in the waters of the Americas. It is a quest that will continue as long as we care about our past.

Glossary

aft toward the stern of a vessel

amidships middle portion of a ship lengthwise or crossways

athwartships from one side of a ship to the other; at right angles to the keel

ballast heavy material in a ship's hold to lower her center of gravity and provide greater stability when she carries little or no cargo

bateau (batteau) flat-bottomed double-ended boat

batten strip of wood used in shipbuilding to reproduce the curves of a vessel's hull

beakhead ship's head forward of the forecastle, forming a small deck over the stem

beam maximum width of a vessel; a horizontal transverse timber forming part of a ship's structure

bergantín a brig (Spanish)

bilge bottom of a ship's hull

bonaventure mizzen second mizzenmast on four-masters

boom spar to which is attached the foot of a fore-and-aft sail

bow forward part of a ship's side, from the point where the planks curve inwards to where they meet at the stem

bower anchor anchor permanently attached to a cable and stowed in the bow ready for use

bowsprit spar projecting forward of a sailing ship's stem

brace rope attached to the boom or yard of a sail, used to control its position; a metal strap used to strengthen the framework of a ship

brig two-masted square-rigger

brigantine two-masted sailing ship, rigged square on the foremast and fore-and-aft with square topsails on the mainmast

bulkhead vertical partition dividing a ship into sections

bulwarks sides of a vessel above the upper deck

buttresses short timbers placed on either side of the keelson and mast step to provide lateral support for the step

caprail timber atop the side planking of a vessel

caravel two- or three-masted sailing ship with broad beam, high poop-deck and lateen rig; used by Spanish and Portuguese in 15th and 16th centuries

carrack round-sterned merchant ship with distinctive triangular bow used in the Mediterranean in the 15th and 16th centuries

carvel-built having the planks all flush from keel to gunwale

carvel planking smooth seamed planking

castle tower or defensive post on the deck of a ship

caulk to stop up the seams between planks

ceiling internal planking of a ship's hull

chine angle at which the side and bottom of a hull join

cleat short projections of wood or metal, used for a variety of purposes

clench bending over and pounding down a bolt or nail

clinker-built said of a vessel whose planks run fore and aft, with the lower edge of one plank overlapping the upper edge of the plank below

clipper fast sailing ship with concave bow, fine lines and raked masts

close to the wind sailing as nearly as possible towards the compass point from which the wind is blowing

composite ship wooden ship with iron or steel framing

deadeye round or pear-shaped wooden block pierced by several holes, used mainly to secure the standing rigging

deadwood blocks of timber attached to top of keel to fill out narrow spaces in hull

dhow lateen-rigged Arab vessel with one or two masts, usually raked

Down-Easter large wooden square-rigger built on the coast of Maine in the late 19th century

draft (draught) the depth of water displaced by a vessel

dunnage brushwood or other material used to protect cargo

fairlead any fixture which leads a rope in the required direction

filler short plank set between frames on the outboard edge of the ceiling to close the gap between frames

flukes triangular extensions to the arms of an anchor

fore in the forward part of a vessel; towards the stem

fore-and-aft rig sails fitted in a fore-and-aft direction and secured on their forward side to a stay or mast

forecastle the raised, forward part of the upper deck, extending from the beakhead to the foremast or just aft of it; the seamen's quarters in a merchant ship

forelock bolt a bolt with a head at one end and, at the other, a slot through which a metal pin or key is thrust to lock the bolt in place

foremast forward mast in a vessel with two or more masts

frames athwartship timbers forming the internal skeleton of a ship

freeboard distance from the waterline up to the rail or gunwale

frigate medium-size square-rigged warship of the 17th through 19th centuries

futtock one of several members joined to form a frame

gaff spar used along the head of a fore-and-aft sail

galleon large sailing ship with three or more masts, lateen-rigged on the after masts and square-rigged on the foremast and mainmast; used as a warship or merchant ship in the 15th through 18th centuries

galley oared warship or merchant ship also propelled by sails

garboard first range of planks above a ship's keel

gondola large, flat-bottomed river or lake barge much like a bateau

gudgeon metal strap with eye, bolted to the sternpost to hold rudder pintle

gunboat a small, shallow-draft armed vessel

gunwale the upper edge of a ship's side

half-deck a deck above the main deck which does not continue the whole length of the vessel

halyard rope or tackle used for hoisting or lowering sails and a vessel's other top gear

hawse-hole hole in bow through which anchor cable passes

hawser a mooring rope or cable

heel knee timber connecting the keel to the sternpost

helm the apparatus by which the ship is steered, consisting of the rudder and a tiller or steering wheel

hogging the result of stress on a ship's hull making her droop at stem and stern while her middle arches

hogging truss a cable running fore and aft, to prevent hogging

ironclad a 19th-century warship sheathed with iron or steel plates

kayak a canoe made of skins stretched over and covering a wooden framework, except for an opening on top for the paddler

keel the lowest longitudinal timber, forming the backbone of a ship

keelson longitudinal timber of a ship, fixed above the frames and to the keel

knarr broad-beamed Viking cargo vessel

knee a piece of timber having an angular bend, used to join two perpendicular members

lapstrake *see* clinker-built

lateen sail a triangular sail extended by a long tapering yard the lower end of which is brought down to the deck

leeward away from the wind; on the side sheltered from the wind

lighter boat used in port for transporting cargo between ship and quay

limber boards ceiling planks which can be removed for cleaning the bilges

mainmast principal mast; chief mast in two-masted vessel; center mast in a three-masted vessel; second mast from stem in others

man-o'-war warship

mast cap two-hole fitting which holds an upper mast in one hole against the top of a lower mast which fits in the other hole

mast partner fitment at deck level to provide additional support for a mast

mast step socket for the heel of a mast; an attachment for fastening the lower end of a ship's mast to the hull

mastercouple the midship frame, usually at the widest part of a vessel

mizzenmast the mast directly aft of the mainmast

mold mark raised line of metal left on shot at the juncture of the two halves of the shot mold

nao merchant ship carrying square fore-, main- and sprit-sails and a lateen sail on its mizzenmast

orlop deck lowest deck in a warship, laid over the beams of the hold

packet 18th-century vessels named after the packets of mail they carried, but from 1818 merchant ships with regular schedules over fixed routes

parral collar by which a yard is fastened to the mast

parral beads wooden beads strung together to facilitate the smooth movement of a parral

pinnace open, general-service vessel propelled by oars or sails

pintle vertical bolt at the back of the rudder which fits into a gudgeon on the sternpost to form a hinge

privateer a privately owned warship under license to the government

prow pointed forward end of a ship

rabbet deep groove or channel cut into a piece of timber to receive the edge of a plank

ribs curved frame-timbers of a ship, to which the sideplanking is nailed

rigging system of ropes used to support the masts and operate the sails

rove small plate or ring on which the point of a nail or rivet is beaten down

row galley early 19th-century term for small oar- and sail-powered warships

rubbing strakes heavy protective side timbers on a ship

scantlings dimensions of any piece of timber used in shipbuilding

scarf lapped joint connecting two timbers or planks

schooner sailing vessel with two or more masts, with all lower sails rigged fore-and-aft

shank shaft forming the principal part of an anchor, connecting the arms to the stock

sheave the wheel of a block

sheet rope controlling the after (lower) corner(s) of a sail

ship-of-the-line warship mounting 50 or more guns

shrouds heavy ropes that brace the mast athwartships

sloop originally a small, single-masted vessel rigged fore and aft with a jib, mainsail and sometimes topsails and staysails; also a war vessel, larger than a gunboat, with guns mounted on a single deck

snag submerged tree stump or branch dangerous to navigation

snag boat steamboat designed to remove snags

spar rounded length of timber such as a yard, gaff or boom

spike heavy nail

sponson structure projecting over the side of a vessel

spritsail small auxiliary sail at the forward end of a ship

sprue mark mark left on cast object where the metal column formed in the entry canal to the mold has been removed

square-rigged said of a vessel rigged with square sails

square-sail four-cornered sail set on a yard athwartships

stays strong ropes to support the mast fore and aft

steamship ship propelled by a steam engine

stem timber forming the front extremity of a vessel

stern rear end of a vessel

sternpost timber at the extreme rear end of a vessel and extending from the keel to deck level or above

stock heavy cross-bar of an anchor

strake one row of planking on the side or bottom of a ship

stringer heavy inside strake secured to the frames

tack forward lower part of a sail

thole wooden or metal pin or peg inserted singly or in pairs in a vessel's gunwale to hold and guide an oar

thwart cross seat in an open boat

tiller lever for controlling a ship's rudder or steering gear

tompion object, usually wooden, placed in the

mouth of a breech chamber to keep the powder dry, or in a gun's muzzle to protect it from corrosion

transom athwartship timber attached to the sternpost

treenail cylindrical wooden fastening

trunnel colloquial term for treenail; also trennel

tryworks place for rendering, or melting out, fat or blubber

tumblehome the sloping-in of a vessel's topsides above the point of greatest width

umiak large open boat made of skins stretched on a wooden framework

wales horizontal planks heavier than the rest, extending along the whole of a ship's sides

yard horizontal athwartships spar fitted to the forward side of the mast, to support square sails

Brief Guide to Museums and Research Institutes

GENERAL

Calvert Marine Museum
P.O. Box 97, Solomons, MD 20688
Chesapeake Bay Maritime Museum
St Michaels, MD 21663
Columbia River Maritime Museum
Astoria, OR 97103
The Great Lakes Historical Society
480 Main St, Vermilion, OH 44089
Maine Maritime Museum
963 Washington St, Bath, ME 04530
The Mariners' Museum
Newport News, VA 23606
M.I.T. Museum and Historical Collection
Hart Nautical Collection, 265 Massachusetts Avenue, Cambridge, MA 02139
Peabody Museum of Salem
East India Marine Hall, Salem, MA 01970
Philadelphia Maritime Museum
321 Chestnut St, Philadelphia, PA 19106
The Smithsonian Institution
National Museum of American History, Washington, D.C. 20560
Vancouver Maritime Museum
1905 Ogden St, Vancouver, British Columbia, V6J 3J9 Canada

CHAPTER ONE

The Cleveland Museum of Natural History
Wade Oval, University Circle, Cleveland, OH 44106
For Ringler dugout canoe
Museo Nacional de Antropología e Historia
Paseo de la Reforma y Ghandi, Mexico 5, D.F., Mexico
For Aztec dugout canoe

CHAPTER TWO

Comision de Rescate Arqueologico Submarino
Museo de las Casas Reales, Calle las Damas Esq. Mercedes, Santo Domingo, Dominican Republic
Responsible for underwater archaeology

CHAPTER THREE

Armed Forces History Collection
National Museum of American History, The Smithsonian Institution, Washington, D.C. 20560
Houses artifacts from the Highborn Cay wreck
The CEDAM Museum
Xelha, Quintana Roo, Mexico
Displays artifacts from the Bahia Mujeres wreck
Departmento del Arqueologia Subacuatica
Museo Nacional de Antropología e Historia, Paseo de la Reforma y Ghandi, Mexico 5, D.F., Mexico
Responsible for shipwreck archaeology in Mexico

Institute of Nautical Archaeology
P.O. Drawer HG, College Station, TX 77841
Conducts research on ships of exploration
The Mariners' Museum
Newport News, VA 23606
Houses artifacts from the Highborn Cay wreck

CHAPTER FOUR

Basque Whaler Project
Department of Indian and Northern Affairs, 1600 Liverpool Court, Ottawa, Ontario K1A OH4, Canada
Conducts Red Bay research

CHAPTER FIVE

Archaeological Research
Division of Historical Resources, Florida Department of State, R. A. Gray Building, Tallahassee, FL 32399-0250
Supervises shipwreck archaeology
Bermuda Maritime Museum
P.O. Box 273, Somerset, Bermuda
For 'San Pedro' and 'San Antonio'
Corpus Christi Museum
1900 North Chaparral, Corpus Christi, TX 78041
For remains of Padre Island wrecks
McLarty State Museum
Sebastian Inlet State Park, Sebastian, FL
For 1715 Spanish plate fleet
Museo de las Casas Reales
Calle las Damas Esq. Mercedes, Santo Domingo, Dominican Republic
For remains of 'Concepcion', 'Tolosa', and 'Guadalupe'
Museo Regional
Campeche, Mexico
For Cayo Nuevo shipwreck
Museo Servicio do Documentacao do Geral da Marinha
Rio de Janeiro, Brazil
For 'Sacramento'
Museum of Florida History
R. A. Gray Building, Tallahassee, FL
For 1715 Spanish plate fleet
St Lucie County Historical Museum
Ft Pierce, FL
For 1715 Spanish plate fleet
Treasure Salvors, Inc. Museum
Key West, FL
For 'Nuestra Señora de Atocha'

CHAPTER SIX

Bermuda Maritime Museum
P.O. Box 273, Somerset, Bermuda
For artifacts from 'Sea Venture'

Jamestown Festival Park
P.O. Drawer JF, Williamsburg, VA 23187
For replicas of 'Susan Constant', 'Godspeed' and 'Discovery'
The Mariners' Museum
Newport News, VA 23606
For remains of Ronson ship
Philadelphia Maritime Museum
321 Chestnut Street, Philadelphia, PA 19106
Pilgrim Hall Museum
75 Court St, Plymouth, MA 02360
For hull remains of 'Sparrow Hawk'
Plimoth Plantation
P.O. Box 1620, Plymouth, MA 02360
For replicas of 'Mayflower' and shallop
Port Royal Museum
Port Royal, Jamaica
Port Royal Project
Nautical Archaeology Program, Texas A&M University, College Station, TX 77843
Excavates Port Royal and conducts summer field school
South Carolina Institute of Archaeology
University of South Carolina, Columbia, SC 29208
For information about Brown's Ferry wreck and underwater archaeology in the state

CHAPTER SEVEN

Adirondack Museum
Blue Mountain Lake, NY
Displays Lake George bateau
Basin Harbor Maritime Museum
Basin Harbor, VT 05491
Exhibit of Lake Champlain's history; also full-scale replica of Lake George bateau
Champlain Maritime Society
P.O. Box 745, Burlington, VT 05402
Machault Museum
Restigouche, Quebec
Artifacts and hull remains of 'Machault'

CHAPTER EIGHT

Armed Forces History Collection
National Museum of American History, Smithsonian Institution, Washington, D.C. 20560
For 'Philadelphia'
Daughters of the American Revolution Museum
1776 D Street, N.W., Washington, D.C. 20006-5392
For 'Augusta'
Maine State Museum
State House Station 83, Augusta, ME 04333
For artifacts from 'Defence'
The Mariners' Museum
Newport News, VA 23606
For artifacts from York River wrecks
Research Center for Archaeology
Division of Historic Landmarks, Commonwealth of Virginia, P.O. Box 424, Yorktown, VA 23690

Yorktown Visitor Center
Colonial National Historical Park, P.O. Box 210,
Yorktown, VA 23690
For Yorktown wrecks

CHAPTER NINE

Hamilton-Scourge Foundation
71 Main Street, Hamilton, Ontario L8N 3T4,
Canada
Historic Naval and Military Establishments
Huronia Historical Parks, P.O. Box 160, Midland,
Ontario L4R 4K8, Canada
Remains of the 'Tecumseth' and naval slip
Historic Naval and Military Establishments
P.O. Box 1800, -C.P.1800, Penetanguishene,
Ontario LoK 1PO, Canada
Marine Museum of Upper Canada
Toronto Historical Board, Exhibition Place,
Toronto, Ontario M6K 3C3, Canada
Model of the 'Nancy' and other 1812 material
Nancy Island Historic Site
c/o Wasaga Beach Provincial Park, Wasaga Beach,
Ontario, Canada
Remains of 'Nancy'
Sackets Harbor Historic Site
Sackets Harbor, NY
Exhibits describe U.S. Naval base
U.S. Flagship Niagara Museum
Erie, PA
Restored 20-gun brig 'Niagara'
U.S. Frigate Constellation
Constellation Dock, Baltimore, MD 21202
U.S.S. Constitution Museum
Box 1812, Boston, MA 02129
Also displays 18th- and 19th-century shipbuilding

CHAPTER TEN

City Hall
Kaslo, British Columbia, Canada
For 'Moyie' (1898, steam-sternwheel)
Duluth, Missabe & Iron Range Railway Co.
Duluth, MN 55801
For 'Edna G.' (1896, steam-screw)
Historic Ships Unit
Golden Gate National Recreation Area,
2905 Hyde St, San Francisco, CA 94109
For 'Eureka' (side-wheel ferry)
The Howard National Steamboat Museum
1101 E. Market St, Jeffersonville, IN 47130
Models, pictures, shipyard tools
Inland Rivers Library
8th and Vine Streets, Cincinnati, OH 45202
Maine Maritime Museum
963 Washington St, Bath, ME 04530
For 'Seguin' (1884, steam-screw)
The Missouri Historical Society
Jefferson Memorial Building, St Louis, MO 63112

Sons and Daughters of Pioneer Rivermen
89 Park St, Canal Winchester, OH 43110
Steamship Historical Society of America
414 Pelton Avenue, Staten Island, NY 10310
Steamboat Photo Company
121 River Avenue, Sewickley, PA 15143
Vermont State Underwater Historic Preserve
Established over wreck of the 'Phoenix'
Visitor Center, Fish and Wildlife Service
Desoto National Wildlife Refuge, U.S. Department
of the Interior, RR 1, Box 114, Missouri Valley,
IA 51555
For artifacts from 'Bertrand'

CHAPTER ELEVEN

Calvert Marine Museum
P.O. Box 97, Solomons, MD 20688
Caswell Neuse Historic Site
Kingston, NC
Remains of CSS Neuse and associated collection
Confederate Museum
St Georges, Bermuda
*Small collection of artifacts associated with blockade
running*
Confederate Naval Museum
201 4th St, P.O. Box 1022, Columbus, GA 31902
*Displays CSS 'Chattahoochee' and CSS
'Jackson'/'Muscogee'*
The Mariners' Museum
Newport News, VA 23606
*Curates artifacts from USS 'Monitor' National Marine
Sanctuary*
Museum of the Confederacy
Richmond, VA
*Curates artifacts associated with Civil War naval
activities*
National Maritime Museum
Greenwich, England
*Plans of blockade runner 'Ella' and other ships register
documents*
New Hanover County Museum
Wilmington, NC
*Displays of Wilmington and Fort Fisher during Civil
War (dioramas with ship models)*
**North Carolina Division of Archives and
History**
109 E. Jones St, Raleigh, NC
*Curates artifacts from blockade runners with additional
collections at: Fort Fisher State Historic Site, Kure
Beach, NC*
North Carolina Maritime Museum
315 Front St, Beaufort, NC 28516
Program in Maritime History
Department of History, East Carolina University,
Greenville, NC 27843
The Science Museum
South Kensington, London, England
Ericsson patent model of USS 'Monitor's' engine

Vicksburg National Military Park
Box 349, Vicksburg, MS 39180
Displays USS 'Cairo'

CHAPTER TWELVE

Bernice P. Bishop Museum
P.O. Box 19000-A, Honolulu, Hawaii 96819
For 'Falls of Clyde' (1878)
Chesapeake Bay Maritime Museum
P.O. Box 636, St Michaels, MD 21663
For 'Edna E. Lockwood' (1889)
Great Britain Foundation
Great Western Dock, Gas Ferry Road, Bristol,
England
For 'Great Britain' (1843)
The Kendall Whaling Museum
P.O. Box 297, Sharon, MA 02067
Maine Maritime Museum
963 Washington St, Bath, ME 04530
Displays remains of 'George R. Skolfield'
Maritime Museum Association of San Diego
1306 North Harbor Drive, San Diego, CA 92101
For 'Star of India' (1863)
Mystic Seaport Museum
Mystic, CT 06355
*For 'Charles W. Morgan' and whaling history, and other
historic vessels*
National Maritime Museum of San Francisco
Golden Gate National Recreation Area,
San Francisco, CA 94123
For holdings of 'Niantic'
**Old Dartmouth Historical Society Whaling
Museum**
18 Johnny Cake Hill, New Bedford, MA 02740
The Peabody Museum of Salem
East India Square, Salem, MA 01970
Philadelphia Maritime Museum
321 Chestnut St, Philadelphia, PA 19106
Ships of the Sea Museum
503 East River St, Savannah, GA 31401
South Street Seaport Museum
207 Front St, New York, NY 10038
Spring Point Museum
SMVTI, Fort Rd, South Portland, ME 04106
Displays bow of extreme clipper 'Snow Squall'

EPILOG

U.S. Naval Academy Museum
Annapolis, MD 21402
U.S. Navy Memorial Museum
Bldg 76, Washington Navy Yard, Washington,
D.C.
U.S.S. Arizona Memorial Park
Honolulu, Hawaii 96818
Woods Hole Oceanographic Institution
Woods Hole, MA 02543
For information on 'Titanic'

Sources of Quotations

CHAPTER ONE　*p.* 19, *col.* 2, *l.* 23–31:
Columbus, C., *The Journal*, 1960; *p.* 19, *col.* 2, *l.*
40–49: author's trans.; *p.* 20, *col.* 1, *l.* 13–16:
author's trans.; *p.* 20, *col.* 2, *l.* 7–11: author's trans.;
p. 22, *col.* 2, *l.* 28–38: Columbus, F., 1959; *p.* 28, *col.*
1, *l.* 13–22: Benzoni, G., 1858.
CHAPTER TWO　*p.* 33, *col.* 1, *l.* 16–19:
Columbus, C., 1960; *p.* 33, *col.* 2, *l.* 28–29:
Columbus, F., 1959; *p.* 38, *col.* 1, *l.* 40–41:
Columbus, C.; *p.* 40, *col.* 2, *l.* 6–8: ibid.; *p.* 40,
col. 2, *l.* 20–29: Columbus, F., 1959.
CHAPTER SEVEN　*p.* 130, *col.* 2-*l.* 26, *p.* 132,
col. 1, *l.* 4: Kalm, P., 1972; *p.* 132, *col.* 1, *l.* 6–11:
ibid.
CHAPTER EIGHT　*p.* 149, *col.* 1, *l.* 37-*col.* 2, *l.*
13: Oswald, R., 'General Observations Relative to
the Present State of the War, London, August 9,
1779', ff. 63–64, William L. Clements Library,
University of Michigan; *p.* 149, *col.* 2, *l.* 31–*p.* 150,

col. 1, *l.* 16: Germaine, Lord G., to Sir H. Clinton,
Whitehall, 8 March 1778, CO 5/95, ff. 35–49,
Public Record Office, London; *p.* 150, *col.* 1, *l.*
21–23: Oswald, R., op. cit., f. 60; *p.* 150, *col.* 2, *l.*
40–43: *The Whalemen's Shipping List*, New Bedford,
Mass., 30 Nov. 1869; *p.* 163, *col.* 1, *l.* 27–35:
Tucker, St G., 'Diary of the Siege of Yorktown',
William and Mary Quarterly, 3rd series, vol. 5 (1948)
391; *p.* 163, *col.* 2, *l.* 15–26: Thacher, J., *A Military
Journal during the American Revolutionary War, from
1775 to 1783*, Boston, Cottons & Barnard 1827, 283.
CHAPTER NINE　*p.* 183, *col.* 1, *l.* 18–25: U.S.
Archives Record Group 45.
CHAPTER ELEVEN　*p.* 209, *col.* 1, *l.* 7–10:
Selfridge, T., *Memories of Thomas O. Selfridge, Jr.
Rear-Admiral U.S.N.*, New York, Putnam 1924; *p.*
209, *col.* 1, *l.* 14–18: Parker, 1883; *p.* 209, *col.* 1, *l.*
32–*col.* 2, *l.* 6: Greene, S. D., 'An Eyewitness
Account: I Fired the First Gun and Thus

Commenced the Great Battle', *American Heritage* 8,
June 1957; *p.* 214, *col.* 2, *l.* 19–22: Bearss, 1966; *p.*
218, *col.* 1, *l.* 11–16: 'Operations of the North
Atlantic Blockading Squadron from October 28,
1864, to February 1, 1865', in *The Official Records of
the Union and Confederate Navies in the War of the
Rebellion*, Washington D.C. 1894–1922, vol. 11; *p.*
220, *col.* 2, *l.* 21–24: Jones, 1961, vol. 2, 375; *p.* 221,
col. 1, *l.* 26–*col.* 2, *l.* 2: Turner, M., *Navy Gray: A
Story of the Confederate Navy on the Chattahoochee
River*, Confederate Navy Museum, Columbus,
Georgia; *p.* 224, *col.* 2, *l.* 1–2: Burnside, A. E.,
Battles and Leaders of the Civil War, The Century
Press, New York, NY 1887, vol. 1, 663; *p.* 230, *col.*
2, *l.* 3–9: Dahlgren, M. V., *Memoires of John A.
Dahlgren, Rear Admiral United States Navy*, Boston
1882.

Further Reading

Abbreviations
IJNA   *International Journal of Nautical
           Archaeology*
JFA   *Journal of Field Archaeology*
MPMAE   *Memoirs of the Peabody Museum of
           Archaeology and Ethnology*
NG   *National Geographic*

CHAPTER ONE
The Earliest Watercraft

ADNEY, E.T. AND H. I. CHAPELLE, *The Bark Canoes
and Skin Boats of North America*, Smithsonian
Institution, Washington, D.C. 1964.
ASHE, G., 'Analysis of the Legends', in Ashe, G.
(ed.), *The Quest for America*, London 1971, 15–52.
BENSON, E. P. (ed.), *The Sea in the Pre-Columbian
World*, Dumbarton Oaks Research Library and
Collections, Washington, D.C. 1977.
BENZONI, G., *History of the New World by Girolamo
Benzoni of Milan Shewing his Travels in America, from
AD 1541–1556*, ed. and trans. by W. H. Smyth,
Hakluyt Society, London 1858.
BLOM, F., 'Commerce, Trade and Monetary Units of
the Maya', *Middle American Research Series
Publication* 4, Tulane University, New Orleans, LA
1932.
BRAY, W., *The Gold of El Dorado*, London 1978.
BROSE, D. S. and I. GREBER, 'An Archaic Dugout
from Savannah Lake, Ohio', *Midcontinental Journal of
Archaeology* 7 (1982) 245–282.
BULLEN, R. P. and H. K. BROOKS, 'Two Ancient
Florida Dugout Canoes', *Quarterly Journal of the
Florida Academy of Sciences* 30 (1967) 97–107.
CLAIBORNE, R., *The First Americans*, New York 1973.
CODEX MENDOZA, *Codex Mendoza: The Mexican
Manuscript, Known as the Collection of Mendoza and
Preserved in the Bodleian Library, Oxford*, 3 vols, ed.
and trans. by J. C. Clark, London 1938.
COLUMBUS, C., *The Journal of Columbus*, abs. by B. de
Las Casas and trans. by C. Jane, New York 1960.
—*Select Letters of Christopher Columbus with Other
Original Documents Relating to His Four Voyages to the
New World*, ed. and trans. by R. H. Major, Hakluyt
Society, London 1870; repr. New York 1961.
—*Select Documents Illustrating the Four Voyages of
Columbus Including those Contained in R. H. Major's
Select Letters of Christopher Columbus* I, ed. and trans.
by C. Jane, Hakluyt Society, London 1930; repr.
Krause Reprints, Germany 1967.
COLUMBUS, F., *The Life of the Admiral Christopher
Columbus by His Son Ferdinand*, trans. and annot. by
B. Keen, New Jersey 1959.
CORTÉS, H., *Letters of Cortés (the Five Letters of
Relation from Fernando Cortés to the Emperor Charles
V)*, 2 vols, trans. by F. A. MacNutt, New York
and London 1908.
CUSHING, F. H., 'A Preliminary Report on the
Exploration of Ancient Key-Dweller Remains on
the Gulf Coast of Florida', *Proceedings of the
American Philosophical Society* 35 no. 135,
Philadelphia, PA 1897.
DE BOOY, T., 'Lucayan Artifacts from the Bahamas',
American Anthropologist 15 (1913) 1–7.
DE LANDA, DIEGO *Yucatan Before and After the
Conquest*, trans. by W. Gates, New York 1978.
DÍAZ DEL CASTILLO, BERNAL, *The Discovery and
Conquest of Mexico 1517–1521*, ed. by G. García and
trans. by A. P. Maudslay, New York 1956.
DURÁN, DIEGO, *The Aztecs: The History of the Indies
of New Spain*, trans. by D. Heyden and F.
Horcasitas, New York 1964.
EDWARDS, C. R., 'Aboriginal Sail in the New
World', *Southwest Journal of Anthropology* 21 (1965)
351–358.
—*Aboriginal Watercraft on the Pacific Coast of South
America*, Berkeley and Los Angeles 1965.
—'Possibilities of Pre-Columbian Maritime Contacts

among New World Civilizations', *Latin American
Center Pamphlet Series* 8, University of Wisconsin,
Milwaukee, WI 1970.
—'Pre-Columbian Maritime Trade in Mesoamerica',
Papers of the New World Archaeological Foundation 40
(1978) 199–209.
FARRIS, N. M. and A. G. MILLER, 'Maritime Culture
Contact of the Maya: Underwater Surveys and Test
Excavation in Quintana Roo, Mexico', *IJNA* 6
(1977) 141–151.
GIDDINGS, J. L., *Ancient Men of the Arctic*, New
York 1967.
GRIEDER, T., 'Periods in Pecos Style Pictographs',
American Antiquity 31 (1966) 710–720.
HAMMOND, N., 'Classic Maya Canoes', *IJNA* 10
(1981) 173–185.
HARRINGTON, J. P., *Tomol: Chumash Watercraft as
Described in the Ethnographic Notes of John P.
Harrington*, ed. and annot. by T. Hudson, J.
Timbrook and M. Rempe, Socorro 1978.
HORNELL, J., *Water Transport: Origins and Early
Evolution*, Cambridge (England) 1946.
INGSTAD, H., 'Norse Explorers', in Ashe, G. (ed.),
The Quest for America, London 1971, 96–112.
—'Norse Sites at L'Anse aux Meadows', in Ashe,
G. (ed.), *The Quest for America*, London 1971,
175–197.
JOHNSTONE, P., *The Sea-Craft of Prehistory*, ed. by
Sean McGrail, London and Cambridge, MA 1980.
KANDARE, R. P., 'Mississippian Dugout Canoes and
the Moundville Phase', MA thesis, University of
Arkansas 1983.
LAING, A., *American Ships*, New York 1971.
LESHIKAR, M. E., 'The Mexica Canoe: An
Archaeological and Ethnohistorical Study of its
Design, Uses, and Significance', MA thesis,
University of Texas at Austin 1982.
—'Construction of a Dugout Canoe in the Parish of
St Ann, Jamaica', *Proceedings of the Sixteenth
Conference on Underwater Archaeology*, Johnston, P. F.
(ed.), *Society for Historical Archaeology Special
Publication Series* 4 (1985) 48–51.
LOTHROP, S. K., 'Metals from the Cenote of
Sacrifice, Chichén Itzá, Yucatan', *MPMAE* 10 no.
2, Cambridge, MA 1952.
LOVEN, S., *Origins of the Tainan Culture, West Indies*,
Göteborg 1935.
LUCE, J. V., 'Ancient Explorers', in Ashe, G. (ed.),
The Quest for America, London 1971, 53–95.
MCFEAT, T. (ed.), *Indians of the North Pacific Coast*,
Seattle and London 1966.
MCGHEE, R., 'Contact between Native North
Americans and the Medieval Norse: A Review of
the Evidence', *American Antiquity* 49 (1984) 4–26.
MCKUSICK, M. B., 'Aboriginal Canoes in the West
Indies', *Yale University Publications in Anthropology* 63
(1960) 3–11.
MARCUS, G. J., *The Conquest of the North Atlantic*,
New York and Oxford 1981.
MEGGERS, B. J., 'Contacts from Asia', in Ashe, G.
(ed.), *The Quest for America*, London 1971, 239–259.
—*Prehistoric America*, Chicago 1972.
MORRIS, E. H., J. CHARLOT and A. A. MORRIS, *The
Temple of the Warriors at Chichén Itzá, Yucatán*, 2
vols, Carnegie Institution of Washington
Publication 406, Washington, D.C. 1931.
OLSEN, O. and O. CRUMLIN-PEDERSEN, *The Skuldelev
Ships*, repr. from *Acta Archaeologica* 38 (1967)
Copenhagen.
—*Five Viking Ships from Roskilde Fjord*, The
National Museum, Copenhagen 1978.
OLSON, R. L., *The Quinault Indians* and *Adze, Canoe,
and House Types of the Northwest Coast*, Seattle and
London 1967.
PHILLIPS, P. and J. A. BROWN, *Pre-Columbian Shell
Engravings from the Craig Mound at Spiro, Oklahoma*,
Cambridge, MA 1978.
SAHAGÚN, BERNARDINO DE, *Florentine Codex*, 12

vols, trans. by A. J. O. Anderson and C. E.
Dibble, The School of American Research and the
University of Utah, Santa Fe, NM 1950–1969.
STEWARD, J. H. (ed.), *Handbook of South American
Indians*, 7 vols, New York 1963.
STURTEVANT, W. C. (ed.), *Handbook of North
American Indians*, Washington, D.C. 1978.
THOMPSON, J. E. S., 'Canoes and Navigation of the
Maya and their Neighbors', *Journal of the Royal
Anthropological Institute* 79 (1949) 69–78.
TLAXCALA, L. DE, *Antigüedades mexicanas, publicadas
por la Junta Columbina de México*, Mexico 1892.
TOZZER, A. M., 'Chichén Itzá and its Cenote of
Sacrifice', *MPMAE* 11 and 12, Cambridge, MA
1957.
VEGA, G. DE LA, *The Florida of the Inca*, ed. and
trans. by J. G. and J. J. Varner, Austin 1980.
WATERMAN, T. T. and G. COFFIN, 'Types of Canoes
on Puget Sound', *Indian Notes and Monographs*, Heye
Foundation, New York 1920.
WAUCHOPE, R. (ed.), *Handbook of Middle American
Indians*, 16 vols, Austin 1964–1984.
WAUGH, F. W., 'Canadian Aboriginal Canoes', *The
Canadian Field-Naturalist* 33 no. 2 (1919) 23–33.
WEST, R. C., 'Aboriginal Sea Navigation Between
Middle and South America', *American Anthropologist*
63 (1961) 133–135.

CHAPTER TWO
The Voyages of Columbus

Columbus
COLUMBUS, C., *The Journal* see Ch. 1.
COLUMBUS, F., *see* Ch. 1.
HARRISSE, H., *Christophe Colomb, son origine, sa vie, ses
voyages, sa famille et ses descendantes*, 2 vols, Ernest
Leroux, Paris 1884–85.
LANDSTRÖM, B., *Columbus*, New York 1966.
LINES, J. A., *Colección de documentos para la historia de
Costa Rica relativos al cuarto y ultimo viaje de Cristóbal
Colón*, Academia de Geografía e Historia de Costa
Rica, San José 1952.
MORISON, S. E., *Admiral of the Ocean Sea. A Life of
Christopher Columbus*, 2 vols, Boston, MA 1942.
—*Journals and Other Documents on the Life and
Voyages of Christopher Columbus*, New York 1963.
NUNN, G. E., *The Geographic Conceptions of Columbus*,
American Geographical Society, New York 1924.

Columbus' Ships
ALBERTIS, E. A. D', *La costruzioni navali e l'arte della
navigazione al tempo di Cristoforo Colombo*, Ministero
della Pubblica Istruzione, Rome 1893.
CONCAS Y PALAU, *La nao historica Santa María en la
celebración del IV centenario del descubrimiento de
América*, Imprenta Alemana, Madrid 1914.
ETAYO ELIZONDO, C., *La 'Santa María', la 'Niña', y
la 'Pinta'*, Graficas Iruña, Pamplona 1962.
FERNÁNDEZ DURO, C., *La nao Santa María, memoria
de la Comisión Arqueológica Ejecutiva*, El Progreso
Editorial, Madrid 1892.
GUILLÉN Y TATO, J. F., *La carabela Santa María,
apuntos para su reconstrucción*, Ministerior de Marina,
Madrid 1927.
MARTÍNEZ-HIDALGO, J. M., *Las naves de Colón*, Museo
Maritimo, Barcelona 1969.
—*A bordo de la 'Santa Maria'*, Museo Marítimo,
Barcelona 1976.
MARX, R. F., *The Voyage of the Niña II*, Cleveland,
OH 1963.
WINTER, H., *Die Kolumbusschiffe*, Robert Loef
Verlag, Magdeburg 1944.

Columbus' Shipwrecks
FRYE, J., *The Search for the Santa María*, New York
1973.
GOODWIN, S. B., *Spanish and English Ruins in Jamaica*,
Boston, MA 1946.

LINK, M. C., *Sea Diver. A Quest for History Under the Sea*, New York 1958.
MORISON, S. E. and M. OBREGÓN, *The Caribbean as Columbus Saw It*, Boston, MA 1964.
SMITH, R. C., 'Fathoming Columbus' Caravels', *Américas* 35:5 (1984) 18–23.
—'The Search for the Caravels of Columbus', *Oceanus* 28:1 (1985) 73–77.

CHAPTER THREE
Shipwrecks of the Explorers

AGRICOLA, G., *De re metallica*, trans. by H. C. and L. H. Hoover, Mineralogical Society of America, New York, NY 1950. Orig. pub. in Basle, 1556.
ARÁNTEGUI Y SANZ, D. J., *Apuntes históricos sobre la artillería española en los siglos XIV y XV*, Establecimiento Tipográfico de Fortaret, Madrid 1887–1891.
ARNOLD, J. B. III and R. S. WEDDLE, *The Nautical Archaeology of Padre Island. The Spanish Shipwrecks of 1554*, New York 1978.
BARKHAM, M. M., *Report on 16th Century Spanish Basque Shipbuilding c. 1550 to c. 1600*, Parks Canada, Ontario 1981.
BIRINGUCCIO, V., *Pirotechnia*, trans. by C. S. Smith and M. T. Gnudi, Cambridge, MA 1943. Orig. pub. in Venice, 1540.
BUSH ROMERO, P., *Under the Waters of Mexico*, Carlton Press, Mexico City 1964.
CHAMBERLAIN, R. S., *The Conquest and Colonization of Yucatan, 1517–1550*, Carnegie Institution, Washington, D.C. 1948.
CHAUNU, H. AND P. CHAUNU, *Séville et l'Atlantique 1504–1650*, 8 vols, SEVPEN, Paris 1955–1957.
FERNÁNDEZ DE NAVARRETE, M., *Colección de los viages y descubrimientos que hicieron por mar los españoles desde fines del siglo XV*, 5 vols, Imprenta Real, Madrid 1825–1829.
HARRISSE, H., *The Discovery of North America*, N. Israel, Amsterdam 1969. Orig. pub. 1892.
IRVING, W., *Voyages and Discoveries of the Companions of Columbus*, Philadelphia, PA and London 1831.
KEITH, D. H. et al., 'The Molasses Reef Wreck, Turks and Caicos Islands, B.W.I: A Preliminary Report', *IJNA* 13 (1984) 45–63.
KEITH, D. H. and J. J. SIMMONS, 'Analysis of Hull Remains, Ballast and Artifact Distribution of a 16th-Century Shipwreck, Molasses Reef, British West Indies', *JFA* 12 (1985) 411–424.
KEMPERS, R. T. W., 'Haquebuts from Dutch Collections', *Journal of the Arms and Armour Society* 11.2 (1983) 56–89.
LINK, M. C., *see* Ch. 2.
MCCLYMONT, J. R., *Vicente Añez Pinçón*, London 1916.
MORISON, S. E., *The European Discovery of America: The Southern Voyages*, New York and Oxford 1974.
—*Portuguese Voyages to America in the Fifteenth Century*, Cambridge, MA 1940.
OLDS, D., *Texas Legacy from the Gulf. A Report on Sixteenth-Century Shipwreck Materials Recovered from the Texas Tidelands*, Texas Antiquities Committee, Austin 1976.
PALACIO, G. DE, *Instrucción nautica para navegar*, Mexico City 1587.
PETERSON, M., 'Exploration of a 16th-Century Bahaman Shipwreck', *National Geographic Society Research Reports, 1967 Projects*, Washington, D.C. 1974, 231–42.
—'Wreck Sites in the Americas', in *Underwater Archaeology: A Nascent Discipline*, UNESCO, Paris 1972.
—'Traders and Privateers Across the Atlantic: 1492–1733', in Bass, G. F. (ed.), *A History of Seafaring*, London and New York 1972, 254–280.
ROSLOFF, J. and J. B. ARNOLD III, 'The Keel of the San Esteban (1554): Continued Analysis', *IJNA* 13 (1984) 287–296.
SAUER, C. O., *The Early Spanish Main*, Berkeley, CA 1966.

SMITH, R. C., D. H. KEITH and D. C. LAKEY, 'The Highborn Cay Wreck: Further Exploration of a 16th-Century Bahaman Shipwreck', *IJNA* 14 (1985) 63–72.
VIGNERAS, L. A., *The Discovery of South America and the Andalusian Voyages*, Chicago 1976.
VIGÓN, J., *Historia de la artillería española*, Instituto Jerónimo Zurita, Madrid 1947.
WEDDLE, R. S., *Spanish Sea, The Gulf of Mexico in North American Discovery 1500–1685*, College Station, TX 1985.

CHAPTER FOUR
Basque Whalers in the New World

ARNOLD, J. B. III and R. S. WEDDLE, *see* Ch. 3.
BARKHAM, S., 'Finding Sources of Canadian History in Spain', *Canadian Geographic* (June 1980) 66–73.
BARKHAM, S. and R. GRENIER, 'Divers Find Sunken Basque Galleon in Labrador', *Canadian Geographic* (Dec. 1978) 60–63.
BÉLANGER, R., *Les Basques dans l'éstuaire du Saint-Laurent*, Montreal 1971.
CUMBAA, S. L., 'Right Whales: Past and Present', *Proc. of Workshop on the Status of Right Whales. Internat. Whaling Commission, Boston, June 1983* (Cambridge, MA 1986) 187–190.
DALEY, T. and L. MURDOCK, 'Polysulfide Rubber and Its Application for Recording Archaeological Ship Features in a Marine Environment', *IJNA* 10 (1981) 337–342.
—'Underwater Molding of a Cross-section of the San Juan Hull', *Proc. of the ICOM Waterlogged Wood Working Group Conference, Ottawa 1981* (1982) 39–40.
GAIZTARRO, M. C., *Los Vascos en la Pesca de la Ballena*, Bibliotheca de Autores Vascos, San Sebastian 1960.
GRENIER, R., 'Excavating a 400 year old Basque Galleon', *NG* (July 1985) 58–68.
GRENIER, R. and J. TUCK, 'A 16th-century Basque Whaling Station in Labrador', *Scientific American* 245 no. 5 (Nov. 1981) 180–188.
JACQUES, R., *Navires et gens de mer à Bordeaux (vers 1400–vers 1550)*, Appendices, École Pratiques des Hautes Études, VIe section, Centre des Recherches Historique, SEVPEN, Paris 1968.
LEBLANC, G. 'Sur les traces des Basques', *Québec Science* 22, no. 11 (July 1984) 17–24.
PROULX, J-P., 'La Pêche à la baleine dans l'Atlantique Nord jusqu'au milieu du XIXe siècle', *Études en Archéologie, Architecture et Histoire*, Parcs Canada, Ottawa (1986) 1–118.
RINGER, R. J., 'Progress Report on the Marine Excavation of the Basque Whaling Vessel San Juan (1565): A Summary of the 1982 Field Season', *Research Bulletin* 206, Parks Canada, Ottawa (1983) 1–20.
—'Sommaire des fouilles archéologiques subaquatiques effectuées à Red Bay en saison de 1984', *Bulletin de Recherche* 248, Parcs Canada, Ottawa (1986) 1–20.
ROSS, L., *Sixteenth-Century Spanish Basque Coopering Technology: A Report of the Staved Containers Found in 1978–79 on the Wreck of the Whaling Galleon San Juan, Sunk in Red Bay, Labrador, 1565*. Manuscript Report no. 408, Parks Canada, Ottawa 1980.
STEVEN, E. W., 'Underwater Research at Red Bay, Labrador: A Summary of the 1981 Field Season', *Research Bulletin* 194, Parks Canada, Ottawa (1983) 1–14.
—'Rapport d'étape sur les fouilles sous-marines à Red Bay, résumé saison 1983', *Bulletin de Recherche* 240, Parcs Canada, Ottawa (1986) 1–16.
STEVEN, E. W. and P. WADDELL, 'Marine Archaeological Research at Red Bay, Labrador: A Summary of the 1985 Field Season', *Research Bulletin* 258, Environment Canada (1987) 1–12.
WADDELL, P., 'The Pump and Pump Well of a 16th Century Galleon', *IJNA* 14 (1985) 243–259.
—'The Disassembly of a 16th Century Galleon', *IJNA* 15 (1986) 137–148.

CHAPTER FIVE
Treasure Ships of the Spanish Main

Spanish Shipping
ANDREWS, K. R., *The Spanish Caribbean. Trade and Plunder 1530–1630*, New Haven 1978.
ARTIÑANO, GERVASIO DE, *La arquitectura naval española*, Oliva de Vilanova, Barcelona 1920.
FERNANDEZ DURO, C., *Armada española desde la unión de los reinos de Castilla y de Aragón*, 9 vols, Museo Naval, Madrid 1973.
HARING, C. H., *Trade and Navigation Between Spain and the Indies in the Time of the Hapsburgs*, Cambridge, MA 1918.
PARRY, J. H., *The Spanish Seaborne Empire*, New York 1966.
WEDDLE, R. S. *see* Ch. 3.
WOOD, P., *The Spanish Main*, Alexendria, VA 1979.

Spanish Shipwrecks
HORNER, D., *The Treasure Galleons*, New York 1971.
NATIONAL GEOGRAHIC SOCIETY, *Undersea Treasures*, Washington, D.C. 1974.
PETERSON, M., 'Traders and Privateers', *see* Ch. 3.
—'Wreck Sites in the Americas', in *Underwater Archaeology: A Nascent Discipline*, UNESCO, Paris 1972, 85–93.
—*The Funnel of Gold*, Boston, MA 1975.
—'Reach for the New World', 152 no. 6 (Dec. 1977) 728–744.

1554 Fleet
ARNOLD, J. B. III, *An Underwater Archaeological Magnetometer Survey and Site Test Excavation Project off Padre Island*, Texas Antiquities Committee, Austin 1976.
—'The Flota Disaster of 1554', in Arnold, J. B. III (ed.), *Beneath the Waters of Time: Proceedings of the Ninth Conference on Underwater Archaeology*, Texas Ant. Comm., Austin 1978, 25–28.
ARNOLD, J. B. III, and R. S. WEDDLE, *see* Ch. 3.
DAVIS, J. L., *Treasure, People, Ships and Dreams*, Texas Ant. Comm., Austin 1977.
HAMILTON, D. L., *Conservation of Metal Objects from Underwater Sites: A Study in Methods*, Texas Ant. Comm., Austin 1976.
MCDONALD, D. and J. B. ARNOLD III, *Documentary Sources for the New Spain Fleet of 1554*, Texas Ant. Comm., Austin 1979.
OLDS, D. L., *see* Ch. 3.
ROSLOFF, J. and J. B. ARNOLD III, *see* Ch. 3.

1622 Fleet
LYON, E. 'The Trouble with Treasure', *NG* 149 no. 6 (June 1976) 787–809.
—*The Search for the Atocha*, New York 1979.
MATHEWSON, D. III, *Archaeological Treasure: The Search for the Nuestra Señora de Atocha*, Seafarers Heritage Library, Woodstock, VT and Key West, FL 1983.

La Concepción
BORRELL, P. J., *Historia y rescate del galeón Nuestra Señora de la Concepción*, Museo de las Casas Reales, Santo Domingo 1983.
EARLE, P., *The Wreck of the Almiranta. Sir William Phips and the Hispaniola Treasure*, London 1979.
GRISSIM, J., *The Lost Treasure of the Concepción*, New York 1980.
KARRAKER, C. H., *The Hispaniola Treasure*, Philadelphia 1934.

1715 Fleet
BURGESS, R. F. and C. J. CLAUSEN, *Gold, Galleons and Archaeology*, New York 1976.
CLAUSEN, C. J., 'A 1715 Spanish Treasure Ship', *Contributions of the Florida State Museum, Social Sciences*, no. 12, Gainesville, FL 1965.
COCKRELL, W. A. and L. MURPHY, '8SL17: Methodological Approaches to a Dual Component Marine Site on the Florida Atlantic Coast', in Arnold, J. B. III (ed.), *Beneath the Waters of Time: Proceedings of the Ninth Conference on Underwater*

Archaeology, Texas Ant. Comm., Austin 1978, 175–180.
WAGNER, K., 'Drowned Galleons Yield Spanish Gold', *NG* 140 no. 1 (Jan. 1965) 1–37.
—*Pieces of Eight: Recovering the Riches of a Lost Spanish Treasure Fleet*, New York 1972.

1733 Fleet
BURGESS, R. F., 'Saga of the *San Jose*', *Oceans* 1 (1974) 66–71.
—*They Found Treasure*, New York 1977.
MEYLACK, M., *Diving to a Flash of Gold*, Garden City, NY 1971.

Guadalupe and Tolosa
BORRELL, P. J., *Arqueología submarina en la Republica Dominicana*, Museo de las Casas Reales, Santo Domingo 1980.
PETERSON, M., 'Graveyard of the Quicksilver Galleons', *NG* 156 no. 6 (Dec. 1979) 850–876.

Portuguese Shipping
BOXER, C. R., *The Portuguese Seaborne Empire: 1415–1825*, New York 1969.
DIFFIE, B. W. and G. D. WINIUS, *Foundations of the Portuguese Empire, 1415–1580*, Minneapolis, MN 1977.
DUFFY, J., *Shipwreck and Empire, Being an Account of Portuguese Maritime Disasters in a Century of Decline*, Cambridge, MA 1955.

Sacramento
GUILMARTIN, J. F. Jr, 'The Guns of the *Santissimo Sacramento*', *Technology and Culture* 24 (1983) 559–601.
PERNAMBUCANO DE MELLO, U., 'The Shipwreck of the Galleon *Sacramento*-1668 off Brazil', *IJNA* 8 (1979) 211–223.

CHAPTER SIX
The Thirteen Colonies

ADAMS, J., 'Sea Venture. A second interim report-Part I', *IJNA* 14 (1985) 275–299.
ALBRIGHT, A. B. and J. R. STEFFY, 'The Brown's Ferry Vessel, South Carolina', *IJNA* 8 (1979) 121–142.
BAKER, W.A., *The Mayflower And Other Colonial Vessels*, London and Annapolis, MD 1983.
DEAN, N., 'Manhattan's Mystery Merchant Ship', *WoodenBoat* 63 (1985) 96–100.
EVANS, C.W., *Some Notes on Shipbuilding and Shipping in Colonial Virginia*, Virginia 350th Anniversary Celebration Corp., Williamsburg, VA 1957.
FLEETWOOD, R., *Tidecraft, The Boats of Lower South Carolina and Georgia*, Coastal Heritage Society, Savannah, GA 1982.
GOLDENBERG, J. A., *Shipbuilding in Colonial America*, Charlottesville, VA 1976.
HAMILTON, D. H., 'The City Under the Sea', *1986 Science Year* (The World Book Science Annual), Chicago, IL 1986, 94–109.
HARRINGTON, F., 'Strawberry Banke: A Historic Waterfront Neighborhood', *Archaeology* 36 no. 3 (1983) 52–59.
HOLLY, H. H., *Sparrow Hawk: A Seventeenth Century Vessel in Twentieth Century America*, Pilgrim Society, Plymouth, MA 1969, and *The American Neptune* 13 no. 1 (1953).
LAVERY, B. (ed.), *Deane's Doctrine of Naval Architecture, 1670*, London 1981.
MADDOCKS, M., *The Atlantic Crossing*, Alexandria, VA 1981.
MORISON, S.E. , *The Maritime History of Massachusetts 1783–1860*, Boston, MA 1979.
ROSLOFF, J. P., 'The Water Street Ship: Preliminary Analysis of an Eighteenth-Century Merchant Ship', MA thesis, Texas A&M University 1986.
SALISBURY, W. and R. C. ANDERSON, *A Treatise on Shipbuilding and A Treatise on Rigging Written About 1620–1625*, Soc. For Nautical Research, London 1958.
SOLECKI, R. S., 'The *Tiger*, An Early Dutch 17th Century Ship, and an Abortive Salvage Attempt', *JFA* 1 (1974) 109–116.
WINGWOOD, A. J., '*Sea Venture*. An Interim Report on an Early 17th Century Shipwreck Lost in 1609', *IJNA* 11 (1982) 333–347.

CHAPTER SEVEN
Struggle for a Continent

GARDNER, J., 'Relics of "Ghost Fleet" are Small Craft Bonanza', *National Fisherman*, Oct. 1966.
HAMILTON, E. P., *The French and Indian Wars*, Garden City, NY 1962.
—*Adventure in the Wilderness: The American Journals of Louis Antoine de Bouganville*, Norman, OK 1964.
KALM, P., *Travels into North America*, trans. by J. R. Forster, The Imprint Society, Barre, MA 1972. Orig. pub. in 1749.
KNOX, J., *A Historical Journal of the Campaigns in North America*, 3 vols, Freeport, NY 1970.
KREUGER, J., A. COHN, K. CRISMAN and H. MIKSCH, 'The Fort Ticonderoga King's Shipyard Excavation', *The Bulletin of the Fort Ticonderoga Museum* 14, no. 6 (Fall 1985).
LAROCHE, D., 'Pas un, mais plusieurs bateaux sous le musée', *L'Escale* 5, no. 4 (May–June 1985).
PARKMAN, F., *Montcalm and Wolfe*, New York 1984.
PROULX, G., *Between France and New France*, Toronto and Charlottetown 1984.
SULLIVAN, C., *Legacy of the Machault*, Parks Canada 1986.
ZACHARCHUK, W. and P. J. A. WADDELL, *The Excavation of the Machault*, Parks Canada 1984.

CHAPTER EIGHT
Gunboats and Warships of the American Revolution

CHAPELLE, H. I., *The History of American Sailing Ships*, New York 1935.
COGGINS, J., *Ships and Seamen of the American Revolution*, Harrisburg, PA 1969.
FORD, B. and D. SWITZER, *Underwater Dig: The Excavation of a Revolutionary War Privateer*, New York 1982.
GOLDENBERG, J. A., *Shipbuilding in Colonial America*, Charlottesville, VA 1976.
JAMES, W. M., *The British Navy in Adversity: A Study of the War of American Independence*, London 1933.
KNOX, D. W., *The Naval Genius of George Washington*, Boston, MA 1932.
LUNDEBERG, P. K., *The Continental Gunboat 'Philadelphia' and the Northern Campaign of 1776*, Smithsonian Institution, Washington, D.C. 1966.
MAHAN, A., *The Major Operations of the Navies in the War of American Independence*, London 1913.
MILLAR, J. F., *American Ships of the Colonial and Revolutionary Periods*, New York 1978.
SANDS, J. O., *Yorktown's Captive Fleet*, Charlottesville, VA 1983.
SYRETT, D., *Shipping and the American War, 1775–83: A Study of British Transport Organization*, London 1970.

CHAPTER NINE
The War of 1812

BRANNAN, J., *Official Letters of the Military and Naval Officers of the United States During the War with Britain in the Years 1812, 1813, 1814, and 1815*, Washington, D.C. 1823.
CAIN, E., *Ghost Ships Hamilton and Scourge: Historical Treasures from the War of 1812*, Toronto and New York 1983, London 1984.
CASSAVOY, K. A., 'The Hamilton and the Scourge: A First Look', in Langley, S. B. M. and Unger, R. W. (eds), *Nautical Archaeology: Progress and Public Responsibility*, 176–198, BAR, Oxford 1984.
CASSAVOY, K. A., B. PENNY and A. AMOS, 'The Penetanguishene Naval Slip', in Skene, M. (ed.), *Archaeological Research Report No. 13*, 153–173, Ontario Historical Research Branch, Toronto 1980.

CHAPELLE, H. I., *The History of the American Sailing Navy*, New York 1949.
CRISMAN, K. J., *The History and Construction of the United States Schooner Ticonderoga*, Alexandria, VA 1983.
—*The Eagle*, New England Press, Shelburne, VT, and The Naval Institute Press, Annapolis, MD 1987.
CRUIKSHANK, E. A., 'The Contest for the Command of Lake Ontario in 1814', *Ontario History* 21 (1924) 99–160.
CUMBERLAND, B., 'The Navies on Lake Ontario in the War of 1812: Notes from the Papers of a Naval Officer then Serving on His Majesty's Ships', *Ontario Historical Society* 8 (1907) 124–142.
DUDLEY, W. S. (ed.), *The Naval War of 1812: A Documentary History*, Naval Historical Center, Dept. of the Navy, Washington, D.C. 1985.
EVEREST, A. S., *The War of 1812 in the Champlain Valley*, Syracuse, NY 1981.
HANNAY, D., *A Short History of the Royal Navy*, vol. 2, London 1909.
HOPKINS, F. and D. SHOMETTE, *War on the Patuxent, 1814*, Calvert Marine Museum, Solomons, MD 1981.
KENNEDY, P. M., *The Rise and Fall of the British Navy*, London 1876.
LOSSING, B., *The Pictorial Fieldbook of the War of 1812*, New York 1868.
MACDONOUGH, R., *Life of Commodore Thomas Macdonough, U.S. Navy*, Boston, MA 1909.
NELSON, D. A., 'Ghost Ships of the War of 1812', *NG* 163 no. 3 (March 1983) 288–313.
PRESTON, R. A., 'The History of the Port of Kingston', *Ontario History* 46 (1954) 202–211.
ROOSEVELT, T., *The Naval War of 1812*, New York 1882.
ROSENBERG, M., *The Building of Perry's Fleet on Lake Erie*, Pennsylvania Historical and Museum Commission, Harrisburg, PA 1974.
STACEY, C. P., 'The Ships of the British Squadron on Lake Ontario, 1812–1814', *Canadian Historical Review* 34 (1953) 311–323.
WOOD, W., *The War with the United States*, Toronto 1915.

CHAPTER TEN
Steamboats on Inland Waterways

ADAMS, R. M., et al., *Survey of the Steamboat Black Cloud*, College Station, TX 1980.
AMBLER, C. H., *A History of Transportation in the Ohio Valley with Special Reference to Its Waterways, Trade, and Commerce from the Earliest Period to the Present Time*, Glendale, CA 1932.
BALDWIN, L. D., *The Keelboat Age on Western Waters*, Pittsburgh, PA 1941.
BATES, A., *The Western Rivers Steamboat Cyclopoedium or American Riverboat Structure & Detail, Salted with Lore with a Nod to the Modelmaker*, Leonia, NJ 1968.
BULLOCK, S., 'The "Miracle" of the First Steamboat', *Journal of American History* 1 (1907) 33–48.
DAVISON, R. (ed.), *The 'Phoenix' Project*, Champlain Maritime Society, Burlington, VT 1981.
DAYTON, F. E., *Steamboat Days*, New York 1925.
DRAGO, H. S., *The Steamboaters, From the Early Side-Wheelers to Big Packets*, New York 1967.
FLEETWOOD, R., *Tidecraft: The Boats of Lower South Carolina and Georgia*, Coastal Heritage Society, Savannah, GA 1982.
FLEXNER, J. T., *Steamboats Come True: American Inventors in Action*, 1944; repr. Boston and Toronto 1978.
GRAHAM, P., *Showboats: The History of an American Institution*, Austin, TX 1951.
HAITES, E. F., J. MAK and G. M. WALTON, *Western River Transportation: The Era of Early Internal Development, 1810–1860. Studies in Historical and Political Science*, Series 93 no. 2, Baltimore, MD 1975.
HUNTER, L. C., 'The Invention of the Western Steamboat', *Journal of Economic History* 3 (1943) 202–220.

—*Steamboats on the Western Rivers: An Economic and Technological History*, Cambridge, MA 1949.
IRION, J. B., *Archaeological Testing of the Confederate Obstructions, 1Mb28, Mobile Harbor, Alabama*, Austin, TX 1985.
LATROBE, J. H. B., *The First Steamboat Voyage on the Western Waters*, Maryland Historical Society Fund Publication, no. 6, Maryland Historical Society, Baltimore, MD 1871.
LESSTRANG, J., *Lake Carriers: The Saga of the Great Lakes Fleet – North America's Fresh Water Merchant Marine*, Seattle, WA 1977.
LINGENFELTER, R. E., *Steamboats on the Colorado River, 1852–1916*, Tucson, AZ 1978.
LYTLE, W. M. and F. R. HOLDCAMPER, *Merchant Steam Vessels of the United States 1790–1868*, ed. and rev. by C. Bradford Mitchell, Steamship Hist. Soc. of America, Staten Island, NY 1975.
MCDERMOTT, J. F. (ed.), *Before Mark Twain. A Sampler of Old, Old Times on the Mississippi*, Carbondale and Edwardsville, IL 1968.
MCDONALD, W. J., 'The Missouri River and Its Victims', *Missouri Historical Review* 21, no. 2 (1927).
MACMULLEN, J., *Paddle-Wheel Days in California*, Stanford, CA 1944.
MERRICK, G. B., *Old Times on the Upper Mississippi: The Recollections of a Steamboat Pilot from 1854 to 1863*, Cleveland, OH 1909.
MORGAN, J. S., *Robert Fulton*, New York 1977.
MORRISON, J. H., *History of American Steam Navigation*, New York 1958.
MYERS, D. P., 'The Architectural Development of the Western Floating Palace', *Journal of the Society of Architectural Historians* 11, no. 4 (1952) 25–31.
OREGON HISTORICAL SOCIETY, *Steamboat Days on the Rivers*, Portland, OR 1969.
PETERSON, W. J., 'Steamboating on the Missouri River', *Iowa Journal of History* 53 (1955) 97–120.
PETSCHE, J. E., 'Uncovering the Steamboat *Bertrand*', *Nebraska History* 51, no. 1 (1970).
—*The Steamboat 'Bertrand': History, Excavation, and Architecture*, National Park Service Publications in Archaeology 11, Washington, D.C. 1974.
PRAGER, F. D., *The Autobiography of John Fitch*, American Philosophical Soc., Philadelphia, PA 1976.
PREBLE, G. H., *A Chronological History of the Origin and Development of Steam Navigation*, Philadelphia, PA 1883.
PURYEAR, P. A. and N. WINFIELD Jr, *Sandbars and Sternwheelers, Steam Navigation on the Brazos*, College Station, TX 1976.
SWITZER, R. R., 'Munitions on the *Bertrand*', *Archaeology* 25/4 (1972) 250–255.
TAYLOR, G. R., *The Transportation Revolution 1815–1860*, Vol. IV in *The Economic History of the United States*, New York 1951.
TURNER, R. D., *Sternwheelers and Steam Tugs*, Victoria, British Columbia 1984.
TWAIN, M., *Life on the Mississippi*, New York 1980.
U.S. CONGRESS, HOUSE, PRESIDENT'S MESSAGE, *Report of the Board of Engineers on the Ohio and Mississippi Rivers Made in the Year 1821*, House Doc. 35, 17th Congress, 2nd Session, Serial Set No. 78, 1823.
WAY, F. Jr, *Pilotin' Comes Natural*, New York and Toronto 1943.

CHAPTER ELEVEN
The Civil War at Sea

AMMEN, D., *The Navy in the Civil War* II. *The Atlantic Coast*, New York 1883.
ANDERSON, B., *By Sea and By River*, New York 1962.
BEARSS, E. C., *Hardluck Ironclad*, Baton Rouge, LA 1966.
BEERS, H. P., *Guide to the Archives of the Government of the Confederate States of America*, National Archives and Records Service, Washington, D.C. 1968.
BERINGER, R. E., H. HATTAWAY, A. JONES and W. N. STILL Jr, *Why the South Lost the Civil War*, Athens, GA 1986.
BOLANDER, L. H., 'The Alligator, First Submarine of The Civil War', *U.S. Naval Institute Proceedings* 64 (June 1938) 843–854.
BULLOCK, J. D., *The Secret Service of the Confederate States in Europe; How the Confederate Cruisers Were Equipped*, 2 vols, New York 1884.
CARSE, R., *Blockade: The Civil War at Sea*, New York 1958.
COCHRAN, H., *Blockade Runners of the Confederacy*, Indianapolis and New York 1958.
DALY, R. W. (ed.), *Aboard the USS Florida: 1863–65*, United States Naval Institute, Annapolis, MD 1968.
—(ed.), *Aboard the USS Monitor: 1862*, United States Naval Institute, Annapolis, MD 1964.
HOBART-HAMPTON, A. C., *Never Caught*, London 1867.
JONES, V. C., *The Civil War at Sea*, 3 vols, New York 1960–1962.
LESTER, R. I., 'The Procurement of Confederate Blockade Runners and Other Vessels in Great Britain During The American Civil War', *Mariners' Mirror* 61 (1975) 255–270.
MACBRIDE, R., *Civil War Ironclads*, Philadelphia, PA 1962.
MERLI, F. J., *Great Britain and the Confederate Navy 1861–1864*, Bloomington, IN 1970.
MILLER, E. M., *USS Monitor, The Ship that Launched a Modern Navy*, Annapolis, MD 1978.
MUNDEN, K. W. and H. P. BEERS, *Guide to Federal Archives Relating to the Civil War*, National Archives and Records Service, Washington, D.C. 1962.
PARKER, CAPT. W. H., *Recollections of a Naval Officer 1841–1865*, New York 1883.
PEAKE, J., *Rudiments of Naval Architecture: or, An Exposition of the Practical Principles of the Science in its Application to Naval Construction; Compiled for the Use of Beginners*, London 1851.
PERRY, M. F., *Infernal Machines: The story of Confederate Submarine and Mine Warfare*, Baton Rouge, LA 1965.
PRICE, M. W., 'Ships that Tested the Blockade of the Carolina Ports, 1861–1865', *The American Neptune* 8 (1948) 196–241.
ROLAND, A., *Underwater Warfare in the Age of Sail*, Bloomington, IN 1978.
SCHARF, J. T., *The History of the Confederate States Navy from Its Organization to the Surrender of Its Last Vessel*, 2 vols, New York 1887.
SEMMES, R., *Service Afloat: The Remarkable Career of the Confederate Cruisers 'Sumter' and 'Alabama', During the War Between the States*, New York 1900.
SOLEY, J. R., *The Navy in the Civil War* I. *The Blockade and the Cruisers*, New York 1883.
STILL, W. N. Jr, *Iron Afloat: The Story of the Confederate Armorclads*, Columbia, SC 1985.
U.S. DEPARTMENT OF THE NAVY, *Civil War Chronology, 1861–1865*, Govt Printing Office, Washington, D.C. 1971.
VANDIVER, F. (ed.), *Confederate Blockade Running Through Bermuda, 1861–1865; Letter and Cargo Manifests*, Austin, TX 1957.
—(ed.), 'The Capture of a Confederate Blockade Runner: Extracts from the Journal of a Confederate Naval Officer', *North Carolina Historical Review* 21 (1944) 136–138.
WAR OF THE REBELLION: *Official Records of the Union and Confederate Navies in the War of Rebellion*, 30 vols, Govt Printing Office, Washington, D.C. 1894–1922.
WATTS, G. P. Jr, *Investigating the Remains of the USS Monitor: A Final Report on 1979 Site Testing in the 'Monitor' National Marine Sanctuary*, North Carolina Division of Archives and History, Wilmington, NC 1982.

CHAPTER TWELVE
The End of the Age of Sail

ALBION, R. G., *The Rise of New York Port, 1815–1860*, New York 1939.
—*Square-Riggers on Schedule*, Princeton, NJ 1938.
—(ed.), *Naval and Maritime History: An Annotated Bibliography*, Marine Historical Association, Mystic, CT 1972.
ALBION, R. G., W. A. BAKER and B. W. LABAREE, *New England and the Sea*, Middletown, CT 1972.
ALLEN, D. E., *The Windjammers*, Alexandria, VA 1978.
AMERICAN NEPTUNE, THE: *A Quarterly Journal of Maritime History*. Peabody Museum of Salem, Salem, MA 1941-present.
ASHLEY, C. W., *The Yankee Whaler*, Boston, MA 1926.
BAKER, W. A., *The Engine-Powered Vessel: From Paddle-Wheeler to Nuclear Ship*, New York 1965.
BENSON, R. M., *Steamships and Motorships of the West Coast*, New York 1968.
BRADLEE, F. B. C., *Some Account of Steam Navigation in New England*, Essex Institute, Salem, MA 1920.
BROUWER, N. J., *International Register of Historic Ships*, Annapolis, MD 1985.
BRYANT, S. W., *The Sea and the States: A Maritime History of the American Merchant Marine* 1950.
CHAPELLE, H. I., *The American Fishing Schooners, 1825–1935*, New York 1973.
—*American Sailing Craft*, New York 1936.
—*American Small Sailing Craft: Their Design, Development and Construction*, New York 1951.
—*The Baltimore Clipper: Its Origin and Development*, Marine Research Society, Salem, MA 1930.
—see Ch. 8.
—*The National Watercraft Collection*, Smithsonian Institution, Washington, D.C. 1960.
—*The Search for Speed under Sail*, New York 1967.
CLARK, A.W., *The Clipper Ship Era: An Epitome of the Famous American and British Clipper Ships . . . 1843–1869*, New York 1910.
CUTLER, C. C., *Five Hundred Sailing Records of American Built Ships*, Marine Historical Association, Mystic, CT 1952.
—*Greyhounds of the Sea: The Story of the American Clipper Ship*, U.S. Naval Institute, Annapolis, MD 1930.
—*Queens of the Western Ocean: The Story of America's Mail and Passenger Sailing Lines*, U.S. Naval Institute, Annapolis, MD 1961.
DALZELL, G. W., *The Flight from the Flag: The Continuing Effect of the Civil War on the American Carrying Trade*, 1940.
DOW, G. F., *Whale Ships and Whaling*, Marine Research Society, Salem, MA 1925.
DUGAN, J., *The Great Iron Ship*, New York 1953.
DUNBAUGH, E. L., *The Era of the Joy Line: A Saga of Steamboating on Long Island Sound*, Westport, CT 1982.
EMMERSON, G. S., *The Greatest Iron Ship: S.S. Great Eastern*, Newton Abbot, England and North Pomfret, VT n.d.
FAIRBURN, W. A., *Merchant Sail*, 6 vols, Fairburn Marine Educational Foundation, Center Lovell, ME 1945–55.
FARR, G. E., *The Steamship Great Britain*, Bristol Branch of the Historical Association, Bristol 1965.
—*The Steamship 'Great Western': The First Atlantic Liner*, Dursley, England n.d.
FASSETT, F. G. (ed.), *The Shipbuilding Business in the United States of America*, 2 vols, Society of Naval Architects and Marine Engineers, New York 1948.
GIBBS, J. A., *Shipwrecks of the Pacific Coast*, Portland, OR 1957.
GOODE, G. B., *The Fisheries and Fishing Industries of the United States*, 8 vols, Govt Printing Office, Washington, D.C. 1884–87.
GREGOR, H., *The S.S. Great Britain*, New York 1971.
HEGARTY, R. B., *Addendum to 'Starbuck' and 'Whaling Masters'*, New Bedford Free Public Library, New Bedford, MA 1964.
HOCKING, C., *Dictionary of Disasters at Sea during the Age of Steam . . . 1824–1962*, 2 vols, Lloyd's Register of Shipping, London 1969.
HOWE, O. T. and F. C. MATTHEWS, *American Clipper Ships 1833–1858*, 2 vols, Marine Research Society, Salem, MA 1926–27.
HOWLAND, S. A., *Steamboat Disasters and Railroad Accidents in the United States*, Worcester, MA 1840.

HUGHES, T., *The Blue Riband of the Atlantic*, New York 1973.

HUNTRESS, K. G., *A Checklist of Narratives of Shipwrecks and Disasters at Sea to 1860*, Ames, IA 1979.

—*Narratives of Shipwrecks and Disasters, 1586–1860*, Ames, IA 1974.

JOHNSTON, P. F., *The New England Fisheries: A Treasure Greater than Gold*, Peabody Museum of Salem, Salem, MA 1984.

—et al., *A Sportdiver's Handbook for Historic Shipwrecks: Tools and Techniques*, Northeast Marine Advisory Council, Durham, NH 1982.

—*Steam and the Sea*, Peabody Museum of Salem, Salem, MA 1983.

KEMBLE, J. H. (ed.), *Gold Rush Steamers*, Book Club of California, San Francisco, CA 1958.

—*Side-Wheelers Across the Pacific*, San Francisco Museum of Science and Industry, San Francisco, CA 1942.

LEAVITT, J. F., *Wake of the Coasters*, Mystic, CT 1970.

LLOYD'S REGISTER OF SHIPPING, London 1764–present.

LUBBOCK, A. B., *The Down Easters, American Deep Water Sailing Ships, 1869–1929*, Boston, MA 1929.

—*The Nitrate Clippers*, Boston, MA 1932.

LYTLE, W. M. and F. R. HOLDCAMPER, *see* Ch. 10.

MCADAM, R. W., *The Old Fall River Line*, New York 1955.

MCFARLAND, R., *A History of the New England Fisheries*, New York 1911.

MCKAY, R. C., *Some Famous Sailing Ships and Their Builder, Donald McKay*, New York 1928.

MCNAIRN, J. and J. MACMULLEN, *Ships of the Redwood Coast*, Stanford 1945.

MADDOCKS, M., *The Atlantic Crossing*, Alexandria, VA 1981.

—*The Great Liners*, Alexandria, VA 1978.

MAGINNIS, A. J., *The Atlantic Ferry: Its Ships, Men and Workings*, London 1900.

MARINER'S MIRROR, THE Society for Nautical Research, London 1911–present.

MARSHALL, D., *California Shipwrecks: Footsteps in the Sea*, Seattle, WA 1978.

MARTIN, W. E., *Sail and Steam on the Northern California Coast, 1850–1900*, San Francisco National

Maritime Museum Association, San Francisco, CA 1983.

MATTHEWS, F. C., *American Merchant Ships 1850–1900*, 2 vols, Marine Research Society, Salem, MA 1930–31.

MORISON, S. E., *see* Ch. 6.

MORRIS, E. P., *The Fore-and-Aft Rig in America: A Sketch*, New Haven, CT 1927.

PARKER, H. and F. C. BOWEN, *Mail Passenger Steamers of the Nineteenth Century*, Philadelphia, PA n.d.

PARKER, W. J. L., *The Great Coal Schooners of New England, 1870–1909*, Marine Historical Association, Mystic, CT 1948.

RIDGELY-NEVITT, C., *American Steamships on the Atlantic*, Newark, DE 1981.

SMITH, E. W., *Passenger Ships of the World, Past and Present*, Boston, MA 1978.

SMITH, M. H., *An Interpretive Study of the Collection Recovered from the Storeship 'Niantic'*, National Trust for Historic Preservation and National Maritime Museum Association, San Francisco, CA 1981.

SPRATT, H. P., *One Hundred Years of Transatlantic Steam Navigation, 1838–1938*, London 1938.

—*Outline History of Transatlantic Steam Navigation*, London 1950.

—*Transatlantic Paddle Steamers*, Brown, Son & Ferguson, Glasgow 1967.

STARBUCK, A., *History of the American Whale Fishery from its Earliest Inception to the Year 1876*, Waltham, MA 1877.

STORY OF YANKEE WHALING, THE, New York 1959.

TOD, G. M., *The Last Sail down East*, Barre, MA 1965.

WEBB, W. H., *Plans of Wooden Vessels . . . Built by William H. Webb in the City of New York . . . 1840–1869*, New York 1895.

WHIPPLE, A. B. C., *The Clipper Ships*, Alexandria, VA 1980.

—*The Whalers*, Alexandria, VA 1979.

EPILOG

BALLARD, R. D., 'A Long Last Look at Titanic', *NG* 170 (Dec. 1986) 698–727.

—'Epilogue for Titanic', *NG* 172 (Oct. 1987) 454–463.

BALLARD, R. D. and J.-L. MICHEL, 'How We Found

Titanic', *NG* 168 (Dec. 1985) 696–719.

BASCOM, W., *The Crest of the Wave*, New York 1988.

—*Deep Water, Ancient Ships*, Garden City, NY 1976.

BASS, G. F., 'The Men Who Stole the Stars', *Sea History* 12 (Fall 1979) 30.

—'Marine Archaeology: A Misunderstood Science' in Borgese, E. M. and N. Ginsburg, (eds.), *Ocean Yearbook 2*, Chicago 1980, 137–152.

—'A Plea for Historical Particularism in Nautical Archaeology' in Gould, R. A. (ed.), *Shipwreck Anthropology*, Albuquerque 1983, 91–104.

—'The Promise of Underwater Archaeology in Retrospect', *Museum* (UNESCO) 137 (1983) 5–8.

—'Archaeologists, Sport Divers, and Treasure-Hunters', *JFA* 12 (1985) 256–258.

CHAMBERLAND, D., 'Titanic: Target of Opportunity', *U.S. Naval Institute Proceedings*, vol. 113/8/1014, Annapolis, Maryland (August 1987) 56–63.

DAVIS, SIR R. H., *Deep Diving and Submarine Operations: A Manual for Deep Sea Divers and Compressed Air Workers*, parts I & II, 5th edn London 1951.

FORSBERG, G., *Salvage from the Sea*, London and Henley 1977.

GORES, J. N., *Marine Salvage: The Unforgiving Business of No Cure, No Pay*, Garden City, NY 1971.

KOSTER, D. A., *Ocean Salvage*, New York 1971.

MACINNIS, J. B., 'Exploring a 140-year-old Ship Under Arctic Ice', *NG* 164 (July 1983) 104A–104D.

MADDOCKS, M., 'A Litany of Disasters on the Devil Sea' in *The Great Liners*, Alexandria, VA 1978: 114–141.

MOSCOW, A., *Collision Course: The 'Andrea Doria' and the 'Stockholm'*, New York 1959.

SEARLE, W. F. and F. R. BUSBY, Prepared Testimony in *Hearing Before the House Merchant Marine and Fisheries Committee on H.R. 3272 The Titanic Maritime Memorial Act of 1985, 29 October 1985*, Serial No. 99-21, Govt Printing Office, Washington, D.C. 1986, 87–107.

SHEPARD, B., *Lore of the Wreckers*, Boston, MA 1961.

THROCKMORTON, P. (ed.), *The Sea Remembers: Shipwrecks and Archaeology*, New York 1987 (publ. in England as *History from the Sea: Shipwrecks and Archaeology*, London 1987).

Sources of Illustrations

TITLE PAGE Photo D. Pagé. Courtesy Parks Canada.

INTRODUCTION Maps by Hanni Bailey.

CHAPTER ONE **1** Department of Library Services, American Museum of Natural History. **2** *PA* 38008, Public Archives Canada. Photo A. P. Low. **3** Department of Ethnography, National Museum of Denmark. Photo T. Krabbe. **4** Courtesy Florida Department of Natural Resources. **5** Cleveland Museum of Natural History. **6** Courtesy Terence Grieder. **7, 8** Courtesy of the Trustees of the British Museum, London. **9** Royal Ontario Museum, Toronto. **10** British Library, London. **11** After *Indian Art of the United States* by F. Douglas and R. D'Harnoncourt (New York 1948). **12** Photo Margaret Leshikar. **13** Photo Janice Rubin. **14** Carnegie Institute of Washington. **15–17** Courtesy Tikal Project, The University Museum, University of Pennsylvania. **18** Photo Norman Hammond. **19** Museo Nacional de Antropología, Mexico. **20** Photo Margaret Leshikar. **21** Museo del Oro, Banco de la Republica, Bogota. **22** From Lienzo de Tlaxcala, *Antiguedades Mexicana* (facsimile, 1892). **23** Drawn by Tatiana Proskouriakoff. Peabody Museum, Harvard University. Photo H. Burger. **24** Drawn by Julio C. Burgos. Museo Antropologico, Banco Central del Ecuador, Guayaquil. **25** Museo

Regional de Arqueologia, Arica. Photo courtesy Callwey Verlag, Munich. **26** Rautenstrauch-Joest-Museum, Cologne. **27** Woodcut of 1565. **28** University Museum, University of Pennsylvania. Photo Max Uhle. **29** After A. Baessler, *Ancient Peruvian Art* (1903). **30** Museum für Völkerkunde, Hamburg. **31** Courtesy Parks Canada. Model by D. Colwell. Photo T. Lackey. **32, 33** © Viking Ship Museum, Roskilde, Denmark. Photo G. Schantz.

CHAPTER TWO **1** From Pedro de Medina, *L'arte de navegar* (Venice 1555). Photo The John Carter Brown Library. **2** Prins Hendrik Maritime Museum, Rotterdam. Drawn by Björn Landström. Courtesy International Book Production, Stockholm. **3** From the *Atlas of Portolan Charts* by Vesconte Maggiolo (Naples 1519). Photo The John Carter Brown Library. **4** From the *Boke of Idrography* by Jean Rotz (1542). Photo The John Carter Brown Library. **5** Chicago Historical Society. Photo C. D. Arnold. **6** Drawn by ML Design. **7** Photo KC Smith. **8** From the *Isolario* by Benedetto Bordoni (1534). **9** Photo KC Smith. **10** Photo R. C. Smith. **11** Photo KC Smith. **12** Museo Navale di Pegli, Genoa. **13** Photo KC Smith. **14** Courtesy Institute of Nautical Archaeology. Photo Bruce Thompson.

CHAPTER THREE **1** Museo Naval, Madrid. Photo Luis Dorado. **2** Bibliothèque Nationale,

Paris. **3** Photo George Eastman House. **4** From the *Instrucción nautica* by Diego Garcia de Palacio (Mexico City 1587). Photo The John Carter Brown Library. **5** Courtesy Texas Antiquities Committee. Photo J. Jenkins. **6, 7** Courtesy Texas Antiquities Committee. **8** Corpus Christi Museum, Texas. **9** After Texas Antiquities Committee. **10–14** Courtesy Texas Antiquities Committee. **15** Photo KC Smith. **16** Photo R. C. Smith. **17, 18** Photos D. D. Denton. **19** Photo R. F. Marx. **20** Photo Susan Samon. **21** Photo KC Smith. **22** Photo Smithsonian Institution. **23** After J. J. Simmons. **24** After J. J. Simmons. **25, 26** Photos D. D. Denton. **27** After D. H. Keith and J. J. Simmons. **28** After D. H. Keith. **29** After J. A. Duff and J. J. Simmons. **30** Photo S. Hoyt. **31** Photo M. D. Myers. **32, 33** Courtesy Institute of Texan Cultures of the University of Texas at San Antonio. **34** Drawn by D. H. Keith and J. J. Simmons. Courtesy Institute of Nautical Archaeology. **35** After J. J. Simmons. **Map** (p. 66) After D. H. Keith.

CHAPTER FOUR **1** After W. Stevens. **2** Drawn by P. Waddell and J. Farley. **3** Drawn by W. Stevens and C. Piper. **4** Photo R. Chan. **5** John Rylands University Library of Manchester. **6** Painting by Abraham Speck. Rijksmuseum, Amsterdam. **7** Photo R. Chan. Courtesy Parks Canada. **8** Photo D. Pagé. Courtesy Parks Canada. **9** Courtesy R. Grenier. **10** Photo D. Pagé. Courtesy

Parks Canada. **11, 12** Musée de la Marine, Paris. **13** Drawn by R. Hellier. **14** Photo P. Waddell. **15** Drawn by S. Laurie-Bourque. **16–18** Photo D. Pagé. Courtesy Parks Canada. **19** Drawn by R. Hellier. **20** Photo D. Pagé. **21–23** Drawn by C. Piper. **24** Photo R. Chan. **25** Drawn by W. Stevens and C. Piper. **26** Photo M. Gingras. **27** Photo R. Chan. Courtesy Parks Canada. **28** Photo D. Pagé. Courtesy Parks Canada.

CHAPTER FIVE **1** Bibliothèque Nationale, Paris. **2** British Library, London. **3** Photo Farley Sonnier. **4, 5** After J. J. Simmons. **6, 7** Courtesy Texas Antiquities Committee. Drawn by J. Rosloff. **8** Institute of Maritime History and Archaeology, Bermuda Maritime Museum. **9** Photo Bermuda Maritime Museum. **10** Drawn by Toni Hepburn. Courtesy Jim Miller. **11** Seventeenth-century engraving. **12** Drawn by Simon S. S. Driver. **13** Museo Naval, Madrid. **14, 15** Courtesy Pedro J. Borrell. **16** Courtesy Florida Bureau of Archaeological Research. **17** Detail of a map from *A Concise Natural History of East and West Florida* by Bernard Romans, New York 1775. British Library, London. **18** Courtesy Florida Bureau of Archaeological Research. **19** Drawn by James B. Levy. Courtesy Florida Division of Historic Resources. **20** Courtesy Pedro J. Borrell. **21** © National Geographic Society. Photo Jonathan S. Blair. **22** Courtesy Pedro J. Borrell. **23** Courtesy Florida Bureau of Archaeological Research. **24, 25** Drawn by Toni Hepburn. Courtesy Florida Division of Historic Resources. **26** Courtesy Florida Bureau of Archaeological Research. **27, 28** Courtesy Florida Division of Historic Resources. Photos R. C. Smith. **29–31** After U. Pernambucano de Mello (*IJNA* vol. 8 no. 3, 1979).

CHAPTER SIX **1** Drawn by ML Design. **2, 3** The Science Museum, London. **4** Courtesy Plimoth Plantation, Plymouth, MA. **5–7** Courtesy Sea Venture Trust. Plan by Jon Adams. **8** After J. Adams. Courtesy Sea Venture Trust. **9** Courtesy Sea Venture Trust. **10** Courtesy of the Pilgrim Society, Plymouth, MA. **11** Photo Alan Albright. **12** Courtesy Institute of Archaeology and Anthropology at the University of South Carolina. **13** Detail from *View of the camp of John Law's concession at New Biloxi, Louisiana, 1720.* Newberry Library, Chicago. **14** Courtesy Plimoth Plantation. Photo Ted Avery. **15** Broadside, London 1692. **16–18** Courtesy Institute of Nautical Archaeology. **19** Photo Shirley Gotelipe. **20–22** Courtesy South Carolina Institute of Archaeology and Anthropology. Photos Gordon Brown. **23, 24** Drawn by Darby Erd. Courtesy South Carolina Institute of Archaeology and Anthropology. **25** Photo Gordon Brown. **26** Photo Alan Albright. **27, 28** Courtesy Jamestown Festival Park. **29** Courtesy the Master and Fellows of Magdalene College, Cambridge. **30** Drawn by J. R. Steffy. **31, 32** Photos J. R. Steffy. **33** Photo Gordon Brown. **34** The Mariners' Museum, Newport News, VA. **35** The Mariners' Museum. Photo Robert Adams. **36** Photo G. Watts. **37** The Mariners' Museum. Photo Robert Adams.

CHAPTER SEVEN **1** The New-York Historical Society, NY. **2** Basin Harbor Maritime Museum, Vermont. **3** Photo Kenneth Garrett. **4** Courtesy Société Immobilière du Québec and the Quebec Ministry of Cultural Affairs. **5** Courtesy Fort Ticonderoga Museum. **6–8** Courtesy K. Crisman. **9** © National Geographic Society. Photo David

Arnold. **10, 11** Drawn by K. Crisman. **12, 13** Basin Harbor Maritime Museum, Vermont. **14** Virginia Canals & Navigations Society. Photo W. E. Trout. **15** Archaeological Society of Virginia. Photo L. E. Browning. **16** Bibliothèque Nationale, Paris. **17** Yale University Art Gallery, Mabel Brady Carvan Collection. **18** Royal Ontario Museum, Toronto. **19–22** Drawn by K. Crisman. **23, 24** Drawn by S. Cooper. **25, 26** Drawn by K. Crisman. **27, 28** Fort Ticonderoga Museum. Photos John Butler. **29** Courtesy Parks Canada. **30** C 13319, Public Archives, Canada. **31** National Gallery of Canada, Ottawa.

CHAPTER EIGHT **1** New York Public Library. I. N. Phelps Stokes Collection. **2** DAR Museum, Washington, D.C. **3** Windsor Castle, Royal Library. © Her Majesty The Queen. **4–6** Smithsonian Institution, NMAH. **7, 8** Photos Carroll and Philip Voss. **9** Virginia Division of Historic Landmarks (VDHL). Photo R. Adams. **10, 11** VDHL. Photos John D. Broadwater. **12** The Mariners' Museum, Newport News, VA. **13, 14** Drawn by Peter Hentschel. Courtesy Institute of Nautical Archaeology (INA). **15** Drawn by Cynthia Orr. Courtesy INA. **16** Maine State Museum, Augusta. **17** Drawn by Sheli Smith. Courtesy INA. **18** The Mariners' Museum, Newport News, VA. **19** Maryland Historical Society, Baltimore. **20** National Portrait Gallery, London. **21, 22** The Mariners' Museum, Newport News, VA. **23** The Science Museum, London. **24** Newberry Library, Chicago. **25** National Maritime Museum, Greenwich. **26** Virginia Division of Historic Landmarks. Photo John D. Broadwater. **27, 28** VDHL. Drawn by John D. Broadwater. **29** VDHL. Drawn by David Hazzard. **30** VDHL.

CHAPTER NINE **1** Yale University Art Gallery, Mabel Brady Garvan Collection. **2** USS *Constitution* Museum Foundation, Boston, MA. **3–5** Library of Congress, Washington, D.C. **6** Drawn by ML Design. **7** Klein Associates. Courtesy Canada Centre for Inland Waters and the Royal Ontario Museum. **8, 9** Courtesy Hamilton-Scourge Project. **10** Courtesy K. Crisman. **11** Historic Naval and Military Establishments, Penetanguishene, Ontario. **12** Courtesy K. Crisman. **13** C 794, Public Archives, Canada. **14** Drawn by K. Crisman. **15** Courtesy K. Cassavoy. **16** © 1983 National Geographic Society. Photo Emory Kristof. Courtesy Hamilton-Scourge Project. **17** Courtesy Hamilton-Scourge Project. **18** © 1983 National Geographic Society. Photo Emory Kristof. Courtesy Hamilton-Scourge Project. **19, 20** Drawn by K. Crisman. **21** Royal Ontario Museum, Toronto. **22** Historic Naval and Military Establishments, Penetanguishene, Ontario. **23** Engraved by B. Tanner after H. Reinagle. 1816. **24–26** Drawn by K. Crisman. **27** Courtesy Ontario Archives. **28** Historic Naval and Military Establishments, Penetanguishene, Ontario. **29** Drawn by K. Crisman.

CHAPTER TEN **1** New Jersey Historical Society, Alofsen Collection. **2** American Society of Mechanical Engineers, New York. **3** New York State Historical Association, Cooperstown, N.Y. **4** American Society of Mechanical Enginers, New York. **5** Peabody Museum of Salem, MA. **6, 7** Drawn by K. Crisman. **8** The Mariners' Museum, Newport News, VA. **9** Wood engraving, 1858. **10** National Archives, Washington, D.C. **11** Robert D. Turner, B.C. Provincial Museum, Victoria. **12**

From *Harper's Weekly*, 1888. **13** Photo R. M. Adams. **14, 15** Drawn by D. H. Keith. **16** Drawn by J. J. Simmons. **17** Public Library of Cincinnati and Hamilton County. **18** Courtesy DeSoto National Wildlife Refuge, U.S. Fish and Wildlife Service. **19** Anglo-American Art Museum, Louisiana State University, Baton Rouge. Gift of Mrs Mamie Persac Lusk. **20–25** Courtesy DeSoto National Wildlife Refuge, U.S. Fish and Wildlife Service. **26** © National Geographic Society. Photo John Fulton. **27** Photo KC Smith. **28** Champlain Maritime Society and the Vermont Division for Historic Preservation 1981. **29** Louisiana Collection, Tulane University Library.

CHAPTER ELEVEN **1, 2** Photo G. Watts. **3** The Mariners' Museum, Newport News, VA. **4** After G. Watts. **5** National Archives, Washington, D.C. **6** From *Harper's Weekly*, 1863. **7** North Carolina Division of Archives and History. **8** Drawn by J. Jannaman. North Carolina Division of Archives and History. **9** Photomosaic U.S. Navy. **10** Photo G. Watts. **11** Drawn by J. Jannaman. North Carolina Division of Archives and History. **12** National Archives, Washington, D.C. **13, 14** National Park Service, Vicksburg. Photo William Wilson. **15, 16** National Park Service, Vicksburg. **17** New Hanover County Museum. **18** Photo James A. Pleasants. North Carolina Division of Archives and History. **19** Merseyside County Museums, Liverpool. **20** Drawn by Julie Melton. Program in Maritime History and Underwater Research, East Carolina University. **21, 22** Courtesy Sam Margolin. **23** The Mariners' Museum, Newport News, VA. **24** National Archives, Washington, D.C. **25–28** James W. Woodruff Confederate Naval Museum, Columbus, GA. **29** Drawn by Kaea Morris, Tidewater Atlantic Research. **30** Photo Wesley K. Hall. **31** From *The Illustrated London News*, 1862. **32** Courtesy Hall Watters. **33** National Archives, Washington, D.C. **34** Courtesy Mrs Thomas Godet, Hamilton, Bermuda. **35, 36** Photos KC Smith.

CHAPTER TWELVE **1–4** Peabody Museum of Salem. **5** Courtesy Maritime Heritage Prints, Boston. **6** Courtesy The Bostonian Society. Photo Peabody Museum of Salem. **7** Courtesy Snow Squall Project. **8** Peabody Museum of Salem, Francis Lee Higginson Steamship Collection. **9** Museum of the City of New York. **10** National Maritime Museum, Greenwich. **11** Photo Associated Press. **12** National Maritime Museum, Greenwich. **13–15** National Maritime Museum, San Francisco. **16, 17** Peabody Museum of Salem. **18** George Eastman House. **19** Metropolitan Museum of Art, New York. **20–22** Peabody Museum of Salem. **23** Courtesy James P. Delgado, National Park Service. **24** Mystic Seaport Museum. **25** Peabody Museum of Salem. **26** Courtesy Howard Wright. **27** Peabody Museum of Salem. **28** Courtesy Society for the Preservation of New England Antiquities.

EPILOG **1** © National Geographic Society July 1983. Photo Emory Kristof. **2** Dr Owen Beattie/University of Alberta. **3** © Woods Hole Oceanographic Institution, MA. **4** Woods Hole Oceanographic Institution, MA. © WHOI & IFREMER. **5** Drawn by T. Gravemaker. **6** From *The Illustrated London News*, 4 August 1956. **7** © The Doria Project. Photo Mark Schreyer. Courtesy Oceaneering International. **8** Official U.S. Navy Photograph. **9** Collection USS *Arizona*, National Park Service. Drawn by Jerry Livingstone.

Index